Watteau to Degas

Watteau to Degas: French Drawings from the *Frits Lugt Collection*

Colin B. Bailey
Susan Grace Galassi
Mària van Berge-Gerbaud

The Frick Collection, New York
in association with
Fondation Custodia, Paris

Published on the occasion
of the exhibition

*Watteau to Degas: French Drawings
from the Frits Lugt Collection*

The Frick Collection, New York
October 6, 2009 – January 10, 2010

Institut Néerlandais, Paris
February 11 – April 11, 2010

Principal funding for the exhibition is provided by
Peter and Sofia Blanchard; Elizabeth and Jean-Marie Eveillard; and
Melvin R. Seiden in honor of Jean Bonna and Eugene V. Thaw.

This publication was organized at The Frick Collection by
Elaine Koss, Editor in Chief, and Julie Di Filippo, Assistant Editor
Index by Susan G. Burke
Designer: Wigger Bierma
Printer: Thoben Offset Nijmegen

Unless otherwise specified, all photographs were supplied by the
owners of the works of art, who hold the copyright thereto, and are
reproduced with permission.

Copyright 2009 The Frick Collection, New York
All rights reserved.
No part of the contents of this book may be reproduced
without the written permission of The Frick Collection.
Library of Congress Control Number: 2009933540

ISBN 978-0912114-45-3

Front cover: Antoine Watteau, *Studies of Seven Heads* (detail), cat. 5
Back cover: François Boucher, *Standing Woman Seen from Behind*, cat. 12

Contents

7   Preface
    Anne L. Poulet and Mària van Berge-Gerbaud

9   Acknowledgments
    Colin B. Bailey and Susan Grace Galassi

12 Frits Lugt – Collector of French Drawings
    Mària van Berge-Gerbaud

25 Catalogue
    Colin B. Bailey, Susan Grace Galassi, and
    Mària van Berge-Gerbaud

183 Provenance, Exhibitions, Bibliography, Notes,
    Comparative Illustrations

267 Selected Bibliography

323 Index of Artists

324 Photograph Credits

325 Index

Preface

It is difficult to think of two collectors less alike than Henry Clay Frick (1849–1919) and Frits (Frederik) Johannes Lugt (1884–1970). The former, a Pittsburgh industrialist of the Gilded Age, moved to New York in 1905 and amassed an incomparable collection of Old Master paintings, sculpture, and decorative arts in a house that would serve, after his death and the death of his wife, "for the use and benefit of all persons whomsoever." Lugt, the only child of a civil engineer in the Amsterdam Public Works Department, began his career at age sixteen in an auction house and would become a prolific scholar, a curator, and a connoisseur primarily interested in prints and drawings, who lived part of his adult life in Paris. Despite their differences, both men were autodidacts, were raised in the Mennonite faith, and showed a precocious interest in art. As an enterprising (but impecunious) twenty-one-year-old seeking a loan from the Mellon bank to finance his acquisition of coal fields, Frick was noted to live in a modest dwelling surrounded by prints and sketches, "some made by himself." Lugt, who at age twelve gained access to the Print Room at the Rijksmuseum to study the Dutch Golden Age drawings, had formed his first collection of "curiosities" four years earlier, catalogued as Het Museum Lugtius, "open when the Director is at home."

Lugt had more in common with Frick's daughter, Helen Clay Frick (1888–1984), founder of the Frick Art Reference Library and an art historian who wrote on Jean-Antoine Houdon. She and Lugt shared many interests and sympathies. In fact, Miss Frick and her staff assisted him on the first volumes of his magnum opus, the *Répertoire des catalogues de ventes publiques intéressant l'art ou la curiosité* – a comprehensive listing and description of auction catalogues between 1600 and 1925, published in four volumes between 1938 and 1987, and still in use today as the standard reference on the subject. Nor was Lugt a stranger to the newly created Frick Collection, which opened its doors to the public in December 1935. During the Second World War, when Lugt and his wife were living in Oberlin, Ohio, The Frick Collection invited him to give a Sunday afternoon lecture on "Old Art Sales Catalogues." In a cordial letter from the director's office, dated June 1942, Lugt was informed "that it is conceivable that circumstances might compel us to withdraw the invitation at short notice, for our small lecture room is not an air-raid shelter." Lugt's lecture was delivered without incident in the Music Room of The Frick Collection on 7 February 1943.

Watteau to Degas: French Drawings from the Frits Lugt Collection is the first collaboration between The Frick Collection and the Fondation Custodia, established by Lugt in 1947 to oversee and administer his collections, as well as the first exhibition and catalogue devoted to a selection of the Fondation's French eighteenth- and nineteenth-century drawings. The project originated in an invitation to Colin B. Bailey, Associate Director and Peter Jay Sharp Chief Curator of The Frick Collection, to select works for an exhibition in New York — to be seen also in Paris in the winter of 2010. He and Susan Grace Galassi, the Frick's Senior Curator and a specialist in nineteenth-century art, have made rigorous choices among the hundreds of sheets at their disposal and have produced the fine catalogue that will now serve as a calling card for Lugt's French holdings.

Such an undertaking could not have been embarked upon without the support of many colleagues and specialists, who are thanked in the authors' acknowledgments that follow. We are above all indebted to the sponsors and funders of this exhibition, who shared our excitement at bringing this group of master drawings to New York for the first time and who supported our undertaking to catalogue them in a scholarly, elegant, and accessible publication. We are most grateful to Peter and Sofia Blanchard; Elizabeth and Jean-Marie Eveillard; Melvin R. Seiden in honor of Jean Bonna and Eugene V. Thaw; the Pierre and Tana Matisse Foundation; Jean Bonna in honor of Mària van Berge-Gerbaud; Dr. and Mrs. Malcolm H. Wiener; Anne Goldrach; Diane Nixon; and those donors who wish to remain anonymous.

While the name of Lugt is known to many historians of the art market and most collectors and curators of Old Master drawings — much as the term Köchel (the surname of the nineteenth-century musicologist Ludwig von Köchel) is familiar to all lovers of Mozart's music — this scholar-collector-philanthropist remains an elusive figure, in keeping with his natural modesty and reserve. It is our hope that in addition to enjoying a rare public viewing of the finest of the Fondation's French eighteenth- and nineteenth-century sheets, audiences in New York and Paris will also become better acquainted with Frits Lugt and his multifaceted collection and will take the opportunity to include the Hôtel Turgot at 121, rue de Lille, in future visits to his adopted city.

Anne L. Poulet
Director, The Frick Collection,
New York

Mària van Berge-Gerbaud
Director, Fondation Custodia,
Paris

Acknowledgments

An avid collector of works on paper from the age of fifteen, and an art historian whose scholarship continues to be cited today, Frits Lugt (1884 – 1970) played a formative role in the history of the graphic arts. In 1947 Lugt established the Fondation Custodia, Paris, to care for and add to his collection, which at the time of his death included some 6,000 Old Master drawings and 30,000 prints (another thousand drawings have been added since then). *Watteau to Degas: French Drawings from the Frits Lugt Collection* brings together, in the first exhibition of French drawings from the Fondation Custodia to be shown in the United States, the collection's most significant eighteenth- and nineteenth-century French works on paper, many acquired by Lugt's successors, Carlos van Hasselt and Mària van Berge-Gerbaud.

We were deeply honored by the invitation to select and catalogue sixty-four drawings, many of which have never been shown before in North America, including works by well-known masters of the French School such as Antoine Watteau, François Boucher, Jean-Honoré Fragonard, Jacques-Louis David, Eugène Delacroix, Jean-Auguste-Dominique Ingres, and Edgar Degas, as well as by important figures who are less familiar to the general public – Pierre-Jean Mariette, Charles-Joseph Natoire, Johan Jongkind, and Léon Bonvin, among others. Our selection ranges from sheets taken from sketchbooks to finished portraits and landscapes; the works present an astounding variety of drawing techniques: red and black chalk renderings, charcoal and pencil sketches, pastels, watercolors, and compositions in pen, ink, wash, and gouache.

Such an undertaking would not have been possible without the support and encouragement of many people, and we thank above all Mària van Berge-Gerbaud, Director of the Fondation Custodia, for placing her confidence in us, providing us with unpublished documentation on every work, and overseeing the myriad details of the exhibition and its accompanying catalogue. The Director of The Frick Collection, Anne L. Poulet, has been an enthusiast for this project from its inception and has ensured that we receive the fullest support for it.

The organization of the exhibition has been overseen at The Frick Collection with customary vigilance and attention to detail by Diane Farynyk, Registrar and Exhibition Manager, and Allison Galea, Assistant Registrar. They have worked seamlessly with Marie-Louise van der Pol, Secrétariat et Intendance, at the Fondation Custodia, as well as with her colleagues. In Paris, above all, *documentaliste* Marie-Claire Nathan provided us with complete documentation for every drawing, much of it previously unpublished. Corinne Letessier, the Fondation Custodia's paper conservator, did an enormous amount of work, choosing each frame and creating special mounts for the presentation in New York. Sylvain Oudry restored the frames, and Pascal and Catherine Faligot of Seventh Square, Paris, were responsible for the excellent photographs of the Fondation Custodia's drawings.

Editing of the catalogue has been undertaken under the tightest of schedules by Elaine Koss, Editor-in-Chief, Julie Di Filippo, Assistant Editor, and Serena Rattazzi, and we are indebted to Wigger Bierma for this handsome, beautifully designed book, a hallmark of the Fondation's publication program. The elegant installation of the exhibition at The Frick Collection is due to Stephen Saitas, and for lighting we thank Anita Jorgensen. For their assistance in many ways in the preparation of the catalogue and the installation of the exhibition we thank Denise Allen, Joseph Godla, Charlotte Vignon, Margaret Iacono, Michael Bodycomb, Julia Day, Joanna Sheers, William Trachet, Adrian Anderson, and Julian Mackler.

The opportunity to publish drawings from the renowned Lugt collection was a challenge as well as a pleasure, and we could not have undertaken this catalogue without the sterling support and assistance of many collaborators. The extraordinary resources of the Frick Art Reference Library sustained us over the course of our research, and we are grateful to our colleagues there, always ready to hunt down the most obscure reference on our behalf: Lydia Dufour, former Chief of Public Services, Suzannah Massen, Don Swanson, Inge Reist, and Debbie Kempe. We are particularly indebted to a group of energetic and resourceful research assistants, Grace Chuang, Cindy Kang, and intern Aurélie Niddam, who worked with David Pullins, former Curatorial Assistant. Curatorial Assistants Nicholas Wise and Caitlin Henningsen have also made an inestimable contribution in assembling the comparative illustrations for the catalogue and in the preparation of the manuscript. We also acknowledge the help of interns Mary Brock, Emily Kaplan, Bérengère Lepine, Camille Mathieu, Ingrid Seggerman, Kabir Singh, Hilary Coe Smith, and particularly Charlotte Healy. Alan Wintermute read the entries for the eighteenth-century drawings most carefully, and each has been improved by his eagle eye. Significant contributions to the content and shaping of the nineteenth-century entries were made by Joanna Sheers and Caitlin Henningsen, Curatorial Assistants. Much is owed to the crucial collaboration of Cindy Kang, whose meticulous research forms the basis for these entries; her many insights into the material, additions to the discussion of drawing techniques, and improvements to the texts are reflected throughout this section of the catalogue.

Among the colleagues and specialists to whom we turned for advice and information, it is a pleasure to thank the following: Stijn Alsteen, Rhea Blok, David J. Burke, Karen Chastagnol, Edouard Kopp, Sonia Couturier, Jean-Pierre Cuzin, Marie-Anne Dupuy-Vachey, Yvonne Elet, Françoise Joulie, Anne Leclair, Christophe Léribault, Laurence Lhinares, Alexandra Libby, Alexandre Maral, Paula M. Mikkelsen, Edgar Munhall, Aileen Ribeiro, Pierre Rosenberg, Guilhelm Scherf, Perrin Stein, Christoph Martin Vogtherr, and Emily H. Vokes.

Colin B. Bailey
Associate Director and Peter Jay Sharp Chief Curator
The Frick Collection

Susan Grace Galassi
Senior Curator
The Frick Collection

Frits Lugt — Collector of French Drawings

The Frits Lugt Collection in Paris houses an exceptional number of drawings, prints, artists' correspondence, and paintings. The greater part of the collection — and the most significant — was brought together by Frits Lugt. Among collectors of drawings and prints Lugt is famous for having compiled *Les Marques de collections de dessins & d'estampes* (1921) and the *Répertoire des catalogues de ventes publiques* (1934–87), still widely consulted, and for his collection in the Institut Néerlandais, which he founded in Paris in 1956.

Early Years

Frits Lugt (Amsterdam 4 May 1884 – 15 July 1970 Paris), an only child, was born to a family whose interest in the arts and sciences reached back to the nineteenth-century horse painter Wouterus Verschuur (1812 – 1874), a relative on his mother's side. His father, a civil engineer in the Amsterdam public works department, imparted to his son a fascination with history and a passion for museum-going in the Netherlands and abroad. After Lugt (fig. 1), like many bright children, had amassed and dispensed with the usual collections of stamps, insects, shells, and other natural curiosities (he is said to have sold his shell collection to the natural history department of Amsterdam's Artis Royal Zoo when he was ten years old), he developed a deep interest in art. His weekly drawing lessons at the Hendrick de Keyser art school in Amsterdam resulted in his persuading, at age twelve, the curator of the Department of Prints and Drawings at the Rijksmuseum to allow him to spend his free Wednesday afternoons studying the Dutch and Flemish drawings in the collection. When

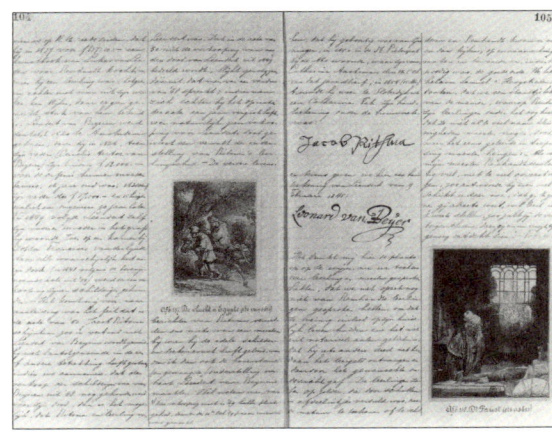

he discovered that there was no catalogue, he started to compile one himself. But what sealed his passion for art was his visit to the major Rembrandt exhibition in Amsterdam in 1898 on the occasion of Queen Wilhelmina's inauguration. On view were no fewer than 123 paintings and more than 300 etchings and drawings attributed to the great Amsterdam artist, which inspired the fourteen-year-old Lugt to write a biography of the Dutch master. Illustrated with his own copies of Rembrandt's etchings and drawings, the biography was dedicated to his parents in June 1900 (fig. 2). In 1899, the year he started work on this biography, he went to an auction in Amsterdam and spent three guilders on his first work of art – Rembrandt's etched portrait of Lieven van Coppenol, accompanied by a sample of calligraphy in the sitter's own hand.

Among those to whom Lugt's father proudly showed the biography was his cousin, co-owner of the renowned Frederik Muller auction house. At Lugt senior's urging, Muller's partner Anton Mensing agreed to give Lugt a job on his return from a study trip to London. Before Lugt set off for England he visited the Rembrandt scholar Abraham Bredius, at that time the director of the Mauritshuis in The Hague, who gave the red-headed boy several introductions to museum directors, collectors, and dealers. Bredius, who regarded Lugt as his protégé, would have liked to see him embark on a career that would ultimately lead to the position of director of the Rijksmuseum. Lugt, however, chose to join the Amsterdam auction house. The sixteen-year-old "connoisseur" could conceive of no better training than a period with Frederik Muller (fig. 3).

On 15 December 1910 Lugt married Jacoba Klever (1888–1969) (fig. 4), the only daughter of one of the founders of the Steenkolen Handelsvereniging, a major coal-trading concern. During his time with Frederik Muller, Lugt was

1. Photograph of Frits, age ten (1894)

2. Page from the Rembrandt manuscript (1899/1900)

3. Self-portrait, 1901
Pencil, 25.2 x 17.5

4. Frits Lugt and Jacoba (To) Lugt-Klever, 1910

not permitted to buy works of art on his own account. The outbreak of World War I, in which the Netherlands remained neutral, soon brought about the collapse of the art market. Lugt was consequently forced to leave Frederik Muller — where he had been a partner since 1911 — and he established himself as an independent art historian, consultant, and dealer in paintings. He was supported in his art dealing by his father-in-law, Josef Klever, who would advance him the necessary funds for major purchases — money that was scrupulously paid back. At this time Lugt was working on his book of Rembrandt's favorite walks in and around the capital — *Wandelingen met Rembrandt in en om Amsterdam* — and on the catalogue of the Dutch royal family's collection of portrait miniatures. It was not until 1917 that he began to collect seriously, and when he did he concentrated on Dutch and Flemish drawings and prints, a field that had interested him since his youth.

The Collector

In 1964 Lugt, who had organized a successful exhibition of French drawings in Dutch collections — *Le Dessin français de Claude à Cézanne dans les collections hollandaises* — in the Institut Néerlandais in Paris (fig. 5), was asked to give a talk about his collecting experiences in the Rijksmuseum, the Dutch venue for the exhibition. He began his talk by attempting to define how he had become a collector. It had happened, he said, without any planning. The need to surround himself with art gradually developed into the determination to build a collection. He felt a passionate desire to create: "It was the closest one could come to a sculptor's urge to form and shape," Lugt explained. During this process "insights mature, relationships clarify and gradually a great thing grows, a living collection with a character of its own." He summed up some of

5. One of the rooms in the exhibition of the *Dessin français de Claude à Cézanne dans les collections hollandaises* in the Institut Néerlandais in Paris, 1964

6. Stefano da Verona, *A Lady and Her Lover*, first half of the fifteenth century. Pen and brown ink, 29.1 x 19.5 (inv. no. 1337)

the qualities of a true collector, using, among others, the word "flair," which in the original French means perspicacity or discernment. Used as a verb, however, in the expressions "flairer une rose" and "flairer un danger," it means to smell or sense – to smell a rose, to sense danger. Both qualities, he believed, also had to be part of the collector's "arsenal": absorbing the "scent" of a work of art, being on guard against pitfalls. He refuted claims made by outsiders that a collector is actually nothing more than a selfish hoarder by arguing that the activity can be "altruistic" – specifically when the collector shares his treasures with the public in the form of an exhibition or a gift to a museum, or by transferring them to a public institution. Here he was undoubtedly referring to the Fondation Custodia, where his collection had been housed since 1947. Thanks in part to the Institut Néerlandais, the Dutch cultural center in Paris, which had been established in 1956 at Lugt's initiative and in cooperation with the Dutch government, it became possible to exhibit his impressive collection.

The Collection

Lugt's first purchases were Dutch and Flemish drawings, but the year 1923 unexpectedly presented the chance to purchase an important group of fifteenth-century Italian drawings, including works by Pisanello's teacher Stefano da Verona (fig. 6). In 1925, equally unexpectedly and within the space of a single week, he acquired three Watteau drawings, two from the Heseltine collection (cat. nos. 2 and 6) and one from the collection of the Goncourts (cat. 5). As he said himself, this was the equivalent of three Rembrandts and there could be no greater praise. In his eyes Watteau was an astounding draftsman whose use of

7. Augustin de Saint-Aubin, *Portrait of P.-J. Mariette*, 1765 (after Cochin). Etching and engraving, 19.5 x 14.1

trois crayons was unmatched. The purchase of these Watteaus encouraged him to continue to collect French drawings, and he was generally prepared to spend quite considerable sums on them – certainly more than he would pay for most of his Dutch drawings.

It should be noted here that the first French drawing Lugt bought was a little portrait of the French collector Pierre-Jean Mariette (1694–1774) by Charles-Nicolas Cochin (cat. 15), which he had acquired together with the print by Saint-Aubin (fig. 7) at the Paris sale of the comtesse de la Bédoyère in 1921. That same year Lugt completed and published *Les Marques de collections de dessins & d'estampes*. In it, under entry number L. 1852, he had written a passionate essay on Pierre-Jean Mariette, the man he revered as the greatest collector of drawings and prints of all time; after all, as Lugt later explained in the exhibition catalogue *Le Cabinet d'un grand amateur P.-J. Mariette* (1967), Mariette was one of those "architects" who knew how to create a coherent and balanced structure. It is about selecting, not amassing ("Il ne s'agit pas d'amasser, mais de choisir"). Anyone can do the latter if he has the money, but to do the former takes taste, expertise, and an eye for quality. In Lugt's opinion, the Mariette collection was the ultimate example of this.

Lugt liked to compare himself with Mariette. They were both good amateur artists, had professional experience in the art market, and had written exemplary catalogues and reference books. As to the matter of expertise – a word Lugt used cautiously – he would have loved to be able to share ideas with Mariette. Whereas his admired exemplar appeared infallible when it came to attributing Italian drawings, Lugt dearly wished he could have challenged him on a number of his attributions to artists from the Netherlands. Both Mariette and Lugt preferred a good drawing by a second-rate artist to a bad drawing by a great master. Another trait the two collectors had in common was that they had both built up their collections with relatively little money — certainly compared with the wealthy of their day. What mattered most were passion, flair, and a certain "curiosity." Lugt also believed that collections acquired with limited resources were often more exciting than the most grandiose ones: "Something 'resonates' in a modest collection that is infinitely preferable to the showy chilliness of large ones."

Lugt the Art Historian

The publication in 1921 of *Les Marques de collections* had brought Lugt considerable international fame. This work and a *Supplément* to it published in 1956 were written in French, the language of the art world at that time. In these volumes Lugt laid the foundations of the history of collecting drawings and prints by recording the activities of a collector and his collection under the different marks, annotations, and stamps found on the sheets. He elaborated on this effort by beginning work on the *Répertoire des catalogues de ventes publiques*, a reference work documenting all auctions of art from the beginning of the seventeenth century through 1925 and the whereabouts of the accompanying sales catalogues with an indication of their various annotations. The *Répertoire* led to a commission from the French authorities to compile the catalogues of the holdings of Dutch and Flemish drawings in the Louvre, the Petit Palais, the Bibliothèque Nationale, and the École des Beaux-Arts in Paris. The result was nine bulky catalogues; the first appeared in 1927 and the last in 1968, two years before Lugt's death (fig. 8).

8. Frits Lugt at his desk, 1967

9. Claude Lorrain, *Sunrise*, c. 1640 – 55
Black chalk, pen and brown ink, gray and brown wash on pink prepared paper, 26.2 x 41.5 cm (inv. no. 5564)

French Drawings

The next major purchase of French drawings – in 1928 – consisted of two small portraits by the seventeenth-century artist Claude Mellan, Boucher's lively drawing of a girl seen from behind (cat. 12), and the large, almost impressionistic boulevard scene by Gabriel de Saint-Aubin (cat. 18). In addition to a landscape by Watteau after Titian from the Rodrigues collection (cat. 3), Lugt also acquired the *Garden of Crozat* by Mariette (cat. 8), one of the few surviving drawings by the amateur artist and great collector. Lugt's collecting in 1929 was particularly strong and varied, with acquisitions of works by Fragonard (cats. 21, 22, and 23), Moreau (cat. 28), and Portail, together with other drawings from the Marius Paulme collection. In 1934 the first Greuze (cat. 24) entered the collection, followed a year later by the first Prud'hon. Just before the

11. *Rustenhoven* in Maartensdijk near Utrecht, rear view (after 1927)

12. The houses at 14 and 15 Lange Vijverberg in the Hague in Lugt's day

10. Claude Lorrain, *Evening Landscape*, c. 1640 – 55
Black chalk, pen and brown ink, brown wash on gray prepared paper, 25.6 x 40.2 (inv. no. 2310)

outbreak of World War II, Lugt acquired his second Claude Lorrain in London. Lorrain's *Sunrise* (fig. 9) made a magnificent pendant to his *Evening Landscape*, which he had bought in 1925 (fig. 10).

Lugt's most important purchases were made in the 1920s, when he and his family – the couple had five children – were living at Maartensdijk, his father-in-law's country estate near Utrecht (fig. 11). In the following decade Lugt, his wife, and their youngest daughter spent a good deal of time in Paris so that he could work on the catalogues he had been commissioned to compile. After the death of his father-in-law in 1935, he and his wife had the means to buy a permanent residence in The Hague – a house on Lange Vijverberg (fig. 12) opposite the Mauritshuis. But in 1939, with World War II impending, he was forced to take steps to safeguard some of his most important prints and drawings, including his French sheets. They were put in fifty envelopes and sent by registered mail to Switzerland for safekeeping.

The Establishment of the Fondation Custodia and the Institut Néerlandais

Lugt spent most of the war years at Oberlin College, Ohio, where he worked primarily on the *Supplément* to the book of collectors' marks, the *Répertoire*, and on assembling documentation for the Netherlands Institute for Art History (RKD) that he had helped to found in The Hague. After returning to Europe and putting his affairs in order – a considerable part of his collection and property had been dispersed – he turned his attention to collecting again.

In the years that followed he acquired a group of Watteaus (cat. 4 and 1) and a number of drawings by Hubert Robert (cat. 19). Meanwhile he and his wife had set up the Fondation Custodia in 1947 with a view to keeping their collection together, and in 1956, after prolonged and difficult negotiations with the Dutch government, the Institut Néerlandais was established. The premises at number 121 rue de Lille, which consist of two buildings – the nineteenth-century Hôtel Lévis-Mirepoix at the front (fig. 13) and the eighteenth-century Hôtel Turgot at the rear (fig. 14) – were a stone's throw away from the apartment on the Place du Palais Bourbon that he and his wife had rented since 1947 for his work in Paris. Save for a few drawings – among them Watteau's *Chaise longue* (cat. 6), which hung on the wall in the apartment behind a small curtain – the collection was housed in the Hôtel Turgot (fig. 15), with its raised garden opening onto the rue de l'Université. Here, too, before long, hung Charles-Nicolas Cochin's small portrait of Louis XVI's former minister of finance, Anne-Robert-Jacques Turgot (cat. 16), who had died there in 1781.

Alongside his regular work on the catalogues, Lugt now directed his energies toward the Institut Néerlandais. An exhibition of Italian drawings in 1962 was followed by a show of French drawings. Of the two hundred drawings lent by seven public Dutch institutions and ten private collectors, forty-seven came from the Frits Lugt collection. The drawings were exhibited in period frames, something to which Lugt attached great importance. Also from the Lugt collection were forty autograph letters from French artists and writers, a field, as he himself said, in which he had not originally collected. But as soon as Lugt encountered an interesting artist's autograph he was compelled to buy it, saying that such an acquisition enabled him to have "an important conversation" with the artist concerned (fig. 16).

13. The Institut Néerlandais in Paris, 121 rue de Lille (1990)

14. The rear of the Hôtel Turgot, 2002

15. Frits and To looking at drawings in the "Dutch room" in the Hôtel Turgot, 1957

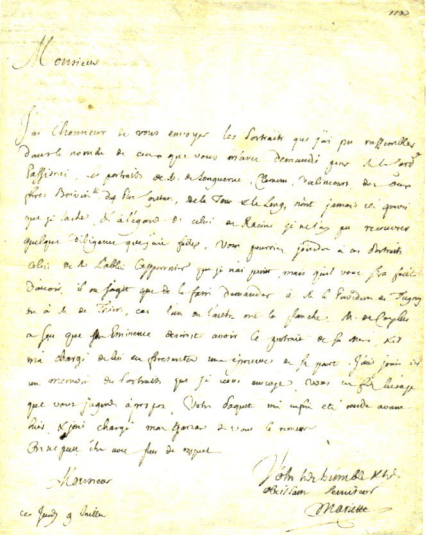

16. Autograph letter by Pierre-Jean Mariette, Thursday, 9 July (1738) (inv. no. 4989)

The nucleus of the French seventeenth-century drawings and the majority of the eighteenth-century ones in the Frits Lugt Collection date from the Frits Lugt period. He had little if any interest in the nineteenth century, unlike the international banker and art collector Franz Koenigs (1881–1941), most of whose holdings eventually found their way to the Museum Boijmans Van Beuningen in Rotterdam. In Koenigs's collection, the finest drawings by Claude Lorrain, Watteau, Boucher, Fragonard, Greuze, and Hubert Robert were accompanied by the work of David, Géricault, Delacroix, Ingres, and Daumier and by magnificent sheets by Manet, Degas, Toulouse-Lautrec, and Cézanne. The occasional drawings by Delacroix (cats. 45–46), Degas (cat. 57), and Berthe Morisot (cat. 62) in the Frits Lugt collection are very much the

exception – they were never collected to be representative of the artists' work, let alone provide an overview of a particular period.

Lugt's successor at Fondation Custodia, Carlos van Hasselt (born in 1929) (fig. 17), who worked closely with him between 1961 and 1970, the year of Lugt's death, continued to build the collection of French drawings in a different way during his time as director (1970–1994). Aside from a superbly preserved Boucher (cat. 13) and works by lesser luminaries of the French Golden Age – artists like Vincent (cat. 29–30), Jeaurat (cat. 9), and de Boissieu – he focused primarily on nineteenth-century French landscapes. Works he acquired include townscapes by Bidauld (cat. 37) and Daubigny (cat. 53), an impressive woodland scene by Gustave Doré (cat. 61), and a sketch of a landscape in De Berry dating from around 1842, painted in oil on paper by the Barbizon landscape painter Théodore Rousseau (cat. 48). After van Hasselt's departure, this area of the collection was augmented with, among other things, an Italian view by Corot (cat. 42), an unusual pastel by Delacroix (cat. 44), an exquisitely drawn landscape by Degas (cat. 56), and a brooding study of the gloomy outskirts of Paris in black chalk by Léon Bonvin (cat. 58). The collection of French drawings had meanwhile grown to number more than eight hundred sheets – including a large studio collection by Hoüel, but not counting the contents of the countless sketchbooks. Thanks to the enthusiasm of Lugt's successors, there are also more than 30,000 French autographs and manuscripts.

Regrettably, Lugt never wanted to write a catalogue of his own collection, let alone his French drawings, which have scarcely been exhibited or published. This, he believed, was a job for his successors. After the catalogue of the

17. Carlos van Hasselt at lunch with the Lugts, 1967

Dessin français of 1964, edited by Carlos van Hasselt – in a sense repeated in 1974 with the *Franse Tekenkunst van de 18de eeuw uit Nederlandse Verzamelingen* in the Rijksprentenkabinet in Amsterdam – a start was made under van Hasselt's guidance on compiling extensive documentation, with the assistance of Pierrette Jean-Richard of the Cabinet des Dessins in the Louvre. Sadly, the small exhibition *Paysage évoqué par la plume et le pinceau. Dessins et autographes d'artistes français du XVIIIe siècle*, staged in 1980 in the Institut Néerlandais with drawings and letters from its own holdings, had to be mounted without a catalogue. It is thanks to Colin B. Bailey, Associate Director and Peter Jay Sharp Chief Curator of The Frick Collection, that this publication marks the first step toward a future catalogue raisonné of the French drawings in the Frits Lugt collection.

Mària van Berge-Gerbaud
Director, Fondation Custodia

Catalogue

Measurements are given
in centimeters.

The initials in the catalogue entries
refer to the following authors:
CBB: Colin B. Bailey
SGG: Susan Grace Galassi
MVB-G: Mària van Berge-Gerbaud
CK: Cindy Kang

1. Antoine Watteau
Valenciennes 1684 – 1721 Nogent-sur-Marne
Three Standing Soldiers, c. 1715
Red chalk | 15.1 x 19.9 | Inv. no. 7208

THREE STANDING SOLDIERS belongs to a group of vigorous drawings in red chalk made around 1715 that relate to one of Watteau's last military paintings, the little-seen panel *Recruits Going to Join the Regiment* (Private Collection), copied by Watteau himself in an etching (fig. 1.1).[1] It was as a painter of military subjects that Watteau established his reputation around 1709, when he emerged from Gillot's and Audran's tutelage. For the comte de Caylus, his unheroic cabinet pictures of soldiers on the march and in repose "were perhaps as beautiful as anything he would produce later in his career."[2] Although many of Watteau's military paintings can be dated to around 1709 and 1710 – years in which he returned home to Valenciennes, a garrison town, during the War of the Spanish Succession – it has long been recognized that the genre occupied him intermittently until 1715 at least.[3]

Watteau's study of an infantry soldier in three different poses pays special attention to the model's body language as well as to details of his costume and armaments. That Watteau was recording the same figure sequentially is suggested by the placement of the model's left hand, tucked into his jacket in both frontal views. The soldier is shown carrying his flintlock musket barrels down, a sword hanging from his waist belt (for use in close combat), and his cartouche (ammunition bag) strapped onto his back. He wears his uniform somewhat casually – the jacket is unbuttoned – and despite the speed with which Watteau worked, we make out the facings on his sleeves, the pockets on the skirt of his jacket, the gaiters over his calves, and even the cockade on his three-cornered hat. It seems probable that Watteau started with the central figure who looks down at us in a slightly intimidating way, then drew closer to the model whom he now showed in profile at left, his cartouche swinging behind him. The third iteration, and the least detailed, is of the soldier from behind, with attention paid to the weight of the cartouche as it is supported on his back. It is this figure that Watteau used for the recruit furthermost to the right in his painting and etching.[4] The confidence with which Watteau fills the page with his three studies, the sinuous, almost balletic relationship between them, and the incisive handling of the brownish sanguine all support a later dating to around 1715.

As Margaret Grasselli was the first to note, the Lugt drawing can be related to a group of military studies in red chalk that share the same mise-en-page of the

[1]

model caught in three different poses.⁵ The closest sheet is *Three Soldiers Advancing* (fig. 1.2), in which the central figure reprises the gesture of the tucked-in left hand; the figure on the right was used for the second soldier at far right in *Recruits Going to Join the Regiment*.⁶ Three other drawings can be included in this group: *Three Studies of Soldiers* (whereabouts unknown) and *Three Soldiers Viewed from Behind* (Kupferstichkabinett, Berlin) – both of which have figures that were preparatory for *Recruits Going to Join the Regiment* – and *Three Soldiers Carrying Muskets* (Private Collection, France), which has been related to the aforementioned composition, even though none of the figures was used for it.⁷ So cohesive is this group that Grasselli has speculated that the drawings may have been made in a single session.⁸ [CBB]

2. Antoine Watteau
Valenciennes 1684 – 1721 Nogent-sur-Marne
Standing Man (Persian), 1715
Red and black chalk | 32.0 x 20.1 | Watermark: coat of arms | Inv. no. 2312

OF THE NINE FIGURE STUDIES by Watteau that can be associated with the state visit to Paris in 1715 of the Persian ambassador Mehemet Reza Beg and his entourage of some twenty men, *Standing Man (Persian)* is the least "oriental" in physiognomy or costume.¹ The absence of any beard or mustache is striking and this "hook-nosed . . . strange little man"² – whose face and hat Watteau recorded for a second time in the *Study of Two Persian Diplomats* (fig 2.1)³ – was traditionally identified as the actor Philippe Poisson (1682 – 1743), who modeled for one of the prints in Watteau's *Figures françoises et comiques*, published in 1715.⁴ More recently, it has been suggested that in *Standing Man (Persian)* Watteau might have dressed one of his friends in a Persian costume from the store of theatrical accessories that he kept on hand in his studio.⁵

Stylistically, this drawing and its cognates bear witness to Watteau's growing fluency in the use of two chalks: his red and black chalk depictions of Savoyards, which also date to 1715, mark an even greater refinement in this regard. Watteau may still not have been "capable of making the sort of continuous, flickering shifts among the three chalks that would become the hallmark of his mature style,"⁶ yet in the Persian and Savoyard sheets his confident, extroverted handling of red and black chalks achieves a "powerful spontaneity."⁷

As is true of many of the Persian drawings, in *Standing Man (Persian)* Watteau's integration of his two chalks is limited. Whereas several sheets in this series were worked up primarily in red chalk, with black used to provide accents and contrast, here black is the dominant color. Watteau's handling of sanguine is fine and delicate in the modeling of the young man's face, head, and hat, more cursory in defining the collarless shirt, and abrupt in delineating the clawlike left hand that holds the garment in place. A richer, more sonorous black chalk is used for the flowing three-quarter-length robe of indeterminate design. Energetic, vivid lines reproduce the rhythms and creases of the costume, rendered at right in stabbing black strokes and dramatically illuminated. Watteau also uses touches of black to delineate the model's hair, eyebrows, and irises, and to enhance the extremities of his fleece-lined, possibly karakul lamb hat.

Although none of the Persian studies was used in any of Watteau's paintings, they are securely documented to 1715 because of the six-month sojourn in Paris of ambassador Mehemet Reza Beg, intendant of Erivan province (the present-day Armenia), and his numerous male entourage, housed between February and August 1715 in the hôtel des Ambassadeurs on the rue de Tournon (Watteau was living nearby on the quai Conti).[8] While the group of nine drawings is less unified than that of the Savoyards, and ranges from summary costume studies to carefully observed portraits, it is generally accepted that all were done from life – even if it has been impossible to explain how (or why) Watteau would have been granted access to members of this official and much publicized mission.[9]

In its swiftness of execution, and separation of red and black chalks, *Standing Man (Persian)* has been associated with the "sub-group" of studies that represent a sympathetic, mustachioed young man, wearing a three-quarter-length jacket and peaked hat, shown seated, standing, and from the back.[10] While the handling of these four sheets is indeed very similar, the model in the Lugt drawing is not the same, as is confirmed by his somewhat spectral reappearance next to one of the higher ranking members of the Persian embassy in *Study of Two Persian Diplomats*. The absence of any facial hair would not have been permissible for a true citizen of the East. As Caylus recalled of his own visit to the Levant in 1716–17, since foreigners were not allowed inside any of the mosques, he had only been able to gain access to the Hagia Sofia by assuming the guise of a slave with "a beautiful moustache."[11] [CBB]

[2]

[3]

3. Antoine Watteau
Valenciennes 1684 – 1721 Nogent-sur-Marne
Landscape with Bear Devouring a Goat, c. 1715 – 16
Red chalk | 20.8 x 29.6 | Watermark: griffin
Inv. no. 3803

LANDSCAPE WITH BEAR DEVOURING A GOAT is a copy in red chalk that Watteau executed around 1715 – 16 after a lost pen-and-ink drawing by Titian, in all likelihood in Pierre Crozat's collection, which was especially rich in landscape drawings by Titian and Domenico Campagnola.[1] Mariette noted that Watteau systematically copied all of Crozat's Campagnolas "and claimed that he had greatly profited from it."[2] Among the portfolios of Watteau's drawings inventoried in May 1735 in the abbé Haranger's estate two were listed as devoted to such copies.[3] The comte de Caylus, who also copied Titian's landscape drawings, claimed that Watteau had been "charmed" by "Titian and Campagnola's fine buildings, beautiful sites, and the tasteful and spirited foliage of their trees."[4] Indeed, Watteau's immersion in these drawings is consistent with Roger de Piles's encouragement to aspiring history painters to copy the sixteenth-century Venetian masters of the pastoral landscape for their "figures, animals, rivers or streams, and trees rustled by the wind."[5]

Titian's lost prototype inspired other copies as well: Rembrandt's pen-and-ink drawing from the 1650s (fig. 3.1), in which the damaged goat's head is difficult to read,[6] and the Carracci school copy of the landscape, without the motif of the warring animals, which had been part of the Jabach collection acquired by Louis XIV in 1671.[7] This latter sheet seems to have been copied by the English connoisseur John Evelyn (1620 – 1706) before it entered the French Royal Collection, since his pen-and-ink drawing is dated "1656."[8]

In a sense, Watteau's copies after sixteenth-century Venetian landscape drawings replaced the exercise of making compositional drawings, an activity that seems to have been abhorrent to him.[9] In the instances in which Watteau's red chalk copies can be compared to their sixteenth-century prototypes, they are meticulous and faithful in nearly every detail, even though by transposing the medium from pen and ink to red chalk, as he always did, Watteau created an atmosphere and luminosity all his own. In the absence of Titian's drawing one is also led to question the identity of the reclining figure who witnesses without emotion the gruesome scene in the foreground.[10] Whereas Rembrandt had depicted this figure as a partially clothed young man, Watteau's naked, epicene onlooker – whose face, buttocks, and knee are vividly accented – is more feminized and evokes the garden statuary that will later populate his fêtes galantes.[11] [CBB]

[4]

4. Antoine Watteau
Valenciennes 1684 – 1721 Nogent-sur-Marne
Study for a Satyr about to Attack, c. 1717
Red, black, and white chalk | 10.8 x 21.2
Verso: to the right, traces of a leg (?) in red chalk
Inv. no. 5923

STUDY FOR A SATYR ABOUT TO ATTACK is one of two known preparatory studies for the figure of Jupiter in Watteau's *Jupiter and Antiope* (fig. 4.1), one of a pair of paintings, probably intended as overdoors, commissioned by Léopold-Philippe-Charles-Joseph, fourth duc d'Arenberg (1690 – 1754). The story of Jupiter, "in a satyr's image hidden . . . filling lovely Antiope with twin offspring," is recounted in the sixth book of Ovid's *Metamorphoses*. In Watteau's composition, the eagle associated with the king of the gods is nowhere to be seen, and the subject was only identified as Jupiter and Antiope by the collector (and donor) Louis La Caze, who acquired the painting in 1868. A variety of sources – from Van Dyck's early *Jupiter and Antiope* (Museum voor Schone Kunsten, Ghent) to Albani's *Diana's Nymphs Disarming Sleeping Cupids* (Musée du Louvre, Paris) to the antique sculpture of *Sleeping Eros* – has been associated with Watteau's composition, which the Goncourts considered a complete appropriation of Titian.[1] It is also clear that Watteau was working from the live model in the elaboration of this rare mythological work.

More brutal and schematic than Watteau's other drawing for the same figure (fig. 4.2), *Study for a Satyr about to Attack* reworks the pose as it appears in the Louvre study to arrive at the squat and undignified position the god will assume in the painting itself.[2] With the oval contours of his composition in mind, perhaps, Watteau compresses the action and elongates the satyr's outstretched right arm, white chalk evoking the drapery between his second and third fingers. This quickly drawn sheet, all stabbing accents and forceful highlights, depicts with extraordinary precision the attitude of the clambering satyr as he pulls himself to the top of the bank, the full weight of his body concentrated in the brutish knee that propels him toward the object of his passion. Although the god's horns, headdress of vine leaves, and cloven hoof are not indicated in this drawing, *Study for a Satyr about to Attack* served as the final blueprint for the figure of the bestial attacker. Even the position of the satyr's naked rump is delineated in red, and such is Watteau's haste that he allows the line to intrude over the contours of the figure's muscular arm.

The two preparatory drawings for *Jupiter and Antiope* have long been related

in style, medium, and function to the group of figure studies for Watteau's Four Seasons, mythological paintings commissioned to complete the decoration of Pierre Crozat's dining room in his hotel on the rue de Richelieu.[3] In its abruptness and ungainliness, *Study for a Satyr about to Attack* is particularly close to *Bacchante Lying on the Ground* (Musée Cognacq-Jay, Paris), a study for one of the recumbent attendants in Watteau's *Autumn*.[4] Together, the drawings of nudes for *Jupiter and Antiope* and the Four Seasons give the lie to Caylus's assertion that Watteau knew "nothing about anatomy," was "incapable of expressing the naked figure," and "never made sketches or noted down his ideas, in however slight or summary a form, for any of his paintings."[5]

Cordelia Hattori's recent redating of the Crozat series has implications for the genesis of *Jupiter and Antiope* as well.[6] Caylus had noted that Watteau's Four Seasons were executed after sketches by Charles de La Fosse (1636–1716), who had been responsible for the ceiling of Crozat's gallery and had introduced Watteau to his patron.[7] Hattori's discovery confirms the fact that La Fosse was the initial recipient of the commission of the Four Seasons, but that he died before starting work on them. Among La Fosse's possessions inventoried after his death in December 1716 were four oval canvases on their stretchers, destined for Crozat's dining room and listed as belonging to him.[8] Only then did the commission pass to Watteau, who must have started work on the series in 1717, the year in which he moved into Crozat's hôtel. The drawings for the Four Seasons cannot date to between 1715 and 1716, as was previously thought, and this would also hold true for the two drawings for *Jupiter and Antiope*. Since Watteau's receipt of 200 livres "for two paintings made for His Highness the duc d'Arenberg" is dated May 1717, this adds further weight to dating the painting, and its related drawings, to that year.[9] [CBB]

5. Antoine Watteau
Valenciennes 1684 – 1721 Nogent-sur-Marne
Studies of Seven Heads, c. 1717 – 18
Red, black, and white chalk, graphite | 22.3 x 28.0
Inv. no. 2319

CELEBRATED SINCE ITS appearance in the *Exposition des dessins des maîtres anciens* in May 1879 – Chennevières pronounced it "the most Watteau of all Watteaus for its splendid, seductive color"[1] – *Studies of Seven Heads* is one of Watteau's rare sheets of multiple heads, a type generally considered "the most immediately recognizable of his drawings."[2] Most likely made in a single session, rather than returned to over a period of time, *Studies of Seven Heads* records the presence of three models: the beautiful, oval-faced girl in a narrow-strapped dress, seen in four different poses in the upper register; a square-faced girl, with dark hair and the hint of a necklace, at lower left; and a young man whose eyelashes are even more luxuriant than his companions' and whose head is studied twice. These last three heads, cast in shadow, create unexpected depth, with the girl emerging from below and the boy's heads establishing a recessive space at the center of the sheet. Rosenberg and Prat have admired "the extraordinarily successful rhythms" of the quartet of female profiles above.[3]

Although heads from this sheet have been considered preparatory for figures in both versions of the *Embarkation to Cythera* (Musée du Louvre, Paris; Schloss Charlottenburg, Staatliche Schlösser und Gärten, Berlin), *The Shepherds* (Schloss Charlottenburg, Staatliche Schlösser und Gärten, Berlin), and the lost *Entretiens badins* (D.V. 95)[4] – supporting a dating to 1716 – 17 – the more cogent relationship is with figures in the second version of the *Embarkation to Cythera*, today in Charlottenburg, made in all likelihood for Jean de Jullienne and executed after Watteau had delivered his reception piece to the Academy in August 1717.[5] (This slightly later dating of the drawing to 1717 – 18 is also commensurate with the use of graphite in the contours of the female heads in the upper register.)[6] As has often been noted, the two studies of the boy's head can be related to the seated male pilgrim (fig. 5.1) who is part of the figural group absent from the first version of the *Embarkation to Cythera*.[7] In his drawing, Watteau was experimenting with different angles and coiffures – and, in the first study, even a hat. He revisited the most fully realized study, in which the boy was initially shown with close-cropped hair, to rework the crown in softer strokes of black. In the painting, this juvenile pilgrim will have a more feline expression and sport a full head of flowing, golden locks.

Of the four studies in the upper register, the head furthest to the right has been associated with that of the seated figure, clad in a red silk mantle, by the tree at right, in *both* versions of the *Embarkation to Cythera*.[8] Watteau appears to have modified this figure in his second painting, and the motif in the Lugt drawing may have served as a blueprint for it (fig. 5.2). The white-chalk highlight visible on the girl's forehead is demarcated in paint in the Berlin *Embarkation to Cythera*, and the position of the girl's eyes, trained to her left, is repeated in this composition.

The model for the four head studies was surely the same young woman who posed for the two figures in the British Museum's *Studies of a Woman and a*

Woman Holding Her Apron (fig. 5.3), as several authors have noted.[9] In the second *Embarkation to Cythera*, Watteau used the motif of the girl with her apron for the figure standing behind the seated woman in red. While in the painting these two adjacent figures have different faces and coiffures, the same model may have served for both. The figure of the dark-haired girl at lower left in the Lugt sheet has been considered preparatory for the rapt companion nestled beside the bagpipe player in *The Shepherds* (Schloss Charlottenburg, Staatliche Schlösser und Gärten, Berlin), but this figure was more likely prepared by another drawing, in which the position of the girl's hands, her expression, and her coiffure are identical to those in the painting.[10] Indeed, as is true of all the sheets of multiple heads, the Lugt drawing is an example of the "extremely complicated" relationship between the drawn motifs and their painted cognates. As Rosenberg and Prat noted, with a hint of exasperation, "Does it happen that Watteau, as he composes his pictures, transforms certain heads that he had studied more meticulously in his drawings?"[11]

Described as in "the finest state of conservation" when it first appeared at auction in April 1791, *Studies of Seven Heads* has suffered from overexposure to natural light, which has darkened the cream paper irrevocably.[12] In this sense, the Lugt drawing may have been a casualty of the rediscovery of the artist in the second half of the nineteenth century. The pride of the Watteaus in the Goncourts' collection — acquired by the brothers for next to nothing from a street vendor in the 1850s[13] — the drawing hung for nearly three decades in the Petit Salon at 53 Boulevard de Montmorency in Auteuil.[14] It was also on display in the Petit Salon of Jacques Doucet's hôtel particulier at 19 rue Spontini, between 1906 and 1912.[15] [CBB]

6. Antoine Watteau
Valenciennes 1684 – 1721 Nogent-sur-Marne
Woman Reclining on a Chaise Longue, c. 1718
Red and black chalk with stumping | 21.7 x 31.1
Inscriptions: recto, at bottom left in graphite,
"Watteau" | Inv. no. 2311

WOMAN RECLINING ON A CHAISE LONGUE is the most introspective of Watteau's intimate studies of a female model captured in a variety of informal but decidedly erotic poses.[1] Probably executed over the course of a few sessions, close in time, this group of drawings is thought to have been made in

rooms rented by the comte de Caylus for the purpose of "posing the model, painting and drawing."[2] In such private quarters, Caylus recalled, "we experienced the pure joy of youth," with the habitually "bilious and timid" Watteau transformed into the artist of his pictures — "agreeable, affectionate, and perhaps even a little rustic."[3]

Were it not for her exposed nipples, highlighted in black chalk, the contemplative young woman in this sheet might be interpreted as an informal variation on a stock fashion type, the *Woman of Quality in Negligent Undress* ("femme de qualité en déshabille negligé"), or even a study in melancholy.[4] Indeed, by comparison with some of the other studies for which the same model posed (fig. 6.1), Watteau's subject here is all propriety. Her hair is gathered tightly in its horseshoe-shaped clip, the sleeve of her *robe volante* drapes over the ample wing of the upholstered *lit de repos* (whose pins are rendered in staccato dashes of black), and her distracted gaze avoids the slightest engagement with the viewer. Yet as Donald Posner eloquently noted — and as the model's décolletage and absence of stays confirm — in this drawing as in the related studies, "What Watteau saw and aimed to express is the voluptuousness of the female body as it surrenders to relaxation, curls, or stretches and turns with feline sensuality."[5]

In *Woman Reclining on a Chaise Longue* Watteau's integration of his red and black chalks is seamless and delicate. The contours of the model's face, upper body, underskirt, and sleeve were initially drawn lightly in red, and then returned to in black — almost too insistently in the space behind her neck, as Rosenberg and Prat have noted[6] — which becomes the dominant tone in evoking the pendulous folds of her costume and the legs and stretchers of the *lit de repos*.[7] Such is Watteau's fluency in alternating between the two colors that we do not immediately grasp that the red stripes at the top of the woman's skirt are rendered in black, as are the creases of the garment as it falls below her waist. White chalk is not used, and liberal stumping adds texture to the wings of the chair and the heft of the woman's robe. Grasselli has noted the drawing's "delicate use of the stump, vaporous atmosphere, gently glowing light, and informal intimacy."[8]

While these erotically charged drawings demonstrably form a distinct group in Watteau's oeuvre, there are considerable variations among them, in mood, pose, and technique.[9] Caylus may have hired more than one model for his friend, but it seems likely that the same model returned for several sessions.[10] In five of the drawings the young woman is shown wearing the same chemise with coquettish bows at the sleeve, an item treated differently in every sheet — as an abstract accent in red and black in the audacious *Woman Reclining on a*

Chaise Longue (see fig. 6.1), as syncopated flourishes anchoring the sprawling figure in *Seated Young Woman* (fig. 6.2, The Thaw Collection, The Morgan Library & Museum, New York).[11] Such is the refinement of the Lugt drawing that this detail is easily overlooked, but the bow is visible inside the model's hanging sleeve as a smudge of black.

While it is agreed that these drawings date to Watteau's maturity, Grasselli and Wintermute have proposed a slightly later dating than Rosenberg and Prat, who placed the series to 1717 – 18. The later dating of 1718 can also be supported by the early history of three of the nudes from the series, first recorded in the Tessin sale of May 1786 (the Lugt sheet is not among them). Since Watteau is known to have destroyed his most licentious paintings and drawings shortly before his death, Count Carl Gustav Tessin (1695 – 1770) is likely to have acquired these three drawings on his second visit to Paris, where he resided between September 1718 and March 1719. Grasselli also speculated that the Swedish art lover and admirer of Watteau might have been among Caylus's party when some of these nude studies were made.[12] [CBB]

7. Anonymous French artist, formerly attributed to Watteau
Study of a Shell (Murex ramosus Linne), c. 1720 – 30
Red and black chalk | 26.2 x 19.6 | Inv. no. 7634

THIS VIGOROUS DRAWING, in red and black chalks, belongs to a group of eight similarly executed studies of seashells, first published by Parker and Mathey as by Watteau in 1957, with the authors also identifying the various species of marine life.[1] Acknowledging that the drawings are of "surpassing beauty," Grasselli rejected the attribution: "The intricately ornamental handling of both the contours and the modeling suggests that they were the work of a designer of decorative pieces, perhaps even a sculptor. Nowhere in Watteau's oeuvre can one find drawings of comparable execution with the same thickly hatched background and the same distinct separation of the red and black chalks."[2] Noting that there were, in fact, certain similarities between the regular hatching strokes in these sheets and Watteau's handling of his chalks in his copies after the Old Masters,[3] Rosenberg and Prat regretfully included the group in their corpus of rejected drawings, proposing that the drawings should be dated to around 1715 – 30, which, they admitted, "resolves nothing."[4] Since the provenance of the eight drawings could only be traced to the

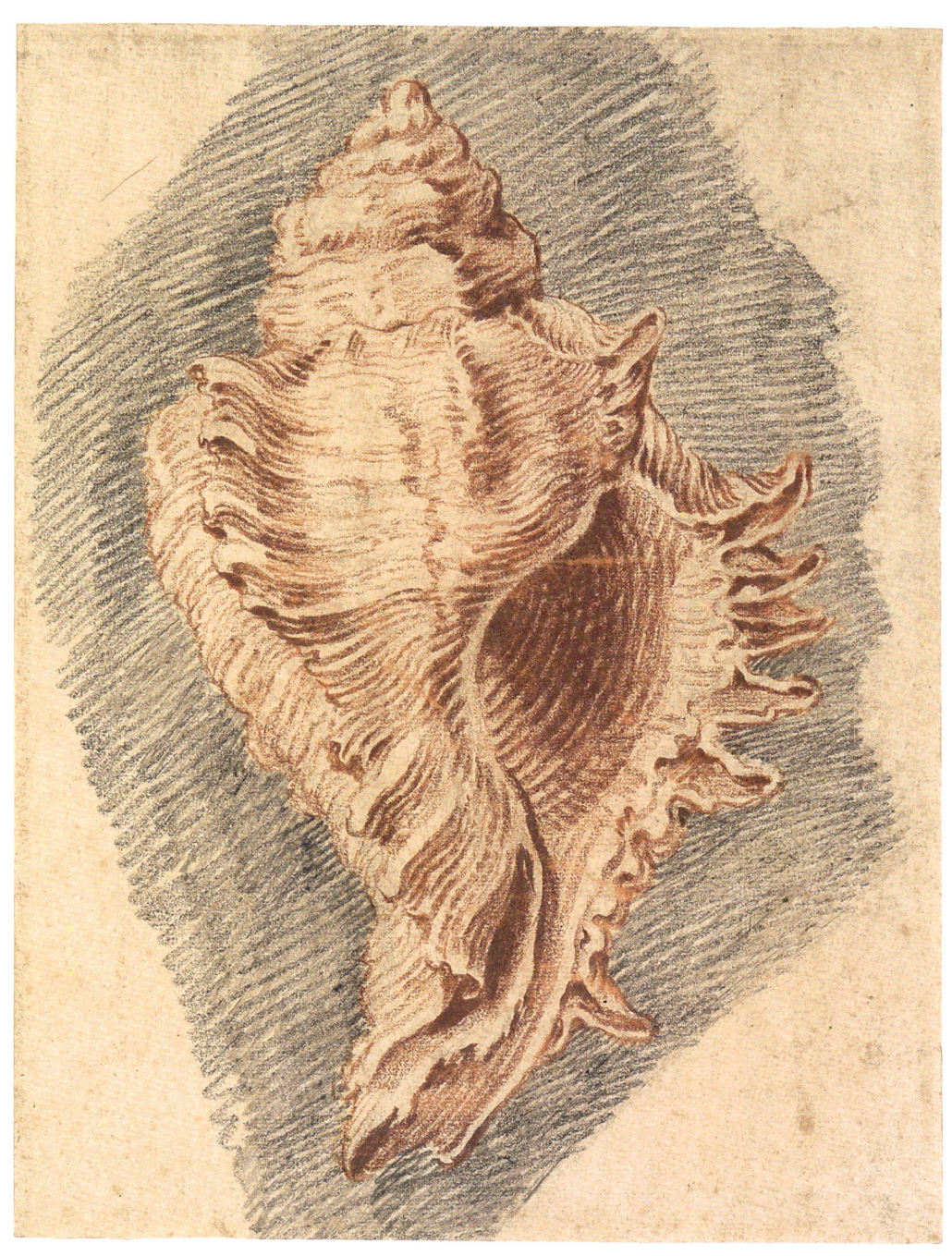

second half of the nineteenth century, eighteenth-century sales catalogues were of no assistance in proposing alternative candidates for authorship.[5]

The seashell in the Lugt collection, classified by Parker and Mathey as *Murex anguliferus*, is a tropical species, found in the Red Sea and the Indian Ocean and distinguished by its "pyriform, angulate shape and short spine."[6] The shell seems to have been portrayed a second time, in a more ungainly "pose," in the sheet from Besançon (fig. 7.1).[7] Twentieth-century classification also identifies the shell as a specimen of *Murex ramosus Linne*, a carnivorous marine gastropod referred to as the subgenus *Chicoreus* (*Chicoreus ramosus* or *Chicoreus virgineus*). Other members of this family include species that provided the famous Tyrian purple dye of antiquity.[8]

Assigning the authorship of this group of drawings to Watteau was also encouraged by his friendship with the dealer Edme Gersaint (1694 – 1750) – in whose premises on the Pont Notre-Dame Watteau lived after returning from England in 1720[9] – who would be responsible for introducing a taste for shells among Parisian collectors in the 1730s and 1740s.[10] Gersaint's annual visits to the Netherlands after 1734 were motivated as much by the burgeoning demand for conchological specimens and other natural curiosities as by the market for Old Master paintings and drawings. The *Mercure de France* dutifully reported on the treasure troves that he negotiated from Dutch collectors, "shells of all types and in the best condition."[11] During Watteau's lifetime, however, Gersaint was renowned as a *marchand-mercier* who specialized primarily in paintings, mirrors, lacquerware, and porcelain; the vogue for natural history collections, in which he would play an instrumental part, was a phenomenon of the decades following Watteau's death.[12]

The function of this group of drawings is also unclear, but it should be noted that they portray the specimens on a monumental scale. The murex represented in the Lugt and Besançon sheets was no larger than four inches, and the cowrie shells and cassidae depicted in drawings at the Morgan Library & Museum and Besançon were even smaller. It was the custom to arrange shells in *coquilliers*, whose drawers might be lined in cloth, or to arrange them in groups or ornamental patterns resembling parterres.[13] The gigantesque presentation in the Lugt drawing and its cohorts, not appropriate for scientific illustration, is another argument in favor of a sculptor or *ornameniste*, one whose distinctive, "Watteauesque" handling of his chalks awaits rediscovery. [CBB]

8. Pierre-Jean Mariette
Paris 1694 – 1775 Paris
View of Crozat's Gardens at Montmorency, dated 1724
Pen and brown ink, brown wash over black chalk, with highlights in white | 40.1 x 26.7 | Inscriptions: in the upper left, in the hand of the artist, in pen and brown ink, "Dans les Jardins de M. Crozat à Montmorenci. 1724."; on the mount, in the cartouche, in brown ink, "Pet. Joan. / Mariette / advivum"
Inv. no. 3787

As noted in mariette's meticulous hand at the upper left of this sheet, this pen and ink drawing of a group of trees towering over a low wall and a disappearing allée was done in "the gardens of M. Crozat at Montmorency." Since 1702 the gardens in question – originally laid out by André Le Nôtre for Charles Le Brun, the first occupant of this property – had belonged to Pierre Crozat (1665 – 1740), the extraordinarily wealthy banker, collector of Old Master drawings, and royal agent. Having acquired the barony of Thionville at Montmorency, thirteen kilometers north of Paris, from Le Brun's heirs, between 1704 and 1709 Crozat engaged the young architect Jean-Sylvain Cartaud (1675 – 1758) to build a new château for him on the southeast corner of the estate, commanding spectacular views of the extensive grounds, which Cartaud also replanted.[1] Le Brun's two-story loggia was gutted and turned into an open-air *maison de plaisance*, which overlooked a long reflecting pool. The most celebrated record of Crozat's gardens at Montmorency was made by Watteau in two drawings; and a view of Le Brun's transformed residence can be seen through the trees in the background of his *La Perspective* of c. 1717 (Museum of Fine Arts, Boston).[2]

On his return from an extended assignment abroad in June 1719, Mariette became an habitué of the select group of connoisseurs, collectors, and artists who met in Crozat's Parisian residence on the rue de Richelieu to study his peerless collection of Old Master drawings. Over the next two decades Mariette would gain an intimate acquaintance with these drawings as he was engaged in cataloguing the 19,000 sheets in Crozat's possession.[3]

As the date on *View of Crozat's Gardens at Montmorency* informs us – and the epithet "advivum" (from life) on the mount's cartouche confirms – the thirty-year-old Mariette made this drawing in situ in 1724. He had studied drawing with the obscure "dessinateur de paysage" Jean Chaufourier (1679–1757) – who would later hold the post of professor of perspective at the Royal Academy – and this rather faltering work may be more indebted to his master than he chose to admit.[4] Nevertheless, it is the most ambitious of Mariette's small oeuvre of original drawings, all landscapes – as opposed to his copies after the masters – to have survived. Jacob Bean aptly characterized the Lugt garden view as "a graceful exercise in the Bolognese vein,"[5] and indeed it is indebted to Annibale Carracci and Guercino, whose landscape drawings Mariette collected, copied, and engraved.[6] Pierre-François Basan also referred to this seventeenth-century Bolognese influence in his catalogue of Mariette's posthumous sale, praising "the foliage of the trees which is done in the grand manner."[7]

View of Crozat's Gardens at Montmorency was one of four landscape drawings of Montmorency retained by their maker for his private collection, which were acquired as a group by his heirs for fifty livres. A sheet from this group, in a characteristic blue mount but without the elaborate Latinate inscription on its cartouche, has recently entered the collection of the Nationalmuseum in Stockholm (fig. 8.1).[8]

Might the Lugt drawing have carried a more personal significance for Mariette and his family? It was made in the year of his marriage to Angélique-Catherine Doyen, daughter of a notary, to whom Mariette had been betrothed since October 1722. The young bride brought a dowry of 40,000 livres to the union; Mariette's father settled 60,000 livres on the couple.[9] If Crozat's grounds at Montmorency with their looming trees and dramatic allées served Watteau as a point of departure for his urbane gardens of love, they may also have conveyed similar (if more discreet) associations for Mariette. [CBB]

9. Étienne Jeaurat
Paris 1699 – 1789 Versailles
View of the Tiber, near the Ripa Grande, Rome,
c. 1724 – 27
Gray ink and wash, white gouache on blue paper | 27.6 x 42.7 | Inscriptions: at lower right, in brown ink, "F Sablet" (partly effaced); on the mount, at bottom, in brown ink, "vue du tibre pres de Ripagrande, a Roma"; verso, at the top of mount, in graphite, "S.vene ACagdou . . . (?)" and "51 x 37"
Inv. no. 1986-T.34

VIEW OF THE TIBER, NEAR THE RIPA GRANDE, ROME, is one of a series of drawings in mixed media on prepared blue paper that Jeaurat made at the encouragement of his protector, director Nicolas Vleughels, during his stay in Rome as a pensionnaire of the French Academy.[1] Like its cognate in the Polakovits collection at the École Nationale Supérieure des Beaux-Arts (fig. 9.1), this quiet, riparian view shows a cluster of buildings in the late afternoon sun set against the lightly trafficked river.[2] The eighteenth-century inscription on the edge of the mount identifies the site as the Ripa Grande, the larger of Rome's two river ports at the foot of the Aventine Hill. As in the drawing in the École Nationale Supérieure des Beaux-Arts, we are shown the irregular cluster of buildings at the upstream edge of the port that constituted the old customs house (the Dogana Vecchia). This was an area under intense redevelopment, site of the future Ospizio Apostolico di San Michele, a gigantic complex of buildings erected between 1693 and 1735, which housed a number of charitable and penal institutions. The buildings of the old customs house would be destroyed in 1734 – 35.[3]

Jeaurat's "poised and placid" drawing,[4] with its interlocking buildings and panoramic vista, avoids any engagement with the active, bustling port, and thus parts company with the traditions of Roman view painting, which portrayed the Ripa Grande's animation and picturesque congestion.[5]

On his return to Paris in 1729, Jeaurat would pursue a career as a history painter, ascending the Academy's hierarchy to become chancellor in 1781 but gaining a reputation in the 1750s and 1760s for his ribald genre scenes of Parisian lowlife (the "genre poissard").[6] The figure studies of his maturity bear little resemblance to this bucolic early Roman view, which may account for the false signature, "F Sablet," probably added to the sheet at lower right when it entered the Lajarriette collection in Nantes in the early nineteenth century. Although catalogued in the financier's posthumous sale of May 1861 as by "Jacob [sic] Sablet," there is no reason to question the attribution to Jeaurat.[7] By a curious coincidence, an authentic work by Jean-François Sablet from the group assembled by Lajarriette, showing *Fisherman in an Italian Landscape during a Storm* (fig. 9.2), was acquired by the Fondation Custodia in 2001. The superficial similarities of media and technique may help explain the fanciful attribution to Jean-François Sablet of Jeaurat's *View of the Tiber, near the Ripa Grande, Rome*. [CBB]

10. Jean-Baptiste Pater
Valenciennes 1695 – 1736 Paris
Standing Soldier with a Pipe, c. 1725 – 30
Red chalk | 18.7 x 9.2 | Inscriptions: at lower left, in pen and black ink, "271" | Inv. no. 7209

STANDING SOLDIER WITH A PIPE is a characteristic mature study by Pater in red chalk on cream paper, preparatory for the languid, tricorne-wearing protagonist of *Troops at Rest* (fig. 10.1).[1] The Lugt study was formerly associated with a similar figure in a related military composition, *Soldiers before an Inn* (Sanssouci Palace, Potsdam), recorded in the Audience Chamber of Frederick the Great's summer palace as early as 1768. While the drawing served for both works, it is closest to the figure in the painting in The Metropolitan Museum of Art, New York, in which the soldier has the same hooked nose and wide-eyed expression. His left hand, with its fingers tapering down, is more or less identical in both the painting and drawing, as is the swagger of his belt. (These details are not repeated in the more refined treatment of the soldier in the later picture in Potsdam, which has been dated by Christoph Vogtherr to between 1730 and 1736.)[2]
Like Watteau a native of the garrison town of Valenciennes, Pater would have had ample opportunity to study soldiers from life during the final years of the War of the Spanish Succession. However, in his bivouac scenes – painted in the peaceful decades of Louis XV's early reign – Pater adhered slavishly to the models established by Watteau, which showed soldiers at rest and far from the arena of battle. Pater had moved to Paris around 1711 – 12 to become Watteau's apprentice (a short and unhappy experience), but it was only in the summer of 1721, when the dying artist, seeking reconciliation, invited him to

Nogent-sur-Marne to resume the twenty-six-year-old's instruction, that Pater became immersed in Watteau's paintings and drawings. He confided to Gersaint that he "owed everything he knew to this brief period of time," and over the next decade and a half he produced an almost endless supply of military subjects, fêtes galantes, and bathing scenes in the manner of Watteau.[3]

At least two dozen red-chalk drawings of soldiers by Pater have been recorded, and the Lugt sheet has been considered exemplary of his standing male figure studies.[4] Pater's distinctive handling involves contours that are smooth, sanguine applied in soft, long strokes, and shadows indicated by rapidly applied accents. Unlike the military studies of his master (see cat. 1), Pater's drawings are all surface elegance and energy, since it was beyond his abilities to convey the underlying structure of the human body. We gain little sense of the model's flesh and bones beneath his costume.

As is confirmed by the truncated tricorne at upper right, the Lugt study has been cut down and mounted onto a second sheet of paper. Indeed, as is true for nearly all of Pater's military drawings, *Standing Soldier with a Pipe* once formed part of a sheet of multiple studies, dismembered to produce single figures in red chalk. The number "271" at lower left indicates that the Lugt drawing was once part of the so-called Groult Album of some five hundred sheets – the majority by Pater, but with examples by Watteau, Claude III Audran (1658 – 1734), and Gilles-Marie Oppenort (1672 – 1742) – compiled in the second half of the eighteenth century, but celebrated once it entered the collection of Camille Groult (1837 – 1908). The album was retained by his descendants until its dispersal after the auction of the family collection in December 1941.[5] [CBB]

11. Jean-Étienne Liotard
Geneva 1702 – 1789 Geneva
Frankish Woman from Galata and Her Servant,
c. 1740 – 42
Black and red chalk on two sheets of paper, joined vertically | 20.4 x 25.0 | Inscriptions: at lower right, in black chalk, "Liotard" | Watermark: on the left-hand sheet, a fragment of a crest with the number "4" and the initials "WR" (interlaced) | Inv. no. 2315

LIOTARD ARRIVED IN Constantinople from Smyrna in June 1738 in the entourage of two English Grand Tourists, the Earl of Sandwich and the Honorable William Ponsonby (whose descendant, the third Earl of Bessborough, would own the Lugt drawing in the 1840s). He remained there for just over four years, sustained by portrait commissions from Western diplomats and merchants, before accepting an invitation from Prince Mavrocordato of Moldavia to spend ten months at his court in Jassy (part of present-day Romania). Bearded, in oriental costume, and now styling himself "le Peintre Turc," Liotard returned to Vienna in September 1743; over the next two decades he established a clientele for his portraits that would include almost every royal family in Europe.[1]

During his four years in the Ottoman empire, Liotard produced a number of black and red chalk drawings of extraordinary refinement, showing well-to-do ladies from the Frankish colony of Pera and Galata with their Turkish servants. Midway between portraits and conversation pieces, these presentation drawings or *tableaux-dessinés* would serve as the basis for future compositions – in painting, pastel, and (occasionally) engraving – later constituting part of the apparatus of Liotard's studio in Geneva, on display to visitors and potential clients.[2] *Frankish Woman from Galata and Her Servant* would be among the sixteen drawings Liotard included in the collection he sold at Christie's in London, in April 1774, toward the end of his two-year sojourn there.[3] At this auction it was paired with *A Georgian*, a drawing whose whereabouts remain unknown.[4]

The subject of the Lugt drawing is provided by the legend accompanying the engraving made jointly in 1745 by Liotard and Giuseppe Camaratta (1713 – 1803) for the Parisian print market (fig. 11.1): "A Frankish Lady from Galata and her Slave who are about to go to Constantinople or another Turkish district. The Slave presents her Mistress with a veil similar to the one she wears

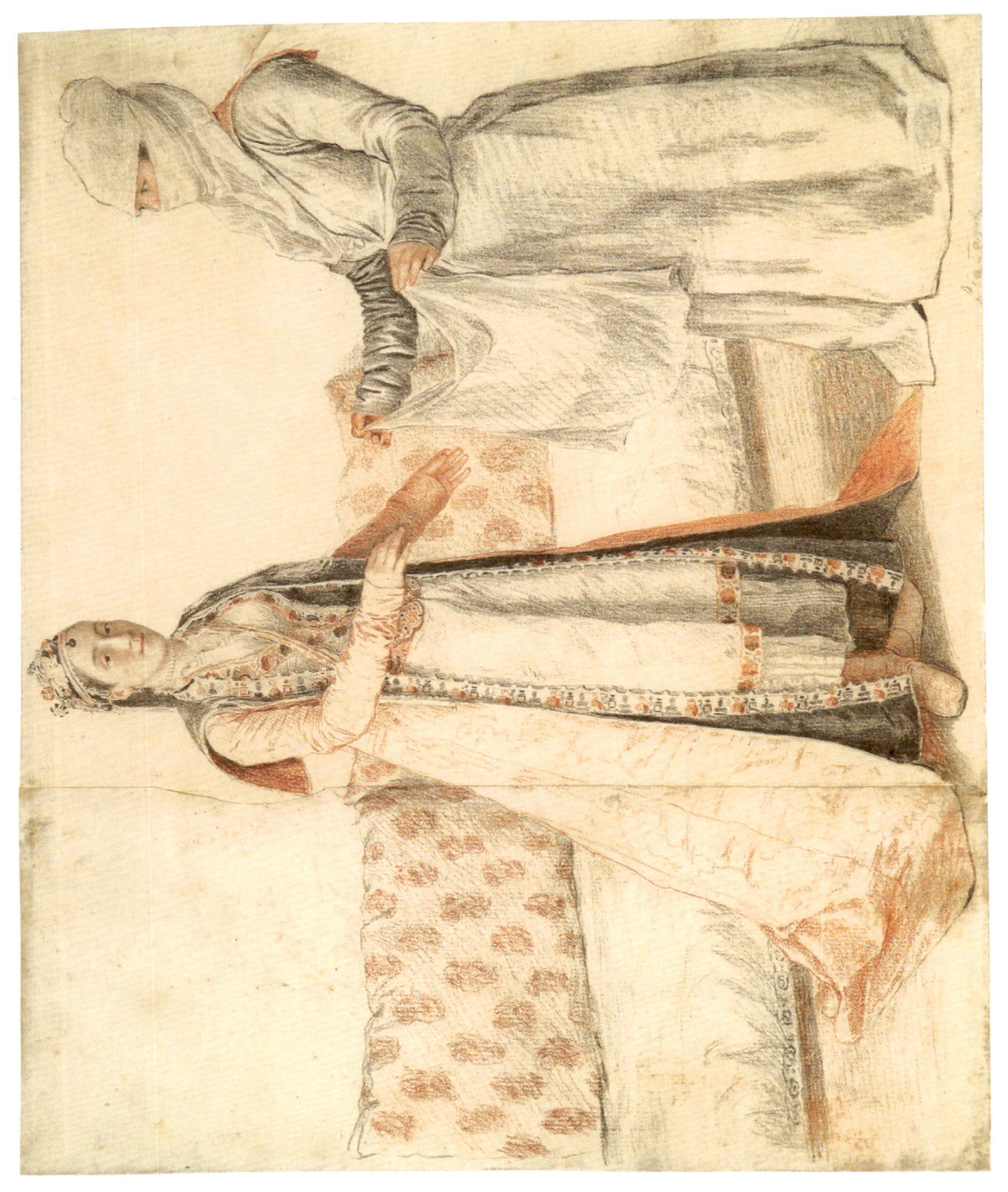

[11]

on her face, without which Turkish Women never go out."⁵ As can be seen from the join in the paper, and as is confirmed by the counterproof of this drawing (fig. 11.2), Liotard initially conceived of his composition as more tightly cropped, with little sense of any interior space. After taking the counterproof, Liotard revised the drawing, extending the Frankish woman's mantle and continuing the sofa to provide depth and air to the scene. This idiosyncratic way of working, a procedure also apparent in the exquisite *Servant Presenting Tea to Her Seated Levantine Mistress* (Oskar Reinhart Foundation Museum, Winterthur, Switzerland), allowed him to revisit the figures of the two women and rework the blacks on the servant's sleeves and the interior of the mistress's cape.⁶ The engraving, for which Liotard etched only the faces, adopts a mise-en-page midway between drawing and counterproof.⁷

In this drawn orientalist conversation piece, Liotard achieves a fragile balance between "an almost photographic obsession with detail and clarity" and an exploration of ritual that eschews stereotype or anecdote.⁸ His approach to his subject is highly mediated: despite Liotard's vaunted naturalism, this is not a scene captured from life. The motif of the veiled servant had first been studied in a drawing made "in the street" in July 1738, one month after his arrival in Constantinople.⁹ His model for the mistress of *Frankish Woman from Galata and Her Servant* was most likely a member of the Christian colony on the north shore of the Golden Horn, who was willing (and allowed) to pose unveiled.

Liotard is fastidious in showing the elaborate dress and coiffure worn by Turkish women of rank, and appropriated by the European settlers. He lingers lovingly over the kid leather shoes, the embroidered smock, the tight-fitting waistcoat ("antery") trimmed with jewels, the ornate girdle, "four fingers broad," and the brocade overmantle ("curdee"). As the legend to the print explains, the Frankish woman is being handed a veil ("asmack"), which she is obliged to wear when visiting the Turkish capital. She and her servant will also cover themselves in a cape and hood known as a "ferigee," "which no woman of any sort appears without."¹⁰

As Lady Mary Wortley Montagu (1689 – 1762), wife of the English ambassador to the Porte, had observed two decades earlier, the women of Pera and Galata had a "perfect aversion" to covering their faces as required by Muslim protocol. "Tis true they wear veils in Pera, but they are such as only serve to show their beauty to more advantage and would not be permitted in Constantinople. These reasons deter almost every creature from seeing it."¹¹ The hesitation of Liotard's young woman, as she accepts the veil from her admiring servant, hints at such coquetry with ineffable grace. [CBB]

12. François Boucher
Paris 1703 – 1770 Paris
Standing Woman Seen from Behind, c. 1742
Black, red, and white chalk, with stumping, on
gray-brown paper | 35.3 x 19.9 | Inv. no. 3552

ONE OF BOUCHER'S MOST vigorous and widely published drawings, *Standing Woman Seen from Behind* relates to the figure of the elegant young woman, lace cap in hand, dancing attendance upon the seated mistress in *A Lady Fastening Her Garter ("La Toilette")* (fig. 12.1).[1] Signed and dated 1742, a commission from the Swedish diplomat and discerning collector of contemporary French art, Carl Gustaf Tessin (1695 – 1770), *La Toilette* was a rare incursion by Boucher into a genre popularized in the 1720s by Jean-François de Troy. It has been recently described as "one of the most evocative images of the pleasure-loving, eighteenth-century Parisian society ever to have been created."[2]

As has also been noted, Boucher's figure study of the woman seen from behind is not, strictly speaking, preparatory for the painting; while very similar, her pose is not identical.[3] In the drawing, her left hand rests by her side, her hips sway to the left — note the angle of the pleats on the back of her jacket — and her feet are in reverse of their position in the final composition. The figure of the young woman is shown with the tiniest of caps, sports no *mouche* on her forehead, and is attired in a different costume from the one in the painting. Her sackback jacket, or *casaquin*, has two sleeve flounces from the elbow, the latest fashion in 1740,[4] and hangs loose over her flounced skirt. Ribeiro also notes that such a jacket would have been too informal for a *modiste* visiting a client, and in the painting she is shown in a full-length *robe à la française*, tucked into the pockets of her petticoat to achieve a swagged look.[5] Nevertheless, as her backless mules confirm, her costume would have been appropriate only for private, indoor wear. It is unlikely that Boucher conceived of this figure as executing a dance step, with her left hand holding up her skirt.[6]

Standing Woman Seen from Behind has little in common with a second preparatory drawing for Tessin's composition, *Study of a Young Woman Tying Her Garter* (Musée des Beaux-Arts, Orléans), a figure study in trois crayons (and in very poor condition) for the seated woman who dominates the composition.[7] Such stylistic incongruities may be explained by the different functions and techniques of the two drawings: the Orléans sheet seems to have been made specifically for the seated figure in Tessin's painting, whereas the Lugt sheet may have started life with another composition in mind, or have been elabo-

[13]

rated at an earlier stage of *La Toilette*'s gestation. *Standing Woman Seen from Behind* relates more easily to other figure studies of the early 1740s, such as the *Head of a Young Woman with Hair Tied Up*, 1740–41, in the Bonna Collection.[8] In its resolute handling of black chalks (with the merest touches of sanguine on the model's cheek and hands) and controlled yet dynamic application of white heightening, *Standing Woman Seen from Behind* bears many of the qualities of Boucher's later autonomous drawings, created as independent works of art to be mounted and framed in the collector's cabinet. Indeed Boucher's flourishes of black and white chalks at the lower right of the Lugt drawing are almost a signature in themselves.

The mature Boucher's lingering debt to Watteau in this figure study has also been widely recognized. His elegant young woman seen from the back, with her hair pulled up and her expression invisible to us, descends from the wistful protagonist of Watteau's *Two Cousins*, c. 1716 (Musée du Louvre, Paris), or the lady in pink in *Gersaint's Shopsign*, 1721 (Schloss Charlottenburg, Staatliche Schlösser und Gärten, Berlin).[9] In his twenties Boucher had been employed to copy Watteau's drawings for Jean de Jullienne's two-volume *Figures de différents caractères*; *Standing Woman Seen from Behind* (Musée du Louvre, Paris, collection Edmond de Rothschild) was among the one hundred etchings he contributed to the project.[10] Such a figure would become one of Boucher's most successful inventions. Shoeless, in rough peasant dress, a basket of laundry or flowers at her side, a baby on her shoulder, she will make an occasional appearance in Boucher's pastorals and rustic landscapes during four decades of his production.[11] [CBB]

13. François Boucher
Paris 1703 – 1770 Paris
View of a Rustic Habitation, c. 1760
Black and white chalk, gray wash and stumping, on blue paper, heightened with black pastel | 23.0 x 35.5
Inscriptions: at the lower right of mount, in pen and black ink, in an eighteenth-century script, "Boucher"
Inv. no. 2007-T.21

THIS ATMOSPHERIC LATE DRAWING — in a superb state of conservation — shows rustic habitations carved into the ruins of an ancient building, anchored by three prominent buttresses heightened in white. Descending the steps at left is a faceless peasant woman, balancing herself as she walks and holding up her skirts with her left hand. Ill-defined farmyard implements rest propped against the wall at the first arched entrance; a basket is almost camouflaged by the stones at the foot of the second buttress; a rope hangs from a pole in the wall at far right, attached to what appears to be a harness on the ground.

The summariness of these staffage elements is in contrast to the powerful presence of the looming, rocky structure itself, with its Piranesi-like portals, stairways, and shutters. Unlike many of Boucher's more finished compositional landscape drawings of the 1740s and 1750s, the Lugt sheet was not made to be engraved, is not patterned after the work of a Northern master, and does not relate to any known painted landscape – either as preparatory study or *ricordo*.[1] The blind stamp and pen-and-ink inscription, "Boucher," on the eighteenth-century mount confirm that this was an autonomous sheet, mounted by Jean-Baptiste Glomy (c. 1720 – 1786), the *marchand-mercier* who specialized in "affixing and matting drawings and prints, carefully and cleanly."[2] The market for collecting the drawings of living French artists was in the ascendant after midcentury, and Boucher, Glomy's best client, was the most senior member of the Royal Academy to profit from it.[3]

Boucher's rustic capriccio, which may be dated to around 1760, conjures memories of the artist's Roman sojourn three decades earlier. The buttresses and doorways emerging from the rock recall the ruins of the Palace of the Caesars on the Palatine Hill, a central motif in the *Capriccio View of the Farnese Gardens*, 1734 (The Metropolitan Museum of Art, New York), and the drawings associated with it.[4] Yet the setting of the Lugt sheet, with its picturesque structures and foliage, is probably intended to evoke the French countryside. Amalgamating such traditions was Boucher's stock-in-trade. As early as 1748, a reviewer of that Salon had noted, "Who is better able than M. Boucher to produce beautiful landscapes in which one sees, with pleasure, that happy mixture of views of Rome or Tivoli, with those from Sceaux and Arcueil?"[5]

Difficult as it is to date Boucher's mature drawings – while he was fairly rigorous about signing and dating his major paintings, he followed no such habit for his graphic work – *Landscape with Ruins* can be assigned to the final decade of his career. In its generalized handling, "all-over" composition (with the rocky architecture expanding beyond the page), and adroit use of stumping, it relates stylistically to sheets that take their point of departure from the drawings of seventeenth-century Northern masters, such as *Study of a Cottage* after Cornelis Decker (fig 13.1), recently dated to around 1760.[6]

Despite the distinctiveness of its presentation, and the vogue for ruins in French art after 1750, in conception the Lugt drawing keeps faith with the principles established by Roger de Piles at the beginning of the eighteenth century. A signal component of the pastoral landscape, as defined by de Piles, was the appropriate portrayal of buildings ("les Fabriques"). They were "a great ornament to the landscape, even when they are Gothic or appear uninhabited and partly in ruins; they raise the imagination by the use they are thought to have been designed for."[7] [CBB]

14. Jean-Baptiste Oudry
Paris 1686 – 1755 Beauvais
Landscape with Bulls Fighting, dated 1751
Brush and black ink, gray wash, heightened with black and white gouache on brownish-gray paper
33.5 x 53.7 | Inscriptions: signed at lower left in pen and brown ink, "JB. Oudry / 1751" | Inv. no. 1980-T.22

ALMOST MONOCHROMATIC IN APPEARANCE — yet a virtuoso display of Oudry's handling of brush, pen, gouache, and wash — *Landscape with Bulls Fighting* has been recently described by Pierre Rosenberg as "an impeccable drawing . . . with a dream of a provenance."[1] It has been associated with the group of sixteen large-format compositional drawings executed in 1745 that served as preliminary designs for a suite of Gobelins tapestries showing wild animals in combat.[2] Oudry seems to have planned this series as a successor to the *Chasses royales de Louis XV*, a set of nine tapestries for the royal hunting lodge at Compiègne, on which he was employed between 1733 and 1746.[3] Only in 1751 did the artist formally approach the Bâtiments with a request to provide the Gobelins with this new series showing different animals fighting; his petition, which fell on deaf ears, listed twelve subjects, many of which conformed to the drawings made six years earlier.[4]

Hal Opperman also identified a group of twelve compositional drawings that showed animals of the *same* species in combat, executed in 1750 and 1751, which Oudry may also have conceived as possible subjects for tapestries.[5] It was in this group that he placed the Lugt drawing, which he knew from documentary sources (the drawing reappeared at auction only in 1979).[6] As is clear from comparing the present sheet with any of those from the series dated 1745 (fig. 14.1), the Lugt drawing is above all a spectacular landscape in which four beautiful, if hardly ferocious, animals engage in an almost courtly encounter.[7] Oudry's earlier proposals for the Gobelins were both more populous and more

bloodthirsty: in those drawings the various wild animals fill the scene in crazed and dramatic confrontation, with the landscape a subsidiary element (as would be appropriate for tapestries twenty feet in scale).

With only an oblique relationship to the Gobelins project, *Landscape with Bulls Fighting* is characteristic of the industrious Oudry's working method. He drew incessantly, for his own purposes, and after his death more than one hundred volumes and portfolios of his drawings were inventoried among the contents of his studio.[8] His first biographer noted that Oudry had been "more attached to his drawings than his paintings, and he considered them a resource to be left to his family; hardly any were available during his lifetime."[9] The Lugt drawing might have been part of a volume devoted to "twenty-nine compositional drawings of animals," appraised at 120 livres in his *inventaire après décès*.[10]

Once Oudry's compositional drawings appeared on the market, however, there was considerable demand for them, and Mariette despaired of the high prices they fetched. "It is the fault of the fashion for finished drawings," he noted, "which satisfies those whose connoisseurship is limited."[11] Thanks to its distinctive dark blue mount and gold filet, it has been possible to identify *Landscapes with Bulls Fighting* as one of the eighteen drawings acquired in July 1755 for Christian Ludwig II, Duke of Mecklenburg-Schwerin (1683 – 1756) – after Louis XV, Oudry's greatest patron. No catalogue was produced for the auction held in the Couvent des Petits Pères on the Place des Victoires, in which the entire contents of Oudry's studio were dispersed. However, from documents in the Schwerin archives, first published in 1890, we know that Christian Ludwig paid 54 livres 5 sous for two drawings representing a "combat de taureaux," and a "combat de cerfs"; the companion to the Lugt drawing has yet to reappear.[12] [CBB]

15. Charles-Nicolas Cochin
Paris 1715 – 1790 Paris
Portrait of Pierre-Jean Mariette, 1756
Graphite with stumping | 11.0 diameter | Inv. no. 709

COCHIN EXECUTED THIS MEDALLION portrait of Pierre-Jean Mariette (1694 – 1774) in 1756, when his sitter was sixty years of age.[1] In all likelihood it was done at one of the Monday dinners hosted by Madame Geoffrin in her hôtel on the rue Saint-Honoré, at which both Cochin and Mariette were frequent guests. His *confrère* at the Royal Library, Hugues-Adrien Joly (1718 –

1800), recalled that "while the others were engaged in conversation, Sieur Cochin would take pleasure in drawing his fellow artists and the other art lovers there."[2] Initially, these portrait drawings may have been intended as gifts for his well-born hosts and were not made to be engraved. To another friend, Cochin later referred to them somewhat dismissively as "little society portrait busts that would make not especially interesting presents."[3] More than two hundred and fifty such medallion portraits are recorded; they follow the same profile format and most are approximately 11 centimeters in diameter.[4] Forty-three of them, including the *Portrait of Mariette*, remained with the descendants of Madame Geoffrin's daughter, the marquise de La Ferté-Imbault, and were sold in June 1921.[5] Madame Geoffrin had apparently promised Cochin that he would be able to retrieve the portraits of his fellow artists from her (or her heirs) in order to leave them to the Royal Academy; a clause to this effect appears in his will but was never carried out.[6] However, Cochin was able to regain temporary possession of the drawing of Mariette in 1765 so that Augustin de Saint-Aubin could engrave it.[7] Saint-Aubin's engraving (fig. 15.1) lists Mariette's titles as "Contrôleur-général de la grande Chancellerie" – the ennobling charge that he had purchased in February 1752, after selling his family's print shop and publishing house and retiring from business in September 1750.[8] Also noted was the title "Honoraire de l'Académie Royale de Peinture et de Sculpture," a post conferred in December 1750, when the former dealer was elected an "Associé-libre" of the Academy.[9]

Dealer, connoisseur, art historian, draftsman (see cat. 8), and collector, Mariette dominated the international art world in the middle decades of the eighteenth century and remains a fertile subject for art historical research today.[10] For Frits Lugt, who contributed a fine study on him in his *Marques de collections*, he was the model collector and a spiritual godfather of sorts.[11] In the charming Preface to the Louvre's celebratory exhibition devoted to Mariette in 1967, Lugt wished his "cher grand Patron" the happiest 273rd birthday and signed himself, "Votre très humble et très obéissant arrière-petit-fils."[12] [CBB]

16. Charles-Nicolas Cochin
Paris 1715 – 1790 Paris
Portrait of Anne-Robert-Jacques Turgot, Baron de l'Aulne, dated 1763
Graphite with stumping | 11.0 diameter | Inscriptions: signed and dated in graphite, "Dis... par Ch... 1763"; on the verso of the mount, in lead pencil, "Mon[s]. Turgot / given to / Mrs Jos Blount / by the / Duchesse D'anville at / La Roche Guyon / 1796" | Inv. no. 8161

COCHIN'S PORTRAIT OF Anne-Robert-Jacques Turgot, baron de l'Aulne (1727 – 1781) – economist, administrator, and reforming contrôleur-général des finances in Louis XVI's first cabinet – commemorates the most prestigious former occupant of the hôtel at 121, rue de Lille in which Lugt established his foundation.[1] In June 1779, three years after his dismissal from office, Turgot purchased this property in the heart of the aristocratic faubourg Saint-Germain, which had been built in 1745 by Pierre Salles, a banker and real-estate speculator, and had already changed hands three times. It was here that Turgot would spend the last two years of his life and where he died from gout in March 1781. In 1953 Lugt acquired the complex of buildings at 121, rue de Lille – part of which had been modernized in 1895 – to house the Fondation Custodia, established in 1947 to oversee his collections; the Institut Néerlandais was officially inaugurated at this site in 1957.[2]

Drawn in 1763 and engraved the same year (fig. 16.1) by Claude-Henri Watelet (1718 – 1785), an associé-libre of the Academy,[3] Cochin's portrait shows the thirty-six-year-old Turgot two years into his post as intendant of Limoges, a large district in central France comprising the poor and overtaxed provinces of Limousin and Angoumois. Turgot would hold this demanding office between 1761 and 1774, and his administration was renowned for its equity and efforts at reform.[4]

The side curls and the long hair falling loosely onto the shoulders were Turgot's customary manner of presenting himself in public and would be reproduced by Houdon in his marble portrait of the minister exhibited fourteen years later at the Salon of 1777.[5] Nonetheless, Cochin's drawing remains a relatively informal, even intimate, portrait of the economist and esteemed administrator. As an old inscription on the mount records, it may well have been made for Turgot's great friend and supporter, the aristocratic bluestock-

ing Louise-Elisabeth de La Rochefoucauld, duchesse d'Enville (1716 – 1797), to whose château at La Roche-Guyon he had retreated after his disgrace in May 1776. The duchesse d'Enville divested herself of this portrait in the year before her death.[6]

Turgot's closest friend and disciple, the physiocrat Pierre Samuel Du Pont de Nemours (1739 – 1817), left an affectionate description of his mentor, which serves to confirm the veracity (and humanity) of Cochin's portrayal. "He had a beautiful face . . . his eyes were a light brown, expressing perfectly the mixture of strength and kindness that characterized him. His forehead was round, high, noble and serene; his features pronounced; his mouth cherry-red and guileless."[7] [CBB]

17. Charles-Joseph Natoire
Nîmes 1700 – 1777 Castel Gandolfo
View of San Giovanni e Paolo in Rome, dated 1757
Brush and gray ink, brown and gray wash, pen and brown ink, and white gouache over black chalk
23.3 x 35.0 | Inscriptions: signed at the bottom right in pen and brown ink, "C. Natoire 1757" and below at left, "[…]ni e Paolo"; collector's mark, "GP" (Pierre Guéraud), at lower right; verso, near center in pen and brown ink, "Charles Joseph Natoire / de Nîmes en 1700 / †1777"; at top in graphite, "158 (?)"; at bottom, "14", "1757", "103", "34 x 45" | Inv. no. 1978-T.10

A REMARKABLY FRESH DRAWING on blue paper – cut down on the left and with pentimenti throughout[1] – *View of San Giovanni e Paolo in Rome* may have been made in the autumn of 1757, after Natoire's recovery from a malignant fever that had left him "at death's door."[2] Incapacitated during the months of July and August, Natoire gradually resumed his official duties as director of the French Academy in Rome. Like the more fully worked-up sheet he composed of the Villa Madama, inscribed "September 1757,"[3] *View of San Giovanni e Paolo* was perhaps another sign of his "perfect recovery."[4]

The early Christian church of San Giovanni e Paolo, built around 410 on the site of the martyred saints' residence and restored in the twelfth century, provides the setting for a bucolic, late-afternoon repose. The basilica was located on the west slope of the Celian hill, and Natoire faithfully records the Clivus Scauri — an ancient, narrow street, crossed by buttressing arches — that ran along the building's southern façade.[5] The ancient church with its triple-storied narthex dissolves in the afternoon sun, partially hidden by the trees that form a screen in the middle ground. Not far from the *petit jardinet* that Natoire had acquired at the foot of the Palatine hills two years earlier,[6] the church of San Giovanni e Paolo would also appear in the more finished *View of San Giovanni e Paolo and San Gregorio* (Graphische Sammlung Albertina, Vienna), signed and dated 1759.[7] In this panoramic view, dominated by Soria's seventeenth-century façade of San Gregorio Magno, the basilica and campanile (the latter not included in the Lugt drawing) are shown at upper left.

In the Lugt drawing, Natoire first establishes the architecture and trees over a characteristically tentative sketch in black chalk.[8] He then adds various staffage elements in pen and ink and wash: a donkey and cart at left, a recumbent, half-naked shepherd and his horse in the middle, and a young peasant family harnessing its horse at right. These groups were initially placed closer to the middle ground of the composition, as can be seen by the naked eye. Natoire brought them forward, almost to the drawing's edge, and cast them in deep shadow, thereby rendering the architecture in the background even more luminous.

Although Natoire's incursions into the Roman countryside anticipate by several years those of Fragonard and Robert — *pensionnaires* at the Palazzo Mancini under his directorship, whose sketching expeditions he encouraged[9] — his pastoral vision remains rooted in traditional view painting. In its deep shadows, spatial organization, and concern for architectural accuracy, *View of San Giovanni e Paolo in Rome* is indebted to contemporary Roman topographical practice and shares affinities with the illustration in the third volume of Giuseppe Vasi's *Delle magnificenze di Roma Antica e Moderna* (fig. 17.1), published in 1753.[10] [CBB]

18. Gabriel de Saint-Aubin
Paris 1724 – 1780 Paris
Le Boulevard, c. 1760
Pen and brown ink, gray and brown wash, over black chalk, with touches of watercolor | 37.1 x 53.8
Inscriptions: at lower left in pen and brown ink, in a nineteenth-century (?) hand, "Benazeht"; at the upper right, possibly an inscription rendered illegible by the wash applied by the artist | Inv. no. 3634

AROUND 1760 SAINT-AUBIN produced a corpus of images in various media that showed citizens promenading on the fashionable, tree-lined boulevard between the porte Saint-Antoine and the porte au Pont-aux-Choux in the east of Paris, on the site of the city's former medieval ramparts.[1] His finest paintings represent such scenes of urban sociability, as does this "large, magnificent" sheet,[2] most likely produced as an autonomous drawing, rather than a preparatory sketch.[3] Well published, and frequently exhibited, *Le Boulevard* has yet to reveal all its secrets: its eighteenth-century provenance is unknown, and the significance of the annotation "Benazeht" at lower left – the name of an early collector, perhaps? – remains to be elucidated.
The central couple in this dynamic composition, each looking in a different direction as they cross the street, are rather more sympathetic iterations of the aristocratic protagonists of *The Meeting on the Boulevard* (Musée Hyacinthe-Rigaud, Perpignan).[4] The young man carries his tricorne tucked under his left arm and trails his sword behind him. The elegant diners at left, approached by an aged beggar, cap in hand and with a walking stick, reappear in the Perpignan painting, in the related watercolor, *Society Promenade* (State Hermitage Museum, Saint Petersburg), and in Duclos's etching after it.[5] The right-hand section of the Lugt drawing, showing rows of carriages coming and going, is reprised in *The Meeting on the Boulevard* and the virtuoso pen and ink drawing, *Street Scene* (Private Collection).[6]
Such is the vibrancy and spontaneity of *Le Boulevard* that it comes as something of a surprise to discover that the essential elements were carefully worked out in a diminutive, preparatory drawing in black and white chalks, formerly in the Goncourt collection (fig. 18.1).[7] In expanding his format, Saint-Aubin developed and enlivened each group at no loss to the general excitement and piquancy that envelops this sweeping composition. His "cuisine" of gray and

brown washes and pen and ink is particularly effective in creating a looming sky that serves as a counterpoise to the activity of the spectators below. As Kim de Beaumont has observed, "Gabriel here uses the same essential elements – receding buildings along the boulevard, trees with slender boles and overarching foliage, rows of carriages advancing and moving away – to impart an energizing sense of movement more closely approximating the actual hustle and bustle of urban existence."[8] "Parisians do not walk, they run, and are always in a hurry." Saint-Aubin joyfully anticipates Sebastian Mercier's insight into city-dwellers at leisure, made in the early 1780s and as relevant today as it was two and a half centuries ago.[9] [CBB]

19. Hubert Robert
Paris 1733 – 1808 Paris
View of an Italian Garden, c. 1760
Red chalk | 39.6 x 49.2 | Inscriptions: verso, at the upper left of mount, in pencil, "N.5"; toward the right, "V206"; and at the lower right, "3256" | Inv. no. 8915

ROBERT'S DAZZLING, sun-filled view of an Italian garden, neither signed nor dated, shows a moment of repose during an afternoon of tree husbandry. The propped ladder and scaffold on wheels on either side of the herm satyr have been used to prune and shape the arbor that protects the dignified female statue with upraised arm. No gardeners are in sight, although a tiny pan (of water?) on the left edge of the scaffold's uppermost plank suggests their recent presence, as does the large basket at the foot of the standing herm in the center of the composition. Through energetic, and at times brutal, hatching lines, Robert creates the sensation of intense sunlight and deep shadow: he uses the whiteness of the paper, sparingly but brilliantly, to enhance this effect.

Victor Carlson assigned the Lugt drawing to 1760 on the basis of stylistic similarities with a group of signed and dated red-chalk counterproofs in the Bibliothèque Municipale, Besançon, that were done in Naples during Robert's six-week visit in the company of the abbé de Saint-Non.[1] The insistent hatching at the left and right edges of the sheets, independent of the motifs described, is a feature also shared by the impressive *Landscape with Stairs* (Museum of Fine Arts, Boston), which must date to around the same time.[2] *View of an Italian Garden* may also be related to another group of vigorous red-chalk drawings showing the Temple of Serapis at Pozzuoli, in which light streams through an arcaded bower.[3]

[19]

Although it is not possible to identify the site of the Lugt drawing—which Carlson assumed to have been done in Naples[4]—it seems likely that it was done after Robert returned to Rome in June 1760. The shaded statue in the center, with its helmet and voluminous drapery, is based on the Minerva Giustiniani, which Robert would have seen in the gallery of the Palazzo Giustiniani, "deservedly esteemed for ancient statues and basso-relievos [*sic*] of which it contains the greatest number of any [palace] in Rome."[5] Robert has placed this celebrated antiquity in a bower of his own invention, guarded by two jocular herm satyrs. Inspired both by his recent trip to Naples and his current immersion in the Roman countryside, *View of an Italian Garden* is an example of Robert's capacity to portray "all that is beautiful, but not truthful . . . a bizarre mixture that exists only in the painter's head."[6]

Although no counterproof of *View of an Italian Garden* is known, it is most likely that Robert made one, if only to fix the chalks of the present drawing. It was assumed that this (lost) counterproof may have provided the model for at least two smaller copies of this composition: a drawing in black chalk, once attributed to Fragonard in the Ringling Museum, Sarasota (fig. 19.1), and a second in black chalk published as by Fragonard when it appeared in the Boussac sale (10 May 1926), but which Eunice Williams recently reattributed to Pierre-Adrian Pâris.[7] In fact, the drawing in Sarasota is an independent (if related) composition by Robert, made at the same time. It shows a similar garden, without ladder or scaffolding, and with a row of antique sculptures—one and a half of which are visible—atop an ornamented plinth at right.[8] [CBB]

20. Jean-Honoré Fragonard
Grasse 1732 – 1806 Paris
View of the Serapeum at Hadrian's Villa, c. 1760
Red chalk, over black chalk underdrawing
35.1 x 48.3 | Signed at bottom right in red chalk, "frago"(now partially truncated); Inscriptions: on the eighteenth-century mount, in pen and black ink, "vüe du canope / de la Ville Adrienne / à Tivoli"
Inv. no. 843

Acquired by lugt in 1922 as by Hubert Robert — the signature, "frago," had been partially removed when the sheet was trimmed at lower right — *View of the Serapeum at Hadrian's Villa* has long been reinstated among Fragonard's pioneering red-chalk landscape drawings made in Tivoli and its environs in the summer of 1760. As a protégé of the abbé de Saint-Non (1727 – 1791), who had rented the Villa d'Este for three months, Fragonard spent at least six weeks sketching in the Roman campagna. Most of his drawings took as their subject the gardens and buildings of the Este property.[1] The *View of the Serapeum at Hadrian's Villa* is one of the rare sheets made on the grounds of Hadrian's Villa, four miles southwest of Tivoli; a second drawing, *The Ancient Theater at Hadrian's Villa*, 1760 (Musée des Beaux-Arts, Besançon), shows the ruined North Theater and the casino Fede, a building erected by the Villa's eighteenth-century owner.[2] Charles de Brosses, president of the Dijon Parlement, visiting in 1739, had admired the Villa's "grand bosquets and fine pools."[3] For Fragonard and his contemporaries a quarter of a century later, Hadrian's Villa was impressive for the "many ruined walls and teeming undergrowth, from which one can only imagine the immensity of its former grandeur and the prodigious number of buildings that were once assembled there."[4]

As with many of the red-chalk drawings made at Tivoli, some of which were exhibited as part of Fragonard's maiden *envoi* at the Salon of 1765, *View of the Serapeum at Hadrian's Villa* was first prepared in a light black-chalk underdrawing, whose contours are easily observed by the naked eye. The purpose of this underdrawing was to block out the general outlines of the composition, since black chalk was more easily effaced or altered than sanguine.[5] Most, but not all, of Fragonard's worked-up landscape drawings were prepared in this way, and most of the horizontal compositions were folded in the middle, as is the Lugt sheet. The counterproof of this drawing, first published in 1999, also bears a crease in the center.[6]

Fragonard's subject in the Lugt drawing is the ruins of a complex of buildings, erected around AD 130 at the end of a 120-meter-long canal in the southern precinct of the Villa. In the eighteenth century the site was known as the Canopus and thought to be Hadrian's re-creation of the Egyptian town and canal with its famous temple dedicated to the Hellenistic-Egyptian god Serapis.[7] Modern scholarship identifies the site as the Great Scenic Triclinium (dining area) or Serapeum, whose soaring, concave vault Fragonard represented with remarkable fidelity (fig. 20.1), although he studiously ignored the canal and its water, which in actuality dominated the foreground of his scene.[8] In 1765 Hubert Robert made an interior view of the same ruined structure, but taking far greater liberties: the vault is shown coffered, and statues are returned to the niches (fig. 20.2).[9] Four years later Piranesi etched the front view of the building, detailing the vault's flattened gores and framing his composition with monumental chunks of fallen masonry.[10]

As Pierre Rosenberg has observed of Fragonard's Tivoli landscape drawings, for all his truthfulness the artist "approached his subject more as a poet than as a surveyor."[11] It is the luxuriance of the foliage, the burning heat of the noonday sun, the insouciance of the three boys, and, above all, the immense silence of the site that most appealed to Fragonard and that he so deftly communicated in this sheet. [CBB]

21. Jean-Honoré Fragonard
Grasse 1732 – 1806 Paris
Le Calendrier des vieillards, c. 1780
Pen and brown ink, brown wash, over black chalk underdrawing | 20.0 x 14.3 | Inv. no. 4068

22. *À Femme avare, galant escroc*, c. 1780
Pen and brown ink, brown wash, over black chalk underdrawing | 20.4 x 14.0 | Inv. no. 4067

FRAGONARD'S LE CALENDRIER DES VIEILLARDS (The Greybeards' Calendar) and *À Femme avare, galant escroc* (The Greedy Woman, Gallantly Deceived) illustrate the eighth and ninth tale in the second part of La Fontaine's *Contes et nouvelles en vers*, first published between 1664 and 1674. They are Fragonard's third, and most "finished," iteration of each composition, worked up in pen and brown ink and brown wash over the faintest of black

chalk underdrawing, and intended for the eventual use of engravers (although they may also have served a secondary purpose as finished drawings for the market).[1] *Le Calendrier des vieillards* would be engraved by Jean Dambrun as plate 9 in the two-volume edition of *Contes et nouvelles en vers par Jean de la Fontaine*, published by Pierre Didot in 1795 (fig. 21.1); Jacques Aliamet, who died in May 1788, engraved *À Femme avare, galant escroc*, which appeared as plate 10 in this edition (fig. 22.1).[2]

Long before Didot's luxury edition appeared, Fragonard had embarked on the project to illustrate La Fontaine's *Contes et nouvelles en vers* as an independent venture. He had first worked out his compositions in black chalk, around 1760, during his time in Rome: forty-two of these drawings have survived and are today in a private collection in New York.[3] A decade later, he elaborated superb pen and ink and bister wash drawings on counterproofs of these black chalk drawings: fifty-seven sheets, mounted in two albums in the early nineteenth century, were acquired by the Petit Palais in 1934. These radiant, life-affirming compositions — exhibited as a group for the first time in 1992, when the albums were temporarily dismantled — are among Fragonard's finest achievements in any medium.[4] The third group of La Fontaine drawings, which may date to around 1780 and to which the Lugt pair belongs, reprise the earlier compositions for the engraver's purposes: their contours are more detailed and articulated, and the washes applied more deliberately.[5]

The dating of each group of drawings in the La Fontaine series remains highly contested, as do Fragonard's reasons for producing them; not at issue, however, are the sympathy and originality of his interpretation of these ribald poems. *Le Calendrier des vieillards*, based on an episode in Boccaccio's *Decameron*, is a cautionary tale about mismatched marriages. The elderly Pisan judge, Richard de Quinzica, has taken the beautiful and well-born young Bartholomée de Galandi for his wife. Although generous with gifts to her, de Quinzica is unable (or unwilling) to acquit his conjugal duties more than four times a year.[6] In support of such abstemiousness, he has created a calendar "Cluttered with dates demanding man's abstention/From husbandly pursuit."

> Time and again
> Some holy office — vigil, mass, or such —
> Gave him much pious pretext not to touch
> Madame his wife. In truth, one long "amen"
> Replaced the pleasures of the bed . . .
> And to excuse his lack, bending the truth,
> He twists the calendar to such degree
> That he convinces her no decent day
> For man-and-wifely folderol exists,
> Insisting that one pure of heart resists.[7]

The second part of the tale describes Bartholomée's abduction, on a fishing trip, by the debonair buccaneer Pagamin de Monègue, who seduces the willing captive – "Delighted, at long last, to sacrifice / That calendar and all its dates red-lettered."[8] The judge tracks down the ship of the honorable pirate, who is ready to restore his wife to him. But Bartholomée is not in the least prepared to return to Richard and, after haranguing him with his inadequacies as a husband, sends him home alone.

Previous publications of the *Contes* had illustrated the later confrontation between Bartholomée and Richard, with the lusty Pagamin and his pirate ship in a supporting role.[9] Fragonard's originality was to show the beginning of the story, setting his composition in Bartholomée's bedroom, with the sun streaming in, as the judge points to an Almanac on the wall and lists the days of abstention to his demure, yet frustrated, wife. The large oval above them shows a young couple adoring a newborn infant; more legible in Dambrun's print (see fig. 21.1), this is a piquant allusion to the unlikelihood of such an event ever taking place in this household.

★ ★ ★

The next tale in La Fontaine's *Contes*, *À Femme avare, galant escroc* – also from Boccaccio's *Decameron* – concerns the well-matched couple Gulphar, "a knavish gent," and the avaricious wife of his friend, Sire Gasparin.[10] The coquette is willing to take Gulphar as her lover only if he agrees to pay her two hundred crowns. Gulphar borrows the money from Gasparin, who has left for the country, and presents his mistress with it in front of her household servants, saying "Madame, please pay this debt for me, / Two hundred crowns I owe our good *messire*." Thinking this a ruse, "She gives him what he paid her for / And several nights thereafter."[11] On Gasparin's return, Gulphar informs him that he had no need of the loan after all, and has entrusted the money to his wife to acquit the debt.

Once again, Fragonard chose an episode from the beginning of the tale – one that was not described in verse[12] – and in so doing deviated from the standard representation, which showed Gasparin writing off the debt in his ledger as Gulphar implements his ruse and the coquettish wife silently expresses her indignation.[13] In an opulent Parisian interior of the 1770s, the eager Gulphar clasps his mistress around her waist, his eyes trained expectantly toward the sofa, with the ornamental nymph on its cartouche casting an anxious look in his direction. Dressed in an elaborate sack dress, a ruff around her neck, the languid young woman is in no hurry to respond to her lover's advances and counts her money, crown by crown.

As comparison with the radiant drawing of this tale from a decade earlier suggests (fig. 22.2), in the final version Fragonard made his protagonists older, and defined the interior decoration, furnishings, and costumes more precisely, bringing them in line with current fashions.[14] The result was a slight diminution in energy and luminosity that would be carried one stage further in the reproductive engraving itself. [CBB]

23. Jean-Honoré Fragonard
Grasse 1732 – 1806 Paris
Portrait of Fragonard Seated in an Armchair, dated 1789
Black chalk, over black chalk underdrawing
17.0 diameter | Inscriptions: at bottom in black chalk, by a later hand, "se ipsum delineabat frago / apud de Bergeret / anno 1789." | Inv. no. 3943

THE LATIN INSCRIPTION at the bottom of this sheet, added by another hand most probably in the nineteenth century, establishes the subject of the drawing: "Frago drew himself in Bergeret's home in the year 1789." Aged fifty-seven, Fragonard is shown casually posed, perhaps recording his reflection as it appeared in one of his host's mirrors. We see him cross-legged, his coat held together by its top button, his expression not in the least ingratiating. Summary and staccato though its handling is, the drawing is elaborated over Fragonard's characteristic underdrawing in black chalk, which suggests a somewhat pondered spontaneity.[1] Although less scrupulous in its facial depiction than the group of roundel self-portraits executed around the same time (fig. 23.1), the Lugt drawing, like them, is a reasonably honest portrayal.[2] In the certificate of residence provided by the Paris Commune five years later (April 1794), Fragonard was described as "four feet eleven inches tall, gray hair and gray eyebrows, a wide forehead, ordinary nose, gray eyes, medium-sized mouth, and a round chin."[3] However, in none of the self-portraits do we see any sign of the smallpox that disfigured his face.[4]

The Latin inscription also stipulates that the drawing was done "apud de Bergeret" (in Bergeret's home).[5] This would be the home of Pierre-Jacques Bergeret de Grancourt (1742 – 1807), who in 1785 had succeeded his father, Pierre-Jacques-Onésyme Bergeret de Grancourt (1715 – 1785), as receveur-général des finances de la généralité de Montauban. One of the country's wealthiest financiers, Bergeret *père* had also been an avid patron of contemporary art. In 1773 he had invited Fragonard and his wife on a two-year Grand Tour of Italy that ended badly when the artist refused to relinquish ownership of the drawings he had made on the trip and successfully sued Bergeret for compensation.[6] The thirty-one-year-old Pierre-Jacques had been part of his father's retinue in 1773 — traveling in the second coach with the cook[7] — and by the late 1770s the family had reconciled with Fragonard. It was to the château de Cassan, Bergeret *fils*'s country estate in L'Isle-Adam, that the Fragonards brought their ailing daughter, Rosalie, in 1779, and it is there that she died, aged nineteen, in October 1788.[8]

Portrait of Fragonard Seated in an Armchair is the only intimate scene commemorating a visit to Pierre-Jacques Bergeret to have survived, although two roundel portraits by Fragonard of his generous amphitryon are known (fig. 23.2).[9] One question that cannot be definitively resolved is in which of Bergeret's many homes Fragonard chose to represent himself. Since his daughter had died in the château de Cassans the previous year, it would seem an unlikely setting for this informal homage.[10] The armchair in which Fragonard slouches may provide a clue to the setting. In its sober, square shape, turned tapered legs, and absence of ornamentation, the armchair is of the latest design and may be related to seating furniture by Jean-Baptiste-Claude Sené (1747 – 1803) and Jean-Baptiste Boulard (c. 1730 – 1789), commissioned for members of the royal family in the mid-1780s.[11] The modernity and stylishness of the armchair suggests a fashionable Parisian habitat — and might situate Fragonard in Bergeret's most recent extravagance, the Chartreuse, or Folie Beaujon, on the rue du Faubourg-Saint-Honoré, which he had acquired in September 1787.[12] [CBB]

24. Jean-Baptiste Greuze
Tournus 1725 – 1805 Paris
Female Nude Kneeling with Outstretched Arms,
c. 1765 – 68
Red chalk | 29.2 x 42.2
Verso, probably by Albert Besnard (1849 – 1934)
Studies of Bare Feet after Greuze's *La Prière du matin*
(Musée Fabre, Montpellier)
Red chalk | Inscriptions: lower left, in the hand of Frits Lugt, in pencil, "Vente collection du peintre Albert / Besnard, Paris 31 Mai – 1er Juin 1934" and "Collection Bon de Schwiter/ (Lugt 1768); Lugt 2565; provient de la Collection du peintre Albert Besnard / …. Juin 1934"; in another hand "J.B. GREUZE"; at the top left, also in pencil, "Aug. Lot 29 / 3 p (?) ; 92 ; [Be]snard (truncated)" | Inv. no. 4837

AS EDGAR MUNHALL HAS NOTED, Greuze's female nudes of the late 1760s "have a muscular solidity totally unlike the luscious softness of his contemporary Boucher's female figures."[1] This vigorous, yet controlled, figure study is one of a large group of red-chalk drawings, made from live models, which relate to Greuze's overdue reception piece for the Royal Academy. "Having decided to present himself as a history painter rather than a genre painter, he experimented with a number of historical and mythological subjects before settling on the confrontation of Septimius Severus and Caracalla."[2] Confiding to Diderot in 1767 that he would very much like to "paint a woman totally nude, without offending propriety,"[3] Greuze explored subjects such as *Danae*, *Lot and His Daughters* (both Musée du Louvre, Paris), *Aegina Visited by Jupiter* (The Metropolitan Museum of Art, New York), *Roman Charity (Cimon and Pero)* (The J. Paul Getty Museum, Los Angeles), and *The Arrest of Sabinus* (Musée Municipal, Chaumont).[4] In keeping with both academic pedagogy and his own practice, he made preparatory drawings for every stage of these compositions. As Diderot had noted in 1763, Greuze "spares neither care nor expense in order to have the models that suit him."[5]

Although the subject of the Lugt drawing has been associated with the fifth-century repentant sinner Saint Mary of Egypt – whom Greuze would portray in paintings and drawings in the late stages of his career[6] – *Female Nude*

Kneeling with Outstretched Arms seems rather to represent a supplicant young woman, in some anguish, kneeling at the foot of a bed or against a slab of stone. Her gesture and expression are directed toward an absent figure: a drunken or imprisoned father, perhaps. Munhall noted the Lugt drawing's stylistic and expressive similarities with such exemplary sheets as *Seated Female Nude* (Fogg Art Museum, Cambridge, Mass.) and *Female Nude with Arms Raised* (Musée Bonnat, Bayonne), the former preparatory for the figure of Pero in *Roman Charity*, the latter for Aegina in *Aegina Visited by Jupiter*.[7] Indeed, the same model of Courbet-like proportions may have posed for all these drawings.[8] Comparison with *Kneeling Female Nude* (fig. 24.1), another preparatory study for *Roman Charity*, is particularly telling, since the model is shown resting her left arm on a plinth not unlike the one in the *Female Nude Kneeling with Outstretched Arms*.[9] Might the Lugt drawing have started life as a study for the figure of Pero, Valerius Maximus's heroine, who will breastfeed her imprisoned father to prevent him from dying of starvation? [CBB]

25. Jean-Pierre-Louis-Laurent Hoüel
Rouen 1735 – 1813 Paris
View of the Colosseum in Rome, c. 1769
Watercolor and gouache, pen and black ink, over a sketch in black chalk | 64.3 x 47.8 | Inv. no. 1999-T.1

THIS IS THE COLOSSEUM seen from the southeast with a view of the masonry connecting the inner wall and the remains of the northern outer wall. This enormous elliptical arena, built and completed between AD 70 and 80, had gradually fallen into decay from the sixth century onward because of earthquakes, the cannibalization of building materials, and the installation of secular and religious structures. In the mid-eighteenth century it was forbidden to dismantle it further, and attempts were made to halt the detrimental overgrowth. It was not until the beginning of the nineteenth century that the ancient building was excavated and the outer wall shown here was buttressed with the massive Pius VII abutment.

This large drawing, which was initially started as a chalk sketch and then finished with a brush in a mixture of watercolors and gouache, was acquired in 1999.[1] A pupil of Jean-Baptiste Descamps, the Rouen-born artist Jean-Pierre Hoüel was apprenticed to the engraver Jacques Philippe Le Bas in Paris from 1755. In the years that followed he "translated" into print countless landscapes

[25]

in the styles of François Boucher and Joseph Vernet, before honing his skills as a painter. In 1769 he went to Rome, where at the end of June he took up the post of "architect" in the French Academy on the recommendation of Blondel d'Azaincourt, Charles-Nicolas Cochin, and others.

As Madeleine Pinault Sørenson, the author of an article about Hoüel's first visit to Italy, observed, the artist began to specialize in landscape during his stay in Rome, with trips to Naples and Sicily.[2] Emulating Italian and French *veduta* painters like Andrea Locatelli and Charles-Louis Clérisseau, he adopted a method involving a combination of watercolor and gouache, wholly in tune with the then predominant fashion of depicting topographical landscapes. This was a technique he developed further and perfected during his second trip to Sicily (1776 – 69).[3]

Unlike these Sicilian *vedute*, the Roman views have as yet been little researched. Here, the artist has succeeded in depicting the typical Roman atmosphere around a somewhat overgrown ancient building against a partly cloudy bright blue sky with a great feeling for the effect of light. The artist's vantage point relative to the ruin is extraordinarily daring. Compared with Hoüel's more familiar Roman views,[4] the technique he uses in the *View of the Colosseum* has more in common with a watercolor than with the gouache and watercolor method he often used later. In this case body color was applied only in the background on the right and in the foreground – probably because after he had painted the ruin Hoüel felt the scene needed more than the sketch of two figures on the left and added the farm cart pulled by oxen in the center. This would seem to be a reason to suggest an early dating, at the beginning of his stay in Rome. [MVB-G]

26. Esprit-Antoine Gibelin
Aix-en-Provence 1739 – 1813 Aix-en-Provence
Interior of a Sculptor's Atelier with the Borghese Gladiator, c. 1770
Pen and brown ink, brown wash over black chalk, on two pieces of paper, joined horizontally | 23.7 x 18.3
Inscriptions: verso, in pencil, "A.E. Gibelin"; and in another hand, "280" | Inv. no. 1978-T. 82

ALONG WITH ITS PREPARATORY drawing in black ink (fig. 26.1), this riveting sheet appeared at auction in 1978 as "French School, 18th century."[1] The attribution to Esprit-Antoine Gibelin – a prolific, but now relatively little-

[26]

known history painter, antiquarian, and museum administrator — was made on the basis of the inscription on the verso of the drawing, "A.E. Gibelin," in a nineteenth-century hand. It must be said that both drawings in the Lugt collection have a fluency, confidence, and command of their medium that are not always discernible in Gibelin's mature graphic work. The wash drawing can best be compared to the signed and dated *Mythological Scene with Horses* (fig. 26.2), in ink and gray wash, that was done in 1770,[2] the year before Gibelin left Rome for Paris, where he would establish a thriving practice as a fresco painter and designer of medals.[3]

Gibelin's dramatic use of wash and the exaggerated musculature of his figures evoke the drawings of the Swedish sculptor Johann Tobias Sergel (1739 – 1814). This is not purely fortuitous, since both men were part of an international circle of artists in Rome, and their intimacy is well documented.[4] Indeed, Sergel may have been the source and inspiration for Gibelin's informed, yet somewhat idealized, view of a sculptor's studio, in which the young master is shown carving a life-size copy of the *Borghese Gladiator* from a monumental block of marble, the edge of which pivots precariously on the makeshift wooden pedestal.

Gibelin's drawing depicts the process of sculptural replication. The sculpture at right, whose mid-section the assistant is measuring with his calipers, is most likely a full-scale plaster model, copied from a mold of the *Borghese Gladiator*, "the most admired work of antiquity in the Villa Borghese for the two centuries of its installation there."[5] The assistant will communicate these dimensions to the sculptor, portrayed with his back to us and shown hatless in the final drawing, who is carving the figure in marble, a mallet in his right hand. Various tools are illustrated: a T-square and calipers — one resting against the tree trunk of the marble, a second perching by the *Gladiator*'s right hand; a set of diminutive chisels on the marble's base; and the "violino" or drill, propped against the wooden crate in the foreground. Above the marble sculpture is suspended a wooden frame, with marks at regular intervals and plumb-lines hanging loose. This would have been used at an earlier stage in the carving, in tandem with a similar frame over the plaster model, with the weighted plumb-lines generating the points on the block for roughing out the final composition.[6] Despite the accuracy of such details, the dark-haired Pygmalion in slippers is attempting a daunting task, since the *Gladiator* is being carved from one block without any sign of the internal armatures that would have been required to attach the figure's arms to his body.

Reduced copies of celebrated antiquities line the shelves in the background at right: the standing *Antinuous*, after the monumental sculpture presented to the

Capitoline Museum in 1742;[7] a roundel of the *Three Graces*, loosely modeled on the "highly restored" group in the Villa Borghese;[8] and the head and torso of the armless *Osiris-Antinuous*, looming above the assistant's head.[9] The bust on the lower shelf is that of the standing *Apollino*, one of the most frequently copied antique statues.[10] Here Gibelin might have intended a discrete homage to Sergel, whose terracotta head, based on the Apollino, was executed in 1771.[11]

Instilled with the optimism of youth, *Interior of a Sculptor's Atelier with the Borghese Gladiator* deserves to be better known as a visual compendium of several of the processes of sculptural replication described and illustrated in the *Encyclopédie*.[12] Late in life, Gibelin would return to the *Borghese Gladiator*, but as an antiquarian rather than an artist. In his *Mémoire sur la statue dite le Gladiateur ou Guerrier combattant*, published in 1807, he entered into an acerbic, and ultimately arid, debate over the identity of this figure, whom Ennio Quirino Visconti (1751 – 1818) had reinterpreted as a heroic warrior being attacked by someone on horseback.[13] Insisting that the subject was an athlete, and that the armband served a gymnastic function, Gibelin identified the figure as a "sphériste" or "joueur de ballon" – from the Greek "sphaerista," a master in the art of playing games with a ball.[14] [CBB]

27. Louis-Jacques Durameau
Paris 1733 – 1796 Versailles
Interior of a Paper Mill, formerly known as *L'Imprimerie secrète*, c. 1770 – 80
Oil on paper | 33.5 x 22.7 | Inv. no. 1972-T.6

ACQUIRED BY THE GONCOURTS for twenty francs in the late 1850s as an oil sketch by Fragonard, this monochrome painting on paper was published by them and by Baron Roger Portalis as an autograph work by the artist. Doubts emerged as early as the sale of Edmond de Goncourt's collection in February 1897, and for the next eighty years the little painting was demoted to "French school, eighteenth century" until its acquisition by the Fondation Custodia from Henri Baderou in 1972, when an attribution to Durameau was first proposed.[1] In her monograph on the artist, published in 2001, Anne Leclair included this work among the paintings "attributed to Durameau," her hesitation owing to the stylistic affinities with the work of Nicolas-Bernard Lépicié (1735 – 1784), which she noted in the portrayal of the seated woman at left.[2] Leclair's reservations may have been overly scrupulous, since the handling of gesture and physiognomy in this work is consistent with Durameau's mature oil sketches. The Lugt sheet is best compared to the sketch for *The Continence of Bayard*, 1776 (fig. 27.1), which entered the Musée des Beaux-Arts, Grenoble, in 1877 as a painting by Fragonard.[3] The sharp noses, lost profiles, elegant choreography of figures, and spatial consistency overall are characteristics common to both works, which bear witness to the enduring fruits of Durameau's training under Jean-Baptiste-Marie Pierre and Carle Van Loo.

The function of Durameau's grisaille painting on paper remains an open question. Its modest scale and relative finish might suggest that it was intended as the model for a print – Durameau's younger brother was an engraver and his brother-in-law a publisher of copperplate engravings[4] – but if that had been its purpose, the seated woman would surely have held the fan in her left hand. If the sketch was preparatory for a painting, the scale of the finished work would have been considerable (and unusual), and no record of such a commission has come down to us.

Where we can add some clarification is with regard to the subject of this oil sketch, which has been widely published under its traditional title of *L'Imprimerie secrète* (a secret printing house), based on a reference that the Goncourts found in an anonymous catalogue of the 1790s.[5] The water wheel, with its rotating wooden beaters in the background at right, provides the clue to the correct identity of the interior represented, which is that of a paper mill in which many of the tasks associated with the fabrication of paper are shown.[6] In front of the mill wheel, two shadowy figures are working in a vat. One vatman stirs the pulped fibers with his stick, while the second is shown with his arms immersed in the receptacle. He is dipping his mold – a rectangular wire mesh, strung with two sets of wires and bounded by a wooden frame – into the mixture from which the embryonic sheet of paper will be formed. Below him, a *coucher* leans forward to flip the mold over onto a piece of felt slightly larger than the paper; he will accumulate a pile of alternating paper and felt until he has 260 sheets (a measure known as a post) ready to be pressed.

The bewigged figure with his back to us in the middle ground at right, formerly identified as the *compositeur* of the print works,[7] is in fact a *formaire*, a well-paid craftsman responsible for repairing old molds and wiring new ones. Unlike the other workers, shown with bare arms and kerchiefs on their heads, he is of a more elevated social status.[8] We also see two workers with reams of paper, the finished product. The first, in the distant background at right, carries a bundle of paper on his head; the second, in the foreground at right, crouches over the block, waiting for a signal from the mill master, who coordinates the various activities around him.

[27]

Finally, in the background at left we see episodes in the later stages of papermaking. The figure leaning forward on the stone table may be the sizerman or *saleran*, sizing the paper, one block at a time, or burnishing the paper after it has been pressed. The standing figure behind him is hanging the paper to dry, sheet by sheet. (This was a task traditionally done by *colleuses* – women who assisted in the sizing and hanging of the wet sheets.)[9] The seated woman in the foreground at left, reclining in relatively informal attire, gazes at the central figure respectfully. The owner's wife, perhaps, she is the only one who is portrayed not working. She holds a fan in her right hand, a necessity in such a hot and humid setting.

From the *Encyclopédie*'s lengthy description (and illustrations) of the Langlée paper factory near Montargis, we know that the machinery and manpower required for the making of paper were far more extensive than those indicated in Durameau's depiction.[10] Durameau has also telescoped the different stages of paper production, bringing the various workers together in a single space and avoiding the depiction of women and children, who carried out many of the most arduous tasks. In its confident, beneficent view of industrial labor, *Interior of a Paper Mill* shares the optimism of Gabriel de Saint-Aubin's *Spinning Factory*, 1776 – 77 (École des Beaux-Arts, Paris), with which it is roughly contemporary in date.[11] How fitting, then, that the true subject of this oil sketch was first identified by Saint-Aubin's champion, Henri Baderou, who noted its title as "Une fabrique de papier" in the documentation he provided to the Fondation Custodia at the time of its acquisition.[12] [CBB]

28. Jean-Michel Moreau, known as Moreau le Jeune
Paris 1741 – 1814 Paris
Portraits of the Artist's Daughter Asleep, c. 1772
Pen and gray ink, gray wash, over black chalk
10.2 x 14.9 (each sheet)
Inscriptions: verso of mount at bottom, in lead pencil, "Catherine-Françoise Moreau le j^ne fille unique de l'artiste qui / deviendra la femme de Carle Vernet … mère d'Horace Vernet" | Inv. nos. 4070A&B

THESE ENCHANTING PEN-AND-INK WASH drawings – "such a paternal double sheet"[1] – are two of the four studies of the sleeping Catherine-Françoise Moreau (1770 – 1821) that her proud father made around 1772. Catherine-Françoise, known as Fanny, was the first and only child, born on 14 February 1770 at two in the afternoon,[2] of Jean-Michel Moreau and Nicole-Françoise Pineau (1740 – 1812), who had married in September 1765 and were living on the rue de la Harpe.[3] In the pair of drawings in the Forsyth Wickes Collection at the Museum of Fine Arts, Boston, the sleeping infant is shown in profile (figs. 28.1, 28.2).[4] In the Lugt drawings, made at the same time, the patient artist has captured her full-faced, showing her angelic features and the details of her night clothes to their best advantage. As the greatest book illustrator of the age and the most acute observer of Paris's fashionable life, Moreau would have ample opportunity to portray happy families in elegant attire. None of his graphic work, however, approaches the affection and sincerity of these vignettes.[5]

Catherine-Françoise would marry the promising history painter Carle Vernet (1758 – 1836) on 29 August 1787, a marriage encouraged by the fathers of both the bride and groom (the couple moved into Joseph Vernet's commodious lodgings in the Louvre).[6] Of their two children, Horace Vernet distinguished himself as the greatest military painter of his generation (see cat. 55). Madame Vernet maintained a deep attachment to her father's work, donating seven volumes of his prints to the Bibliothèque Nationale, to which she appended a notice of his life.[7] Her relations with her husband were less cordial. In April 1815 Dominique Vivant, Baron Denon, director of the Louvre, approached the intendant-général de la Couronne on Carle Vernet's behalf, explaining that the artist had been ruined by his wife's excesses: "Married for thirty years to a woman who constantly tormented him and forced him into debt, [and who]

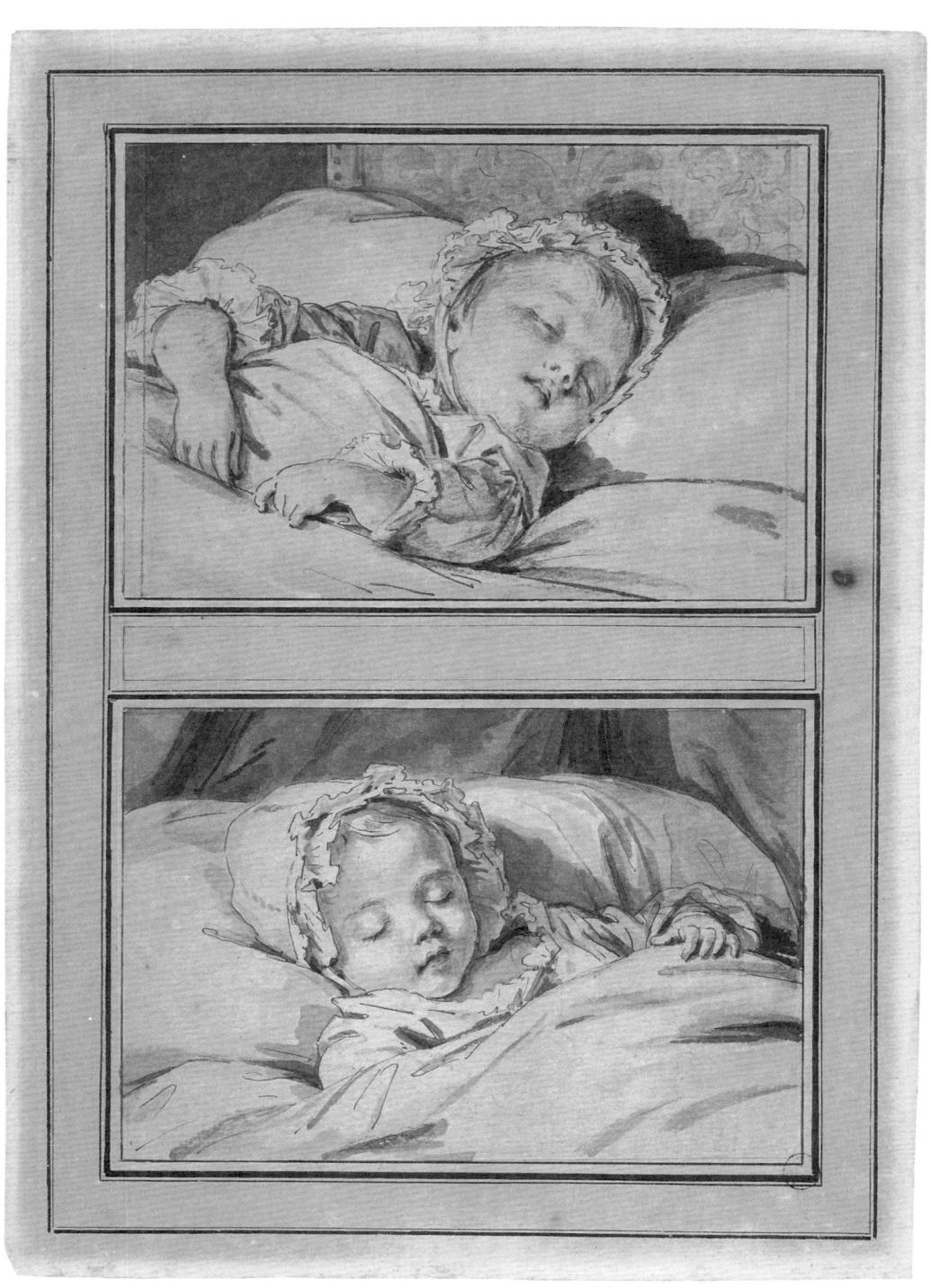

now, as an ultimate indignity, has initiated a legal separation in order to retain the inheritance provided by her father, the deceased M. Moreau, and is bringing him before the tribunal for the return of her dowry."[8]

Despite being drawings from life, Moreau's portraits relate to the iconography of infancy inspired by Greuze's domestic genre scenes of the 1750s and 1760s. Precursors in this tradition would also include tender family drawings by engravers such as Augustin de Saint-Aubin (1736 – 1807) and Jean-Baptiste Delafosse (1721 – 1808).[9] In Nicolas Ponce's engraving after Bounieu's *Innocence Watched over by Fidelity* (fig. 28.3), a devoted dog guards the sleeping child, who, prettily attired and enveloped by fine linens, has become a symbol of unsullied purity.[10]

It is tempting to associate these drawings with enlightened opinion regarding family life in the last decades of the ancien régime, and more particularly with Jean-Jacques Rousseau's proposals for a more humane upbringing of infants and his strictures on the evils of wet nursing.[11] Moreau, a great reader and acolyte of Rousseau's, was the illustrator of his collected works, including *Émile ou de l'éducation*.[12] Certainly, little Catherine-Françoise, shown in comfortable dress, is not constrained or swaddled, and is obviously well cared for. However, as the child of a fairly privileged Parisian household, she was dispatched to a wet nurse, as her mother had been before her. The family armorial kept by her grandfather, the sculptor Dominique Pineau (1718 – 1786), noted that she was nursed in the village of Grand Besson, on the outskirts of the city.[13] [CBB]

29. François-André Vincent
Paris 1746 – 1816 Paris
Studies of Cats and a Donkey, dated 1772
Red and black chalk | 47.7 x 34.7 (six joined sheets)
Inscriptions: at bottom left, signed in pen and brown ink, "Vincent à Rome 1772."; verso, in pencil, "4a / 11 Avril 1873 / Vendredi St Sap . . ."
Inv. no. 1974-T.60

VINCENT'S MONUMENTAL *Studies of Cats and a Donkey* was acquired for the Fondation Custodia four years after Lugt's death from the dealer and collector Henri Baderou (1910 – 1991), whom Lugt had known since the 1930s,[1] and whose immense collection of drawings would enter the Musée des Beaux-Arts, Rouen, in 1975.[2] *Studies of Cats and a Donkey* is a composite drawing made up of six sheets of various sizes – cut from the pages of sketchbooks, perhaps – that was mounted by the artist, dated "Rome, 1772," and signed by him with a flourish, most likely in the following decade.[3] Despite his delicate health and poor eyesight, the twenty-five-year-old laureate would spend four immensely productive years as a pensionnaire at the French Academy in Rome, where the formal curriculum of copying from antiquity and after Old Master paintings was supplemented by studies from nature in the surrounding countryside. Vincent's graphic output during his Roman sojourn was protean and ranged from heroic compositional studies and académies, to caricatures, genre scenes, and landscapes (see cat. 30).[4]

Studies of Cats and a Donkey is an assemblage of life studies of cats sleeping and preening themselves. The sheet at upper left shows a short-haired male, sleeping on the matted seat of a fairly rustic chair and portrayed a second time below, licking his paws.[5] The same cat is shown in the sheet at upper right, cleaning his foreleg. As an impeccably trained history painter, Vincent treats his subject as he might a male nude: he isolates the cat's ear and front paws and revisits them in the two studies below. Two sheets in the center of the drawing portray a sleeker animal, in animated, almost convoluted, poses: lively sketches, midway between Watteau and Delacroix, which are not without their humor. At lower left, Vincent returns to the rotund Tom cat, but this time in black chalk. The sheet is completed by a supine donkey, who might have made its way into this feline menagerie from a drawing by Hubert Robert.

Vincent's self-contained cats, abstracted from their domestic setting, do not engage the viewer directly but are absorbed in quotidian activities. Good only for chasing mice, in Buffon's opinion, cats were faithless, malicious, and thieving.[6] Buffon conceded, however, that their "bodies and temperaments were in accord with nature: the cat is pretty, supple, adroit, clean and voluptuous."[7] These are the very qualities that Vincent chose to explore. Although, as has been noted, Vincent did not use any of these studies in his current (or future) paintings, the exercise of studying animals from life served him well.[8] Two years later, in February 1774, he surprised Fragonard's patron, the financier Bergeret de Grancourt, with a sympathetic portrait of his greyhound, Diane, seated on a tasseled velvet cushion (fig. 29.1).[9] This privileged canine inhabits a world far removed from the modest interiors and rough-and-tumble existence hinted at in these red-chalk vignettes, in which Vincent's handling is "intelligent, precise, clean and soft, and of great effect."[10] [CBB]

30. François-André Vincent
Paris 1746 – 1816 Paris
Artists in a Landscape, near Tivoli, dated 1773
Black chalk and graphite | 26.7 x 40.5 | Inscriptions:
at bottom left, signed in pen and brown ink,
"vincent.f.Tivoly.1773." | Inv. no. 1974-T.23

WERE IT NOT FOR THE INSCRIPTION at lower left identifying the site as "Tivoly," there would be few clues to the view depicted in this drawing, since Vincent avoided any hint of the picturesque villas and gardens that had attracted an earlier generation of French artists to this hilltop town (see cat. 20). In this "probing and precise" sheet, Vincent's calligraphic virtuosity is placed at the service of a deliberate, unvarnished rendering of the motif.[1] We are presented with two artists, fellow pensionnaires no doubt, one of whom is hard at work drawing the site – an early instance of a pictorial *mise en abyme* – while the other takes his ease, no portfolio in sight.[2] As Jean-Pierre Cuzin has noted, Vincent's spirited handling is "quasi-documentary," his zigzags and curlicues subordinated to an unexpectedly austere depiction.[3] Equally rigorous is the artist's construction of space, with the empty white paper in the left foreground providing the most intensely lit section of the composition. With an eye to later developments in the genre, Peter Galassi has written eloquently of such nature drawings, which documented "the modest spirit of freedom and release these history painters brought to their outdoor studies."[4]

Outdoor sketching had always flourished at the French Academy in Rome, and both Vleughels and Natoire had encouraged the students under their charge to penetrate the surrounding countryside and draw from nature (see cats. 9 and 17). Vincent benefited from the relative informality of the final years of the aging Natoire's directorship to experiment in a variety of genres and to gain mastery over a wide array of techniques.[5] A red-chalk drawing made the same year shows two students, one with a portfolio on his knees, by the parapet of the Torretta (or observatory) in the Farnese Gardens (fig. 30.1). Although in the medium beloved by Fragonard and Robert, this sheet manifests a similar "predilection for the real," with Vincent literally (and figuratively) turning his back on the picturesque panorama of the Forum below.[6] Even Vincent's most finished, elaborate landscape drawing made in 1773, the splendid *View of the Gardens of the Villa Negroni* (fig. 30.2), shares the acuity and rigor of these outdoor studies.[7] One should be careful, however, of importing too much restraint

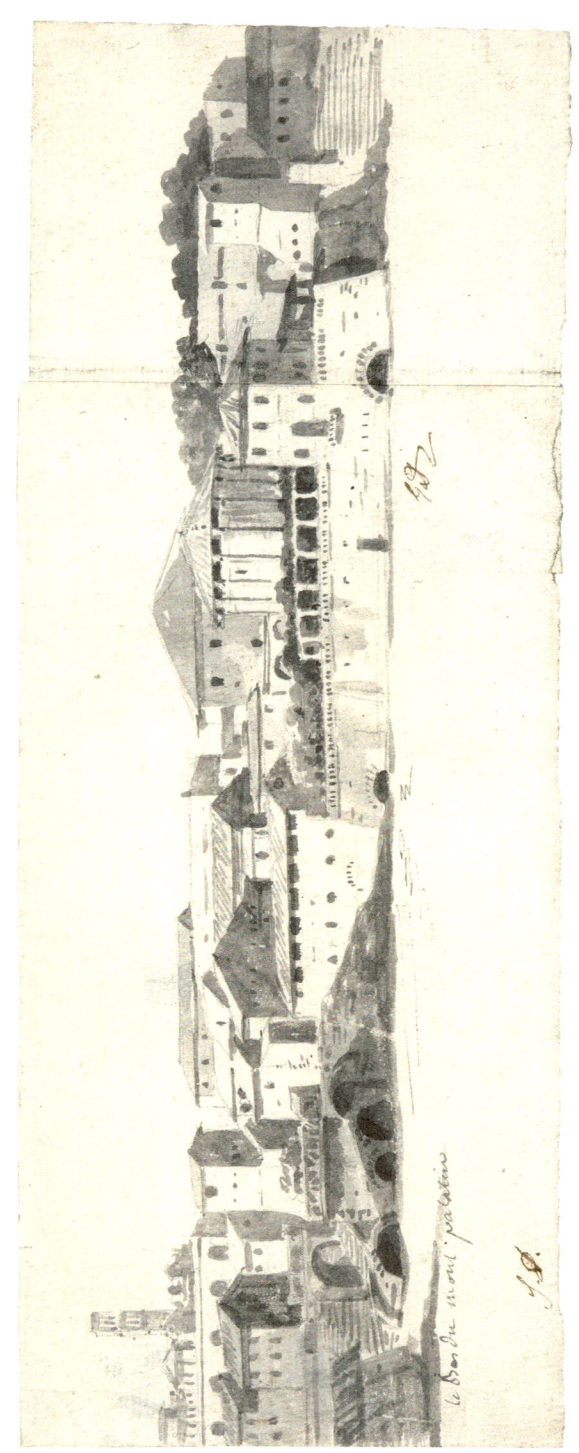

to the Protestant Vincent. Hitherto unremarked in the Lugt drawing is the line of washing hanging out to dry in front of the entrance to the semicircular ruins in the middle ground at right. Although there are no laundresses in sight, this fanciful intrusion suggests that Robert's influence remained potent for the next generation of fledgling academicians.[8]

The date of the Lugt drawing has given rise to some confusion. Although quite clearly inscribed "1773" at lower left, the last digit has often been misread and the drawing incorrectly dated to "1775," the final year of Vincent's residence (he would leave Rome in early October 1775).[9] The artist's enthusiasm for working en plein air, attested to by a number of signed and dated Roman drawings,[10] had given his family cause for concern, since he was "greatly incommoded by the heat." In May 1775 they had requested that he return home before finishing his studentship, to avoid the dangers of another summer.[11] The *premier peintre*, Jean-Baptiste-Marie Pierre, intervened to allay the family's concerns, noting that Vincent "could profit from the time that is left to him in studying in the interiors of churches and palaces."[12] Indeed, by the end of his four-year stay at the Palazzo Mancini, Vincent's interest in landscape may have waned. Natoire informed d'Angiviller in May 1775 that the artist had recently painted a number of "very good portraits . . . and it seems to me that this will be the genre in which he is most likely to specialize."[13] [CBB]

31. Jacques-Louis David
Paris 1746 – 1825 Brussels
View across the Tiber with the Temple of Vesta,
1775 – 80
Gray ink and gray wash over black chalk on two sheets of paper | 10.5 x 28.3 (10.5 x 21.2; 10.3 x 7.1; covered width: 3.7) | Verso, *Sketch of Buildings*, graphite
Inscriptions: bottom left in black ink, "le Bas du mont palatin" | Marks: initials in pen and brown ink of, bottom left, Jules David, *JD*. (L. 1437); bottom right, Eugène David, *ED* (L. 839); verso, left edge, touches of gray ink | Inv. no. 2006-T.6

ON LEAVING FRANCE FOR HIS state-sponsored program of study in Italy, David was determined not to succumb to the pull of antiquity. But by the time he reached Rome, he was overcome by what he saw and expressed shame of his own ignorance.¹ During his years as a pensionnaire at the French Academy from 1775 to 1780, he drew incessantly after works by the Old Masters, antique statuary, and architecture and made landscape sketches and urban scenes. He returned to Paris with more than a thousand drawings and tracings in notebooks, which he kept in his studio as source material for his paintings.²

Here, as in a few other examples from his notebooks (fig. 31.1), David uses a horizontal panoramic format for his topographical view. However, the Lugt work is unique among David's Roman sketches—he extended the sheet by pasting another piece of paper to the right-hand side, carefully lining up the lines of the laid paper, to accommodate the view. David sketched the buildings in black chalk on site, and later in the studio he filled in the shadows with gray wash.³ In this urban landscape, David concentrates on the purity of the architecture seen in a bright, cold light. The scene is devoid of human figures, and trees appear only minimally.

David took his viewpoint from the east side of the Tiber looking across the west bank to the base of the Palatine Hill. In the center of the drawing is the Piazza Bocca della Verità (in ancient times known as the Forum Boarium, an animal or cattle market); to the right of the piazza, David would have identified the round monument as the Temple of Vesta (recognized today as the Temple of Hercules Olivarius) and to the left, the long rectangular Temple of Fortuna Virilis (the Temple of Portunus), of which only the roof is visible. The dark semicircular opening on the edge of the river near the center of the drawing is the mouth of the famous Cloaca Maxima, one of the earliest sewers ever built (dating from c. 600 BC).⁴ To the far left toward the back rises the thirteenth-century bell tower of the church of San Giorgio al Velabro, which once stood on the site of a Roman basilica, a part of which is incorporated into its façade. David's years in Rome were crucial to his movement away from rococo art to neoclassicism. In this drawing, a new aesthetic vocabulary is already in evidence in the relief-like composition, architectonic structure, clear distinction of light and dark, and emphasis on geometric forms. [SGG]

[32]

32. Pierre-Paul Prud'hon
Cluny 1758 – 1823 Paris
The Cellist, half-length, three-quarter back view, turned toward the left, 1777 – 78
Pen and black ink, gray wash over graphite; framing lines in pen and gray ink and brown ink | 28.2 x 43.6
Verso, on mount: preliminary sketch of cellist in graphite | Inscriptions: bottom left of mount in pencil, "13-21/ 1019"; bottom right, "3" | Inv. no. 2004-T.35

THE CELLIST is an early work by a great and idiosyncratic master whose life spanned the turbulent periods of the French Revolution, the First Empire, and the Restoration. The son of a stonemason, Pierre Prud'hon was educated by Benedictine monks in his native town of Cluny. In 1774 the bishop of Mâcon (Gabriel-François Moreau) secured for the sixteen-year-old student a scholarship to attend the École gratuite de dessin in Dijon, one of the most important art schools in France outside Paris. Under the tutelage of the school's founder and primary teacher, François Devosges, Prud'hon progressed swiftly through the curriculum, which heavily favored drawing. In 1777 Prudhon added "Paul" to his first name in honor of Rubens and an apostrophe to his family name to give it an aristocratic ring. Prud'hon's fluency in drawing brought him to the attention of the baron de Joursanvault of Beaune (1748 – 1792), an enlightened art patron and amateur printmaker and musician who took talented students and local artists under his wing.[1] For the next three years, Prud'hon enjoyed the baron's patronage, friendship, and occasional collaboration on projects.

The present drawing is a preparatory sketch for an engraving to illustrate baron de Joursanvault's *Méthode de basse*, a treatise he wrote on his technique for playing the cello.[2] He commissioned Prud'hon to execute at least twelve illustrations as well as a frontispiece for the treatise. The drawings feature the baron, his father (M. de Bessey), his curate (fig. 32.1), and another unknown young man, depicted half or full length from the front in profile, or, as here, from the back, demonstrating different arm and hand positions.[3] The treatise was never published, however, nor were the illustrations engraved.

The thirty-year-old baron is the model in the Lugt drawing, executed, like most of the others in the series, in pen and ink and gray wash over graphite.

He is represented in profile from the back, facing left, his hair pulled back in a black taffeta bag in the fashion of the late eighteenth century.[4] With his left hand he presses his fingers on the strings while gazing out into space as if attentively listening. The strong contrasts between light and dark give the drawing a dramatic, sculptural quality, a style that reflects that of the artist's teacher Devosges.[5] As Prud'hon's drawing developed into a softer and more personal mode, some of the idiosyncratic elements of this early work — the elongated arm and slight awkwardness of the hand — remained consistent.[6] This sheet passed through the hands of several notable figures, among them Alexander Dumas *fils* and Anatole France. It remains a testament to the vital relationship between patron and artist, one that had a formative influence on Prud'hon's art. [SGG]

33. Pierre-Paul Prud'hon
Cluny 1758 – 1823 Paris
Study for a Curtain, c. 1806
Black chalk, stumped, heightened with white chalk on blue paper (slightly discolored) | 30.2 x 22.8
Inscriptions: verso, bottom right in pencil, "6829"
Stamps: bottom right in red ink, monogram of Charles-Boulanger de Boisfremont (L. 353)
Inv. no. 1971-T.38

A PAINTER OF PORTRAITS, allegorical subjects, and large decorative works, Prud'hon has a reputation today that rests to a large degree on his drawings, his preferred medium of expression. His primary artistic interest was in the design of his work and in the creative process itself. Prud'hon experienced great difficulty in finishing his paintings and relied on the centuries-old workshop practice of working with others, already begun with his first patron, the baron de Joursanvault (see cat. 32).
This drawing stems from his most important and long-lasting collaboration with a highly accomplished artist, Marie Françoise Constance Mayer-Lemartinière (1775 – 1821), who entered his studio in 1803 as a former student of Jean-Baptiste Greuze, an artist they both admired.[1] After Prud'hon's mentally unstable wife was committed to an institution in 1803, Mayer became his artistic partner as well as his unofficial wife and surrogate mother to his five children. She translated his drawings into paintings for him, while he provided extensive preparatory sketches for her paintings, which she exhibited at the

Salon under her name alone.[2] Their highly productive collaboration lasted until Mayer, despairing of ever becoming Prud'hon's legal wife, took her own life at age forty-six.

The Lugt drawing is thought to be a preparatory sketch by Prud'hon for Mayer's painting *Full-length Portrait of Madame B. Putting on Her Earrings* (also known as *La Toilette*), which she exhibited at the Salon of 1806 (fig. 33.1).[3] Another Prud'hon drawing at the Louvre (fig. 33.2) has been securely identified as a preparatory sketch for the curtain that hangs behind Madame B. While the positioning of the curtain in the painting, with the shadow at the far side, more closely resembles the Louvre drawing, the cord that catches and gathers the drapery is probably taken from the Lugt drawing. Additional known compositional studies and drawings of details for this painting from Prud'hon's hand—of the mirror and the woman's head—demonstrate the degree of involvement he had in the planning stages of her works.[4]

In the Lugt drawing, Prud'hon first lightly outlined most of the curtain in black chalk on a sheet of blue paper, which serves as a middle tone. He applied black chalk to the left of the curtain and then stumped it to create a smooth dark shadow on the wall. The projecting folds of the cloth are suggested through subtle transitions from dark to light. In certain areas the black and white chalks are smoothly blended; in others delicate black hatch marks are applied over the intermediary blended gray tones. White highlights sometimes forcefully shoot down the edge of a long fold, and in other areas lie on the surface in a web of gossamer strokes. The variety of methods of applying the chalk make for a sparkling, luminous surface suggesting the density and weave of the cloth, while the powdery substance of the chalk contributes texture and softness to the image. Prud'hon's mastery of chiaroscuro in this drawing of a relatively minor detail for a painting, and the care he lavished on it, substantiate his reputation as "the French Correggio" and as one of his country's leading draftsmen. [SGG]

34. Pierre-Paul Prud'hon
Cluny 1758 – 1823 Paris
Queen Hortense and Her Two Children in a Park, c. 1811
Black chalk, stumped, heightened with white chalk
on blue paper, largely faded; black chalk framing lines
Image: 30.3 x 20.5; sheet: 32.7 x 22.8 | Verso, traces
of a study of drapery in black chalk | Stamps: bottom
left in red ink, monogram of Charles-Boulanger de
Boisfremont (L. 353) | Inv. no. 2008-T.16

UNDER THE FIRST EMPIRE, Prud'hon painted some of his best-known works, including the celebrated outdoor portrait *Empress Josephine at Malmaison* (1805 – 9).[1] Josephine, lost in reverie, is seated on a rock in the park of her country retreat outside Paris. When the emperor and empress divorced in 1809, Josephine retired to this villa. Prud'hon carried out extensive commissions for Josephine, as well as for her daughter from her first marriage, Queen Hortense of Holland, the subject of this drawing.[2] Hortense is depicted in the same park at Malmaison with two of her sons, Napoleon-Louis on the left and Charles-Louis-Napoleon, the future Napoleon III, on the right.[3] This drawing is one of six known preparatory studies for a portrait that was never realized.[4] In the Lugt drawing, Prud'hon experiments with the positions of the intertwined figures in a pyramidal composition. The queen stands beside the rock, with one knee resting on it. She wears a fashionable high-waisted, flowing Empire-style dress with puffed sleeves, and her short curls are held in place with a bandeau in the style of the time. Her head is frontal, and she looks out at the viewer, while her body in a graceful serpentine pose turns gently to the right. She appears to be rising while clasping her youngest son to herself, as he thrusts his small body into her arms, lifting him off the rock. To her right, her older son stands detached, holding flowers and looking off beyond the space of the image. In another preparatory sketch for the portrait, the boy faces his mother and looks up at her (fig. 34.1). The arrangement of figures and the intimacy among them recall Leonardo da Vinci's well-known cartoon *The Virgin and Child with Saint Anne and Saint John the Baptist* (fig. 34.2). Prud'hon revered Leonardo, whose works he had studied during his years in Rome (1784 – 88), calling him "my master and hero."[5]

Following his normal practice, Prud'hon worked on blue paper (which has now

[34]

faded to beige) to create an intermediate tone between the depths and heights of black and white chalk. As opposed to the smooth and subtle handling of the detailed study of a curtain (see cat. 33), however, here Prud'hon uses a rougher, more rapid drawing style appropriate to a compositional sketch. The figures are drawn in bold, dark outlines, and the forms are developed with energetic, crude hatch marks — black to suggest the abstract patterns of the folds of drapery flowing over the figures and in white rapid strokes to create the sensation of fleeing light drifting across faces, limbs, the rock, and ground. The forked tree behind, summarily drawn and heavily stumped, sets off the rough, calligraphic execution of the figures against a vague, smoky background. Edmond de Goncourt described Prud'hon's style in this drawing as "of the largest facture and in the darks executed with the audacity and brutality that only the great masters possess."[6] [SGG]

35. Louis-Jean Desprez
Auxerre 1743 – 1804 Stockholm
The Slaves of Vedius Pollio Thrown Alive to the Moray Eels, 1777 – 79
Pen and gray ink, watercolor over traces of black chalk | 22.2 x 15.1 | Inscriptions: verso at center in graphite, "2"; on the mount from the Paignon Dijonval collection, at top, in graphite, "*O abla guld* (?)" | Watermark: [J.] Honig Zoonen
Inv. no. 1986-T.46

THANKS TO THE RECENT publication of Vivant Denon's manuscript for the *Voyage pittoresque . . . de Naples et de Sicile* — acquired by the Fondation Custodia in 2000 — the subject and history of Desprez's frightening watercolor can be fully elucidated.[1] As the late Philip Conisbee noted, this delicate, crystalline sheet presents a "gruesome historical scene ... showing bodies dumped in a pool."[2] The pool in question was one of the fish tanks of the Villa Pausilypon, home of the notorious Publius Vedius Pollio (d. 15 BC), "famous for his wealth and for his cruelty." In the *Roman History*, Cassius Dio noted that Vedius Pollio "kept in reservoirs huge lampreys that had been trained to eat men, and he was accustomed to throw to them such of his slaves as he desired to be put to death."[3]

In an opening of the lateral wall at right, two of Vedius Pollio's henchmen have just propelled a hapless slave headlong into the pool. The distended bodies of at least two victims can be seen floating in the water, circled by the man-eating moray eels (also referred to in the literature as lampreys). Tiny figures in classical garb stand on the bridge, their backs to the terrible scene. All is calm and orderly in this limpid reconstruction of the Villa Pausilypon; the rearing equestrian statue glimpsed through the arcade is perhaps a reference to Vedius Pollio's rank as an "eques" or knight.[4] In such an unhurried depiction, Desprez approaches the banality of evil with a modernist's insight.

Desprez was a thirty-four-year-old laureate studying architecture at the French Academy in Rome, who had won the Grand Prix on his sixth attempt and arrived in August 1777 to take up residence at the Palazzo Mancini.[5] He was soon co-opted by Vivant Denon (1747 – 1825), "gentilhomme ordinaire du roi," in Italy to provide the text and oversee the illustrations for the *Voyage pittoresque ou description des royaumes de Naples et de Sicile* – a grandiose publication, financed jointly by Jean-Benjamin de Laborde and the abbé de Saint-Non, which would eventually appear in five folio volumes between 1781 and 1786.[6] Denon, who had left Marseilles on 4 November 1777 in the company of the draftsman Claude-Louis Châtelet (c. 1750 – 1795),[7] persuaded Desprez and his fellow pensionnaire Jean-Augustin Renard (1744 – 1807) to join him on the expedition to seek out and illustrate sites in Naples and southern Italy.

We now know that Denon and his *équipe* traveled along the coast of Posillipo at the northern edge of the Gulf of Naples in late November 1777.[8] At Marechiaro the intrepid Desprez scaled one of the rocks on the coast to take the view of the Bay of Naples and Vesuvius.[9] "When we came for him," Denon recalls, "he was besieged by waves, which seemed determined to wrest from him his portrait of the place they so cherished and caressed so constantly."[10] Since this was also the site of the ruins of Vedius Pollio's villa, the "unworthy friend of Augustus," Denon had his illustrators record the "pools or breeding grounds, which still exist in their entirety."[11]

Desprez made three drawings of this site: the villa's courtyard, the interior of the pool as it then existed (fig. 35.1), "and a third, of the pool reconstructed as it had been in Vedius's time, with the odious, inhuman usage that he made of it."[12] None of these drawings would make their way into the second volume of Saint-Non's publication, which nonetheless included a brief description of Vedius's notorious harvesting of moray eels, "which were fed on the blood and flesh of the slaves whom he had thrown alive into his pools for the least infraction."[13]

Previously confused with another horrific episode from Roman history,

Tiberius having the condemned thrown to their deaths from his Villa Jovis in Capri[14] — a subject proposed by the artist to the comte d'Angiviller, who wished to commission a pair of paintings by Desprez for his private collection (fig. 35.2)[15] — *The Slaves of Vedius Pollio* was one of several drawings made at Denon's instigation that were rejected by Saint-Non and not engraved for the *Voyage pittoresque*.[16] It seems likely that Desprez completed the sheet after returning to the Palazzo Mancini in January 1779. In April 1779 the new director, Joseph-Marie Vien, reported to d'Angiviller that Desprez had been "fully occupied since his return from Sicily in finishing those views that are to be used in M. Laborde's publication, which he had only sketched in situ."[17] The black-chalk grid, visible through the layers of wash and watercolor, and the treatment of light and shade against the bricks and water suggest the deliberation and meticulousness with which Desprez prepared and completed his view. [CBB]

36. Nicolas Lavreince
Stockholm 1737 – 1807 Stockholm
The Stolen Kiss, c. 1785 – 90
Pen and black and brown ink, brown and gray wash, heightened with white gouache
26.1 x 31.5 | Inv. no. 7492

UNSIGNED, UNDATED, and never reproduced in an engraving, Lavreince's ambitious gouache drawing is immediately recognizable within the repertory of licentious, gallant imagery that proliferated in Paris in the 1780s.[1] Slight oxidization of the white gouache highlights owing to the sheet's overexposure to light has somewhat compromised the refinement of Lavreince's finish, but the care with which he elaborated this amorous encounter suggests that this was a drawing intended for reproduction, perhaps by Jean-François Janinet (1752 – 1814), his most successful collaborator during the 1780s.[2]

In an aristocratic residence, a smartly dressed man draws the stately, standing woman close to him to steal a kiss. Her female companion, who wears a mob cap, has fallen asleep at her sewing, and work has yet to begin on the small oval canvas resting on the easel. (Lavreince's heroine most likely paints for her own amusement.) That this is an illicit interlude is also suggested by the disapproving expression of the portrait of a male figure in military costume — an absent husband, perhaps — who looks down on the couple from the overdoor at upper left.

A miniaturist by training, Lavreince had already approached the theme of the stolen kiss in a tiny watercolor and gouache painting, in which the female lover is represented as an amateur musician (fig. 36.1).[3] In the more expansive format of the Lugt drawing, he is able to pay greater attention to the details of the mirrored and paneled room – no artist's studio, this! – lingering over details such as the variously patterned parquet floor, the rectilinear boiseries and Corinthian pilasters on either side of the mirror, and the various pieces of Louis XVI furniture.[4] Lavreince depicts a small round worktable at far right, with its straight, tapered legs, on which the sleeping woman rests her left arm;[5] the chair on which she is seated has a curving crest rail and side rails surmounted by knobs.[6] Glimpsed under the mirror, behind the easel, is a *bergère* with a semicircular back and ample seat cushion, protected by a makeshift cover from the amateur painter's handiwork.[7]

It is the clothing and coiffures of the protagonists of Lavreince's not especially dangerous liaison that establish a date in the mid- to late 1780s. The ardent suitor wears a frock coat, cut narrow across the shoulders, with the fronts curving away to reveal a relatively short waistcoat.[8] Both women are dressed in *robes à l'anglaise*, with the wide hairstyles that became fashionable in the mid-1780s, comprising a "mass of frizzled curls and long, unraveling ringlets." The standing woman wears a "vast plumed and ribboned hat," also typical of that period.[9]

One final argument for dating Lavreince's composition to the late 1780s are its formal (and conceptual) similarities to Fragonard's *Stolen Kiss (Le Baiser à la dérobée)* (fig. 36.2) engraved by Nicolas-François Regnault in June 1788.[10] The flowing curtain, ardent hand gestures, and, above all, the woman's half-hearted resistance make one wonder if Lavreince had been given access to Fragonard's genre painting even before its translation into print. [CBB]

37. Joseph Bidauld
Carpentras 1758 – 1846 Montmorency
View in Rome, c. 1785 – 90
Watercolor, graphite underdrawing and framing lines | 19.2 x 25.4 | Inv. no. 1983-T.4

JOSEPH BIDAULD WAS A LEADING NEOCLASSICAL LANDSCAPE PAINTER of the first decades of the nineteenth century.[1] As a promising young artist, he obtained a stipend from the art dealer Antoine-Charles Dulac to travel to Italy

in November 1785. There he joined the circle of northern artists connected with the French Academy, where a return to classicism was in full swing. This new generation of landscape painters looked back to the examples of Nicolas Poussin (1594 – 1665) and Claude Lorrain (1600 – 1682), whose structured landscapes, often with historical, biblical, or mythological figures, evoked an idealized world. While their highly detailed exhibition pieces were executed entirely in the studio, the neoclassicists' painting practice rested on a foundation of plein-air sketching, that is, drawing and painting directly from nature.[2] Bidauld remained in Italy for five years and traveled extensively throughout the peninsula, recording his observations of picturesque architecture in rugged landscapes or urban environments.

The intimate view encountered on a walk or seen from a window in the Lugt watercolor has the characteristic sense of structure of Bidauld's oil paintings. Using a horizontal format, he laid out his strictly ordered composition in graphite in three bands. In the foreground, low ground cover and a row of luxuriant bushes flank a high wall. A lone tree provides a counterpoint to the architecture in the middle ground. A row of taller trees with two umbrella pines in the background runs parallel to the bushes. The focus of the drawing is the villa in the center constructed of simple geometric shapes; the stacking of cubes with arched and rectangular windows culminates in a curious tower or lookout. An outdoor loggia is seen on the left side of the house. The carefully placed dots and dashes on the surface of the architecture describe the textural details of the crumbling stucco-covered masonry as well as the regularly spaced putholes for the scaffolding used in the construction of the building.

The harmony of clearly defined parts, balance of cool greens against warm ochers, sharp divisions of light and shadow, and lack of incidental detail or figures give the picturesque scene a sense of timelessness. Bidauld's meticulous application of watercolor in small, delicate strokes of dense, opaque color underlies the stability of his image. Only in the light blue sky with vaporous white clouds and in the swath of green in the foreground does he exploit the transparency of the medium in fluid veils of color. Indeed, the atmospheric treatment and diffuse light of the sky seems at odds with the strong contrasts of light and dark that define the architectural shapes.

Although the Lugt work was undoubtedly sketched on site, it exhibits the fastidious detail and finish of a studio painting. For Bidauld, plein-air sketching did not necessarily entail a loose handling of the medium and spontaneous effects. It was an exercise in close observation to aid him later in composing his idealized historical landscapes. Writing in 1849 shortly after Bidauld's death, a critic noted that he "had pushed his passion for landscape to a point where he established himself for months at a time in front of a view . . . to paint all day . . . in spite of accidents even of temperature, and did not leave his place until after finishing his painting."³

Bidauld's dedication to plein-air sketching and keen attention to the details of nature earned him the esteem of Camille Corot (see cat. 42) in the next generation of artists. Of the then unfashionable Bidauld, Corot said: "Bidauld! . . . he was certainly a master and sometimes one of the most exquisite of them. Several of his small canvases were masterpieces. . . . I admire him and I respect him."⁴ [SGG]

38. Louis-Roland Trinquesse
Bourgogne c. 1746 – c. 1800

Portrait of a Man Looking Right, dated 12 October 1797
Red chalk | 23.8 diameter | Inscriptions: at the bottom, signed in red chalk, "desine par Trinquesse. ce 12.obre 1797."; verso, on the mount, in pen and brown ink, "149", and in lead pencil, "95" and "77" (encircled) | Inv. no. 1979-T.14

TRINQUESSE REMAINS ONE of the least studied artists working in the last quarter of the eighteenth century.¹ A specialist in ambitious, oversize genre paintings and conversation pieces in the "Metsu manner," he was also an able and prolific portraitist who received important commissions without the benefit of an affiliation with the Royal Academy. Although in 1770 as a young man he had won two prizes for drawing,² he did not compete for the Grand Prix to study in Rome and from 1779 chose to exhibit at the Salon de la Correspondance, outside the precincts of the official establishment.³ Trinquesse seems to have had a change of heart in August 1789, when he apparently considered presenting a work to the Academy in order to become an associate member (agréé) of the institution, and thus become eligible to exhibit in the biennial Salon.⁴ Although, in the end, he failed to appear before his academic peers, with the suppression of the Academy in 1793 and the open Salons of the 1790s, he was able to exhibit his work regularly in that decade. A measure of how little is known of him is the absence of any documentation for either his birth or death. Trinquesse's last dated drawing was done in 1798, and it is assumed that he died around 1800.⁵

Medallion male portraits in red chalk, modeled after examples by Bouchardon

and Cochin,[6] were a distinct category of Trinquesse's production, beginning as early as 1771, with the signed and dated portrait of the landscape painter Joseph Vernet (Musée Carnavalet, Paris).[7] Over the next twenty-six years the artist would continue to produce several such effigies, nearly always signed within the framing lines, and sometimes dated to the very day.[8] Certain of his portraits of established artists and professional men were engraved — some as beribboned medallions, following a conceit established by Cochin and Augustin de Saint-Aubin.[9] However, some of his most striking, naturalistic portrait drawings were made of less well-known men (fig. 38.1) — or those yet to make a name for themselves[10] — with whom Trinquesse may have enjoyed a personal connection.[11]

The large roundel portrait of an unknown sitter catalogued here is likely to have been such a case in point. The handsome young man is shown informally, his hair unstyled and his collar without a cravate, dressed in working clothes, perhaps. Trinquesse's intense parallel hatches establish a luminous background in which the sitter's face is almost chiseled in red chalk. The white paper functions as the brightest part of the composition, providing the sheen on the sitter's wavy, unkempt hair and modeling his left cheekbone. In keeping with Trinquesse's approach to his male sitters, the subject's gaze resolutely avoids our own; he is presented modestly, with an intense expression that lacks the swagger and confidence of some of the other male portraits in Trinquesse's repertory.

We have no idea of the identity of the sitter, although the care with which Trinquesse dated the roundel — "drawn by Trinquesse this 12th October 1797" — may provide a clue. Two red-chalk medallion portraits of Dom Claude-Pierre Clavelin (b. 1736) and his wife are documented as having been done at the same time. The portrait of the Madame Clavelin was drawn on Friday, 13 October 1797, the day after the Lugt roundel; that of her husband is dated "Monday, 6 November 1797."[12] Dom Clavelin, a robust sixty-one-year-old, had been the archivist at the Benedictine abbey of Molesmes, in Burgundy. He was one of the few priests who had supported the Revolution's ecclesiastical reforms and rejected celibacy, as the companion portrait suggests.[13] If Trinquesse, a native of Burgundy, was visiting friends in the autumn of 1797, is it possible that the *Portrait of a Man Looking Right* may represent someone in Clavelin's household — an acquaintance, or someone in his employ. [CBB]

39. Jean-Auguste-Dominique Ingres
Montauban 1780 – 1867 Paris
Medallion Portrait of Julie Forestier, 1806
Graphite pencil, heightened with watercolor and white gouache on transfer paper, mounted on board; oval framing lines in graphite | 9.0 x 7.2
Inscriptions: at lower right, in graphite pencil, *J.I.* [?]
Inv. no. 2004-T32

THIS EXQUISITELY RENDERED, intimate drawing is likely to have been traced by Ingres from his portrait of the Forestier family in the Musée du Louvre, Paris (fig. 39.1). The drawing of the family was made shortly after Ingres's engagement in June 1806 to Julie Forestier (1782 – 1824), a painter and talented musician, a few months before his departure for the French Academy in Rome.[1] Although Ingres was entitled to spend four years in Italy as a Prix de Rome winner, Julie's father agreed to the engagement on the condition that he return at the end of the first year to marry her.

In the Louvre drawing—of which two other versions exist—Julie Forestier is depicted in full length, standing at a clavier and looking out at the viewer.[2] Her father and mother are seated on either side of her, with her uncle and a servant on the left and her dog at her feet. Ingres singled out the figure of his fiancée for the small-scale Lugt drawing, representing her in half length in an oval format, reminiscent of a medallion. She wears a loose gown with a ruffled collar, a tie under the bodice, puffed sleeves, and a softly pleated skirt. The pure oval of her head, her almond-shaped eyes, upturned lips, and the curves of her gown and figure are echoed in the format of the sheet.

Ingres drew on a variety of materials and techniques to create the Lugt drawing.[3] The paper was first coated with gum arabic to give it a luster that suggests vellum or ivory, materials commonly associated with portrait miniatures. He then traced the figure and a section of the decorative wall frieze from the original drawing in a fine graphite line. Using the edge of a soft graphite pencil, he shaded the lower part of the wall behind Julie and subtly contoured her face, while with a harder pencil he reinforced the outlines of her dress and strongly incised the pleat lines of her skirt. Ingres's departures from the original drawing include the gold pendant Julie now wears around her neck and her gently parted lips.[4] With watercolor he rendered her blond and blue-eyed and added white gouache highlights to her costume to enhance the curves of her bodice

and sleeve. Finishing touches of gouache enliven both the surface and the likeness, giving light to Julie's eyes, brilliance to her gold earring, and a slight shimmer to her lips. With these changes, Ingres transformed his tracing into a unique work of art evoking the fineness and intimacy of a painted miniature. The artist appears to have taken this portrait with him to Rome, as he refers to it in letters to Julie; writing on 19 October 1806, he teasingly complains: "I speak to you, but alas! You do not respond."[5] Julie's absence, as well as negative criticism of works he exhibited at the Salon, contributed to Ingres's deep unhappiness during his early days in Rome. But after a period of adjustment, he decided to stay on at the end of his first year, and Julie's father offered to release him from his engagement.[6] The original drawing of the Forestier family was returned to Ingres by Mlle Forestier after they parted. Ingres remained in Rome for the next fourteen years, breaking yet another engagement before marrying Madeleine Chapelle in 1813.[7] Julie continued to exhibit at the Salon, but never married. Ingres's early biographer, Henry Lapauze, ascribed to her the following (probably apocryphal) remark: "When one has had the honor of being engaged to Mr. Ingres, one does not marry."[8] [SGG]

40. Théodore Géricault
Rouen 1791 – 1824 Paris
Forest with Two Figures and a Cow, c. 1813 – 14
Graphite | 12.7 x 20.4 | Inscriptions: verso, upside down, in graphite, "Bas Breau 10 mai" | Stamps: bottom left in black ink, Coutan-Hauguet-Schubert (L. 464); bottom right in blue ink, Nikos Dikeos (mark not catalogued by Lugt) | Inv. no. 2007-T.13

GÉRICAULT WAS A LARGELY self-taught artist and is regarded as a pioneer of Romanticism. He burst on the scene at the Salon of 1812 with his heroic canvas *The Charging Chasseur*, which earned him a gold medal. His magnum opus, *The Raft of the Medusa* of 1819, heralded a new type of subject matter drawn from contemporary life but expressive of universal themes of man versus nature. Landscape played a minor role in his oeuvre, although in 1816 Géricault traveled to Italy, and in 1818 he produced a monumental cycle of Italianate vistas entitled *The Times of Day*.[1]
The Lugt drawing, based on direct observation, is very different in spirit from the artist's proto-Romantic works. It has only recently come to light and has

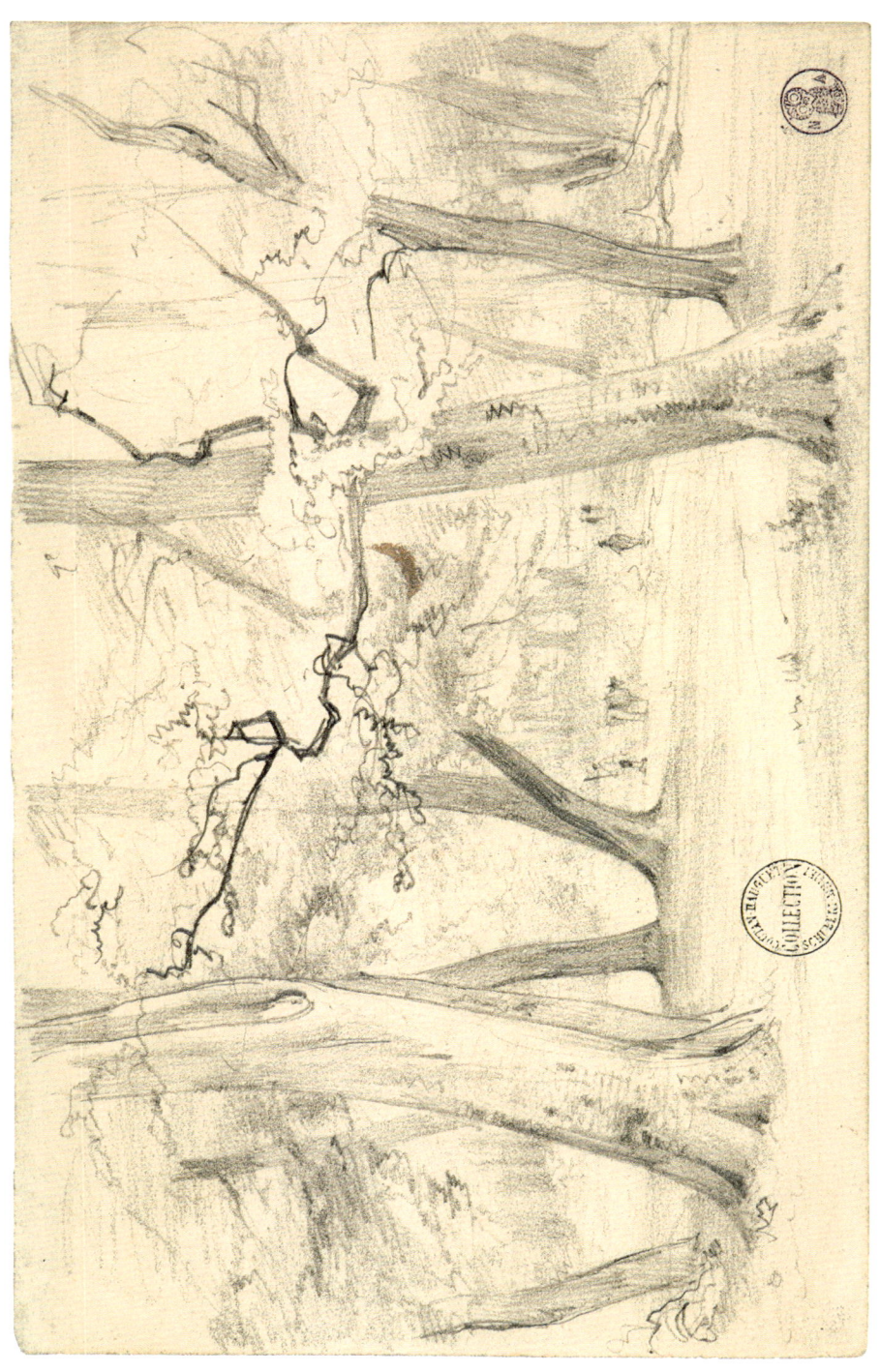

[40]

not been previously published. Here, Géricault sketched a slice of wooded land. A stout pair of trees with tall trunks bending toward each other forms an archway leading into the wood or park. Behind them, slender trees with supple curving trunks spread across the sheet. Further back in the center of the composition is a vignette of two figures with a cow and other strolling figures leading back to the stand of trees in the depth. The dramatic contrast of scale between the foreground trunks and the figures, and the fact that the tops of the trees are cut off by the upper edge of the sheet contribute to a sense of engulfment in the scene. The theme of the *sous-bois* would become a favored motif among the later Barbizon artists.

Working in graphite, Géricault uses a range of expressive marks and modes of drawing. The branches in the foreground are drawn in hard, jagged, and strikingly dark lines; they stand out against the smoothly rendered contours of trunks, shaded with long vertical strokes of the pencil and marked by zigzag lines that suggest the rough texture of bark and lichen. Foliage is indicated in summary scalloped shapes. On the basis of the stylistic analysis, Bruno Chenique has related the Lugt sheet to an album in The Art Institute of Chicago (fig. 40.1), and has dated the drawing to 1813–14.[2] In the Chicago sketchbook, Géricault made graphite studies of parks around Paris and animals in a naturalistic style alongside loose pen and wash sketches of imagined compositions.[3] A nearly contemporary sketchbook at the Louvre known as the Zoubaloff album demonstrates that the artist was also executing drawings in a classical mode at this time. The Lugt drawing thus fits into this fruitful period in which Géricault, following his early triumph, recommitted himself to artistic study by exploring a range of drawing styles as well as sketching directly from nature. [SGG]

41. Achille-Etna Michallon
Paris 1796 – 1822 Paris
View from the Vatican, 1818 – 21
Graphite | 28.3 x 43.6 | Inv. no. 2006-T.32

BORN IN PARIS, Achille-Etna Michallon was the son and nephew of sculptors Claude Michallon and Claude Francin. He learned to draw at an early age and studied with the two leading neoclassical painters, Jacques-Louis David and Pierre-Henri de Valenciennes, and later with Jean-Victor Bertin. Michallon made his debut at the Salon in 1812 with three landscape paintings and, in 1817, won the Prix de Rome in the newly established category of historical landscape. During his stay in Italy from January 1818 to the autumn of 1821, he sketched in and around Rome and traveled to southern Italy and Sicily, carrying Valenciennes's treatise *Eléments de perspective pratique* with him as his guide.[1] He painted oil sketches and made some 800 drawings in pastel, gouache, watercolor, and pen and ink, although most of them were pure landscapes in pencil.[2]

In the Lugt drawing, Michallon took his viewpoint from the Vatican. This extensive landscape is drawn in delicate contour lines with a minimal use of shading, a style that is characteristic of many of Michallon's Italian drawings and recalls the purity of Ingres's landscape sketches. The master was still in Rome when Michallon arrived and, as Stefani has speculated, he must have seen some of Ingres's landscape drawings as he chose several of the exact same sites.[3] The Lugt sheet, in fact, was attributed to Ingres when it came to light and was exhibited at the Fondation Custodia in 2001 but later reattributed to Michallon by Stijn Alsteens, who discovered an identical drawing made on tracing paper in the Louvre that was securely Michallon's (fig. 41.1).[4]

This sheet is unusual in Michallon's drawn oeuvre in its representation of architecture. Yet unlike Ingres's Italian landscape drawings, where the focus is on the architecture, here Michallon concentrates on the extensiveness of the view into which the buildings are folded.[5] The degree of clarity in the Lugt drawing varies from the summarily executed trees in the foreground to the more finely rendered buildings at the horizon. Some of the monuments have been identified: the walls of Urban VIII at left, the Torre delle Milizie at the center, and the Capitoline Hill at right. Behind the Capitoline are the Janiculum, Sabine, and Alban hills.[6]

Michallon returned to Paris in 1821 and opened a studio, where Corot was briefly his student (see cat. 42). His historical landscape paintings earned him the reputation of leading painter in that genre, in which he combined a Poussinesque sense of structure with direct observation. His promising career was cut short by pneumonia, however, and he died in 1822 at the age of twenty-six. [SGG]

42. Jean-Baptiste-Camille Corot
Paris 1796 – 1875 Paris
Landscape with Rocks near Marino, dated 1827
Pencil on paper | 29.2 x 27.3 | Verso: Sketch with Rocks and Trees | Inscriptions: lower right of recto in pencil, "Marino Mai 1827" | Inv. no. 2001-T.2

THE CLASSICAL LANDSCAPE tradition that began with Poussin and Claude in the seventeenth century and flourished among the international group of neoclassicists who gathered in Rome in the late eighteenth century culminated in the work of Camille Corot. Born in Paris, he received his early training in the studio of Achille-Etna Michallon (see cat. 41) and Jean-Victor Bertin, both of whom had been students of Pierre-Henri de Valenciennes, the leading painter of historical landscapes. In November 1825 Corot left for Italy and joined the community of landscapists around Théodore d'Aligny in Rome. During his visit, he traveled to the well-known sites on the sketching route visited by generations of artists since Claude – Tivoli and the villa d'Este, Civita Castellana, Lake Nemi, and Marino – making oil sketches and some two hundred drawings along the way. These fresh works, usually inscribed with the location and date, served to sharpen his powers of observation and provided him with a repertoire of motifs for later use.

The Lugt sheet dates from May 1827, the year that Corot made his debut at the Salon in Paris with two paintings sent from Rome.[1] In this drawing executed in Marino, a small town that was part of the Castelli Romani on the Alban hills southeast of Rome, Corot focuses on an unprepossessing slice of nature seen from close up. A boulder and smaller rocks form a frieze sloping slightly downhill across the lower half of the vertical sheet. The peak of the rocky outcropping is just left of center, and three trees form a screen behind the rocks, their height diminishing from left to right. The curving trunks and twisting branches of these slender trees are almost balletic in their movement. In this beautifully balanced composition, Corot gives equal value to the forest floor in the foreground, the rocks, the trees actively straining toward the light, and the sky.

[43]

André and Renée Jullien have identified the site in this drawing as the same that appears in a larger pen-and-ink sheet executed during the same period, *Vallée avec un cavalier et une italienne*.[2] Corot would often sketch the same site multiple times and leave his drawings in a relatively unfinished state. Drawing for Corot was not only a tool for observation and documentation, but also a process of experimentation and exploration. As Peter Galassi has argued, Corot's working process eroded the neoclassical tradition barriers between plein-air sketching and studio painting while also prefiguring the modern taste for the unfinished aesthetic.[3]

The Lugt work is executed in hard, fine lines for contours and softer graphite for shading. Commenting on the precision and vigor of Corot's pencil-drawing technique, Moreau-Nélaton noted that "The fine black point . . . dug a deep furrow that risked puncturing the sheet" and quoted Corot as having remarked: "I had great pencils back then! They never broke; they would rather take a piece with them."[4] The neoclassical drawing style, exemplified by Ingres, was strictly linear with shading indicated by regular parallel hatching. Over the course of his Italian stay, Corot shifted away from this austere style and developed a more tonal approach to drawing, evidenced by the Lugt sheet. The variation and sometimes complete obliteration of line in the shading of the boulders and tree trunks attest to Corot's increasing concern with areas of light and dark as opposed to contours of forms.[5] Corot's keen sensitivity to changing qualities of light would influence generations of artists, including Rousseau, Millet, and Harpignies (see cats. 48, 51, 52, and 63). [SGG]

43. Louis-Gabriel-Eugène Isabey
Paris 1803 – 1886 Paris
Boat in a Storm, c. 1828
Pen and brown ink, watercolor heightened with white gouache over black chalk underdrawing on irregularly cut paper | 20.7 x 32.9 | Inscriptions: verso, bottom right in graphite, "020577" | Inv. no. 2003-T.13

A MINOR ROMANTIC MASTER, Isabey was known for his marine scenes, though his subjects ranged widely from landscapes to historical fantasies. This drawing from Eugène Isabey's youth is connected with his oil *The Smugglers*, which was exhibited to acclaim in 1828 at the Louvre by the Société des Amis des Arts.[1] The same precariously tossed boat in the drawing appears in the painting as well as in the etching after it (fig. 43.1); in the oil and the print, however, the jagged cliffs loom directly over the boat, suggesting its imminent destruction. The drawing was passed down through the family of the artist as part of an album of landscapes, seascapes, and figures.[2]

With the advent of Romanticism, the sea with its uncontrollable power and mystery gained currency as a motif in the visual arts and literature in France in the first half of the nineteenth century. Géricault's epic canvas *The Raft of the Medusa*, exhibited at the Salon in 1819, and Delacroix's *The Barque of Dante* (Salon of 1822) set a new bar for the subject of man pitted against the sea; they serve as obvious precedents for Isabey's *Smugglers* and his other seascapes and shipwrecks, which he continued to produce even after the subject became less favored.

In this painterly sketch, Isabey freely employs a variety of materials to powerful effect. The desolate setting is established in broad sweeps of the brush. Transparent, watery veils of gray wash, rapidly applied, suggest storm clouds and rolling waves. The horizon is marked by a long swath of opaque black pigment representing dark water with the intensity of oil paint.[3] At right rise the rough silhouettes of the mountains, also rendered with layers of this dense watercolor. A slash of white gouache behind the mountains conjures up a bolt of lightning, which discharges its electrical energy into the atmosphere as it illuminates the boat below; Isabey's use of a dry brush in parts of the sky conveys a sense of the air crackling from the storm. The texture of crumbly strokes of black chalk in the waves heightens the drama of the image.[4] Switching to pen and ink, Isabey minutely outlines the boat and defines the smugglers, their goods, and even their hats and jackets with precise, calligraphic lines. The oars, also depicted in fragile, thin lines, threaten to snap in the tumultuous sea.

Isabey was one of the first French artists to embrace the new developments in watercolor technique introduced by British contemporaries, most notably Richard Parkes Bonington (1802 – 1828), who would, in his very short life, exert a significant influence on French art. Isabey had traveled to the Normandy coast with Bonington and Delacroix in 1825 and was evidently inspired by the Englishman's skillful combination of media to achieve great expressivity.[5] Isabey emulated Bonington's loose brushwork and dazzling atmospheric effects, in turn influencing a younger generation, as seen in the work of his student Jongkind (see cat. 50). The Lugt drawing, executed about the year of Bonington's death, shows Isabey's mastery of his exuberant approach to watercolor, through which he achieves a spontaneity and intensity most appropriate to an image of the elements unrestrained. [SGG]

44. Eugène Delacroix
Charenton Saint Maurice 1798 – 1863 Paris
Near Gibraltar, 1832
Pastel and black chalk | 15.8 x 21.5 (bottom and left edges irregular) | Inscriptions: bottom left in graphite, "21 jv / Pres de Gibraltar"
Inv. no. 2005-T.24

IN THIS PASTEL STUDY, everything contributes to a sense of tranquillity, a quality not generally associated with Delacroix. A stretch of rugged mountain coast rises from the water. Two peaks frame a middle rise and a more distant snow-capped range. The blue and buff mountain formations are bathed in an even light, and darker jagged recesses give a sense of volume. The water is rendered in long horizontal strokes of the pastel crayon in gradations of tone. The focus of the drawing is on the atmospheric light that unites land, water, and sky in shades of blue, from a deep blue black, where the water meets the land, to the palest shimmer in the sky. Except for a tiny boat at the foot of the mountain at the left, the scene is devoid of signs of human life or habitation.

The drawing was made aboard a ship, *La Perle*, which had been sent by Louis-Philippe on a diplomatic mission to the sultan of Morocco in 1832. Delacroix served as official artist to this delegation headed by Charles-Henri-Edgar, comte de Mornay (1803 – 1878).[1] Although pastel was not a medium Delacroix frequently used, its portability would have made it ideal for capturing transitory observations en route.[2] This sketch of the Spanish coast was made on 21 January 1832 near the outset of the journey. The ship had put down anchor between Algeciras and Gibraltar to refresh provisions and was becalmed for two days. Delacroix sketched not only to pass the time, but also to document the expedition. In addition, he kept an extensive journal of his experiences, colorfully recording his impressions of the landscape among other observations.[3]

Over the course of his voyage to Tangier, Delacroix made several other studies in watercolor and pastel of the rugged Spanish coastline with its rising mountains and "eternally snow-capped" peaks and pure sky (fig. 44.1).[4] Remarkable for their simplicity and sensitivity to atmosphere, these pastel drawings also presage the turning point in Delacroix's art marked by his encounter with the vivid colors and intense light of Morocco, Spain, and Algeria during his six-month journey. [SGG]

[44]

45. Eugène Delacroix
Charenton Saint Maurice 1798 – 1863 Paris
Study of a Wild Feline Facing Left, c. 1847
Pen and brown ink | 10.2 x 13.0 | Stamp: bottom right corner, cursive initials in red ink, "ED" for artist's estate sale | Inv. no. 2507 A

46. *Study of a Wild Feline Facing Right*, c. 1847
Pen and brown ink | 10.1 x 13.0 | Stamp: bottom right corner, cursive initials in red ink, "ED" for artist's estate sale | Inv. no. 2507 B

THIS PAIR OF QUICK, assured sketches of large felines demonstrates Delacroix's remarkable ability to seize the essence of his subject through highly economical means.[1] In these studies of movement and expression, Delacroix presents his subjects — most likely panthers — in an empty background facing in opposite directions; whether they were sketched from life or from memory is not clear.[2] In each, he outlines the animal in broken contour lines of varied widths and uses broad, energetic, parallel hatch marks to suggest the body's volume, musculature, and weight, as well as the shadow it casts. A "colorist" in painting, Delacroix defended his improvisatory manner of drawing, in opposition to that of the smooth classical mode of his archrival, Ingres: "Say you have outlined my form on a writing slate ... if you are a colorist, with that simple line you will manage to make it clear I have a density, a relief, a body. How will you manage it? By not making the outline consistently even, by making it ductile, almost broken off in places, accentuating it in other places by a second line and if needed a third, or else by a widened, thickened line that will strive not to look like a piece of wire."[3]
Accordingly, in the drawing of the panther facing right, Delacroix describes his subject with a great deal of verve and variety of line. The swiftness of his hand and the varied patterns of curved, spiraling, and spiky lines underlie the unleashed power of the animal springing diagonally forward. The panther's uncoiling motion begins in its round haunches, rises through the sinewy torso and the rippling muscles of the shoulders, and projects outward through the long neck, small head, and open mouth. The forward thrust of the head and left foreleg is counterbalanced by the downward pressure of the right paw on the

ground. The animated calligraphy verges on the decorative and abstract. Hatch marks are rapid and various, conveying a sense of energy that radiates into the abstract space of the background in long parallel strokes.

In the image of the panther facing left, Delacroix presents the body full-length in profile with more restrained supple outlines; spare hatching reinforces the feeling of energy held in reserve. The animal's head is lowered with ears laid back, and its curved tail, tip twitching, weighs heavily on the ground. The panther's silent stalking is conveyed through a sense of shifting weight, particularly onto the muscular left foreleg that strikingly resembles a human forearm. Indeed, Delacroix would later relate to the art critic Hippolyte Taine that while sketching a lion at the Musée d'histoire naturelle in Paris he noticed that "the lion's foreleg was the monstrous arm of a man, but twisted and reversed."[4] Delacroix's remark indicates his fascination with the new and hotly debated science of comparative anatomy, led by the naturalists Georges Cuvier and Étienne Geoffroy de Saint-Hilaire during the early to mid-nineteenth century.[5]

Delacroix's initial involvement in the subject of wild animals is traditionally dated between 1827 and 1833, a period of close collaboration with his friend the animal sculptor Antoine-Louis Barye. Together they attended dissections of lions in the laboratory of the Musée d'histoire naturelle and drew Bengal tigers at a traveling menagerie in St. Cloud.[6]

Delacroix's visit to North Africa (see cat. 44) in 1832 exposed him to a greater variety of exotic animals and deepened his interest in wild felines.[7] When the Musée d'histoire naturelle acquired several new animals in 1847, he began sketching regularly again in the Jardin des Plantes where they were kept. Indeed, these new arrivals seem to have sparked in Delacroix a creative renewal; after his trip to Morocco, the artist had ceased writing in his journal and this fifteen-year hiatus was broken only by a revelatory visit to the Jardin des Plantes. His inaugural journal entry of 19 January 1847 enthusiastically describes the breathtaking diversity of the animals there, and he comments: "How necessary it is to give oneself a shaking up, to get one's head out, to try to read in the book of creation, which has nothing in common with our cities and the works of men!"[8]

The Lugt drawings are tentatively dated to this period in the late 1840s, when the number of Delacroix's drawings of large felines greatly increased and sparked a wider vogue for the theme among French artists.[9] A similar style of execution is evident in *Tiger Lying Down* in the Musée du Louvre (fig. 45.1), which has also been placed in this period. While the Lugt drawings reveal the continuing inspiration Delacroix found in the world of exotic animals, they also make clear the special character he attributed to line in his oeuvre. [SGG]

[45]

[46]

47. Hippolyte-Jean Flandrin, Lyon 1809 – 1864 Rome; or Paul-Jean Flandrin, Lyon 1811 – 1902 Paris
View from the Summit of Vesuvius, 1838
Watercolor over graphite or black chalk
13.4 x 18.8 | Inscriptions: verso, top left, in graphite, "du Sommet du Vesuve" | Inv. no. 1989-T.21

WHETHER THIS PANORAMIC vista is by Hippolyte-Jean Flandrin – a painter of religious murals and a disciple of Ingres – or his brother Paul-Jean, a specialist in academic landscapes, has not been determined with certainty. The two brothers had a close working relationship.[1] Paul, who was also a student of Ingres, often assisted his more renowned older brother on his commissions and thus remained largely in his shadow. Paul's adherence to the neoclassical style of landscape painting, which had fallen out of repute with the advent of Impressionism, contributed as well to his obscurity.[2]

The Lugt sheet comes from an album that was passed down through the family containing sketches made by Hippolyte during his years in Italy (1833 – 38) with some sheets by Paul as well. When Hippolyte left for his residency at the French Academy in 1833 as a Rome Prize winner, Paul joined him there a year later.[3] This unsigned watercolor of Mount Vesuvius was made during a trip to southern Italy just before the brothers returned to France. A diary entry by Hippolyte dated 12 June 1838 gives a colorful description of their ascent of the mountain and of the volcano's awesome power.[4] Yet there is no evidence of smoke, lava, and chaos in this composed image. The emphasis is on neoclassical qualities of measured and enduring stasis.

Volcanic rock formations encircle the dark purple crater wall in the foreground, formed of cooled layers of lava and volcanic ash.[5] The rocky slopes fall into a rhythmic sequence of pointed shell shapes, listing right. Their concave sides are painted purple, while their rounded backs are covered in low green vegetation. At the far edge of the crater to the left, seven minute figures are indicated with dots of white and red watercolor. A second mountain range, probably the Apennines, runs behind the volcanic slopes and their vivid blue color suggests their relative distance through aerial perspective. A few streaks of pink and gray appear on the otherwise untouched upper two-thirds of the sheet. The artist's drawing technique gives this image a sense of palpable solidity. The contours of the mountains are precise and the areas of color within the land formations are kept within distinct boundaries. The dense pigment is built up with short strokes of the brush and the artist makes use of the paint's substance to emphasize the materiality of the geological formations.

[48]

Paul discovered his bent as a landscape painter while in Italy, while Hippolyte turned to this genre only occasionally. Examples by both brothers from the 1838 trip provide a basis for comparison with the Lugt sheet. In the *Bay of Naples*[6] and *Vesuvius* (fig. 47.1), Hippolyte applies the paint in liquid, transparent washes, capturing the overall quality of light in which the land formations are subsumed, an approach opposite to what is seen in this drawing. Paul's *The Environs of Naples*,[7] however, shares with the Lugt sheet a similar tendency toward clear definition of form. The affinities of the Lugt sheet with the latter has led Jacques Foucart to lean toward Paul in considering the sheet's authorship.[8] [SGG]

48. Théodore Rousseau
Paris 1812 – 1867 Barbizon
Riverbank in Le Berri, 1842
Watercolor, brown wash, heightened with oil in brown, blue, and white, over traces of black chalk; pencil framing lines | 28.9 x 43.6 | Stamp: bottom left in black ink, "TH R" for artist's estate sale (L. 2436) | Watermark: [F]ABRIANO
Inv. no. 1990-T.16

THÉODORE ROUSSEAU, generally acknowledged as the leader of the Barbizon school of painters, suffered the humiliating repeated rejection of his landscape paintings from the Paris Salon from 1834 to 1841, which earned him the sobriquet "le Grand Refusé." In June 1842 he left for a six-month sojourn in the remote, unspoiled region of Le Berry in central France, living in the tiny hamlet of Fay. There he carried on his longstanding practice of drawing directly from the site, of which this large sheet is a fine example.

In this sparse and luminous work of a gently rising riverbank, Rousseau laid out his composition in light touches of black chalk and went over them in brush and brown wash, leaving much of the buff paper bare. The long rectangular shape of the bank is bisected into light and dark areas, indicating sun and shadow. Two clumps of trees stretching across the bank are silhouetted against the sky. Rousseau makes use of a variety of lively marks—commas, dashes, and lines—to suggest their vitality and fullness of form. A few bold strokes of blue oil paint in the center of the drawing between the two masses of trees suggest

the water beyond the bank. Either on site, or later in his studio, Rousseau added strokes of white oil paint to the sky, between the groups of trees, and along the top of the riverbank at the right, all of which contribute to the luminosity of the work. He also reinforced some of the tree trunks and the edge of the land in brown oil paint. The drawing, the only one made in Le Berry that incorporates oil paint, looks forward to the examples of *dessin-peint* – a hybrid of oil sketching and drawing – he would make later in the 1840s.[1]

The simplicity of the composition, ordinariness of the scene, its horizontal format, low horizon and large sky, as well as its golden tonality, are reminiscent of Rembrandt's drawings of similar views. Rousseau owned prints after Dutch landscape painters, such as Ruisdael, and the influence of such masters pervades the French artist's work.

Rousseau kept most of his drawings until his death. As a result, he was not particularly known for his draftsmanship during his lifetime. The catalogue of his estate sale in 1868, which included this drawing, aptly described the works made in Le Berry as "petit poëmes intimes."[2] [SGG]

49. François-Marius Granet | Aix-en-Provence 1775 – 1849 Malvalat (near Aix-en-Provence)
View of Mont Sainte-Victoire from the Terrace of Malvalat, 1844?
Watercolor partially heightened with gum arabic, graphite underdrawing | 10.5 x 16.9 | Inscriptions: "malavala terrasse" in pencil on the former mount (removed but conserved) | Inv. no. 1995-T.18

A NATIVE OF AIX-EN-PROVENCE, Granet lived in Rome for more than twenty years and gained recognition for his quiet, meditative Salon paintings of cloisters and monasteries with narrative or religious subject matter. In contrast to his official work, he also made luminous, fresh, and spontaneous watercolors from nature as a form of relaxation and never exhibited them during his lifetime.[1] The Lugt sheet belongs to his Provençal watercolors, most of which were made after 1844, when he began to spend longer periods of time in his native area. The arid climate of the south and the quality of its light, as well as the artist's deep roots in the region, give these watercolors a personal significance while also locating them within the established tradition of Provençal landscape painting.[2]

[50]

The viewpoint of the Lugt watercolor is from the terrace of Granet's country house outside Aix, Le Petit Malvalat, which he purchased in 1825. The artist has deftly combined architectural elements with landscape, giving the scene a structured quality, like an outdoor room. A stone ledge enclosing the terrace extends from the lower left corner across to the opposite side. It is bisected by a stone path that leads to an opening in the low wall for an invisible set of stairs to the grounds below. The sunlight flooding the terrace creates sharp divisions of light and shadow. To the right of the intersection, resting on the ledge almost in the center of the composition, stands a terracotta pot with a cascading plant of orange flowers and yellow light-reflecting leaves. It serves as a warm, glowing focal point of the composition, almost a surrogate sun. One lone slim tree on the terrace with delicate branches and sun-dappled leaves stands out against the amorphous mass of trees composing the natural landscape in the middle ground of the watercolor. The view centers on the familiar landmark of the region, the triangular, stony peak of Mont Sainte-Victoire, represented in delicate, watery strokes of cool violet and blue that contrast in tone with the orange and yellow of the potted plant (fig. 49.1). To add interest to the surface of the watercolor, Granet selectively applied the shiny substance of gum arabic to areas that reflect sunlight, such as the vegetation. In contrast, he left matte the dusty stone path and rocky mountain peak which absorb light.

Just as Granet effected a dynamic balance between architecture and landscape, his exuberantly fluid washes are set off by the more meticulously defined foreground elements. Granet's reputation today largely rests on the virtuosity of his watercolor technique.[3] These private, deeply personal sketches have become some of his most publicly recognized works. [SGG]

50. Johan Barthold Jongkind
Latrop 1819 – 1891 Grenoble
View of Montmartre, c. 1849
Brush and brown ink, watercolor over black chalk mounted onto Japan paper | 25.7 x 41.5 | Signed lower left in pen and brown ink, "Jongkind" | Verso, visible through the mount, is a sketch in black chalk of trees, figures, and a house | Inscriptions: center of verso in graphite, "57,55" | Inv. no. 2000-T.1

ORIGINALLY A SACRED SITE, Montmartre, the mount of martyrs, was associated with political radicalism during the Paris Commune of the 1870s and by the last decades of the century established a reputation as a district of pleasure and vice through the cabarets made famous in the posters of Toulouse-Lautrec. Johan Barthold Jongkind, a Dutch artist who moved to Montmartre in 1846 to work in the studio of Eugène Isabey (see cat. 43) near the Place Pigalle, lived on the Butte when it was still semirural in character and located outside the walls of Paris. (It became the eighteenth arrondissement in 1860.) Living among fellow artists such as Théodore Rousseau (see cat. 48), Jongkind strolled the streets of his quartier carrying his paper in a large portfolio (as seen in a self-portrait, fig. 50.1) recording sights in watercolor, chalk, and graphite. In his selection of motifs and his treatment of them, he brought a Dutch sensibility to his French surroundings, having trained in the Netherlands with Andreas Schelfhout.[1] This drawing with its glowing buff, gold, green, and pale blue tones, unprepossessing subject matter, long horizontal composition, and low horizon has affinities with seventeenth-century Dutch art, such as the landscapes of Jacob van Ruisdael and Jan van Goyen.[2]

Absent in this scene are the notable landmarks of the district, such as its windmills, churches, and picturesque winding streets. The white substance at the left foreground, represented by the white of the paper, is probably gypsum, which was mined in Montmartre and was the essential ingredient for plaster of Paris.[3] The rustic buildings with triangular roofs at mid-ground are probably structures related to the mines. Just beyond them, an open area of golden earth is balanced by a tree-crowned section, which may be the Montmartre cemetery. In the far distance we see smokestacks belching gray soot, rendered with smudges of black chalk. Tiny dashed-off figures can be seen here and there. Jongkind developed a looser style of watercolor painting that differed from the more precise approach of Schelfhout. As in this work, he laid in his scenes lightly in chalk and applied color freely in brushstrokes that do not necessarily conform to the drawn contours. Instead of the thick paper normally used for watercolor, he chose thin smooth sheets that did not completely absorb the water and allowed the pigments to migrate to the edges of the wash. The resulting spontaneity, evident here, earned him the respect of later artists, such as Monet, and a reputation as a pre-Impressionist. [SGG]

51. Jean-François Millet
Gruchy 1814 – 1875 Barbizon
A Gleaner (study of Ruth for *Harvesters Resting*), 1851 – 53
Black conté crayon on beige paper | 31.0 x 15.5
Stamps: bottom right in black ink, "J.F.M" for artist's estate sale (L. 1460) | Inv. no. 3018

THIS DRAWING IS A STUDY for the figure of Ruth in one of Millet's most important paintings, *Harvesters Resting (Ruth and Boaz)* (Museum of Fine Arts, Boston), exhibited in the Salon of 1853 (fig. 51.1).[1] The painting refers to a story of Ruth and Boaz from the Book of Ruth in the Old Testament.[2] In this painting and others of peasant life, Millet modulated his depictions of the harsh reality of contemporary rural life with a sense of timelessness through allusions to the Bible and paintings by Old Masters.[3] In *Harvesters*, viewers of his era would have recognized his reference to Poussin's famous *Summer: Ruth and Boaz*, in the Musée du Louvre.[4]

The Lugt sheet is one of some fifty preparatory drawings for this painting, including studies of the composition, groups of figures, and individuals made after a nude and clothed model.[5] In this extraordinarily lively drawing, Millet works out the details of the pose and costume of the main character. He blocks out the figure with vigorous, assured strokes, paying particular attention to the outlines of her dress and the broad divisions of light and dark. Shadows, laid in with straight, definite lines, are juxtaposed with areas of untouched paper that serve as highlights. In contrast, the young woman's face under a hooded head gear is delicately veiled in shadow. Millet pays particular attention to the costume and the glistening sheath of wheat, represented in a vibrant alternating pattern of light and dark. In the costume, he balances the downward motion of the mantle falling behind the girl's shoulders with the upward lift of her apron. A shadow cast on the ground behind the figure is the only suggestion of a setting.

In her final form in the canvas, the figure loses some of the energy of her appearance in this drawing. Her posture is slumped rather than erect, and her face, which is partially concealed, appears older. Changes occur as well in the pose and costume. While the sheath of wheat was bundled in her apron in the drawing, in the painting she holds it loose in her arms. Another preparatory sketch of Ruth, now lost, presents an intermediary stage between the Lugt sheet and the finished painting.[6] In the drawing, the backbreaking work of gleaning has

taken its toll on Ruth, who is depicted slouching and weary. The evolution of the Ruth figure from the Lugt sketch to the Boston canvas is a testament to Millet's attentive observation of peasant life. [SGG]

> 52. Jean-François Millet
> Gruchy 1814 – 1875 Barbizon
> *Landscape near Gruchy*, c. 1854 (?)
> Pen and brown ink, watercolor | 21.8 x 28.4, irregularly cut | Inscriptions: at lower left, in pen and gray ink, signed "MILLET"; on verso, at lower left, in pencil, "(2)"; at lower right, in blue chalk, "4", crossed out in pencil; below, in pencil "43 – p9 blanc" (?), partly erased | Inv. no. 2007-T.33

THIS PREVIOUSLY UNKNOWN and unpopulated landscape is not easy to place in Millet's drawn oeuvre, which consists on the one hand of sketches of figures, usually as preliminary studies for his paintings (see cat. 51), and on the other of completed compositions of his favorite subjects from peasant life. He worked in charcoal initially, but from the 1850s onward adopted black conté crayon with great flair. In the second half of the 1860s – after a hesitant start when he combined pastel with the black crayon – Millet concentrated primarily on depicting rural scenes in pastel alone. By contrast, he used pen and ink less often, and the combination with watercolor is only found in the pure landscape drawings that he made for the most part during the summers of 1866 and 1867, when he accompanied his wife to Vichy to take the waters.

Here, however, it seems that the artist has drawn the landscape near Gruchy, the village where he was born. It lies on the coast, seventeen kilometers to the east of Cherbourg in Normandy, and it was in Cherbourg in the 1830s that the young farmer's son had his first lessons before he won a scholarship and was apprenticed to Paul Delaroche in Paris in 1837. After stays in Cherbourg, Le Havre, and Paris, he settled in Barbizon in 1849 and remained there until his death. The genre in which Millet was to excel was the direct result of his submission of his painting *The Sower* to the Salon the following year.

Thanks to surviving correspondence and the biography by his friend and patron Alfred Sensier, we know that in the summer of 1854 Millet returned to Gruchy, where, as well as making twenty or so drawings, he filled two albums with sketches with the intention of using them later.[1] He adopted the same

method during his stay in and around Vichy, making a large number of annotated sketches in pen and ink on the spot and completing them in watercolor later at home.[2]

Compared with the watercolors we know of from the Allier – the département in which Vichy is situated – this landscape is more of a painted composition than a drawing illuminated with watercolors. The landscape, cursorily indicated in pen and ink, is almost entirely covered in color and even the sky is depicted – masterfully – in blue and gray strokes. The dominant dark bluish-green color also evokes the hilly landscape of Normandy rather than the countryside around Vichy. A watercolor of almost the same size in a sale at Christie's in New York (2002) also depicted a landscape of green fields enclosed by hedges typical of Normandy.[3] Nevertheless, in one of his letters to the collector Émile Gavet in 1866 he described the countryside around Vichy as an area that in many respects was "not unlike parts of Normandy, the greenery and fields surrounded by hedges."[4] [MVB-G]

53. Charles-François Daubigny
Paris 1817 – 1878 Paris
View of Paris from the Tour Saint-Jacques, 1852
Graphite with stumping on beige paper | 35.2 x 47.9
Inscriptions: signed bottom right in graphite, "C. Daubigny"; verso, traces of charcoal and inscribed in the center in black chalk, "123"; bottom right in graphite, dealer's mark? | Inv. no. 1979-T.7

A YEAR AFTER DAUBIGNY made this topographical drawing of Paris, Napoleon III ordered Baron George-Eugène Haussmann to raze decaying congested areas and impose on the city a rational plan of wide, straight boulevards, open parks, and improved sanitation.[1] This drawing belongs to Daubigny's work as an illustrator, although its exact purpose is not known.[2] In the late 1850s, the photographer Charles Marville (1816 – 1879) was employed by Haussmann to document the streets and neighborhoods the baron was planning to tear down. The Lugt sheet perhaps arose from a similar documentary impulse to preserve the memory of the old Paris. Indeed, during Haussmannization, Daubigny made a drawing of full-grown trees being transplanted to line the grand boulevards.[3]

Daubigny's viewpoint is from the top of the fifty-two-meter Tour Saint-

Jacques, a remnant of a medieval church that afforded a bird's-eye view of the city looking south over the Île de la Cité and the Left Bank beyond it. The densely packed, ramshackle buildings at the foot of the tower in the place du Châtelet are laid in quickly with broad hatch marks. They were soon to be demolished by Haussmann, who described the area as "a shabby part" of town and constructed in their place a splendid new theater.[4] Clearly depicted in the bottom right-hand corner is the Colomne du Châtelet, a seventy-foot column rising from a fountain and surmounted by a gilded figure of Victory. Ordered by Napoleon to commemorate various battles, it was completed in 1808 and moved during Haussmannization.[5]

Leading the viewer from the chaotic Right Bank to the more meticulously drawn Île de la Cité are three bridges. On the right-hand side is the Pont au Change, which connects the rue Saint Denis with the boulevard du Palais. The Pont de Nôtre Dame appears just to the left of center, connecting the rue Saint Martin on the Right Bank with the rue de la Cité, and further to the left is the Pont d'Arcole. After Haussmannization, the rues Saint Martin and Saint Denis were no longer the main north-south arteries of Paris as circulation was redirected onto the grand boulevard de Sébastopol.[6]

Paris's historic monuments rise above the continuous fabric of multistory residential, governmental, and commercial buildings of the Cité and Left Bank. Daubigny underlined the importance of the city's most prestigious and largest structure, the Gothic cathedral of Nôtre Dame, through his use of dark lines and stumping. Details are carefully observed, including even the rose window on the west façade, seen here at an oblique angle. In contrast, the equally imposing Renaissance Palais de Justice and Gothic Conciergerie on the quai to the right are more lightly drawn. The tall elliptical dome of Soufflot's neoclassical masterpiece, the Panthéon, is silhouetted against the horizon toward the back at left, and the mismatched towers of the church of Saint-Sulpice are seen at the right. Figures represented by dots and dashes crossing the bridges, as well as a few barges on the river, indicate the scale of the built environment and the flow of human life and activity within its constricting web, a city poised on the brink of modernization. [SGG]

54. Auguste-Joseph Bracquemond, called Félix Bracquemond
Paris 1833 – 1914 Sèvres
Portrait of Charles Daubigny, 1853
Lead pencil and graphite | 15.7 x 11.7 | Inscriptions: bottom left in black chalk, "B" | Inv. no. 1994-T.22

Félix Bracquemond – a printmaker and draftsman, designer of furniture, jewelry, and tableware, and art theorist – was a well-connected member of the Parisian art scene of the mid- to late nineteenth century.[1] Bracquemond counted among his friends many major figures of the artistic and literary avant-garde, including the Goncourt brothers, Manet, and Daubigny (see cat. 53), the last of whom is portrayed here in a preparatory sketch for an etching. Bracquemond was a major figure in the etching revival in France, along with Charles Meryon (1821 – 1868) and Alphonse Legros (1837 – 1911). He co-founded both the Société des Aquafortistes Français (in 1862) and the Société des Peintre-Graveurs Français (in 1890) to promote the employment and appreciation of etching as an art form.[2]

This drawing and the etching after it (fig. 54.1) are testaments to his friendship with the landscape painter and printmaker Charles Daubigny (1817 – 1878). Executed in 1853, it dates from the early years of Bracquemond's long career when, as he recalled in a memoir, he often dined at Daubigny's house in the company of fellow artists such as Corot (see cat. 42) and Daumier.[3] Daubigny's long curly black hair and dark pointed beard set off the paleness of his face, with light falling on his slightly balding head and his temple. In contrast to the finely rendered head, his jacket or smock is represented more freely with strong accent lines. Bracquemond's use of a strict profile follows a Renaissance tradition (one that itself looks back to antique medals and coins), perhaps alluding to Daubigny's interest in the masters of this period. Here, the profile, in combination with the sitter's lowered eyelids, contributes to a feeling of introspection and of remove from the viewer and the "real" world. The forest background, drawn in a sketchy, spontaneous manner, reads ambiguously both as the outdoors and as a landscape painting hung on a wall. Bracquemond thus presents Daubigny, who holds his palette and brushes as a kind of professional attribute, as a plein-air painter.

Comparing the drawing with the etching, we can see that Bracquemond selected and exploited the properties of his drawing implements to approximate the tonal range and technique of an etching. The palette of graphite and lead pencil varies from a silvery gray to the deepest velvety black, replicating the different degrees of "bite" of an acid bath on the etched plate. Furthermore, the hardness of graphite produces a fine, sharp line, which Bracquemond uses to imitate the etching needle in passages such as the hatching in Daubigny's forehead, nose, and cheek. Conversely, the friability of the lead pencil allows him to execute subtle gradations of tone as well as stark contrasts of light and dark. Bracquemond's employment of both graphite and lead pencil permits the striking combination in this drawing of meticulous detail and quick, rough shading that ingeniously anticipates the etching. [SGG]

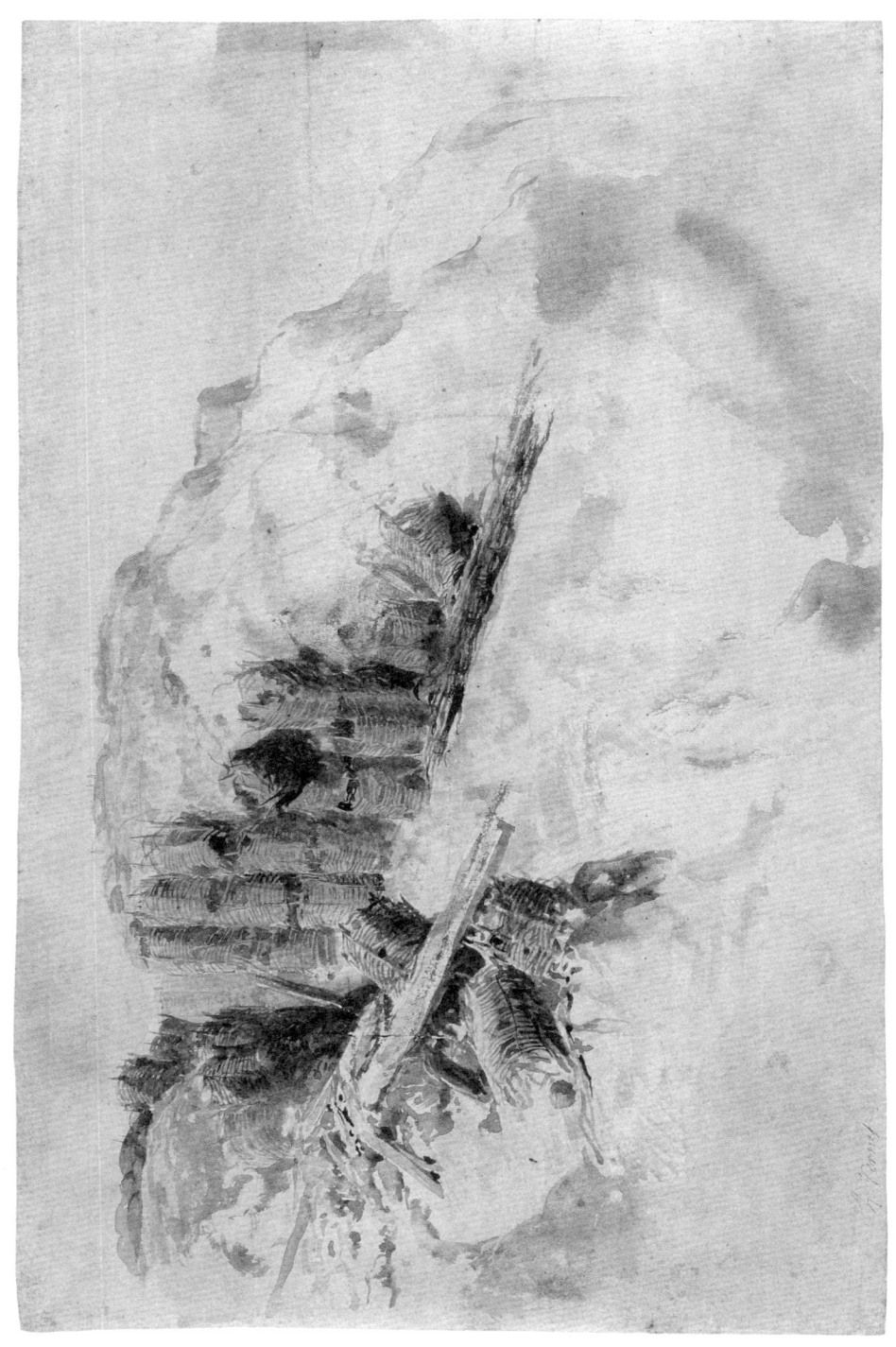

55. Horace Vernet
Paris 1789 – 1863 Paris
Study of Gabions in the Trenches of the Crimean War,
1854 – 55
Pen and brown ink, brown and gray-brown wash, over traces of graphite on discolored paper | 20.7 x 32.0
Verso, geometric patterns with notations about color, graphite | Inscriptions: bottom left in pen and brown ink, "h Vernet"; on the former mount in pen and brown ink, "H. Vernet étude guerre de Crimée"
Watermark: present but difficult to make out
Inv. no. 1991-T.17

THE EERIE STILLNESS OF this scene of abandoned gabions in a desolate mountain landscape conveys something of the harshness of the Crimean War (1853 – 56).[1] Some of these cylindrical structures – portable wicker baskets that can be filled with soil or rock and used to shore up the embankments of trenches – are still stacked up in an orderly fashion; others tumble down, and some are upended in a heap along with planks of wood in the foreground of the drawing. Depicted in pen and brown ink, the gabions are set off by the more abstract rendering in soft brushstrokes of the anonymous landscape lightly covered in snow. Although the military structures are rendered in a precise manner, the drawing leaves to the imagination the human misery that took place in the deserted trench, or what lies beneath the snow.

Horace Vernet, a member of an artistic dynasty and a staunch liberal, was the foremost painter of military battles of mid-nineteenth-century France.[2] He enjoyed the patronage and support of the duc d'Orléans, who ascended the throne as King Louis-Philippe in 1830. Vernet has been described as the first modern military painter who eschewed allegory in favor of straightforward reportage of contemporary events based on his own eyewitness experience at the front and presented in his paintings and drawings in exacting detail.[3] Under Louis-Philippe, Vernet traveled to North Africa in the 1830s and 1840s during the French conquest of Algeria, and even after the king was deposed, he covered the French siege of Rome in 1849. The combination of his meticulous style, official success, and widespread popularity elicited contempt from Charles Baudelaire, who famously dismissed Vernet as "a soldier who paints."[4]

Twentieth-century scholarship, however, has reevaluated his journalistic eye and "anti-compositions" as a contribution to the realism and modernism hailed in the work of Courbet and Manet.[5]

The Lugt sheet relates to the arduous and brutal Siege of Sebastopol. In June of 1854, at age sixty-five, Vernet traveled unofficially to Varna on the coast of Turkey in present-day Bulgaria to observe the British, French, and Turkish armies prepare for battle. They set sail in September for the Crimean Peninsula with the aim of taking Fort Malakoff in Sebastopol, Russia's main stronghold, and seizing control of the Black Sea area. The onset of winter immobilized the Allies, who dug trenches south of the city to wait it out, but the harsh weather, lack of supplies, and continual attacks left them decimated.[6] Vernet is thought to have returned to France by December as he was unable to withstand the physical rigor of the front.[7] The siege continued through September 1855, eventually ending in Allied victory. Whether the Lugt drawing was made on site or after a photograph, either while in the Crimea or afterward, cannot be determined with certainty, but it is thought to depict the early stages of the so-called winter troubles. It would have had deep resonance for viewers of the time, who were following the events of the war as portrayed in newspapers and photographs.

On his return to France, Vernet carried out three paintings commemorating the Crimean War.[8] Although none of them include gabions, the paintings undoubtedly benefited from observational studies of the details of war similar to the Lugt drawing. As a self-standing depiction, *Study of Gabions* is a powerful testament to the grim reality of trench warfare. [SGG]

56. Edgar Degas
Paris 1834 – 1917 Paris
View of the Saône River with the Sérin Bridge near Lyon, 1855
Black chalk on paper | 47.4 x 31.2 | Inscriptions: bottom right in graphite, "du haut du rocher de PierSiz" | Stamps: verso, bottom right in red ink, oval "ATELIER/ ED. DEGAS" (L. 657)
Inv. no. 1997-T.8

THIS DRAWING DATES from mid-July to mid-September 1855, the summer following Degas's first year at the École des Beaux-Arts in Paris. The young art student followed his teacher Louis Lamothe to Lyon, where he was assisting his own master, Hippolyte Flandrin, on mural decorations for the church of Saint Martin-d'Ainay. While there Degas filled a notebook of seventy-five sheets with drawings after plaster casts of sculpture in the École des Beaux-Arts and paintings by Renaissance masters in the Lyon museum, as well as views of the city, the Saône River, and the surrounding area.

Degas took his viewpoint in this drawing looking southward from the top of a cliff at the northern entrance to the city of Lyon, where the Pierre-Scize fortress had once stood.[1] This imposing structure, atop a massive rock formation rising dramatically from the river, was frequently represented by seventeenth-century northern artists who stopped in Lyon (known as the antechamber to Italy) on their voyage south (fig. 56.1).[2] By the time Degas reached Lyon, however, Pierre-Scize had been demolished. Instead of illustrating the fortress, he depicts the bird's-eye view it would have afforded over the extensive landscape. Degas rotated his large sheet of paper to a vertical format, which was best suited to representing the depth of space before him. The sense he achieves of a disembodied eye hovering over the landscape is emphasized by the emptiness of the foreground, filled with water. The unfolding of the vast space of the landscape is contained within two horizontals: the multiarched Pont Sérin spanning the riverbanks in the foreground, which anchors the scene at the bottom of the image, and a range of distant mountain peaks at the top.[3] The eye is drawn to the middle ground in between these framing elements through the rapidly narrowing and curving river.

A group of buildings on the right-hand side of the drawing, identified as the quartier Sérin, juts into the center of the composition in a triangular wedge. A row of buildings, perhaps warehouses, represented in simple geometric shapes, line the quai. Other structures — houses or farms — interspersed with trees, climb the hill above the walkway. A few local landmarks, the Granary of Abundance at the end of the quai and the sixteenth-century Fort Saint Jean above it, stand out among the more generalized forms of buildings.[4] On the left, an open landscape with a few scattered villas balances the cluster of buildings on the right and leads the eye back through successive planes to the distant mountain range at the top of the drawing.

Known primarily as a figurative artist, Degas is said to have had little interest in landscape, and professed disdain for the plein air tradition.[5] As Richard Kendall has noted, however, the Lugt sheet and his notebook sketches from Lyon, as well as notebook drawings made during his Italian stay (1856 to 1859) and his period in Normandy in the late 1860s reveal Degas's enduring love for the genre.[6] In this rare, early drawing, Degas remained true to his classical training at the École des Beaux-Arts and the influence of Ingres, first assimilated through Lamothe and Flandrin, the latter a direct disciple of the master.[7] The carefully balanced composition, the delicacy and precision of his handling of the charcoal, and the emphasis on line and simple geometric shapes are elements of his enduring Ingrisme. [SGG]

57. Edgar Degas
Paris 1834 – 1917 Paris
Head of a Soldier, 1857 – 59
Watercolor, gouache, and red chalk wash over graphite
25.6 x 21.0 | Inscriptions: on the mount bottom right in graphite, "Flor. 1857"; on the verso of the former matte (removed but conserved) in black ink, "Vente Pra/ Paris 1938 / (7 juin)" | Stamp: bottom left in red ink script, "Degas" (L. 658) | Inv. no. 5488

FOR DEGAS, imitation and originality were complementary terms. When asked how an artist learns the métier of painting, he famously replied: "One must copy and recopy the masters, and only after having given all the proof of being a good copyist can one reasonably be expected to draw a radish from nature."[1] Degas began copying works at the Louvre and the Bibliothèque

Nationale in 1853, concentrating largely on Italian art of the fifteenth and sixteenth centuries. After a brief period of study at the École des Beaux-Arts in Paris in 1855, he traveled in Italy for three years, spending time in Naples, Rome, and Florence. He returned to Paris in 1859 with hundreds of copies in addition to his own original drawings and oil sketches.[2]

This unique work, with its unusual combination of media, appears to draw from a mixture of Italian Renaissance and Mannerist sources; it is a "creative" as opposed to a straightforward copy.[3] From August 1858 to March 1859, Degas was in Florence sketching regularly at the Uffizi Galleries. The small figure of the knight on horseback at the far left of the Lugt drawing is taken from Paolo Uccello's *Battle of San Romano*, a painting that Degas copied in graphite at the Uffizi in early 1859 (fig. 57.1).[4] The bust of the young man has affinities with the various versions of Agnolo Bronzino's portrait *Cosimo I in Armor*. Bronzino's renowned half-length painting of the Medici duke, resplendent in an elaborately decorated suit of Austrian armor, had been on display at the Uffizi since the late eighteenth century, as had a miniature form of the portrait replicating only the bust (fig. 57.2).[5] It is likely that the miniature portrait in oil on tin served as a source for the Lugt drawing.[6] In both works, the tightly cropped head pressed close to the picture plane directs the viewer's focus to the duke's intense expression rather than to his spectacular suit of armor. Indeed, Degas's bold use of broad sweeps of white gouache elides any detail of the armor and instead emphasizes its metallic luster; it also, perhaps, evokes the sheen of oil on tin as opposed to the more matte texture of the tempera on wood used for the half-length portrait. Degas's skillful manipulation of red chalk wash conveys the warm, rich flesh tones that he admired in Renaissance drawings and accentuates the duke's expressive visage.[7]

Despite its clear basis in Italian Renaissance art, the Lugt drawing noticeably differs from its sources and adopts a Romantic tone reminiscent of Delacroix, whom the young Degas greatly admired. The young man's tousled hair is set against a stormy sky, and his pensive gaze is focused inward on his own thoughts. Behind him, the indication of multiple armed figures riding toward an arched gateway in an imaginary landscape suggests a dramatic narrative of battle. In the Lugt sheet, Degas seems to have filtered his Old Master sources through Romanticism, drawing out the latent suggestion of psychological portraiture in the Bronzino and pairing it with an enigmatically poetic reading of the Uccello. The drawing's idiosyncratic combination of disparate sources and styles attests to Degas's creative approach to the copy and his remarkable sense of invention. [CK and SGG]

[58]

58. Léon Bonvin
Paris 1834 – 1866 Meudon
The Plain of Vaugirard, dated 1856
Black chalk with stumping | 17.3 x 26.5 | Verso, traces of black chalk | Inscriptions: bottom right in black chalk, "1856, L. Bonvin" | Inv. no. 2008-T.8

LÉON BONVIN WAS LARGELY self-taught, though he briefly attended the École de dessin in Paris with the help of his older half-brother, François, an established realist painter. The Lugt drawing belongs to a series of early black chalk and charcoal sketches that share an austere treatment of light and form (fig. 58.1).[1] In this desolate, dark landscape, the only signs of life are the spindly, leafless branches of trees atop a high retaining wall to the right. The blank wall of a building runs along the right-hand side of the drawing, but most of the image is made up of sky and a flat stretch of land, bisected by a road rapidly receding from the foreground to a point on the distant horizon. The overall dark tonality and headlong rush of perspective convey an unsettling impression of gloom – or doom.

Nearly the entire sheet is covered with black chalk, which Bonvin applied to the paper in a number of ways. In the sky, Bonvin appears to have turned the stick broadside and dragged it lightly across the paper and then stumped it, leaving narrow bands of white paper untouched. The overall effect is a luminescent gray; as the sky meets the horizon, the bands of white expand in width, suggesting the rising or setting sun. He applied greater pressure to his implement in the retaining wall and parts of the ground to create a thick, velvety, matte surface, while in the brick wall he skims the friable medium lightly across the textured paper, leaving deposits of the material in the crevices to achieve a modulated play of light and dark.

The wall at right most likely represents a side of the family tavern in Vaugirard, an area then on the outskirts of Paris where Bonvin worked as a waiter. After his father's death, Léon took over the inn, which became a meeting place for artists, such as Félix Bracquemond (see cat. 54).

The blank exterior wall of the inn appears to function as a symbolic barrier between the artist and the world around him, and indeed the grueling work of running the establishment left Bonvin little time for his art. Furthermore, the inn was not profitable, and Léon's mounting debts, coupled with the lack of recognition for the art he was able to produce,[2] led him to his take his own life at age thirty-two.

In their restricted range of tones and radical simplicity of form, Bonvin's black chalk and charcoal sketches appear to anticipate the innovative tonal drawings of Georges Seurat from the early 1880s. Although it is uncertain whether Seurat knew of Bonvin's work, the affinity between their drawings is striking. The Lugt sheet bears testament to the visionary sensibility of a gifted draftsman, whose life was cut short by insurmountable obstacles of circumstance and temperament. [SGG]

> 59. Paul Huet
> Paris 1803 – 1869 Paris
> *View near Apt*, 1862
> Watercolor over black chalk | 22.0 x 35.3
> Inscriptions: bottom right in black ink, "Apt"; on the former mount in pen and black ink by René-Paul Huet, "PAUL HUET / 1803 – 1869 / 'Apt.1865'"
> Stamp: bottom right in red ink, artist's studio (L. 1268) | Inv. no. 1994-T.3

PAUL HUET WAS a leading figure in French landscape painting whose career unfolded through the movements of Romanticism and Realism and led up to the cusp of Impressionism. He was instrumental in promoting a break with Neoclassicism's grand manner and focus on Italy and redirecting landscape painting to a naturalistic mode with roots in Dutch art and a preference for the French countryside. Huet studied with Pierre Guérin and later with Antoine-Jean Gros; at the Académie Suisse he met Delacroix and formed a lifelong friendship with the older artist (see cats. 44 – 46). Huet was already a devotee of plein-air sketching when Constable's revelatory naturalistic landscapes made their appearance at the Salon of 1824 and deeply impressed French artists.[1] Constable and the Dutch masters remained major sources of inspiration for Huet throughout his life. He traveled constantly in France, working from direct observation to capture the unique character of each region.
The Lugt watercolor, inscribed "Apt," dates from 1862, a year in which Huet's travels took him to Normandy, England, Berry, Avignon, and Grenoble. On 26 September 1862 he wrote to his wife that he was eager to reach Apt, an old market town near Avignon, which he had visited several times previously, noting, "I hope to commune a bit seriously with the beautiful nature around Apt and see if I am still good at something and a little more than *an old fool*."[2]

This light-filled landscape, painted in warm earth tones with touches of orange under a blue sky, is characteristic of Huet's innovative handling of the watercolor medium in his late work. Over a light underdrawing in black chalk, he rapidly and broadly brushed in the sky with wet, unbroken strokes stretching from one end of the sheet to the other, allowing slivers of bare paper to shine through. The luminosity of the wash technique used in the sky contrasts with the more detailed rendering of the landscape. A wide stream or rivulet cuts through a scene of rocky ledges, sandy banks, and scrubby trees leading from foreground to the middle ground. (The outline of a small figure in black chalk, which gives a sense of the scale of the landscape, can be seen on the banks of the stream.) Further back, a Provençal house is seen at left, and at right, a cluster of buildings stands before a low ridge. Huet delineated these landscape elements in small, deft strokes emphasizing their materiality. In certain areas, however, such as the large boulder on the left, the blue and green reflections of the sky and trees in the water, and in the foliage, he suggests form more freely through juxtaposed, spontaneous touches of color, a method that has been characterized as proto-Impressionist.[3]

Like Constable, Huet felt a deep emotional attachment to nature and attempted to grasp the spirit of each landscape he depicted.[4] He would write fervently in a letter of 1868, "The landscapist is, of all artists, the one who communicates most directly with nature, with the veritable soul of nature."[5] [SGG]

60. Eugène-Emmanuel Viollet-le-Duc
Paris 1814 – 1879 Lausanne
View of the Alps, dated 1875
Watercolor heightened with yellow gouache over a pencil drawing on blue paper | 14.4 x 23.7
Inscriptions: lower right, in pen and black ink, "au dessus dulac Blanc" and "9 Sept / 75," repeated below in pencil; various inscriptions in pencil on image; above in pen and black ink, "Porphire"
Inv. no. 1995-T.12

BEST KNOWN AS AN ARCHITECT and theorist dedicated to the restoration of medieval churches, Viollet-le-Duc was also an amateur geologist and glaciologist. He was a prolific writer and draftsman, having taught at the École de dessin during the 1830s. In the latter years of his life, he undertook an extensive geological survey and comprehensive map of the massif of Mont Blanc in the Haute Savoie, a region annexed by France from Piedmont in 1860. Viollet-le-Duc spent every summer from 1868 to 1876 in the Alps conducting research for the project, which he published in his book *Le Massif du Mont Blanc* of 1876.[1] As part of this endeavor, he produced some 600 topographical drawings of the mountain. Viollet-le-Duc's interests in geology, architecture, and restoration were interconnected and mutually reinforcing.[2] As he noted in the introduction to his book, "To analyze carefully a group of mountains, the manner in which they were formed, and the causes of their ruin . . . is to devote oneself to a work of methodical analysis which is, on a grander scale, analogous to that to which the practical architect and the archeologist applies himself when drawing conclusions from the study of buildings."[3]

This drawing, dated 9 September 1875, and inscribed "au dessus dulac Blanc" (above Lac Blanc), depicts an area located at the foot of the Aiguille du Belvédère, the highest peak of the Aiguilles Rouges, a mountain chain opposite the massif of Mont Blanc. Viollet-le-Duc outlined the majestic Alpine vista in pencil on site and made annotations directly on the sheet so that he could complete the image with the proper colors in gouache and watercolor later on. Written on the drawing are "gla" for *glacier*, and "n" for *neige* (snow) or *névé* (refrozen snow) and "*porphire*" for the reddish porphyry stone just below the inscription. Viollet-le-Duc makes use of the gray-blue paper as a neutral tone

that represents the hazy, changeable atmosphere, setting off patches of bright blue sky and white fleeting clouds. Surveying the scene from an altitude of some 10,000 to 12,000 feet, Viollet-le-Duc presents an image of total engulfment in a mineral world devoid of human life. He combines a naturalist's eye for the accurate rendering of small details, such as the rough texture of the ore in the middle of the sheet represented by thick, dry ocher gouache,[4] with a Romantic's sensibility for the awe-inspiring grandeur of the Alps, the archetypal symbol of the Sublime in the work of previous artists such as Turner and Ruskin.[5] Viollet-le-Duc's cycle of Mont Blanc drawings was integral to his geological project. In his autobiographically based book of 1879, *Histoire d'un dessinateur: comment on apprend à dessiner*, he sets forth his belief in drawing as an epistemological tool with his well-known words, "to draw is to see, to see is to know."[6] In a charming passage in a chapter of the book entitled "Twelve Days in the Alps," he has a fictional character, M. Majorin, instruct a certain petit Jean:

> take your time with these rocks; they demand to be drawn with precision, and these forms are not due to chance. There are major principal lines that you must first indicate; then, when these are faithfully outlined, taking into account the angles and gradients, you must fill in the details according to their importance . . . each kind of rock affects special forms and you must not neglect them as you would not neglect to observe the features of a face . . . .[7]

The Lugt drawing, and others in the group, such as his *View of White Lakes* made in the same week as the present work (fig. 60.1), exemplify the method described here and bear testament to the lifelong passion of an architect/restorer for mountains, which were for him "gigantic ruins, which the imagination endeavors to restore."[8] [SGG]

61. Paul-Gustave Doré
Strasbourg 1832 – 1883 Paris
View of the Forest at Westbridge, dated 1879
Watercolor and gouache over graphite | 74.3 x 52.7
Inscriptions: bottom right in black ink, "G Doré /
Wesbridge / 1879" | Inv. no. 1987-T.9

A PROLIFIC AND LARGELY self-taught artist, Gustave Doré painted colossal canvases and experimented with sculpture, but his reputation rests primarily on the some ten thousand drawings he made to illustrate classics of world literature and original works, such as his celebrated *London, A Pilgrimage* (1872) written by Jerrold Blanchard. He is regarded as the greatest illustrator in France during the second half of the nineteenth century, and his fame was even greater in England. From 1868 to 1892, the Gallery Doré on New Bond Street featured his latest graphic work and paintings, receiving more than two million visitors.

Until Doré began to travel regularly to Great Britain, watercolor remained a minor part of his oeuvre. It was for him primarily a medium for note taking, and for the purposes of his illustrations he often mixed watercolor with gouache.[1] Under the impact of the English watercolorists, however, he explored the possibilities of pure watercolor executed in a more spontaneous wash technique and became increasingly drawn to landscape. In 1878 he became a member of the newly formed Société des Aquarellistes Français and exhibited sixteen watercolors with them the following year.[2] In his impressive *View of the Forest at Westbridge*, made the same year, he combined watercolor and gouache, working in a somewhat meticulous style that recalls his earlier use of the watercolor medium. Another watercolor by Doré entitled *Landscape at Westbridge* also dates to 1879. The exceptionally large scale and finish of these works suggest that they were conceived as independent paintings made for exhibition.[3]

In the Lugt sheet, low leafy plants and ferns cover the slanted forest floor and are balanced by the strip of blue sky and pink-tinged clouds at top, which suggest the diffuse light at the end of day. Massed beech trees with tall trunks and slender, whiplash branches – bare or in leaf – seem to march forward from the depths of the forest in a continuous formation.[4] The sheet is signed and dated 1879 and inscribed with the word "Wesbridge" (*sic*), which may refer to a part of Sussex County.[5] A guidebook to England and Wales of 1813 describes a large

track of forest in Sussex, known as the Weald, of which the distinctive feature is "its timber, which overspreads its every direction . . ."[6] It is precisely this sense of endlessness that Doré's image conveys. Though presumably inspired by life, the image transcends everyday reality to suggest something enchanted, claustrophobic, and impenetrable. There is no sign of human, animal, or even mineral life in this environment of pure flora. In a precise style, Doré conveys a sense of magical reality that has little in common with the inviting forest interiors of his contemporaries Courbet and the Barbizon artists, and instead looks forward to Symbolism.[7] [SGG]

62. Berthe Morisot
Bourges 1841 – 1895 Paris
Swans on the Lake of the Bois de Boulogne, 1885
Pastel on blue paper (slightly discolored) | 28.5 x 40.0
Inscriptions: verso, lower right in lead pencil,
"Je certifie que ce pastel / est bien de ma nièce /
Berthe Morisot / J. Manet" | Inv. no. 6841

BERTHE MORISOT BEGAN working en plein air during the 1860s in Pontoise, Normandy, and Brittany under the guidance of Camille Corot (see cat. 42). This pastel of 1885 exemplifies the improvisational methods in which Morisot excelled as a plein-air artist as well as the decorative character of her later work. Lively scribbles of chalk convey the rippling reflections of foliage and sky in the water, here represented by the blue sheet. Their swift execution attests to the deftness of the artist's hand hovering over the sheet. The clearly planned composition of the drawing, however, belies its improvisatory effect. Two graceful swans in white chalk face each other just off-center. They are anchored by a duck in the upper-left corner and his barely sketched-in counterpart in the lower right. The four birds balancing one another are connected through a web of colorful strokes.

Morisot noted in her sketchbook, "My ambition is limited to the desire to capture something transient, and yet, this ambition is excessive."[1] Swans breaking the placid surface of the water provided her with an apposite image of delicate transience, and this pastel forms part of a group of works on the same theme of waterfowl in the pond in the Bois, only steps from her house on rue Villejust (fig. 62.1), later renamed rue Paul Valéry.

Nevertheless, capturing such ephemeral spontaneity proved to be frustrating. The painter Jacques-Émile Blanche recalled: "She destroys everything that she makes at this time . . . this morning, once again, in desperation, she threw into the lake of the Bois de Boulogne a study of swans that she was following in a boat."[2]

Morisot's fascination with the swan has been connected with its currency in Symbolist literature, a movement to which she was connected through her close friendship with the poet Stéphane Mallarmé. Yet, this colorful pastel has little of the melancholy of Mallarmé's famous poem "Le Vierge, le vivace . . ." (1885), in which the swan is interpreted as a symbol of the artist's alienation and isolation.[3] It is instead playful and exuberant, recalling the decorative quality of the rococo. During this period of her artistic career, Morisot increasingly looked back to the masters of the eighteenth century, and in 1884 she copied a detail of François Boucher's *Venus at Vulcan's Forge* (1757) at the Louvre. Her use of pastel on blue paper is also reminiscent of rococo artistic practices. Her technique, however, combines the virtuosity of eighteenth-century artists with the innovations spearheaded by her Impressionist colleague Edgar Degas (see cats. 56, 57)[4]: blended passages describe the downy feathers of the swans; soft vaporous touches appear in the water; and bold strokes of vibrant green and blue are layered directly on top of each other to capture the effect of light and shadow in the vanishing ripples of the lake. [SGG]

63. Henri-Joseph Harpignies
Valenciennes 1819 – 1916 Saint-Privé
Studio of the Artist, dated 1909
Watercolor over black chalk | 29.1 x 22.9
Inscriptions: bottom left in black ink, "Coin de mon Atelier/ h^iharpignies"; bottom right in black ink, "Fevrier 1909"; verso: bottom left in graphite, "Tout blanc"; bottom center in black chalk, an illegible annotation; bottom right, in purple pencil, "Verdun" | Stamps: on verso, HARPIGNIES / VENTE ATELIER R. VERDUN / ORLÉANS - 1978 in an oval, not catalogued by Lugt | Inv. no. 1980-T.31

IN THIS WATERCOLOR, Harpignies's perennial subject, landscape, is represented through images of his paintings hung on a wall in a corner of his studio. Eleven rectangular canvases, vertical and horizontal, small to medium in size,

form an orderly decorative pattern above the chair rail. A framed canvas hangs on the rail and below it a drawing in a white matte, perhaps of a figure, along with a white plaster mask and a white porcelain electrical outlet. All the paintings are landscapes and their modest scale and seemingly informal execution suggest they were made directly from nature. At right, a door leads to another room, and a few larger canvases – one of which appears to be an unfinished landscape – are propped up on the floor in or beyond the doorway. Artwork is represented in different forms and various stages of creation: the small oil sketch, the finished work, the canvas in progress awaiting the artist's brush, framed and unframed works, drawing and sculpture. A red and black coat or cape carelessly draped on a tapestry-covered armchair in the foreground conjures up an image of the absent artist and adds contrast to the watercolor's gray tonality and rectilinear composition. Here, the studio is represented not as a space for art making, but as a staging area or sanctuary for the artist's contemplation of works created beyond its confines. Harpignies plays with the concept of the painting as a window on the world and the boundary between inside and outside space.[1] The door serves as a hinge between these spaces as well as between the flat surface of the paper support and the illusion of depth.

Harpignies was born in Valenciennes in northern France of Belgian parents. Roughly the same generation as the Barbizon artists, he remained faithful to a naturalistic mode of painting throughout his long career. He traveled to Germany and Italy, where he spent two years in the early 1850s, but is associated primarily with Saint Privé about fifty kilometers east of Auxerre, where he spent his summers from 1879 onward, and the area around Menton on the Riviera, his winter home in later years. The Lugt watercolor, made in February 1909, most likely depicts his atelier in Menton. Harpignies was then eighty-nine years old.

In his later years, Harpignies won recognition for his oil paintings at the Salon and he rose through the ranks of the Légion d'honneur to become a grand officier at the end of his life. Watercolor played a particularly important role in his oeuvre. He became a member of the Societé des Aquarellistes in 1881 and taught watercolor painting at a school which he opened in Paris in 1884. The Lugt sheet, with its silvery tones and sense of order, and the theme of the studio itself, reflect his lifelong admiration for his older contemporary Corot, who had encouraged him in his youth and remained his constant source of inspiration (see cat. 44). The fluid washes and loose touch add to the poetic, evocative nature of this unpretentious personal work and is characteristic of the style of his late years, in which clarity of parts gave way to an overall unity of composition. [SGG]

Provenance, Exhibitions, Bibliography, Notes,
Comparative Illustrations

1. Antoine Watteau
Valenciennes 1684–1721 Nogent-sur-Marne
Three Standing Soldiers, c. 1715
Red chalk | 15.1 x 19.9 | Inv. no. 7208

Provenance: Jean-Pierre Norblin de la Gourdaine (1745–1830); Martin Norblin de la Gourdaine (1781–1854); baronne de Conantré; baronne de Rublé; Mme de Witte; marquise de Bryas (Orange); Galerie Cailleux, Paris, 1958; Frits Lugt (1884–1970), Paris (L. 1028), acquired 6 November 1958.
Exhibitions: Paris and Amsterdam 1964; Paris 1968.
Bibliography: Goncourt 1875, pp. 241, 251, 300, under nos. 361, 412, 669; Cailleux 1959, pp. i–v, vii, fig. 1; Gordon 1965, p. 38; Paris and Amsterdam 1964, p. 36, no. 37, pl. 25; Paris 1968, no. 36, repr.; Eidelberg 1977, pp. 112, 133, note 77; Roland Michel 1984, pp. 166–67, fig. 153; Washington, Paris, and Berlin 1984, pp. 97–98, under no. 33, fig. 1; Grasselli 1987a, pp. 199, 227, 409, 474, no. 110, fig. 210; Rosenberg and Prat 1996, vol. I, pp. 330–31, no. 209, repr.; Grasselli 2001, p. 314; Boorsch and Marciari 2006, pp. 188–89, under no. 62, fig 62b.

Fig. 1.1
Antoine Watteau, *Recruits Going to Join the Regiment*, c. 1715, etching, 24.8 x 34.8, Bibliothèque Nationale, Paris, D. V. 178-1

Fig. 1.2
Antoine Watteau, *Three Soldiers Advancing*, c. 1715, red chalk on cream paper, 14.5 x 20.0, Private Collection, Paris

Notes

1. Watteau's etching was retouched by Henri-Simon Thomassin for a print announced in 1729 and included in the *Recueil Jullienne* (DV 178); see Parmentier in Washington, Paris, and Berlin 1984, pp. 236–37. Each soldier would be reproduced separately, in the same direction as the drawing, by Louis Desplaces for Jullienne's *Figures de différents caractères* (nos. 59, 13, 290); Desplaces etched a second version of the third figure, *Soldat vu du dos*, in a landscape setting. See Rosenberg and Prat 1996, vol. I, p. 330.

2. "Ces premiers tableaux ont peut-être égalés à ce qu'il a fait de plus beau dans la suite"; Rosenberg 1984, p. 62.

3. For recent surveys of Watteau's military paintings, see Opperman 1987, Munhall 1992, and Plax 2000, pp. 53–107. It should be noted that the previously lost *Escorte d'équipages*, a painting on panel securely dated to around 1715, recently reappeared at Christie's, New York, 28 January 2009, no. 89.

4. Rosenberg and Prat (1996, vol. I, p. 330) have observed that the attitude of this soldier appears more hunched over in the painting and etching.

5. Grasselli in Washington, Paris, and Berlin 1984, pp. 95–96; Grasselli 1987a, pp. 199–200.

6. Rosenberg and Prat 1996, vol. I, p. 276, where an earlier dating of the sheet to 1712–13 is advanced.

7. Ibid., pp. 272–75, nos. 176, 177 (dated by the authors to 1712–13), and pp. 438–39, no. 278 (dated by them to 1714–15). The middle figure in *Three Studies of Soldiers* (RP 176) was used for the soldier third from the right in *Recruits Going to Join the Regiment*; the right-hand figure in *Three Soldiers Viewed from Behind* (RP 177) was preparatory for the fifth soldier from the right in the painting and etching.

8. Grasselli 2001, p. 314.

2. Antoine Watteau
Valenciennes 1684–1721 Nogent-sur-Marne
Standing Man (Persian), 1715
Red and black chalk | 32.0 x 20.1 | Watermark: coat of arms | Inv. no. 2312

Provenance: Richard Fisher (1809–1890), Midhurst (Sussex); John Postle Heseltine (1843–1929), London (L. 1507 & Suppl.); Stettiner & Co., Paris; Frits Lugt (1884–1970), Maartensdijk and Paris (L. 1028), acquired 15 June 1925.

Exhibitions: London 1909a; London 1909b; Paris 1913; Amsterdam 1926; Amsterdam 1935; London 1952; Paris and Amsterdam 1964; London 1968; Amsterdam 1974; Washington, Paris, and Berlin 1984.

Bibliography: Heseltine 1900, pp. 48–49, no. 3, repr.; London 1909a, p. 166, no. 56; London 1909b, p. 98, no. 56; Guiraud 1913, no. 98, repr.; Paris 1913, p. 53, no. 98; Amsterdam 1926, p. 99, no. 203; Dimier 1928, p. 54, no. 45; Parker 1931, p. 20; Amsterdam 1935, p. 8, no. 12; Mathey 1939, p. 159; London 1952, p. 102, no. 163; Parker and Mathey 1957, vol. II, p. 351, no. 799; Bean 1964, p. 294; Paris and Amsterdam 1964, p. 39, no. 42, pl. 36; London

Fig. 2.1
Antoine Watteau, *Study of Two Persian Diplomats*, 1715, black, red, and white chalk, 43.3 x 24.0, Private Collection, New York

1968, p. 133, no. 765; Amsterdam 1974, pp. 105–107, 166, no. 132, repr.; Sérullaz 1981, pp. 30–32, note 7, fig. 6; Washington, Paris, and Berlin 1984, pp. 114, 116, no. 49, repr.; Grasselli 1987a, pp. 169–70, 481, no. 130, fig. 162; Moureau and Grasselli 1987, p. 248; Rosenberg and Prat 1996, vol. I, pp. 450–51, no. 286, repr.

Notes

1. Rosenberg and Prat 1996, vol. I, pp. 442–57, nos. 281–89; for the most recent study of this group, see the excellent chapter "Drawing the Persian Embassy" in Weisberg-Roberts 2005, vol. I, pp. 127–62.
2. "Un étrange petit homme au nez crochu"; Rosenberg and Prat 1996, vol. I, p. 444.
3. Ibid., pp. 452–53, no. 287; for this sheet, see, most recently, Wintermute in New York 2008, no. 16.
4. Grasselli in Washington, Paris, and Berlin 1984, p. 107; Rosenberg and Prat 1996, vol. I, pp. 512–13, no. 318; Watteau's red and black chalk drawing of *The Actor Philippe Poisson*, 1715, is in the British Museum, London.
5. Wintermute in New York and Ottawa 1999, p. 114; Caylus noted that Watteau owned "des habits galants, quelques-unes de comiques, dont il revêtait les personnes de l'un et de l'autre sexe"; Rosenberg 1984, pp. 78–79.
6. Wintermute in New York and Ottawa 1999, p. 26.
7. Grasselli 1987a, pp. 170–71.
8. Bouret 1982.
9. Weisberg-Roberts 2005, vol. I, p. 134. Grasselli (1987a, p. 167) speculated that Watteau might have been introduced to the Persians by Antoine Coypel, his sponsor at the Academy, who had been commissioned to record the embassy's audience at Versailles in February 1715.
10. Grasselli in Washington, Paris, and Berlin 1984, pp. 112–14, nos. 47–49; Rosenberg and Prat 1996, vol. I, pp. 446–49, nos. 283–85; Wintermute in New York and Ottawa 1999, p. 114.
11. Caylus's memoir of his voyage to Constantinople, in Schazmann 1938, p. 117.

3. Antoine Watteau
Valenciennes 1684–1721 Nogent-sur-Marne
Landscape with Bear Devouring a Goat, c. 1715–16
Red chalk | 20.8 x 29.6 | Watermark: griffin |
Inv. no. 3803

Provenance: Bibliothèque Doucet; Georges Bourgarel (sold Paris, Drouot, 15–16 June 1922, no. 74, repr., as "École française (XVIIIe siècle)"); Eugène Rodrigues (1853–1928), Paris (L. 897 & Suppl.; sold Paris, Drouot, 28–29 November 1928, no. 242, pl. XXXVII, to Lugt); Frits Lugt (1884–1970), Maartensdijk and Paris (L. 1028).

Exhibitions: Amsterdam 1935; Paris 1935; Paris and Amsterdam 1964; Paris 1968; Florence and Paris 1976; London 1977; Paris, Institut Néerlandais, 1980, *Le Paysage évoqué par la plume et le pinceau* (no catalogue); Washington 1988.

Bibliography: Parker 1931, p. 43, no. 23, repr.; Amsterdam 1935, p. 14, no. 45; Paris 1935, p. 36, no. 11; Parker and Mathey 1957, vol. I, p. 58, no. 437, repr.; Paris and Amsterdam 1964, pp. 34–35, no. 35, pl. 45; Cailleux 1967b, p. 56; Paris 1968, no. 17; White 1975, pp. 375–78, fig. 1; Florence and Paris 1976, p. 30, no. 19, repr.; Washington, Dallas, and Detroit 1976, p. 100, note 9; London 1977, p. 27, no. 20; Jacoby 1979, pp. 261, 268, note 2; Roland Michel 1984, pp. 145–47, note 10, fig. 121; Washington 1988, pp. 154, 158–59, 178, note 48, no. 75, fig. 144; Eidelberg 1995, pp. 114–15, notes 34–35; Rosenberg and Prat 1996, vol. II, pp. 718–19, no. 432, repr.; Berge-Gerbaud 1997, pp. 46–48, under no. 18.

Notes

1. Rosenberg and Prat (1996, vol. I, pp. 402–11, 546–53, nos. 252, 254–59, 341–45; vol. II, pp. 716–21, nos. 430–34) have catalogued the seventeen extant landscape copies in three groups, suggesting that this was an activity that absorbed Watteau intermittently between 1714 and 1716.

2. "Vateau les copia tous, étant chez M. Crozat, et il avouoit qu'il en avoit beaucoup profité"; Mariette/Chennevières and Montaiglon 1851–60, vol. I, p. 294.

3. "Cinquante paysages dont la plus grande partye par Watteau d'après Le Titien et Le Campagnolle, priséz 5 liv." and "Trente-un paysages d'après Le Titien et Le Campagnol par Watteau, prisés 6 liv."; Rosenberg and Prat 1996, vol. III, p. 1420, reproducing the notary's listing in Haranger's post-mortem inventory.

4. "Les belles fabriques, les beaux sites, et le feuillé plein de goût et d'esprit des arbres du Titien et du Campagnol . . . le charmèrent"; Rosenberg 1984, p. 75. Caylus's etching after a landscape by Titian in the French

Fig. 3.1
Rembrandt Harmenszoon van Rijn, *Landscape with Bear Devouring a Goat*, 1650s, pen and brown ink with corrections in white gouache on brown paper, 20.3 x 29.4, Fondation Custodia, Paris, Inv. no. 6584

Royal Collection is illustrated and discussed in Jacoby 1979, pp. 264–65.
5. "Les Figures, les Animaux, les Eaux, les Arbres agitez du vent"; De Piles 1708, pp. 254–55; for François Boucher's early copies after Campagnola, see Jacoby 1979.
6. White 1975; Berge-Gerbaud 1997, pp. 46–48.
7. White 1975, p. 377, fig. 2; *Landscape with Man Seated near a Farm*, pen and ink, inv. no. 8084.
8. Berge-Gerbaud 1997, p. 48; Evelyn's copy is in the collection of the Yale Center for British Art, New Haven, B 1977.7.3, see Godfrey 1994, p. 149, no. 114, repr.
9. Wintermute in New York and Ottawa 1999, pp. 22–24.
10. Parker and Mathey (1957, vol. I, p. 58) described this as "une figure de femme . . . très sommairement indiquée."
11. For a recent discussion of the ways in which Watteau incorporated his copies of Venetian landscape drawings in his fêtes galantes, see Eidelberg 1995 and Valenciennes 2004, pp. 202–4.

4. Antoine Watteau
Valenciennes 1684–1721 Nogent-sur-Marne
Study for a Satyr about to Attack, c. 1717
Red, black, and white chalk | 10.8 x 21.2 |
Verso, to the right, traces of a leg (?) in red chalk |
Inv. no. 5923

Provenance: M Lindon; Hans Maximilian Calmann (1899–1982), London; Frits Lugt (1884–1970), The Hague and Paris (L. 1028), acquired 9 January 1947.
Exhibitions: Paris and Amsterdam 1964.
Bibliography: Adhémar 1950, p. 225, under no. 180; Parker and Mathey 1957, vol. I, pp. 72, 74, no. 517, repr.; Mathey 1959, p. 36, fig. 75; Paris and

Amsterdam 1964, p. 51, no. 58, pl. 47; Cormack 1970, p. 28, under pl. 44; Eidelberg 1977, pp. 35, 55, notes 66, 67; Posner 1984, pp. 80, 282, note 41; Washington, Paris, and Berlin 1984, pp. 329, 332, under no. 36, fig. 8; Grasselli 1987a, p. 262, no. 184, fig. 318; Paris 1987, p. 72, under no. 95; Paris, Philadelphia, and Fort Worth 1992, pp. 186–93, under no. 14, fig. 6; Rosenberg and Prat 1996, vol. II, pp. 620–21, no. 376, repr.

Fig. 4.1
Antoine Watteau, *Jupiter and Antiope*, c. 1717, oil on canvas, 73.5 x 107.5, Musée du Louvre, Paris, MI 1129

Fig. 4.2
Antoine Watteau, *Study of a Nude Man Kneeling and Holding Drapery*, c. 1717, black, red, and white chalk on brown paper, 24.5 x 29.8, Musée du Louvre, Paris, Inv. no. 33360

Notes

1. Washington, Paris, and Berlin 1984, pp. 135–36 (entry by Grasselli), 329–33 (entry by Rosenberg); Bailey in Paris, Philadelphia, and Fort Worth 1992, pp. 186–93. The companion to *Jupiter and Antiope*, an oval of similar dimensions it is to be assumed, remains unrecorded.
2. Rosenberg and Prat 1996, vol. II, pp. 618–19, no. 375.
3. Grasselli in Washington, Paris, and Berlin 1984, pp. 127–32; Grasselli 1987a, pp. 261–63; Rosenberg and Prat 1996, vol. II, pp. 608–17, nos. 370–74.
4. See, most recently, Burollet 2008, pp. 246–48.
5. "En effet, n'ayant aucune connaissance de l'anatomie, et n'ayant presque jamais dessiné le nu, il ne savait ni le lire, ni l'exprimer . . . Jamais il n'a fait ni esquisse ni pensée pour aucun de ses tableaux, quelques légères et quelque peu arrêtées que ç'a pu être"; Caylus in Rosenberg 1984, pp. 72, 78. Caylus's criticisms are to be understood in part as a rearticulation of academic orthodoxy in keeping with the reformist agenda of the late 1740s, Caylus's "Life of Antoine Watteau" having been written as a lecture for the Academy in February 1748.
6. Hattori 2001.
7. "Il les ait exécutées d'après les esquisses de M. de la Fosse"; Caylus in Rosenberg 1984, p. 73.

8. "Quatre toilles ovales avec leur chassis prisé la somme de douze livres. Après avoir inventorié dudit article cy dessus la dite dame de La Fosse a declaré que lesdits quatres toilles et chassis appartiennent au s[ieu]r Crozat qui estaient destinées pour placer dans sa salle à manger . . ."; Hattori 2001, p. 57.

9. Watteau's receipt is reproduced in Dacier, Vuaflart, and Hérold 1921–29, vol. I, p. 77; for d'Arenberg's peregrinations after the War of the Spanish Succession, see Descheemaeker 1969, pp. 177–201.

5. Antoine Watteau
Valenciennes 1684–1721 Nogent-sur-Marne
Studies of Seven Heads, c. 1717–18
Red, black, and white chalk, graphite
22.3 x 28.0 | Inv. no. 2319

Provenance: Jean Baptiste Pierre Lebrun (1748–1813) (sale, Paris, Lebrun, 11–30 April 1791, one of two drawings in lot 344, for 97 livres, to Daudet, according to marginalia in the copy of the auction catalogue in the Rijksbureau voor Kunsthistorische Documentatie, The Hague); Daniel Saint (1778–1847) (sale, Paris, Defer, 4–7 May 1846, probably no. 297, for 48 francs); acquired by Edmond (1822–1896) and Jules (1830–1870) de Goncourt, before 1857 (L. 1089 & Suppl.; sale, Paris, Goncourt, 15–17 February 1897, no. 344, repr., for 17,500 francs, to Jacques Doucet); Jacques Doucet (1853–1929), Paris (sale, Paris, Galerie Georges Petit, 5–8 June 1912, no. 66, repr., most likely for 78,100 francs, to Edwin Marriott Hodgkins); Edwin Marriott Hodgkins (sale, Paris, Galerie Georges Petit, 30 April 1914, no. 54, repr., for 60,000 francs); Seymour de Ricci, Paris; Reginald Davis, Paris; Frits Lugt (1884–1970), Maartensdijk and Paris (L. 1028), acquired 20 June 1925.

Exhibitions: Paris 1860; Paris 1879; Amsterdam 1926; Amsterdam 1935; Paris and Amsterdam 1964; Amsterdam 1974.

Bibliography: Paris 1860, p. 60, no. 289; Goncourt 1875, pp. 346–47; Paris 1879, p. 124, no. 472; Chennevières 1880, p. 93; Goncourt/Pety and Galantris 1881/2003, vol. I, p. 173; Amsterdam 1926, p. 97, no. 199; Parker 1931, pp. 34, 45, pl. 52; Amsterdam 1935, p. 12, no. 33; Adhémar 1950, p. 220, no. 153; Parker and Mathey 1957, vol. II, p. 342, no. 744; Bauër 1959, no. 36; Paris and Amsterdam 1964, pp. 51–52, no. 59, pl. 48; Amsterdam 1974, pp. 99–100, 163–64, no. 122, repr.; Sutton 1976, pp. 246–47, fig. 9; Chapon 1984, pp. 78, 153; Washington, Paris, and Berlin, 1984, pp. 174, 178 (fig. 1), 378, 401 (fig. 18), 406; Grasselli 1987a, pp. 265 (notes 46–47), 312–14, 346, 350 (note 43), 361, 427, no. 234, fig. 386; Roland Michel 1987, pp. 179, 182, fig. 209; Launay 1991, p. 59, fig. 11, pp. 504–6, no. 373; Grasselli 1993, p. 119, no. 12; Rosenberg and Prat 1996, vol. II, pp. 944–45, no. 557, repr.

Figs. 5.1 and 5.2
Antoine Watteau, *Embarkation to Cythera* (details), 1717–19, oil on canvas, 129.0 x 194.0, Schloss Charlottenburg, Staatliche Schlösser und Gärten, Berlin

Fig. 5.3
Antoine Watteau, *Studies of a Woman and a Woman Holding Her Apron*, c. 1717–18, black and red chalk, 20.9 x 14.8, British Museum, London, Inv. no. 1846-11-14-23

Notes

1. "L'un des plus Watteau de tous, par son éblouissante et séduisante couleur"; Chennevières 1880, p. 93. For the pastiches and copies of this sheet, see Rosenberg and Prat 1996, vol. II, p. 944; Jules de Goncourt's etching of the first three heads in the upper section is also reproduced in Launay 1991, p. 505, fig. 344.

2. Wintermute in New York and Ottawa 1999, p. 31.

3. "L'extraordinaire réussite du rythme avec lequel s'enchaînent les quatre têtes du régistre supérieur"; Rosenberg and Prat 1996, vol. II, p. 945.

4. Washington, Paris, and Berlin 1984, pp. 400, 410 (entry by Rosenberg); Grasselli 1987a, p. 361; Rosenberg and Prat 1996, vol. II, p. 945 (fig. 557i).

5. See Rosenberg's thorough entry in Washington, Paris, and Berlin 1984, pp. 406–11. First recorded as in Jullienne's collection only in 1733, the more populous version of *The Embarkation to Cythera* must have been painted at some point between September 1717 and Watteau's departure to London in late 1719.

6. As noted in Grasselli 1987a, p. 313.

7. Ibid., p. 312; Rosenberg and Prat 1996, vol. II, p. 944, fig. 557f.

8. Rosenberg and Prat 1996, vol. II, p. 945, figs. 557g, 557h.

9. Grasselli 1987a, p. 313; Rosenberg and Prat 1996, vol. II, pp. 922–23, no. 545; Stein in New York and London 2005, pp. 110, 222 ("her features and the manner of drawing both find parallels in a sheet of studies in the

Institut Néerlandais"). Rosenberg and Prat (1996, pp. 752–53, no. 454, and pp. 1082–83, no. 634) consider the same model to have been used in two beautiful sheets of head studies in the Rijksmuseum, Amsterdam, and the Teylers Museum, Haarlem. These wash drawings, which they date to 1718–19, while stylistically comparable to the *Studies of Seven Heads* (as Grasselli pointed out in Washington, Paris, and Berlin 1984, pp. 177–78), would appear to represent a different woman.

10. See note 4; for *The Seated Women, Leaning Forward*, Rosenberg and Prat 1996, pp. 822–23, no. 491.

11. "L'extrême complication des rapports entre tableaux et dessins amène à émettre une hypothèse: arrivait-il à Watteau de composer un tableau, puis de transformer par la suite certains visages lorsqu'il les avait étudiés de façon plus poussée par le crayon?" Rosenberg and Prat 1996, p. 688, no. 415, in their entry on the *Sheet of Eight Heads, with a Right Hand Holding a Mask* (Musée du Louvre, Paris).

12. "Ces charmantes etudes . . . sont de la plus belle conservation." *Catalogue d'objets curieux du plus beaux choix . . . provenant du Cabinet de M. Lebrun*, Paris, 11 April 1791, no. 344.

13. Launay 1991, p. 505. The illustrator, journalist, and collector Maurice Feuillet (1873–1968) informed Lugt in May 1929 that Edmond de Goncourt (whom he had visited as a young man) told him that he had acquired this drawing around 1860, "chez un brocanteur, roulé, pour ainsi dire dans la boue, pour un prix dérisoire, disons 30 sous." In a later reminiscence of August 1947, Feuillet claimed that this had been one of the Goncourts' first acquisitions and that the *brocanteur* was at the marché Saint-Martin; Lugt's records of these conversations are in the curatorial files at the Fondation Custodia.

14. Goncourt/Pety and Galantris 1881/2003, vol. I, p. 173; Launay 1991, pp. 95–101.

15. Paris 1982a, pp. 80–81.

6. Antoine Watteau
Valenciennes 1684–1721 Nogent-sur-Marne
Woman Reclining on a Chaise Longue, c. 1718
Red and black chalk with stumping | 21.7 x 31.1 |
Inscriptions: recto, at bottom left in graphite, "Watteau" | Inv. no. 2311

Provenance: Richard Bull, second half of the eighteenth century, Ongar (Essex), and his daughters (cf. L. 314 & Suppl.; sold London, Sotheby's, 29 April 1880, no. 885, to Donaldson, as part of a collection, for 1,800 livres);

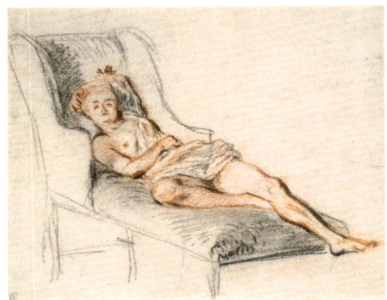

Fig. 6.1
Antoine Watteau, *Woman Reclining on a Chaise Longue*, c. 1718, black and red chalk, 20.4 x 25.6, Private Collection

Fig. 6.2
Antoine Watteau, *Seated Young Woman*, c. 1718, black, red, and white chalk, 17.4 x 20.6, The Morgan Library & Museum, New York. Thaw Collection. 2000.53

Donaldson, London (sold, London, Sotheby's, 23 May 1881, no. 164, to Thibaudeau, for Heseltine); John Postle Heseltine (1843–1929), London (L. 1507 & Suppl.); J. Klener, according to Parker and Mathey 1957; Stettiner & Co., Paris; Frits Lugt (1884–1970), Maartensdijk and Paris (L. 1028), acquired 15 June 1925.

Exhibitions: London 1909a; London 1909b; Paris 1913; Amsterdam 1926; Amsterdam 1935; London 1952; Paris and Amsterdam 1964; Paris 1968; Amsterdam 1974; Washington, Paris, and Berlin, 1984.

Bibliography: Heseltine 1900, pp. 72–73, no. 27, repr.; London 1909a, pp. 162, 164, no. 44, repr.; London 1909b, p. 93, no. 44; Guiraud 1913, no. 82, repr.; Paris 1913, p. 45, no. 82; Amsterdam 1926, p. 98, no. 201; Dimier 1928, p. 53, no. 20; Parker 1931, p. 48, no. 80, pl. 80; Amsterdam 1935, p. 11, no. 29, repr.; Hennus 1950, p. 134, repr.; London 1952, pp. 106–7, no. 172, fig. 9b; Bouchot-Saupique 1953, pl. 7; Parker and Mathey 1957, vol. II, p. 315, no. 607, repr.; Bean 1964, p. 294; Hasselt 1964, p. 378, fig. 14; Paris and Amsterdam 1964, pp. 43–44, no. 47, pl. 31; Paris 1968, no. 42, repr.; Posner 1973, pp. 54–55, fig. 22; Amsterdam 1974, pp. 103–4, 165, no. 129, repr.; Posner 1984, pp. 99, 283, note 50; Sollers and Violette 1984, pp. 74–75, repr.; Washington, Paris, and Berlin 1984, pp. 193–94, no. 114, repr.; Grasselli 1987a, pp. 369, 535, no. 272, fig. 457; Moureau and Grasselli 1987, pp. 249–50, fig. 8; McPherson 1990, p. 34, fig. 1; Rosenberg and Prat 1996, vol. II, pp. 994–95, no. 585, repr.

Notes 1. For the eight drawings in this group, see Rosenberg and Prat 1996, vol. II, pp. 982–95, nos. 578–85.

2. "En quelques chambres que j'eus en différents quartiers de Paris, qui ne nous servaient qu'à poser le modèle, à peindre et à dessiner"; Caylus in Rosenberg 1984, pp. 71–72.

3. "Nous éprouvions, lui et moi . . . la joie pure de la jeunesse . . . l'auteur qu'ils font imaginer, agréable, tendre et peut-être un peu berger"; ibid., p. 72. Caylus noted the presence of another young "ami commun," Nicolas Hénin (1691–1724), conseiller du roi, at these drawing sessions.

4. See DeJean 2007, p. 43.

5. Posner 1984, p. 99.

6. Rosenberg and Prat 1996, vol. II, p. 994.

7. The chair, a late seventeenth-century *lit de repos* with upholstered wings to shield the sitter's face from direct heat and drafts, appears in seven of the eight intimate studies, but also in two sheets not associated with the drawing sessions in rented rooms: the counterproof *Young Woman in a Bonnet on a Chaise Longue* (Musée Magnin, Dijon), c. 1714–15 (RP 274), and *Two Studies of Women* (Nationalmuseum, Stockholm), c. 1716–17 (RP 488).

8. "L'usage délicat de l'estompe, l'atmosphère vaporeuse, la douceur d'une lumière diaphane, le naturel de la pose et de son caractère intime"; Washington, Paris, and Berlin 1984, p. 193–94.

9. As noted by Grasselli in Washington, Paris, and Berlin 1984, pp. 192–93, and Wintermute in New York and Ottawa 1999, pp. 162–65.

10. Rosenberg and Prat (1996, vol. II, p. 986) noted that the model portrayed giving herself a pedicure in the striking *Study of a Semi-Nude Woman Seated on a Chaise Longue* (British Museum, London) differs from the others in being "plus jeune et plus avenant."

11. See Rosenberg and Prat 1996, vol. II, pp. 984–85, nos. 579–80, and pp. 990–95, nos. 583–85; and on the two drawings cited, Wintermute in New York and Ottawa 1999, pp. 162–65.

12. Grasselli 1987a, p. 367; Wintermute in New York and Ottawa 1999, p. 162.

7. Anonymous French artist, formerly attributed to Watteau
Study of a Shell (Murex ramosus Linne), c. 1720–30
Red and black chalk | 26.2 x 19.6 | Inv. no. 7634

Provenance: Camille Groult (1837–1908); Jean Groult (1868–1951), his son; Pierre Bordeaux-Groult, his son (sale, Paris, Palais Galliéra, 11 April 1962, no. 41, pl. 30, as Watteau, to Lugt); Frits Lugt (1884–1970), Paris (L. 1028).
Exhibitions: Paris and Amsterdam 1964 (as Watteau); Copenhagen 1983 (as Watteau).
Bibliography: Parker and Mathey 1957, vol. II, pp. 369, 373, no. 902, repr.;

Paris and Amsterdam 1964, p. 37, no. 39, pl. 47; Sérullaz 1981, pp. 31–32, fig. 10; Copenhagen 1983, pp. 95–96, no. 22, repr; Paris 1984, p. 47, under no. 68; Washington, Paris, and Berlin 1984, p. 57, fig. 4; Aaron 1985, pp. 72, 112, no. 70, repr.; Gruber 1994, p. 396, repr.; New York 1995, p. 14, under no. 3, fig. 1; Rosenberg and Prat 1996, vol. III, pp. 1284–85, no. R513.

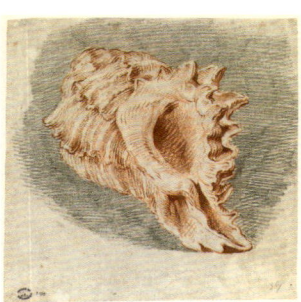

Fig. 7.1
Anonymous French artist, formerly attributed to Antoine Watteau, *Study of a Shell (Murex anguliferus)*, identified here as *Murex ramosus Linne*, c. 1720–30, black and red chalk, 23.6 x 24.0, Musée des Beaux-Arts et d'Archéologie, Besançon, Inv. no. D. 1739

Notes

1. Parker and Mathey 1957, vol. II, p. 373, nos. 901–7; Rosenberg and Prat 1996, vol. III, pp. 1160–61, nos. R43, R44, R74–76, R395, R543.
2. "D'une grande beauté . . . le traitement excessivement complexe du contour et du modelé suggère qu'ils sont l'oeuvre d'un ornameniste, peut-être meme un sculpteur. Nulle part dans l'oeuvre de Watteau, on ne trouve pas des études d'une exécution comparable, avec cet arrière-plan grossièrement hachuré et une séparation aussi nette entre la sanguine et la pierre noire"; Washington, Paris, and Berlin 1984, pp. 55–57.
3. See Watteau's copies after Venetian sixteenth-century paintings, in particular the figure of the woman seen from the back in Gerolamo Bassano's *Deluge* (RP 348) and the copy after Veronese's Saint Catherine (Private Collection, United Kingdom) (RP 354).
4. "Qu'il n'est pas absolument impossible que Watteau en soit l'auteur, mais que rien ne vient appuyer cette thèse"; Rosenberg and Prat 1996, vol. III, p. 1160.
5. Ibid.; the authors note that Berlin's *Study of a Shell* (RP R43) had been previously attributed to François Boucher—a great collector of shells—as well as to Louis-Roland Trinquesse (see cat. 38), before being published by Watteau in 1957.
6. Tryon 1879–98, vol. II, p. 93.
7. Parker and Mathey 1957, vol. II, p. 373, no. 901; Rosenberg and Prat 1996, vol. III, p. 1168, no. R74.
8. Wye 1991, p. 130, and email correspondence from Dr. Emily Vokes, Tulane University, 8 February 2009.
9. As suggested by Denison in New York 1995, p. 14; this would have assigned a late date to the drawings (for Watteau), incompatible with his stylistic development in these years.
10. Glorieux 2002, pp. 279–81.

11. "Le Sieur Gersaint . . . a rapporté tout nouvellement d'Hollande une collection considérable de coquilles de toute espèce et des mieux conservés"; *Mercure de France*, November 1735, cited in Glorieux 2002, p. 280.
12. Sargentson 1996, pp. 64–66; Pomian 1987.
13. MacGregor 2007, pp. 136–39; New York 2007, p. 24.

8. Pierre-Jean Mariette
Paris 1694–1775 Paris
View of Crozat's Gardens at Montmorency, dated 1724
Pen and brown ink, brown wash over black chalk, with highlights in white | 40.1 x 26.7 | Inscriptions: in the upper left, in the hand of the artist, in pen and brown ink, "Dans les Jardins de M. Crozat à Montmorenci. 1724."; on the mount, in the cartouche, in brown ink, "Pet. Joan. / Mariette / advivum"
Inv. no. 3787

Provenance: Pierre-Jean II Mariette (1694–1774), Paris (L. 1852 & Suppl.; sold Paris, Pierre François Basan, 15 November 1775–30 January 1776, p. 195, part of no. 1284, to Mariette fils [either Jean-Pierre or Corneille-Guillaume]); Eugène Rodrigues (1853–1928), Paris (L. 897 & Suppl.; sold Paris, Drouot, 28–29 November 1928, no. 150, to Lugt); Frits Lugt (1884–1970), Maartensdijk and Paris (L. 1028).
Exhibitions: Paris 1935; Paris and Amsterdam 1964; Paris 1967; London 1977; Paris, Institut Néerlandais, 1980, *Le Paysage évoqué par la plume et le pinceau* (no catalogue).
Bibliography: Basan 1775, p. 195, no. 1284; Lugt 1921, p. 332; Paris 1935, p. 41, no. 27; Bean 1964, p. 294, pl. 42; Paris and Amsterdam 1964, p. 62, no. 76, pl. 57; Paris 1967, p. 175, no. 299; Schneider/Ekkart 1932/1973, p. 285; London 1977, pp. 30–31, no. 80, repr.; Bacou 1981, p. 19, fig. 4; Roland Michel 1987, pp. 250–51, fig. 301.

Notes
1. Krause 1996, pp. 266–70; on Crozat, see Stuffmann 1968.
2. Wintermute in Ottawa, Washington, and Berlin 2003, pp. 126–28. Watteau's drawing *À Montmorency* is known only from Caylus's engraving; his *Allée Bordered by Trees*, a drawing in red chalk engraved by Boucher for the *Figures de différents caractères*, is in The State Hermitage Museum, Saint Petersburg; see Rosenberg and Prat 1996, vol. I, pp. 378–79.
3. Paris 1967, pp. 17–18, 25–27.

Fig. 8.1
Pierre-Jean Mariette, *View of a Park*, c. 1724, pen and black ink, brown wash, 25.5 x 38.2, Nationalmuseum, Stockholm, NMH 237/1968

4. "Il s'étoit fait une manière qui étoit petite et mesquine"; Mariette/Chennevières and Montaiglon 1851–60, vol. I, pp. 364–66. For an example of Chaufourier's landscape drawings, see David Mandrella's entry on *River in Undergrowth* in Weimar, New York, and Paris 2005, pp. 150–51, no. 48.
5. Bean 1964, p. 294.
6. Mariette's pen and ink copy of Annibale Carracci's *Study of a Tree* is in the Louvre (inv. no. 30880); Carracci's drawing was sold most recently at Christie's, London, 9 April 1990, no. 32. In Basan 1775, p. 50, nos. 306–7, it was noted that Mariette's drawing was "une très bonne copie de ce Dessin, faite à tromper." Mariette also copied, "supérieurement bien," eight landscape drawings by Guercino in his collection; see Basan 1775, p. 16, no. 153. One of these, *Landscapes with Rocks and Trees*, was acquired by Lugt in 1937 (inv. no. 5223); see Bacou 1976, p. 382. Lugt (1921, p. 332) noted that Mariette's etchings after Guercino's pen and ink landscape drawings were done in 1724 and dedicated to Antonio Zanetti.
7. "Le feuiller des arbres y est fait dans le grand style"; Basan 1775, p. 195, no. 1284.
8. "Quatre Etudes d'Arbres & Paysages, dessinés en 1724 d'après nature, dans les jardins de M. Crozat à Montmorenci"; ibid. *View from a Park* is catalogued in Bjurström 1982, no. 1063, and New York and Edinburgh 1987, p. 127, no. 76.
9. Paris 1967, p. 26; Préaud in Mariette/Mandroux-França and Préaud 2003, vol. I, p. 349.

9. Étienne Jeaurat
Paris 1699–1789 Versailles
View of the Tiber, near the Ripa Grande, Rome,
c. 1724–27

Gray ink and wash, white gouache on blue paper | 27.6 x 42.7 | Inscriptions: at lower right, in brown ink, "F Sablet" (partly effaced); on the mount, at bottom, in brown ink, "vue du tibre pres de Ripagrande, a Roma"; verso, at the top of mount, in graphite, "S.vene ACagdou" and "51 x 37" | Inv. no. 1986-T.34

Provenance: M. de Lajarriette, Nantes (sale, Paris, Drouot, 4–9 March 1861, part of no. 1333, as "Jacob [*sic*] Sablet"); Private Collection; Paul Prouté, S.A., Paris; Fondation Custodia, Paris, acquired 10 April 1986.
Exhibitions: Paris 1986; Paris 1994b.
Bibliography: Paris 1986, p. 15, no. 23, repr. (as Jeaurat); Roland Michel in Paris 1989, p. 200, under no. 80; Arizzoli-Clémentel in Paris 1994b, pp. 90–91, no. 39, repr.

Fig. 9.1
Étienne Jeaurat, *View of the Dogana Vecchia near the Port of Ripa Grande, on the Banks of the Tiber*, c.1724–27, black chalk, brown wash, white gouache on blue paper, with touches of indigo wash, 24.5 x 37.0, École Nationale Supérieure des Beaux-Arts, Paris, PM 2545

Fig. 9.2
Jean-François Sablet, *Fisherman in an Italian Landscape during a Storm*, c. 1793, brush and black ink, gray wash, heightened with white gouache on blue-gray paper, 41 x 54, Fondation Custodia, Paris, Inv. no. 2001-T.25

Notes
1. See Arizzoli-Clémentel in Paris 1994b, p. 90, and Brugerolles in Paris, Sydney, and Ottawa 2003, pp. 202–9. One of this group, *View of the Tiber at San Bartolomeo*, is dated "30 September 1725"; see London 1990, no. 34. The National Gallery of Canada, Ottawa, has recently acquired *Landscape with Two Figures*, signed and dated 1726 (inv. no. 41422), which probably shows the church of Santa Sabina all'Aventino overlooking the Tiber.
2. For the *Vue de la Dogana Vecchia près de l'embarcadère du port de Ripa Grande au bord du Tibre*, signed "jeaurat.f," see Brugerolles in Paris, Sydney, and Ottawa 2003, pp. 208–9.
3. Gross 2004, pp. 22–23.
4. Conisbee 1986, p. 532.
5. See, for example, Giovanni Battista Falda's *Altra Veduta di Ripa Grande*,

1677, in *The Illustrated Bartsch* (Strauss 1978–), vol. 47, part 2, commentary, *Italian Masters of the Seventeenth Century: Giovanni Battista Falda*; and Gaspar Van Wittel's *Vedute* in the Accademia di San Luca, Rome, and the Musée des Beaux-Arts, Tours.

6. See, most recently, the entry on *Prostitutes Being Led off to La Salpetrière*, 1757 (Musée Carnavalet, Paris), in Ottawa, Washington, and Berlin 2003, pp. 208–9.

7. *Catalogue d'Estampes . . . Livres à figures, Portraits, Dessins Anciens & Modernes, formant la 1re partie du cabinet de Feu M. de Lajarriette, Ancien Receveur des Finance à Nantes*, Paris, Drouot, 4–9 March 1861, no. 1333. Among the eleven drawings catalogued under this lot, the *Vue du Tibre, près de Ripa Grande, à Rome* most likely refers to the sheet by Jeaurat.

10. Jean-Baptiste Pater
Valenciennes 1695–1736 Paris
Standing Soldier with a Pipe, c. 1725–30
Red chalk | 18.7 x 9.2 | Inscriptions: at lower left, in pen and black ink, "271" | Inv. no. 7209

Provenance: Possibly anonymous sale, Douai, 7 July 1772, no. 32, part of "Desseins reliés. 500 Desseins au Crayon rouge en 157. feuilles, par Watteau et Pater"; Camille Groult (1837–1908); his son, Jean Groult (1868–1951); Galerie Cailleux, 1958; Frits Lugt (1884–1970), Paris (L. 1028), acquired 6 November 1958.

Exhibitions: Paris and Amsterdam 1964, London 1968.

Bibliography: Paris and Amsterdam 1964, p. 54, no. 63, pl. 54; London 1968, p. 107, no. 546, pl. 20, fig. 91; Cambridge, Mass., Toronto, Paris, Edinburgh, New York, and Los Angeles 1998, p. 200, under no. 47, fig. 2; Rosenberg 2003, p. 34.

Fig. 10.1
Jean-Baptiste Pater, *Troops at Rest*, c. 1725–30, oil on canvas, 54.0 x 65.4, The Metropolitan Museum of Art, New York, Bequest of Ethel Tod Humphrys, 1956. (56.55.2)

Notes

1. Ingersoll-Smouse 1928, p. 370, no. 417, fig. 126; Baetjer 1995, p. 370; Baetjer in Martigny 2006, pp. 189–94. A reduced autograph variant of the Metropolitan Museum's composition, oil on paper laid down on canvas, appeared at Sotheby's, New York, 27 January 2005, no. 14.

2. I am most grateful to Christoph Vogtherr for allowing me to see a draft of his entry on the painting in Potsdam for the forthcoming catalogue raisonné of this collection. See also Paris and Amsterdam 1964, p. 54, no. 63 (which notes the variant composition now in The Metropolitan Museum of Art); and Paris 1963a, no. 17.

3. "Il m'a avoué depuis qu'il devait tout ce qu'il sçavait à ce peu de temps qu'il avait mis à profit"; from Gersaint's biography of Pater, in his *Catalogue raisonné des diverses curiosités du cabinet de feu M. Quentin de Lorangère*, Paris 1744, reprinted in Ingersoll-Smouse 1928, p. 19. For the most recent assessments of Pater's style, see Wintermute in New York and Ottawa 1999, pp. 232–37, and especially Grasselli in New York and Ottawa 1999, pp. 56–59, and Grasselli 2000.

4. See the partial listing in New York and Ottawa 1999, p. 234, and Rosenberg 2003, p. 34. For Pater's drawings in the Louvre, see Legrand 1997, pp. 223–27.

5. Rosenberg 2003, and see Provenance in this volume. The discovery of the Douai album also confirms that the habit of cutting down Pater's sheets of military studies was established well before Groult's lifetime; see also the *Standing Man* (inv. no. 33369) and *Soldier Walking to the Right* (inv. no. 33369 bis), which entered the Louvre as part of the Saint-Morys collection in June 1796; see Legrand 1997, pp. 225–26. For a rare example of a sheet with more than one male figure (and not owned by Groult), see *Studies of a Soldier with a Rifle*, Sotheby's, New York, 8 January 1991, no. 84.

11. Jean-Étienne Liotard
Geneva 1702–1789 Geneva
Frankish Woman from Galata and Her Servant,
c. 1740–42
Black and red chalk on two sheets of paper, joined vertically | 20.4 x 25.0 | Inscriptions: at lower right, in black chalk, "Liotard" | Watermark: on the left-hand sheet, a fragment of a crest with the number "4" and the initials "WR" (interlaced) | Inv. no. 2315

Provenance: Jean-Étienne Liotard (sale, London, Christie's, 15–16 April 1774, part of no. 31, to Lord Bessborough, for £4); Horace Walpole (1717–1797), Fourth Earl of Orford, London and Strawberry Hill, Twickenham (cf. L. 1386 & Suppl.; not in the Strawberry Hill estate sale of 25 April–24 May, 1842); Frederick Ponsonby, Third Earl of Bessborough (1758–1844), London (sale, London, Christie's, 1 April 1848, part of no. 1 or 8); Charles Sackville Bale (1791–1880), London (cf. L. 640–41 & Suppl.; sale, London, Christie's, 9–14 June 1881, no. 2239); John Postle Heseltine (1843–1929), London (L. 1507 & Suppl.); Stettiner & Co, Paris; Frits Lugt (1884–1970), Maartensdijk and Paris (L. 1028), acquired 15 June 1925.

Exhibitions: Paris 1771; Paris 1911b; Paris 1913; London 1950; Paris and Amsterdam 1964; Utrecht 1985; Geneva and Paris 1992.

Bibliography: Paris 1771 (Lauts 1977), p. 8, no. 5 (p. 64); Humbert, Revilliod, and Tilanus 1897, p. 149, under nos. 22, 23; repr.; Paris 1911b, no. 199bis; Guiraud 1913, no. 49, repr.; Paris 1913, p. 29, no. 49; Fosca 1928, p. 151; London 1950, p. 16, no. 47b; Paris and Amsterdam 1964, p. 64, no. 78, pl. 56; Aaron 1985, pp. 66, 111, repr.; Utrecht 1985, p. 80, no. 5, repr.; Starcky 1988, pp. 250–51, no. 374, repr.; Boppe 1989, p. 285, no. 54; Monneret 1989, p. 111; Geneva and Paris 1992, pp. 112–13, no. 55, repr.; Bull 2002, p. 11, fig. d.; Roethlisberger 2002, p. 395.

Fig. 11.1
Giuseppe Camaratta and Jean-Étienne Liotard, *A Frankish Lady from Galata and Her Slave*, 1745, engraving, 30.8 x 24.7 (plate), Fondation Custodia, Paris, Inv. no. 2315A

Fig. 11.2
Jean-Étienne Liotard, *Frankish Woman from Galata*, c. 1740–42, counterproof, black and red chalk, 20.0 x 16.0, Musée du Louvre, Paris, RF1393

Notes

1. For convenient summaries of Liotard's biography and career, see De Herdt in Geneva and Paris 1992 and Bull 2002.

2. De Herdt in Geneva and Paris 1992, pp. 112, 277–81 (nos. 22–79), for the drawings done in Constantinople. A young aristocrat from Karlsruhe visiting Liotard in his studio in Geneva in June 1761 noted "On y voit aussi un grand nombre de beaux dessins, qu'il a fait surtout en Turquie et souvent d'après nature"; see Geneva and Dijon 1984, p. 64.

3. *Catalogue of the Select, Well-Chosen Collection of Italian, French, Flemish and Dutch Pictures (Principally CABINET) of Mons. Liotard of Great Marlborough Street, . . . Sold by Auction by Mr Christie*, London, 15 April 1774, no. 31. See De Herdt in Geneva and Paris 1992, p. 281, no. 78, and Roethlisberger 2002, p. 395. In 1778 Liotard would sell a group of thirty drawings, including the counterproof of *Frankish Woman from Galata*, to the comte de Montigny; see Starcky 1988, p. 235.

4. See De Herdt in Paris and Geneva 1992, p. 281, no. 78, and Roethlisberger 2002, p. 395.

5. "Une Dame Franque de Galata et son Esclave qui sont sur le point d'aller à Constantinople ou autre quartier turc. L'Esclave présente à sa Maîtresse un voile semblable à celui qu'elle a sur le visage et sans lequel les Femmes Turques ne sortent jamais"; in Starcky 1988, pp. 250–51.

6. Geneva and Paris 1992, pp. 94–95, nos. 44 and 45. In *Servant Presenting Tea to Her Seated Levantine Mistress*, the transformation was more extreme, Liotard starting with the motif of the servant carrying in the teapot, which he counterproofed, and extending the sheet by almost two-thirds to include the seated mistress taking tea on the sofa.

7. Starcky 1988, pp. 250–51, no. 374.

8. Bull 2002, p. 11.

9. For the Morgan Library & Museum's *Veiled Turkish Woman* (inv. no.1989.50), inscribed "femme/Turque/dans les rues/Juillet 1738," see Wintermute in New York and Ottawa 1999, pp. 224–25.

10. Montagu 1837, vol. I, pp. 240–42; the terms for the various elements of female Turkish apparel come from the elaborate description in Lady Montagu's letter to the Countess Mar, 1 April 1717.

11. Ibid., vol. I, p. 289, undated letter (1717) to the Countess of Bristol.

12. François Boucher
Paris 1703–1770 Paris
Standing Woman Seen from Behind, c. 1742
Black, red, and white chalk, with stumping, on gray-brown paper | 35.3 x 19.9 | Inv. no. 3552

Provenance: Unidentified eighteenth-century collector, mark of Jean-Baptiste Glomy (c. 1720–1786), Paris (L. 1085 & Suppl.); probably M. de Cypierre (sale, Paris, 10 March 1845 and following days, no. 167, for 81 francs); Frédéric Villot (1809–1875) (sale, Paris, Drouot, 16–18 May 1859, no. 92, for 30 francs); Private Collection of R.M . . . (sale, Paris, Drouot, 3 June 1908, no. 6, repr., to Ducrey, for 760 francs.); Georges B. Lasquin (sale, Paris, Galerie Georges Petit, 7–8 June 1928, no. 21, pl. V, to Houthakker); Bernard Houthakker (1884–1963), Amsterdam (cf. L. 1272); Frits Lugt

(1884–1970), Maartensdijk and Paris (L. 1028), acquired 19 June 1928.
Exhibitions: Paris 1951; Paris and Amsterdam 1964; London 1968; Paris 2003b.
Bibliography: A. Michel 1906, p. 125, no. 2261; Hennus 1950, p. 135, repr.; Jaccottet 1952, p. 185, no. 57, repr.; Paris 1951, no. 11; Bauër 1959, pl. 20; Paris and Amsterdam 1964, p. 70, no. 86, pl. 71; Ananoff 1966, p. 57, no. 135, repr.; London 1968, p. 53, no. 98, fig. 139; Ananoff and Wildenstein 1976, vol. I, p. 324, under no. 208, fig. 1; Washington, Detroit, Minneapolis, Cleveland, Los Angeles, Denver, Fort Worth, Kansas City, and New York 1979, p. 138, under no. 46; Ananoff 1980, p. 102, under no. 213; Tokyo and Kumamoto 1982, pp. 18, 26, fig. E; Brunel 1986, pp. 76–77, repr.; New York, Detroit, and Paris 1986, p. 195, under no. 38; Karlsruhe 1999, p. 117, under no. 16, fig. 2; New York and Fort Worth 2003, p. 130, under no. 44; Ottawa, Washington, and Berlin 2003, p. 363, under no. 52, note 2; Paris 2003b, pp. 64–65, no. 26, repr.; Hedley 2004, pp. 70–71, fig. 57.

Fig. 12.1
François Boucher, *A Lady Fastening Her Garter ("La Toilette")*, dated 1742, oil on canvas, 52.5 x 66.5, Museo Thyssen-Bornemisza, Madrid, 58 (1967.4)

Notes

1. See, most recently, Laing in New York, Detroit, and Paris 1986, pp. 195–97; Bailey in Ottawa, Washington, and Berlin 2003, pp. 222–23, 263; and Hedley 2004, pp. 70–71. While previous authors have assumed that the figure seen from behind is a lady's maid ministering to her mistress, Ribeiro (2002, pp. 38, 179) makes the interesting observation that she is a *marchande de modes* plying her wares.
2. Laing in New York and Fort Worth 2003, p. 130.
3. First noted in Washington, Detroit, Minneapolis, Cleveland, Los Angeles, Denver, Fort Worth, Kansas City, and New York 1979, p. 138, "[a drawing] in which the connection may be superficial, but which might have been adapted for the figure of the maid." See also Laing in New York, Detroit, and Paris 1986, p. 195. In earlier catalogues the drawing was given the title "Jeune femme marchant, vue de dos."
4. Ribeiro 2002, p. 136.
5. Ibid., p. 179, and email communication to the author, 28 January 2009.
6. A suggestion made by Laing in New York and Fort Worth 2003, p. 130.

7. Most fully catalogued in ibid., pp. 130–31; see also Joulie in Paris 2003b, p. 64.
8. Ibid., pp. 162–63; Laing in Paris and Geneva 2006, pp. 173–75.
9. Hedley 2004, p. 71; Joulie in Paris 2003b, p. 64.
10. Jean-Richard 1978, pp. 54–55, no. 117; for Boucher's involvement in Jullienne's publication, see Roland Michel 1987, pp. 122, 126.
11. New York and Fort Worth 2003, p. 141, for an iteration of the motif in the 1760s. For examples of paintings in which such a figure appears (by no means an exhaustive list), see Ananoff and Wildenstein 1976, nos. 40, 74, 175, 260, 321, 327, 458, 532, 655.

13. François Boucher
Paris 1703–1770 Paris
View of a Rustic Habitation, c. 1760
Black and white chalk, gray wash and stumping, on blue paper, heightened with black pastel
23.0 x 35.5 | Inscriptions: at lower right of mount, in pen and black ink, in an eighteenth-century script, "Boucher" | Inv. no. 2007-T.21

Provenance: Unidentified eighteenth-century collector, mark of Jean-Baptiste Glomy (c. 1720–1786), Paris (L. 1085 & Suppl.); possibly sale of Jean-Paul de Meulemeester, Brussels; Private Collection, Paris, 1975; Fondation Custodia, Paris, acquired 11 June 2007.
Exhibitions: Paris, Institut Néerlandais, 1980, *Le Paysage évoqué par la plume et le pinceau* (no catalogue).
Bibliography: Méjanès 1976, pp. 396–98, fig. 5.

Fig. 13.1
François Boucher, *Study of a Cottage*, c. 1760, black chalk with white highlights, 40.5 x 29.0, Musée du Louvre, RF 14757

Notes 1. For recent discussions of Boucher's mature landscape drawings, see Laing in New York and Fort Worth 2003, pp. 219–31, and Méjanès in Paris 2003b, pp. 66–83.
2. "Son talent de coller et ajuster les dessins et estampes avec soin et propreté"; *Mercure de France* (April 1771), cited by Bailey in New York and Ottawa 1999, p. 79. The inscription on the mount is also found on other drawings by the artist, such as Boucher's early *A Soldier Spreading Alarm in Chilperic's Camp*, Private Collection, New York. The identity of this eighteenth-century collector remains unknown; see New York and Fort Worth 2003, p. 244, no. 5.
3. Bailey in New York and Ottawa 1999, pp. 78–86.
4. Laing in New York, Detroit, and Paris 1986, pp. 151–54; Jacoby 1986, pp. 171, 252–53; Slatkin 1971.
5. "Qui pourra mieux rendre que M. Boucher . . . ces beaux Païsages où l'on reconnait avec plaisir un heureux mélange des vûes de Rome et de Tivoli, avec celles de Sceaux et d'Arcueil?" *Lettre sur le Salon de 1748*, cited in Dijon and London 2004, p. 93.
6. Dijon and London 2004, pp. 85–89, 97, 100. Joulie has identified late drawings by Boucher that are based on works by Cornelis Saftleven, Nicolaes Berchem, and Jan Asselijn.
7. "Les Fabriques en general [*sic*] sont d'un grand ornement dans le Paisage, quand même elles seroient Gottiques ou qu'elles paroîtroient inhabitées & à moitié ruinées: elles élevent la pensée par l'usage auquel on s'imagine qu'elles ont été destinées"; De Piles 1708, pp. 221–22.

14. Jean-Baptiste Oudry
Paris 1686–1755 Beauvais
Landscape with Bulls Fighting, dated 1751
Brush and black ink, gray wash, heightened with black and white gouache on brownish-gray paper
33.5 x 53.7 | Inscriptions: signed at lower left in pen and brown ink, "JB. oudry / 1751" | Inv. no. 1980-T.22

Provenance: Posthumous sale of Jean-Baptiste Oudry (without catalogue, Paris, 7 July 1755, sold with another drawing representing *Combat de cerfs*, to the Duke of Mecklembourg-Schwerin, for 54 livres 5 sols); Christian Ludwig II, Duke of Mecklembourg-Schwerin (1683–1756), Schwerin; disappeared from the print collection of Schwerin between 1798 and 1890; Private Collection (sale, Paris, Drouot, 23 February 1979, no. 7, repr.); Galerie de Bayser,

Paris; Fondation Custodia, Paris, acquired 19 February 1980.
Exhibitions: Paris 1979b; Paris, Institut Néerlandais, 1980, *Le Paysage évoqué par la plume et le pinceau* (no catalogue); Paris 1994b.
Bibliography: Seidel 1890, p. 105, no. 7; Locquin 1912, p. 137, no. 793; Opperman 1972, vol. I, pp. 111–12; vol. II, p. 756, no. D658; Opperman 1973, p. 64, no. 30; Paris 1979b, no. 31, repr.; Rosenberg in Paris 1994b, pp. 88–89, no. 38, repr.

Fig. 14.1
Jean-Baptiste Oudry, *Lions and Bears Fighting*, 1745, pen and black and brown ink, brush in gray and white, gray wash, heightened with white, over black chalk, on blue paper, 31.5 x 54.0, Museum Boijmans Van Beuningen, Rotterdam, MB 342 (PK)

Notes

1. "Le *Paysage avec combat de taureaux* d'Oudry est un nouvel exemple de cette passion pour les dessins impeccables; la provenance de la feuille fait rêver"; Paris 1994b, p. 88.
2. Opperman 1973.
3. See, most recently, Fontainebleau and Versailles 2003.
4. For Boucher and Oudry's joint proposal in October 1751, with Boucher suggesting eight episodes of the *Aventures de Renaud et Armide* and Oudry the *Combat de différents animaux*, see Engerand 1896, p. 146. Neither artist was awarded a commission; see Laing in New York, Detroit, and Paris 1986, pp. 27–28, and Opperman 1973, pp. 59–60.
5. Opperman 1973, pp. 62–64.
6. Ibid., p. 64, no. 30; see also Opperman 1972, p. 756, no. D658.
7. For a rather more vigorous depiction of bulls fighting, see Oudry's illustration to "Les Deux Taureaux et une grenouille," in the second book of La Fontaine's *Fables*, published posthumously between 1755 and 1759; La Fontaine/Selliers 1668–94/1992, vol. I, p. 93.
8. Bailey in Los Angeles, Houston, and Schwerin 2007, p. 25, referring to the 110 items listed under "Etudes, desseins de composition, esquisse et autres," in Oudry's unpublished posthumous inventory.
9. "M. Oudry étoit en quelque sorte plus attaché à ses dessins qu'à ses tableaux. Il les regardoit comme un fonds qu'il accumuloit pour sa famille. On n'en a presque point eu de son vivant"; from the abbé Louis Gougenot's "Vie de M. Oudry," published in 1761, cited by Bailey in ibid., p. 28, note 120.

10. Archives Nationales, *Minutier Central*, LIII/345, "Inventaire après décès," Jean-Baptiste Oudry, 7 May 1755; appraisal of "Etudes, desseins de compositions, esquisses et autres," made on 16 May 1755, "no. 20, Item un volume contenant vingt-neuf desseins de composition d'animaux dont il y a quelques contre epreuves . . . prisés 120 #."

11. "La mode y est; ils sont terminés; cela suffit pour quelqu'un dont les connoissances ne sont pas fort estendues"; Mariette's comments in his *Abécédario*, cited in Paris 1982b, p. 203.

12. Seidel 1890, pp. 104–5; Opperman 1972, p. 310. The eighteen drawings were framed and displayed in the print room of the old gallery at Schwerin, which may account for the fading of the blue paper in the Lugt sheet.

15. Charles-Nicolas Cochin
Paris 1715–1790 Paris
Portrait of Pierre-Jean Mariette, 1756
Graphite with stumping | 11.0 diameter
Inv. no. 709

Provenance: Marie-Thérèse Rodet Geoffrin (1699–1777); her daughter, the marquise de La Ferté-Imbault, née Marie-Thérèse Geoffrin (1715–1791); comtesse de la Bédoyère, Paris (sale, Paris, Galerie Georges Petit, 8 June 1921, no. 45, repr., to Lugt); Frits Lugt (1884–1970), Paris and Maartensdijk.
Exhibitions: Paris and Amsterdam 1964; Paris 1967; Amsterdam 1974.
Bibliography: Francis 1931, p. 159; Hennus 1950, pp. 132–33, repr.; Paris and Amsterdam 1964, pp. 72–73, no. 89, pl. 79; Cailleux 1967a, p. i, fig. 1; Paris 1967, p. 170, no. 285, repr.; Huyghe 1971, no. 11, repr.; Amsterdam 1974, pp. 31–32, 135, no. 25, repr.; Sutton 1976, pp. 8–9, fig. 7; Bacou 1981, p. 8, fig. 2; Munhall 1982, p. 63, repr.; Mandroux-França 1983, p. 321, no. 8, repr.; Bertrand 1991, pp. 19, 25, repr.; Rosenberg 2000, p. 34, fig. 34; Mariette/Mandroux-França and Préaud 2003, vol. I, p. 348, fig. 72; Atlanta 2006, p. 118, repr.

Fig. 15.1
Augustin de Saint-Aubin after Cochin, *Portrait of Pierre-Jean Mariette*, 1765, engraving, 17.1 x 12.2, Fondation Custodia, Paris, Inv. no. 1975-P.14

Notes

1. "Dessiné par C. N. Cochin en 1756" is inscribed at lower left in Saint-Aubin's engraving; see Bocher 1879, p. 64.
2. "Tandis que les uns sont à la conversation, le S. Cochin se recrée à dessiné [*sic*] ou de ses confrères ou amateurs"; Joly/Johnson 1772–89/1988, p. 8.
3. "Des petits portraits de société en buste . . . ce ne serait pas un cadeau intéressant"; Cochin to Pujol, 20 July 1779, cited in C. Michel 1993, p. 398.
4. Ibid., pp. 173, 617–26, for a listing of all the engraved portraits.
5. *Catalogue de huit tableaux par Hubert Robert, Quarante-trois dessins par Cochin . . . appartenant au Comte de La Bédoyère*, Paris, 8 June 1921, nos. 9–51.
6. "Je donne et lègue à la dite Académie les différents portraits d'aucuns de Messieurs les academiciens que j'ay dessinés"; "Testament de Cochin," 28 April 1790, cited in Henry 1880, p. 189.
7. The two joined forces in a commercial venture that year, Saint-Aubin charging 240 livres to engrave a portrait, and Cochin needing to sell a minimum of 150 prints to recoup his investment. Christian Michel (1993, pp. 172–74) has established that the diffusion of these portraits became a source of income for Cochin only after the mid-1760s.
8. Préaud in Mariette/Mandroux-França and Préaud 2003, vol. I, p. 349.
9. Paris 1967, p. 28.
10. With the support of the Association Mariette, Pierre Rosenberg is currently preparing a facsimile edition of the catalogue of Mariette's posthumous sale of November 1775 (Lugt 2453), illustrated by Gabriel de Saint-Aubin, in the collection of the Museum of Fine Arts, Boston. The publication of Kristel Smentek's doctoral dissertation, "Art, Commerce and Scholarship in the Age of the Enlightenment: Pierre-Jean Mariette and the Making of Art History" (University of Delaware, 2008) is eagerly anticipated; see also her recent article on Mariette as a collector of drawings, Smentek 2008.
11. Lugt 1921, pp. 331–38.
12. Paris 1967, pp. 13–15.

16. Charles-Nicolas Cochin
Paris 1715–1790 Paris
Portrait of Anne-Robert-Jacques Turgot, Baron de l'Aulne, dated 1763
Graphite with stumping | 11.0 diameter | Inscriptions: signed and dated in graphite, "Dis... par Ch... 1763"; on the verso of the mount, in lead pencil, "Mon^s. Turgot / given to / Mrs Jos Blount / by the / Duchesse D'anville at / La Roche Guyon / 1796" | Inv. no. 8161

Provenance: Louise Elisabeth de La Rochefoucauld, duchesse d'Enville (1716–1797); Mme Jos Blount; Eliot Hodgkin, London; Frits Lugt (1884–1970), Paris (L. 1028), acquired 22 May 1964.
Exhibitions: Paris and Amsterdam 1964 (not in catalogue); Amsterdam 1974.
Bibliography: Huyghe 1971, no. 10, repr.; Amsterdam 1974, pp. 32, 135, no. 26, repr.; Sutton 1976, pp. 8–9, fig. 6; Paris 1983, pp. 98–100, no. 141, repr.

Fig. 16.1
Claude-Henri Watelet after Cochin, *Portrait of Anne-Robert-Jacques Turgot, Baron de l'Aulne*, 1763, engraving, 19.4 x 14.0, Château de Versailles et de Trianon, INV.GRAV.LP 83.40.2.

Notes

1. Faure 1961 remains the classic study.
2. Paris 1983, pp. 98–100.
3. C. Michel 1993, p. 618. Watelet, receveur-général des finances for the generality of Orléans, was the author of *L'Art de peindre* (1760), a contributor to the *Encyclopédie*, and an associé-libre of the Academy since September 1747; he would have met Turgot at Madame Geoffrin's dinner table; see Bailey 2002, pp. 65–68. Watelet's engraving is inscribed "A. B. (*sic*) J. Turgot / Intendt de Limoges... Cochin.fil.del.1763 / C.H.Watelet sc.1763."
4. Hill 1999, pp. 27–49.
5. Scherf 2006, p. 100.
6. On the friendship between Turgot and the duchesse d'Enville, see, most recently, Vaugelade 2001, pp. 169–90.
7. "Sa figure était belle... Ses yeux, d'un brun clair, exprimaient parfaitement le mélange de fermeté & de douceur, qui faisait son caractère. Son front était arrondi, élevé, ouvert, noble & serein; ses traits prononcés; sa bouche vermeille & naïve"; Du Pont de Nemours 1788, vol. II, p. 219.

17. Charles-Joseph Natoire
Nîmes 1700–1777 Castel Gandolfo
View of San Giovanni e Paolo in Rome, dated 1757
Brush and gray ink, brown and gray wash, pen and brown ink, and white gouache over black chalk | 23.3 x 35.0 | Inscriptions: signed at the bottom right in pen and brown ink, "C. Natoire 1757"; and below at left "[…]ni e Paolo"; collector's mark, "GP" (Pierre Guéraud), at lower right, verso, near center in pen and brown ink, "Charles Joseph Natoire / de Nîmes en 1700 / †1777"; at top in graphite, "158 (?)"; at bottom, "14", "1757", "103", and "34 x 45" | Inv. no. 1978-T.10

Provenance: Eugène Rodrigues (1853–1928), Paris (L. 897 & Suppl.); Pierre Guéraud (1870–1948) (sale, Enghien-les-Bains, 20 November 1977, no. 84, to Petithory); Jacques Petithory (1929–1992), Paris; Fondation Custodia, Paris, acquired 6 January 1978.
Exhibitions: Paris, Institut Néerlandais, 1980, *Le Paysage évoqué par la plume et le pinceau* (no catalogue); Paris 1994b.
Bibliography: Paris 1994b, pp. 92–93, no. 40, repr.

Fig. 17.1
Giuseppe Vasi, *Chiesa dei SS Giovanni e Paolo*, from *Delle magnificenze di Roma Antica e Moderna*, 1753, vol. III, pl. 53, Avery Architectural and Fine Arts Library, Columbia University, New York

Notes

1. Natoire had inscribed the name of the church, "Giovanni e Paolo," at lower left; only the last two letters ("ni") of the first name are visible today; also missing now is the edge of the framing line in black chalk (my thanks to Perrin Stein for this observation). The sheet may have originally been a little longer. It is also worth noting that the church's name is in a different hand from the "signature" at right. Such double notations appear on several of the landscape drawings, for example *A Farmhouse at Frascati*, "signed" "C. Natoire 1757" at lower left and inscribed (by Natoire) "Cam. de Frascati 1756" at lower right; this drawing most recently appeared at Christie's, New York, 28 January 1999, no. 128.

2. See the letter of 20 July 1757 from Natoire's sister to the marquis de Marigny, explaining that "il vient d'essuyer tous les dangers d'une fièvre maligne qui l'a mis aux portes de la mort"; Montaiglon and Guiffrey 1887–1908, vol. XI, p. 190.
3. See Christie's, New York, 28 January 1999, no. 127; the drawing is inscribed on the rock at right "Villa madama/ Sept 1757/ c.n."
4. Marigny congratulated Natoire in a letter of 12 September 1757 on his "parfait rétablissement"; see Montaiglon and Guiffrey 1887–1908, vol. XI, p. 195,
5. Webb 2001, pp. 101–4.
6. Natoire to Marigny, 11 June 1755; see Montaiglon and Guiffrey 1887–1908. vol. XI, p. 93. For Natoire's drawings of his "Villa" in the Schlossmuseum, Weimar, the Musée Atger, Montpellier, and the Städelsches Kunstinstitut Frankfurt, see Duclaux 1991, p. 29, nos. 38, 39, and Weimar, New York, and Paris 2005, pp. 174–75.
7. As noted by Duclaux in Paris 1994b, p. 92; see also Busiri Vici 1976, p. 38.
8. For a discussion of his working method, see Stein 2000, p. 179.
9. Rosenberg in Paris and New York 1987/1988, pp. 61–65.
10. Vasi 1747–61, vol. III, pl. 53.

18. Gabriel de Saint-Aubin
Paris 1724–1780 Paris
Le Boulevard, c. 1760
Pen and brown ink, gray and brown wash, over black chalk, with touches of watercolor
37.1 x 53.8 | Inscriptions: at lower left, in pen and brown ink, in a nineteenth-century (?) hand, "Benazeht"; at the upper right, possibly an inscription rendered illegible by the wash applied by the artist | Inv. no. 3634

Provenance: Private Collection, Switzerland; S. Meller, Munich; Frits Lugt (1884–1970), Maartensdijk and Paris (L. 1028), acquired 25 October 1928; J. Klever, his father-in-law, Maartensdijk; Mme J. Klever-Schmidt, his widow; Frits Lugt, repurchased from Mme J. Klever-Schmidt in 1940.
Exhibitions: Brussels and Paris 1949; Vienna 1950; Paris 1951a; Rome and Milan 1960; Paris and Amsterdam 1964; London 1968; Amsterdam 1974; London 1977; New York and Paris 2007 (only exhibited in Paris).
Bibliography: Dacier 1929–31, vol. I, pl. 6, vol. II, pp. 90–91, no. 525; Brussels and Paris 1949, no. 99; Vienna 1950, p. 31, no. 108; Paris 1951, p. 8,

no. 137; Jaccottet 1952, p. 178, no. 71, repr; Rome and Milan 1960, p. 56, no. 79, pl. 39; Cailleux 1960, p. iii; Paris and Amsterdam 1964, p. 81, no. 98, pl. 82; London 1968, p. 116, no. 625, fig. 325; Amsterdam 1974, pp. 90–91, 160, no. 109, repr.; London 1977, p. 56, no. 62, repr.; McCullagh 1981, p. 191; Aaron 1985, p. 46, fig. 36; de Beaumont 1998, pp. 293–94; Toulouse 2001, p. 184, under no. 77, repr.; Ottawa, Washington, and Berlin 2003, pp. 242–43, note 2, under nos. 61, 62; New York and Paris 2007, pp. 204–5, no. 47, repr.

Fig. 18.1
Gabriel de Saint-Aubin, *Le Boulevard*, c. 1760, black and white chalk, 14.0 x 19.0, Location unknown

Notes

1. See the entries by Bailey and de Beaumont in New York and Paris 2007, pp. 194–201, 206–11.
2. Cailleux 1960, p. iii.
3. For the suggestion that the drawing was made in preparation for an oil painting, see de Beaumont in New York and Paris 2007, p. 204.
4. New York and Paris 2007, p. 199.
5. Ibid., pp. 195, 200. Only three people are seated at table in the Lugt drawing; a fourth—a woman with her back to us—is included (less harmoniously) in other the compositions.
6. Ibid., pp. 199, 201; *Street Scene* appeared most recently at Christie's, Paris, 21 November 2007, no. 104.
7. Dacier 1929–31, vol. II, p. 90, no. 523; Launay 1991, p. 453, no. 304. The drawing, whose present whereabouts are unknown, was previously unpublished.
8. De Beaumont in New York and Paris 2007, p. 204.
9. "Les Parisiens ne se promènent point, ils courent, ils se precipitent"; Mercier/Delon and Baruch 1783–89/1990, p. 188, from "Promenades Publiques" in *Tableau de Paris*, published between 1783 and 1789.

19. Hubert Robert
Paris 1733–1808 Paris
View of an Italian Garden, c. 1760
Red chalk | 39.8 x 49.5 | Inscriptions: verso, at the upper left of mount, in pencil, "N.5"; toward the right, "V206"; and at the lower right, "3256" | Inv. no. 8915

Provenance: Robert Goelet (sale, London, Sotheby's, 6 July 1967, no. 33, repr., to Lugt); Frits Lugt (1884–1970), Paris (L. 1028).
Exhibitions: London 1968; Amsterdam 1974; Washington, 1978; Paris, Institut Néerlandais, 1980, *Le Paysage évoqué par la plume et le pinceau* (no catalogue).
Bibliography: London 1968, p. 114, no. 610; Amsterdam 1974, p. 84, 157–58, no. 100, repr.; Méjanès 1976, p. 401, pl. 15; Washington 1978, p. 44, no. 9, repr.; Christie's Monaco 1995, p. 110, under no. 101; Turner 2001, p. 251, under no. 81.

Fig. 19.1
Hubert Robert, *The Vaulted Garden*, c. 1760, black chalk, 20.6 x 28.7, Collection of The John and Mable Ringling Museum of Art, the State Art Museum of Florida, a Division of Florida State University, Sarasota, Museum purchase, 1959, SN710

Notes

1. Washington 1978, p. 44, citing *Vue d'une ancienne maison à Naples*, *Jardin et palais à Portici, près de Naples*, and *Vue dessinée d'après nature*, all dated 1760 and inscribed with their location by Robert; see Feuillet 1926, nos. 61, 62, 68. Robert and Saint-Non left for Naples on 17 April 1760 and were back in Rome on 4 June. Natoire informed Marigny in a letter of 4 June 1760 that "Ils ont parcouru tous les environs et n'ont rien négligé pour mettre à profit leurs fatigues; ce pensionnaire ne peut que tirer de très grand fruit de cette promenade"; Montaiglon and Guiffrey 1887–1908, vol. XI, p. 343 (letter of 4 June 1760).
2. Munger, Zafran, Poulet, et al. 1992, pp. 38 (pl. XV), no. 136 (the Forsyth Wickes drawing at the Museum of Fine Arts, Boston, is neither signed nor dated). The Lugt drawing is also stylistically close to *Farmyard with Two Figures by a Well* (The J. Paul Getty Museum, Los Angeles), which, like it, was formerly in the Robert Goelet collection; see Turner 2001, pp. 250–51.

3. See Rome 1990, pp. 99, 127 (pl. XV).
4. Washington 1978, p. 58, an observation made in the entry on *Fountain in the Garden of the Villa d'Este*, The Philips Family collection, New York, which Carlson assigned to the late summer of 1760.
5. Northall 1776, p. 328; Haskell and Penny 1981, pp. 269–71; my thanks to Denise Allen for her eagle eye.
6. "Tout ce qu'il y a de beau, mais non pas de vrai . . . mélange bizarre qui n'existe que dans la tête du peintre"; Paciaudi to Caylus, 22 July 1760, Serieys 1802, pp. 158–59; Paciaudi was in the process of engaging Robert to copy antiquities for Caylus's publications.
7. Christie's, Monte Carlo, 30 June 1995, under no. 101.
8. Carlson and Williams (in Washington 1978, p. 44) considered this sheet to be by neither Fragonard nor Robert, but a "free copy by another student at the French Academy." The drawing, which I am here attributing to Robert, was acquired by the Ringling Museum as by Fragonard in 1959 (SN 710).

20. Jean-Honoré Fragonard
Grasse 1732–1806 Paris
View of the Serapeum at Hadrian's Villa, c. 1760
Red chalk over black chalk underdrawing | 35.1 x 48.3 | Signed at bottom right in red chalk, "frago" (now partially truncated); inscriptions on the eighteenth-century mount, in pen and black ink, "VÜE du CANOPE / de la Ville Adrienne / à TIVOLI"
Inv. no. 843

Provenance: Gutekunst & Klipstein, Bern; Frits Lugt (1884–1970), Maartensdijk and Paris, acquired 23 May 1922.
Exhibitions: Amsterdam 1926 (as Hubert Robert); Copenhagen 1935; Paris and Amsterdam 1964; Amsterdam 1974; Paris, Institut Néerlandais, 1980, *Le Paysage évoqué par la plume et le pinceau* (no catalogue); Rome 1990.
Bibliography: Amsterdam 1926, p. 96, no. 194; Copenhagen 1935, p. 114, no. 375; Ananoff 1961–70, vol. II, p. 119, no. 884, fig. 232 and vol. III, p. 330; Paris and Amsterdam 1964, pp. 90–91, no. 110, pl. 99; Ananoff 1965, p. 87, repr.; Amsterdam 1974, pp. 40–41, 139–40, no. 38, repr.; Méjanès 1976, pp. 400–402, fig. 12; Paris and New York 1987/1988, p. 98, under no. 24, fig. 5; Rome 1990, pp. 130–31, no. 75, repr.; MacDonald and Pinto 1995, p. 233; Paris 1999, p. 280, under no. 119; Besançon 2006, p. 59.

Fig. 20.1
The Serapeum at Hadrian's Villa

Fig. 20.2
Hubert Robert, *View of the Serapeum at Hadrian's Villa*, 1765, red chalk, 43.4 x 34.9, Bibliothèque municipale de Besançon, vol. 452, no. 23 BM

Notes

1. Rosenberg in Paris and New York 1987/1988, pp. 94–97; Rome 1990, pp. 110–34; Rosenberg 2006, pp. 51–55.
2. MacDonald and Pinto 1995, p. 233. The site of the Besançon drawing has sometimes been confused with that of the Lugt sheet, as by Rosenberg in Besançon 2006, p. 59.
3. "De grands bosquets et de belles pièces d'eau," from de Brosse's *Lettres sur l'Italie*, cited in MacDonald and Pinto 1995, p. 231.
4. "Un grand nombre de murailles ruinées et de débris sans forme, d'après lesquels l'on doit seulement conjecturer de la grandeur immense dont elle étoit et du nombre prodigieux de Bâtiments qui y étoient rassemblés"; abbé de Saint-Non, *Journal ou Nottes sur un Voiage fait en Italie*, 1759–60, in Rosenberg and Brejon de Lavergnée 1986, p. 160.
5. As first noted by Williams in Washington, Cambridge, Mass., and New York, 1978, p. 42.
6. Roland Michel in Paris 1999, p. 280, no. 119.
7. MacDonald and Pinto 1995, pp. 108–12. In the course of the seventeenth century, the Villa's property had fallen into shared ownership, with tenant farmers cultivating fields and pasturing sheep there; de Brosses noted that the Canopus belonged to the Jesuits. The site of Hadrian's Villa extended over three hundred acres and originally comprised some sixty structures.
8. Ibid., pp. 44–45, 233.
9. Loukomski and Nolhac 1930, pl. 77; MacDonald and Pinto 1995, pp. 233–34, the authors noting that in 1765 Robert inscribed his signature in a niche in the north flank of the Circular Hall.
10. Wilton-Ely 1994, vol. I, p. 266, no. 223, *Avanzi del Tempio del Dio Canopo nella Villa Adriana in Tivoli*; MacDonald and Pinto 1995, p. 258.
11. Rosenberg in Paris and New York 1987/1988, p. 96.

21. Jean-Honoré Fragonard
Grasse 1732–1806 Paris
Le Calendrier des vieillards, c. 1780
Pen and brown ink, brown wash, over black chalk underdrawing | 20.0 x 14.3 | Inv. no. 4068

Provenance: Possibly Jean-Benjamin de Laborde (sale, Paris, 16 May 1783, no. 55, to Paillet); M. de Jamonières (anonymous sale, Paris, 24 February 1883, part of no. 13); A. Piat (sale, Paris, Drouot, 22–23 March 1897, fifth item of no. 50); Gaston Le Breton (sale, Paris, Galerie Georges Petit, 6–8 December 1921, no. 60, pl. 4, to Paulme); Marius Paulme (1863–1928), Paris (L. 1910 & Suppl.; sold Paris, Galerie Georges Petit, 13 May 1929, no. 90, pl. 61, to Lugt); Frits Lugt (1884–1970), Maartensdijk and Paris, (L. 1028).
Exhibitions: Copenhagen 1935; Paris and Amsterdam 1964; London 1968; Amsterdam 1974.
Bibliography: Copenhagen 1935, pp. 113–14, no. 374; Paris and Amsterdam 1964, pp. 96–97, no. 118, pl. 90; London 1968, p. 74, no. 255; Ananoff 1961–70, vol. IV, p. 236, no. 2706; Roland Michel 1970, p. v, fig. 5b; Amsterdam 1974, pp. 48–49, 141–42, no. 48b, repr.; Roland Michel 1987, p. 150, fig. 170; Paris 1992, p. 211, under no. 136.

22. Jean-Honoré Fragonard
Grasse 1732–1806 Paris
À Femme avare, galant escroc, c. 1780
Pen and brown ink, brown wash, over black chalk underdrawing | 20.4 x 14.0 | Inv. no. 4067

Provenance: Possibly Jean-Benjamin de Laborde (sale, Paris, 16 May 1783, no. 55, to Paillet); M. de Jamonières (anonymous sale, Paris, 24 February 1883, part of no. 13); A. Piat (sale, Paris, Drouot, 22–23 March 1897, third item of no. 50); Gaston Le Breton (sale, Paris, Galerie Georges Petit, 6–8 December 1921, no. 61, pl. 4, to Paulme); Marius Paulme (1863–1928), Paris (L. 1910 & Suppl.; sale, Paris, Galerie Georges Petit, 13 May 1929, no. 89, pl. 61, to Lugt); Frits Lugt (1884–1970), Maartensdijk and Paris (L. 1028).
Exhibitions: Copenhagen 1935; Paris and Amsterdam 1964; London 1968; Amsterdam 1974; Paris 2007a.
Bibliography: Copenhagen 1935, p. 113, no. 373; Paris and Amsterdam 1964, pp. 95–96, no. 117, pl. 91; London 1968, pp. 73–74, no. 254; Ananoff

1961–70, vol. IV, pp. 235–36, no. 2704; Amsterdam 1974, pp. 48–49, 141–42, no. 48a, repr.; Roland Michel 1987, pp. 147, 150, fig. 165; Paris 1992, pp. 192–93, fig. 97, pp. 212–13, under no. 137; Rosenberg 2000, p. 154, fig. 199; Paris 2007a, p. 58, no. 15, repr.

Fig. 21.1
Jean Dambrun, after Fragonard, *Le Calendrier des vieillards*, published 1795, engraving, Private Collection, New York

Fig. 22.1
Jacques Aliamet, after Fragonard, *À Femme avare, galant escroc*, engraving, published 1795, engraved before 1788, Beinecke Rare Book and Manuscript Library, Yale University, New Haven

Fig. 22.2
Jean-Honoré Fragonard, *À Femme avare, galant escroc*, c. 1770, black chalk, brown ink and wash, 20.4 x 14, Musée du Petit Palais, Paris, L.Dut. 1173

Notes

1. See Roland Michel 1987, pp. 149–50, for illustrations of all three versions of *Le Calendrier des vieillards*, and Dupuy-Vachey in Paris 2007a, pp. 58–59, for all three versions of *À Femme avare, galant escroc*. We know that certain of the finished drawings circulated in the 1780s; see the Boileau sale of 4 March 1782, no. 155, "Quatre sujets des Contes de La Fontaine, Composition de M. *Fragonard*, qui seront vendus par couple," and the La Borde sale of 16 May 1783, no. 55, "Deux Dessins agréables lavés au bistre sur papier blanc, sujets des Contes de La Fontaine."

2. Delignières 1896, pp. 28, 211–13. The project to engrave Fragonard's drawings for an illustrated La Fontaine may have originated with a group of engravers around 1788–89, but it was realized only after Didot published a new edition of the *Contes et nouvelles en vers* in 1795, into which twenty illustrations, sixteen after drawings by Fragonard, were to be inserted (the first fascicle of engravings was announced in September 1796); see Roland Michel 1970, Osborne 1985, pp. 70–79, and Schroder 1996.

3. Roland Michel 1987, pp. 17–18, and Dupuy-Vachey in Paris 2007a, pp. 53–57. Dupuy-Vachey compares the first group of La Fontaine drawings stylistically to Fragonard's black-chalk copies after the Old Masters, done

in Saint-Non's company between March and September 1761.

4. Los Llanos in Paris 1992, pp. 193–274; Bailey 1992; the series in the Petit Palais has been beautifully republished in La Fontaine/Selliers 1664–74/1994.

5. For a listing of several of these drawings, see Schroder 1996.

6. La Fontaine/Ferrier and Collinet 1664–74/1980, pp. 142–47; I have used the excellent English translation in La Fontaine/Shapiro 1664–74/1992, pp. 71–87.

7. "Qui mainte fête à sa femme allégua, / Mainte vigile, et maint jour fériable. / Et du devoir crut s'échapper par là . . . Pour s'excuser, et pour la contenir, / Ne rencontrait point de jour en l'année, / Selon son compte et son calendrier, / Où l'on se pût sans scrupule appliquer / Au fait d'hymen; chose aux vieillards commode, / Mais dont le sexe abhorre le méthode." La Fontaine/Shapiro 1664–74/1992, pp. 71, 73; La Fontaine/Ferrier and Collinet 1664–74/1980, pp. 142–43.

8. "Elle oublia ce beau calendrier / Rouge partout, et sans nul jour ouvrable." La Fontaine/Shapiro 1664–74/1992, p. 79; La Fontaine/Ferrier and Collinet 1664–74/1980, p. 145.

9. Romeyn de Hooghe's illustration to this tale has an angry Bartholomée opening the door of her cabin to show Richard out; see La Fontaine 1664–74/1685, p. 60; Eisen included Pagamin in a window above the couple, in La Fontaine 1664–74/1762, vol. I, p. 68. For Boucher's painting *en camaieu brun*, dated 1740 and engraved by Nicolas de Larmessin, which set the scene in an exotic harbor, see Los Llanos 1995, p. 83.

10. La Fontaine/Shapiro 1664–74/1992, pp. 91–95; La Fontaine/Ferrier and Collinet 1664–74/1980, pp. 148–49.

11. "Voilà, dit-il, deux cents écus comptants, / Qu'à votre époux vous donnerez, Madame . . . Le drôle en prit ce jour et les suivants / Pour son argent, et même avec usure." La Fontaine/Shapiro 1664–74/1992, p. 93; La Fontaine/Ferrier and Collinet 1664–74/1980, p. 149.

12. As noted in Los Llanos in Paris 1992, p. 212.

13. See Romeyn de Hooghe's illustration of the passage, "J'ai votre argent à Madame rendu / . . . Déchargez-en votre livre de grâce," in La Fontaine 1664–74/1685, p. 70. Lancret's painting of the same subject, engraved by Larmessin, was shown at the Salon of 1738, Wildenstein 1924, p. 114, no. 644.

14. As he does in nearly all of the drawings made to be engraved, as noted by Dupuy-Vachey in Paris 2007a, p. 56.

23. Jean-Honoré Fragonard
Grasse 1732–1806 Paris
Portrait of Fragonard Seated in an Armchair, dated 1789
Black chalk, over black chalk underdrawing | 17.0 diameter | Inscriptions: at bottom in black chalk, by a later hand, "se ipsum delineabat frago / apud de Bergeret / anno 1789." | Inv. no. 3943

Provenance: Pierre-Jacques Bergeret de Grancourt (1742–1807); possibly Colonel de la Girennerie, his descendant (cf. Walferdin sale, no. 274); Hippolyte Walferdin (1795–1880) (sale, Paris, Drouot, 12–16 April 1880, no. 274, to Lefilleul, for 415 francs); probably Camille Groult; Eugène Paillet, 1889; Anonymous collection (sale, Paris, Drouot, 19 December 1928, no. 5, to Féral, for 25,500 francs); Jean Féral, Paris; Frits Lugt (1884–1970), Maartensdijk and Paris (L. 1028), acquired 20 February 1929.

Exhibitions: Paris 1935; Paris and Amsterdam 1964; Amsterdam 1974; Paris and New York 1987/1988; Barcelona 2006.

Bibliography: Gonse 1889, p. 75, repr.; Portalis 1889, pp. 224, 268, repr.; Goncourt and Goncourt/Neveux 1859–75/1927, vol. III, p. 280; Guimbaud 1928, p. 92, repr.; Grappe 1929, p. 216, pl. 56; Paris 1935, p. 120, no. 250; Hennus 1950, p. 133, repr.; Paris and Amsterdam 1964, p. 89, no. 108, pl. 89; Ananoff 1961–70, vol. III, p. 58, no. 1315, fig. 386; Amsterdam 1974, pp. 39, 139, no. 35, repr.; Tokyo and Kyoto 1980, repr.; Cuzin 1987, p. 243, fig. 306, p. 257, note 1; Paris and New York 1987/1988, pp. 557–58, no. 290, repr.; Roland Michel 1996, p. 443, note 25 (p. 446); L'Isle-Adam and Grasse 2001, p. 90, repr.; Barcelona 2006, p. 168, no. 102, repr.

Fig. 23.1
Jean-Honoré Fragonard, *Self-Portrait, Seen Full Face*, late 1780s, black chalk heightened with colored pencil, 12.9 diameter, Musée du Louvre, Paris, RF 41192

Fig. 23.2
Jean-Honoré Fragonard, *Portrait of Pierre-Jacques Bergeret*, late 1780s, black chalk, 18.0 diameter, Musée des Beaux-Arts et d'Archéologie, Besançon, Inv. no. D. 2874

Notes

1. Cuzin (1987, p. 257, no. 1) has described the Lugt drawing as "the most fascinating image of the artist, but of almost spectral imprecision" ("l'image la plus fascinante, mais d'une imprécision quasi fantomatique").
2. For Fragonard's seven black-chalk portraits, acquired by the Louvre in 1986 (three of which are self-portraits), see Rosenberg in Paris and New York 1987/1988, pp. 553–56, and Roland Michel 1996.
3. "Taille de quatre pieds onze pouces; cheveux et sourcils gris front haut, nez ordinaire yeux gris bouche moyenne menton rond"; from Fragonard's certificate of residency, dated 24 germinal an II (13 April 1794) in the Bibliothèque d'Art et d'Archéologie, Paris, in Paris and New York 1987/1988, pp. 585–86.
4. Ibid., "Marqué de petite verole."
5. The incorrect use of the particle "de" suggests that the inscription was made by someone other than the sitter, who had been proposed as the author by Rosenberg in Paris and New York 1987/1988, p. 558. (We agree that the Latin inscription is not by Fragonard himself.)
6. Rosenberg 2000, pp. 35–36; L'Isle-Adam and Grasse 2001, for the most recent survey of the Bergeret dynasty.
7. "Mon fils suit dans un cabriolet avec un cuisinier"; Bergeret's Journal entry for 5 October 1773, cited in Paris and New York 1987/1988, p. 364.
8. L'Isle-Adam and Grasse 2001, p. 22.
9. Rosenberg in Besançon 2006, pp. 174–75. The inscription on the mount of the portrait in Besançon, "Xbre (October) 1787- mlle Gerard," continues to perplex, since the attribution of the drawing to Fragonard seems certain.
10. Rosenberg in Paris and New York 1987/1988, pp. 557–58.
11. For Séné and Boulard's seating furniture for Madame Elisabeth's château de Montreuil, ordered in 1788, see Pallot 1993, pp. 174–76; my thanks to Joseph Godla and Charlotte Vignon for their assistance.
12. Gady 1994, pp. 357–58, noting that Bergeret acquired the Folie Beaujon furnished, and that the "salon octogone" had a suite of twelve mahogany armchairs. Among the 275 drawings by Fragonard in the Walferdin sale of 12 April 1880, no. 269, "Neuf dessins au crayon noir dans le même cadre," included "Fragonard et la famille Bergeret (no. 1)," and "Folie Beaujon (no. 5)"; no. 273 contained "11 Dessins aux crayons noir et rouge pour la Folie Beaujon et la famille Bergeret." None of these drawings is known today, but reference to them substantiates Fragonard's familiarity with Bergeret's new residence.

24. Jean-Baptiste Greuze
Tournus 1725–1805 Paris
Female Nude Kneeling with Outstretched Arms,
c. 1765–68
Red chalk | 29.2 x 42.2 | Verso, probably by Albert Besnard (1849–1934):

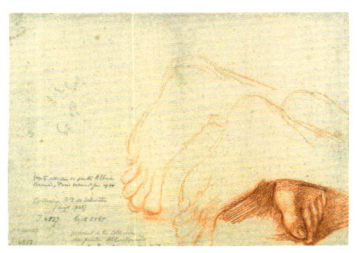

Studies of Bare Feet after Greuze's *La Prière du matin* (Musée Fabre, Montpellier)
Red chalk | Inscriptions: lower left, in the hand of Frits Lugt, in pencil, "Vente collection du peintre Albert / Besnard, Paris 31 Mai – 1er Juin 1934" and "Collection Bon de Schwiter/ (Lugt 1768); Lugt 2565; provient de la Collection du peintre Albert Besnard / …. Juin 1934"; in another hand "J.B. GREUZE"; at the top left, also in pencil, "Aug. Lot 29 / 3 p (?) ; 92 ; [Be]snard (truncated)" | Inv. no. 4837

Provenance: Hippolyte Walferdin (sale, Paris, Drouot, 12–16 April 1880, no. 312); Baron Louis Auguste de Schwiter (1805–1889), Paris (L. 1768; sale, Paris, Drouot, 20–21 April 1883, no. 61, for 88 francs); Albert Besnard (1849–1934), Paris (sale, Paris, Galerie Charpentier, 31 May–1 June 1934, no. 283, repr., to Lugt); Frits Lugt (1884–1970), The Hague and Paris.
Exhibitions: Brussels and Paris 1949; Paris and Amsterdam 1964; Amsterdam 1974; Hartford, San Francisco, and Dijon 1976.
Bibliography: Mauclair 1905, p. 136, repr.; Martin 1908, p. 80. no. 1311; Brussels and Paris 1949, no. 81; Bauër 1959, no. 19; Paris and Amsterdam 1964, pp. 75–76, no. 92, pl. 74; Amsterdam 1974, pp. 53–54, 144, no. 55, repr.; Hartford, San Francisco, and Dijon 1976, p. 131, no. 58, repr.; Raleigh and Birmingham, Ala. 1986, p. 30, under no. 15, fig. 18.

Fig. 24.1
Jean-Baptiste Greuze, *Kneeling Female Nude, Study for "Cimon and Pero: Roman Charity,"* c. 1765–68, red chalk on cream paper, Jeffrey E. Horvitz Collection, Boston, Inv. no. D-F-820

Notes

1. Hartford, San Francisco, and Dijon 1976, p. 138.
2. Ibid, p. 140; for the most recent study of *Septimius Severus Reproaching Caracalla*, 1769 (Musée du Louvre, Paris), see Tournus 2005.
3. "Je voudrais bien peindre une femme toute nue, sans blesser la pudeur"; Diderot 1767/1995, p, 152.
4. Tournus 2005, pp. 24–29.

5. "Il n'épargne ni soins ni dépense pour avoir les modèles qui lui conviennent"; Diderot 1759, 1761, and 1763/1984, p. 238.
6. Munhall's observation, made in Hartford, San Francisco, and Dijon 1976, p. 131; for the fine wash drawing in Dijon, dated by Munhall to c. 1790, see New York and Los Angeles 2002, pp. 263–65.
7. Ibid., pp. 184–85; Hartford, San Francisco, and Dijon 1976, p. 138.
8. See also the Louvre's *Seated Female Nude Leaning Forward*, in New York and Los Angeles 2002, pp. 182–83; not only the proportions but also the coiffures of these models are very similar.
9. Reproduced in New York and Los Angeles 2002, p. 184.

25. Jean-Pierre Louis Laurent Hoüel
Rouen 1735–1813 Paris
View of the Colosseum in Rome, c. 1769
Watercolor and gouache, pen and black ink, over a sketch in black chalk | 64.3 x 47.8
Inv. no. 1999-T.1

Provenance: Private Collection, Paris; Thomas Le Claire, Kunsthandel, Hamburg; Fondation Custodia, Paris, acquired 6 January 1999.
Exhibitions: New York 1998.
Bibliography: New York 1998, no. 24, repr.; Blok 1999, pp. 47–48, pl. 6.

Notes
1. J-P. Hoüel's workshop stock has been in the Frits Lugt collection since 1998. It includes 236 drawings and sketches, among them many animal and figure studies, portraits, genre scenes, and landscapes (but no gouaches).
2. Pinault Sørensen 1996, pp. 501–28.
3. See Paris 1990b. The majority (originally 500 gouaches, 260 of which are still traceable) are in The State Hermitage Museum, Saint Petersburg, and 46 gouaches are in the Musée du Louvre, Paris.
4. See the *View of the Gardens of the Villa d'Este* in the Frits Lugt collection (Pinault Sørensen 1996, p. 507, fig. 8) and *View of the Organ Fountain at the Villa d'Este* in the Prat collection in Paris (New York, Fort Worth, Ottawa 1990, no. 55, repr.).

26. Esprit-Antoine Gibelin
Aix-en-Provence 1739–1813 Aix-en-Provence
Interior of a Sculptor's Atelier with the Borghese Gladiator, c. 1770
Pen and brown ink, brown wash over black chalk, on two pieces of paper, joined horizontally | 23.7 x 18.3 | Inscriptions: verso, in pencil, "A.E. Gibelin"; and in another hand, "280" | Inv. no. 1978-T. 82

Provenance: Private Collection (sale, Paris, Drouot, 11 December 1978, part of no. 48, to Petithorry, for the Fondation Custodia); Fondation Custodia, Paris.
Exhibitions: never before exhibited
Bibliography: no known references

Fig. 26.1
Esprit-Antoine Gibelin, *Study for Interior of a Sculptor's Atelier with the Borghese Gladiator*, c. 1770, pen and ink, pencil, 23.9 x 18.2, Fondation Custodia, Paris, 1978-T.81

Fig. 26.2
Esprit-Antoine Gibelin, *Mythological Scene with Horses*, dated 1770, ink wash, 23.9 x 30.5, Musée du Louvre, Paris.

Notes
1. Drouot Rive Gauche, Paris, 11 December 1978, no. 48, "Ecole Française XVIIIe."
2. The drawing is signed "Spiritis Gibelin invenit, 1770"; see Bukowskis Stockholm, 28 November 2007, no. 574.
3. See the very thorough biographical entry by Alexandre Maral in Saur 1992–2009, vol. 53, pp. 318–21, which, however, does not mention the drawings in the Lugt collection.
4. In Gibelin's pornographic wash drawing, *Roman Bacchanalia with Sergel*, in the Nationalmuseum, Stockholm, done around 1770; see Cederlöf 1979 and Myrone 2005, pp. 174–75.
5. Haskell and Penny 1981, p. 221.

6. For a discussion of the phases of executing marble statuary, with reference to Canova's studio practice, see Honour 1972, pp. 148, 154, and more generally Wittkower 1977, pp. 222–24. See also Francesco Chiaruttini's view of Canova's studio, reproduced in Mellini 1999, p. 299. My thanks to Denise Allen for helping me understand this process.

7. See the entry on Hubert Robert's red-chalk drawing, *Antiquities of the Capitoline Museum* (Musée des Beaux-Arts, Valence), in Paris, Ottawa, and Vienna 1994, pp. 78–79.

8. Haskell and Penny 1981, pp. 103–4.

9. Paris, Ottawa, and Vienna 1994, pp. 46–47.

10. Haskell and Penny 1981, pp. 146–48.

11. Stockholm 1990, pp. 208–9; Sergel's marble copy of the *Apollino* would be installed in the Hall of Mirrors in the Royal Palace of Stockholm by 1782.

12. Diderot and d'Alembert 1751–76, vol. XIV, pp. 841–42, article "Sculpture en Marbre," and *Recueil des Planches*, vol. VIII, plate "H," *L'Opération d'élever un bloc de marbre*, plate "L," *Différentes opérations pour le travail du marbre*.

12. Haskell and Penny 1981, p. 222.

13. Gibelin 1807, pp. 3, 10.

27. Louis-Jacques Durameau
Paris 1733–1796 Versailles
Interior of a Paper Mill, formerly known as *L'Imprimerie secrète*, c. 1770–80
Oil on paper | 33.5 x 22.7 | Inv. no. 1972-T.6

Provenance: Charles Gasc (?–c. 1850), Paris (L. 543 & Suppl.); Edmond (1822–1896) and Jules (1830–1870) de Goncourt, acquired before 1857 for 20 francs (sale, Paris, Drouot, 15–17 February 1897, no. 86, as "attributed to Fragonard," to Hodgkins, for 370 francs); Private Collection of L. B*** (sale, Paris, Drouot, 12 May 1905, p. 11, no. 21, as "attributed to Fragonard," to Bertaux, for 180 francs); Jacques Guérin (sale, Paris, Drouot, 20–21 December 1922, p. 23, no. 75, as "French school, Eighteenth century"); D. David-Weill (sale, Paris, Drouot, 9–10 June 1971, no. 178, as "French school, Eighteenth century," for 5,500 francs); Henri Baderou (1910–1991), Paris; Fondation Custodia, Paris, acquired 19 January 1972.
Exhibitions: Paris 1974; Strasbourg and Tours 2003.
Bibliography: Goncourt/Pety and Galantris 1881/2003, vol. I, p. 78 (as Fragonard); Portalis 1889, p. 303 (as Fragonard); Mireur 1911–12, vol. III, p. 201; Goncourt and Goncourt/Neveux 1859–75/1927, vol. III, p. 430; Wildenstein

1960, p. 31, note 3; Ananoff 1961–70, vol. IV, p. 29, no. 1971; Castelot and Decaux 1970–75, vol. VIII, p. 169, repr.; Paris 1974, p. 10, no. 23, pl. 36 (as Durameau); Sandoz 1980, p. 121, no. F, pl. IX (as attributed to Durameau); Launay 1991, p. 282, no. 81, fig. 131 (as Durameau); Leclair 2001, p. 184, pl. 117 (as attributed to Durameau); Strasbourg and Tours 2003, p. 206, no. 75, repr. (as attributed to Durameau).

Fig. 27.1
Louis-Jacques Durameau, *The Continence of Bayard*, 1776, oil sketch on canvas, 39.5 x 29.0, Musée de Grenoble, MG 828

Notes

1. See the excellent entries in Launay 1991, p. 282, and Leclair 2001, pp. 184–85.

2. Leclair 2001, p. 184; also Jacquot in Strasbourg and Tours 2003, pp. 206–7.

3. Leclair 2001, pp. 46–47, 162; *The Continence of Bayard* was commissioned by the Bâtiments in March 1776 as a cartoon for a Gobelins tapestry.

4. Ibid., pp. 15, 321. Jacques-Philippe Durameau succeeded his father as a copperplate engraver; Jean-Joseph Oger, husband of Durameau's sister, Marie, is listed in documents as "imprimeur en taille douce."

5. First noted in Goncourt/Pety and Galantris 1881/2003, vol. I, p. 78, where the source was not identified and has not since been discovered. For contemporary paintings by Léonard Defrance that do indeed represent the interior of a printing press, see Dehousse, Pacco, and Pauchen 1985, pp. 167–68, nos. 314–16.

6. My thanks to Don Swanson, Chief of Collections Preservation at the Frick Art Reference Library, for his assistance on the history of papermaking. For an excellent introduction to papermaking in eighteenth-century France, see Rosenband 2000, pp. 3–21.

7. "L'ouvrier compositeur est assis devant un tréteau en forme du pupitre et on devine qu'il va disposer les caractères métalliques pour former les lettres de chaque mot"; Leclair 2001, p. 184.

8. Rosenband (2000, p. 10) notes that the *formaires* were "the most highly prized—and highly paid—workers in the industry . . . [who] wandered from mill to mill."

9. Ibid., p. 13.

10. "Papeterie," Diderot and D'Alembert 1751–76, vol. XI, pp. 834–45. See also the clear explanations of the *Encyclopédie*'s illustrations in Diderot and D'Alembert/Gillispie 1751–76/1959, vol. II, pl. 359–67.

11. De Beaumont in New York and Paris 2007, pp. 224–27.

12. "Une fabrique de papier," Baderou's handwritten notes in the curatorial files of the Fondation Custodia.

28. Jean-Michel Moreau, known as Moreau le Jeune
Paris 1741–1814 Paris
Portraits of the Artist's Daughter Asleep, c. 1772
Pen and gray ink, gray wash, over black chalk | 10.2 x 14.9 (each sheet) | Inscriptions: verso of mount at bottom, in lead pencil, "Catherine-Françoise Moreau le j^{ne} fille unique de l'artiste qui / deviendra la femme de Carle Vernet . . . mère d'Horace Vernet" | Inv. nos. 4070A&B

Provenance: Marius Paulme (1863–1928), Paris (L. 1910 & Suppl.; sale, Paris, Galerie Georges Petit, 14 May 1929, no. 176, pl. 119, to Lugt); Frits Lugt (1884–1970), Maartensdijk and Paris.

Exhibitions: Haarlem 1931; Copenhagen 1935; Paris 1951; London 1952; Paris and Amsterdam 1964; Amsterdam 1974.

Bibliography: Haarlem 1931, p. 20, no. 391; Copenhagen 1935, p. 133, no. 451; Paris 1951, no. 93; London 1952, pp. 69–70, no. 111; Rotterdam, Paris, and New York 1958a, p. 63, under no. 66; Rotterdam, Paris, and New York 1958b, under no. 66; Rotterdam, Paris, and New York 1958c, p. 61, under no. 66; Ananoff 1964, p. 55, repr.; Paris and Amsterdam 1964, pp. 103–4, nos. 128, 129, pl. 108; Amsterdam 1974, pp. 64–65, 149, nos. 71a–b, repr.; Hattis 1977, pp. 117, 121, under no. 78, figs. 78a–b; Aaron 1985, pp. 28–29, 102, figs. 12, 13; Zafran in Munger, Zafran, Poulet, et al. 1992, p. 131, under no. 78; Dupuy-Vachey in Paris and Geneva 2006, p. 191, under no. 44, ill. 3, 4.

Notes

1. "Ce double dessin si paternal"; in Goncourt and Goncourt/Neveux 1859–75/1927, vol. III, p. 67, a reference to the related sheet in the Museum of Fine Arts, Boston, which the brothers had owned.
2. "à deux heur de l'aprémidi" (*sic*); Biais 1892, p. 95.
3. Mahérault 1880, p. x; Delaroche-Vernet 1907, pp. 5–7. Cathérine-Françoise died in June 1821 and is listed in the family genealogy as an engraver.

4. Munger, Zafran, Poulet, et al. 1992, pp. 129–31; Launay 1991, p. 377.

5. Moreau would make two sketches of Fanny as a married woman in his notebook in the Louvre; see Marcel 1914, vol. II, pp. 22, 25. Two other portrait drawings supposedly of Catherine-Françoise are attributed to Moreau, the *Portrait of the Artist's Daughter* in the British Museum, London (1954, 1009.1), in trois crayons, and the *Portrait of the Artist's Daughter* in the Achenbach Foundation for Graphic Arts, Fine Arts Museums of San Francisco (1967.17.74), in black and white chalks. The handling of these sheets has little in common with the wash drawings in Boston and Paris.

6. Dayot 1925, pp. 33–36.

7. Moureau 1893, pp. 10–11.

8. Denon to Montalivet, 10 April 1815, in Dupuy, Le Masne de Chermont, and Williamson 1999, vol. II, p. 1,155, letter 3428.

9. See Dupuy-Vachey's excellent entry on Jean-Baptiste Delafosse's *Portrait of Marie Nicole Delafosse* in the collection of Jean Bonna, in Paris and Geneva 2006, pp. 188–91, no. 44.

10. Nicolas Ponce's engraving of *L'Innocence sous la garde de la fidélité* is illustrated in Sims Reed Ltd., London, *Prints and Printmakers*, Summer 2003, no. 201.

11. See the classic article, Duncan 1973.

12. Moureau 1893, p. 88; Bocher 1882, p. 514; Moreau provided thirty-one drawings for the edition of Rousseau's collected works published in London in 1774.

13. "Ma petite fille né [*sic*] 14 février 1770 . . . Noury au Grand Besson, proche Paris"; Biais 1892, p. 95.

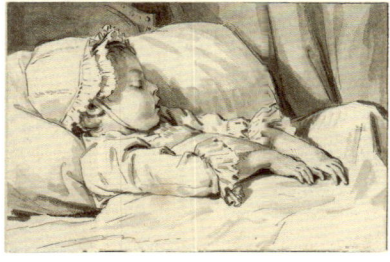  

Fig. 28.1
Jean Michel Moreau, known as Moreau le Jeune, *The Artist's Daughter Asleep (facing right)*, c. 1772, pen and black ink and wash over charcoal, 10.3 x 13.5, Museum of Fine Arts, Boston, Bequest of Forsyth Wickes—The Forsyth Wickes Collection, 65.2592

Fig. 28.2
Jean Michel Moreau, known as Moreau le Jeune, *The Artist's Daughter Asleep (facing left)*, c. 1772, pen and black ink and wash over charcoal, 10.2 x 15.1, Museum of Fine Arts, Boston, Bequest of Forsyth Wickes—The Forsyth Wickes Collection, 65.2593

Fig. 28.3
Nicolas Ponce, after Bounieu, *Innocence Watched over by Fidelity*, engraving, 25.0 x 30.5, Grosvenor Prints, London.

29. François-André Vincent
Paris 1746–1816 Paris
Studies of Cats and a Donkey, dated 1772
Red and black chalk | 47.7 x 34.7 (six joined sheets) | Inscriptions: at bottom left, signed in pen and brown ink, "Vincent à Rome 1772."; verso, in pencil, "4a / 11 Avril 1873 / Vendredi St Sap . . ." | Inv. no. 1974-T.60

Provenance: Henri Baderou (1910–1991), Paris; Fondation Custodia, Paris, acquired 3 June 1974.
Exhibitions: Besançon 1992.
Bibliography: Gelder 1976, p. 95, fig. 16; Foucart-Walter and Rosenberg 1987, p. 37, repr. (detail); Cuzin 1988, p. 18, no. 8, repr.; Besançon 1992, p. 59, no. 26, repr.

Notes

1. Baderou had assisted Lugt on his catalogue of Dutch drawings in the École des Beaux-Arts, "pendant les dernières années d'avant-guerre"; see Lugt 1950, p. x.
2. The Donation Suzanne et Henri Baderou, consisted of more than 4,000 drawings and 300 paintings; see Avril 1980.
3. The form of the signature, more elaborate than those of the 1770s, is similar to that on the *Head of a Young Woman*, 1782 (Albertina, Vienna); see Cuzin 1988, no. 37. Vincent used the same composite approach in his *Sheet of Studies for Aria and Poetus* 1784 (Private Collection, Paris), comprising nine separate sheets mounted together by the artist; see ibid., no. 42.
4. Cuzin 1983 and Cuzin 1988, pp. 5–7, nos. 1–28, remain the standard accounts.
5. My thanks to Dr. Thomas de Vincentis of The Country Vet for his assistance.
6. Buffon's memorable chapter in the sixth volume of his *Histoire naturelle* opens, "Le chat est un domestique infidèle qu'on ne garde que par nécessité, pour l'opposer à un autre ennemi domestique encore plus incommode"; Buffon 1749–67, vol. VI, p. 3.
7. "La forme du corps et le tempérament sont d'accord avec le naturel, le chat est joli, léger, adroit, propre et voluptueux"; ibid., p. 4.
8. Foucart-Walter and Rosenberg 1987, p. 37.
9. Besançon 1992, pp. 50–55.
10. "Une manière d'ombrer au crayon rouge . . . qui est . . . spirituelle, nette, propre et douce, de beaucoup d'effet"; Chaussard 1806, p. 110. This subtle appreciation of Vincent's red-chalk manner appeared in Chaussard's detailed and eulogizing obituary in *Le Pausanias français ou Description du Salon de 1806*.

Fig. 29.1
François-André Vincent, *Portrait of Diane, Greyhound of Bergeret de Grancourt*, 1774, oil on canvas, 61.0 x 73.5, Musée des Beaux-Arts et d'Archéologie, Besançon, Inv. no. 991.6.1

30. François-André Vincent
Paris 1746–1816 Paris
Artists in a Landscape, near Tivoli, dated 1773
Black chalk and graphite | 26.7 x 40.5 | Inscriptions: At the bottom left, signed in pen and brown ink, "vincent.f.Tivoly.1773." | Inv. no. 1974-T.23

Provenance: Charles Gasc (? – c. 1850), Paris (L. 543 & Suppl.); Private Collection (sale, Paris, Drouot, 7 November 1973, no. 131, repr., to Leroux); Jacques Petithory (1929–1992), Paris; Fondation Custodia, Paris, acquired 15 November 1973.
Exhibitions: Amsterdam 1974; Paris, Institut Néerlandais, 1980, *Le Paysage évoqué par la plume et le pinceau* (no catalogue); Besançon 1992; Paris 1994b.
Bibliography: Amsterdam 1974, pp. 95, 162, no. 116, repr.; Méjanès 1976, p. 402–3, fig. 15 (dated 1775); London 1977, p. 96, under no. 127; Washington 1978, p. 155, fig. 10; Cuzin 1983, p. 117; Cuzin 1988, p. 17, no. 6, repr.; Rome 1990, p. 247, under no. 174; Galassi 1991, p. 23, fig. 19 (dated 1775); Besançon 1992, p. 63, no. 29, repr.; Paris 1994b, pp. 104–5, no. 46, repr.; Montpellier 1996, p. 25, repr. (dated 1775); Galassi 1998, pp. 403, 416, fig. 9 (dated 1775).

Notes
1. Cuzin in Paris 1994b, p. 104.
2. Méjanès 1976, pp. 402–3, identified the two artists as Jean-Benoit Suvée (1743–1807) and Louis Chaÿs (c. 1740–1811), both of whom made landscape drawings in black chalk. Since Chaÿs was not a pensionnaire at the Palazzo Mancini, more promising candidates for the second figure would be Jean-Simon Berthélemy (1743–1811) and Pierre-Adrien Pâris (1745–1819), who, along with Suvée, were classmates of Vincent's in Rome.
3. Cuzin in Paris 1994b, p. 104.
4. Galassi 1991, p. 23.

5. See Cuzin 1980; Cuzin 1988, pp. 5–8.

6. Korchane in Orléans and Vevey 2006, pp. 24–25.

7. See Holmes in New York 1999, pp. 160–61; and Grasselli in New York and Washington 2007, pp. 156–57.

8. Carlson in Washington 1978, p. 155.

9. First "corrected" in Méjanès 1976, p. 402, the later date was also given to the drawing in Carlson in Washington 1978, p. 155, Rome 1990, p. 247, and Galassi 1991, p. 23.

10. In addition to the works cited above, there is the *View of an Italian Park*, c. 1774 (National Gallery of Art, Washington, D.C.), formerly attributed to Fragonard; see Cuzin 1988, no. 18; *The Young Man at the Villa Doria*, 1774 (Musée des Beaux-Arts, Rouen), see Washington, New York, Minneapolis, and Malibu 1981, pp. 92, 155, no. 118, pl. 81; *View of Steps Leading to the Villa Doria Pamphili*, Sotheby's, New York, 12 January 1994, no. 137, repr.; and *Classical Statue in a Niche*, 1774 (Private Collection), Cambridge, Mass., Malibu, Montreal, and New York 1980, p. 160.

11. "On n'informe que le Sr. Vincent . . . est fort incommodé de la chaleur et que ses parents désireroient qu'il revînt en France avant l'été"; d'Angiviller to Natoire, 18 May 1775, Montaiglon and Guiffrey 1887–1908, vol. XIII, p. 64.

12. "Il pourroit profiter du temps que lui reste en étudiant dans des églises et dans des palais qui sont frais en la saison de la chaleur extérieure"; undated memorandum, c. August 1775, ibid., p. 117.

13. "Le sr Vincent a fait quelques portraits . . . d'un très bon goût; il me paroit que ce sera la partie où il voudra le plus s'occuper"; Natoire to d'Angiviller, 17 May 1775, ibid., p. 63.

Fig. 30.1
François-André Vincent, *Artist Sketching in the Farnese Gardens*, 1773, red chalk, 27.3 x 39.2, Musée des Beaux-Arts d'Orléans, Inv. no. 1141

Fig. 30.2
François-André Vincent, *View of the Gardens of the Villa Negroni*, 1773, black chalk heightened with white, on tan paper, 34.1 x 44.4, Private Collection

31. Jacques-Louis David
Paris 1746–1825 Brussels
View across the Tiber with the Temple of Vesta, 1775–80
Gray ink and gray wash over black chalk on two sheets of paper | 10.5 x 28.3 (larger sheet 10.5 x 21.2; smaller sheet 10.3 x 7.1; covered width: 3.7) | Verso, *Sketch of Buildings*, graphite | Inscriptions: bottom left in black ink, "le Bas du mont palatin" | Marks: initials in pen and brown ink of Jules David, *JD.* (L. 1437) at bottom left and Eugène David, *ED* (L. 839) at bottom right; verso, left edge, touches of gray ink | Inv. no. 2006-T.6

Provenance: Studio of Jacques-Louis David (1746–1825), the artist, recorded in his postmortem inventory, 25 February 1826, part of nos. 19–27 (first sale of the artist's estate, Paris, 17 April 1826, part of no. 66, not sold); Mme David, his wife, recorded in her postmortem inventory, 27 June 1826, no. 19 (second sale of the artist's estate, Paris, 11 March 1835, part of no. 16); Galerie Terrades, Paris, at the Salon du Dessin 2006; Fondation Custodia, Paris, acquired 21 March 2006.
Exhibitions: Paris 2006.
Bibliography: Paris 2006, p. 62, repr.

Fig. 31.1
Jacques-Louis David, *View of Rome with the Tower of Milizie and the Church of San Pietro in Vincoli*, 1775–80, gray wash over black chalk, 15.5 x 21.1, Nationalmuseum, Stockholm, NMH 82/1969

Notes

1. "À peine fus-je à parme que voyant les ouvrages du Corrège je me trouvait déjà ébranlé, à bologne je commençai à faire des tristes reflections [*sic*], à florence, je fus convaincu mais à rome, je fus honteux de mon ignorance…"; Rome 1981, p. 64; also cited in Galerie Terrades 2006.
2. After David's death, his heirs organized the drawings into twelve albums for the sale of the contents of his studio in 1826. Two of these albums have since disappeared. According to Pierre Rosenberg, the Lugt sheet was originally part of album no. 2, one of the two albums that are missing today

(Galerie Terrades 2006). On the twelve Roman albums of David, see Rosenberg and Prat 2002, pp. 391–407.
3. Ibid., p. 495
4. These monuments are identified in Galerie Terrades 2006.

32. Pierre-Paul Prud'hon
Cluny 1758–1823 Paris
The Cellist, half-length, three-quarter back view, turned toward the left, 1777–78
Pen and black ink, gray wash over graphite; framing lines in pen and gray ink and brown ink | 28.2 x 43.6 | Verso, on mount, preliminary sketch of cellist in graphite | Inscriptions: bottom left of mount, in pencil, "13-21/ 1019"; bottom right, "3" | Inv. no. 2004-T.35

Provenance: Jean-Baptiste-Anne-Geneviève Gagnaire, Baron de Joursanvault, Beaune, by bequest from the artist; M. Tainturier; Mme Tainturier; Dr. Roux; Alexandre Dumas fils (1824–1895) (sale, Paris, Galerie Georges Petit, 2–3 March 1896, no. 114, to Anatole France, for 580 francs); Anatole-François Thibault, called Anatole France (1844–1924), Paris and Saint-Cyr-sur-Loire; Private Collection; Galerie *Les Autographes*, Paris; Fondation Custodia, Paris, acquired 23 November 2004.
Exhibitions: Paris 1874.
Bibliography: Paris 1874, p. 126, no. 416; Goncourt 1876, p. 267; Guiffrey 1924, p. 384, no. 1019.

Fig. 32.1
Pierre-Paul Prud'hon, *Seated Cellist, front view (curate of baron de Joursanvault)*, 1777–78, pen and black ink, gray wash over graphite, 27.8 x 21.4, Fondation Custodia, Paris, Inv. no. 2004-T.37

Notes
1. Only ten years older than Prud'hon, the baron had been a member of the king's light cavalry and had since retreated to his hôtel in Beaune and his château in Jours-en-Vaux in the nearby countryside. For Prud'hon's relationship with his patron, see Guffey 2001, pp. 21–30.

2. Ibid., p. 30. The instrument was previously identified as a bass viol; however, a bass viol has six strings, frets, and a perfectly flat back. The cello, as illustrated in the Lugt drawing, has four strings, a smooth fingerboard, and a slightly convex back. The cello is the bass instrument of the violin family. Laveissière 2005, p. 18, note 2, points out this mistake.

3. Guiffrey 1924, pp. 383–85, lists and describes the twelve drawings; however, he erroneously identifies M. de Bessey as the baron and the baron as the son of the baron de Joursanvault. Four of the drawings depict details of the left arm and left hand on the fingerboard and of the right hand holding the bow. Nine of the twelve drawings are owned by the Fondation Custodia.

4. There has been some confusion as to which catalogue number in Guiffrey 1924 corresponds to which drawing in this series; however, no. 1018 is the only drawing in which the figure's hair is described as tied back in a bag and must therefore be matched with the present drawing.

5. Paris and New York 1998, p. 36.

6. Guffey 2001, p. 21.

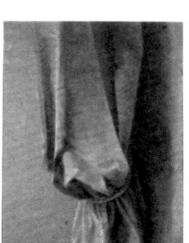

33. Pierre-Paul Prud'hon
Cluny 1758–1823 Paris
Study for a Curtain, c.1806
Black chalk, stumped, heightened with white chalk on blue paper (slightly discolored) | 30.2 x 22.8 | Inscriptions: verso, bottom right in pencil, "6829" | Stamps: bottom right in red ink, monogram of Charles-Boulanger de Boisfremont (L. 353) | Inv. no. 1971-T.38

Provenance: Pierre-Paul Prud'hon (1758–1823), the artist; Charles-Boulanger de Boisfremont (1773–1838), Paris, bequest of the artist in his will (L. 353); Mme Émilie Power, née de Boisfremont, his daughter, by inheritance (sale, Paris, Galerie Georges Petit, 15–16 April 1864, no. 203, for 18 francs); Lucien Huteau (1878–1975), Paris (sale, Paris, Drouot, 5 May 1971, no. 56, to the Fondation Custodia); Fondation Custodia, Paris.
Exhibitions: Paris 1974.
Bibliography: Guiffrey 1924, p. 466, no. 1294; Paris 1974, p. 25, no. 64, pl. 37; Laveissière 1997, pp. 52–53, repr.; Paris 1997a, p. 566, under no. 2068; Bibliothèque de l'Image 2002, p. 78.

Notes
1. Mayer had previously studied with Joseph-Benoit Suvée and had been exhibiting at the Salon since 1796. See Weston 1980, pp. 15–17.

2. On their working process, see Guffey 2001, pp 180–81.
3. For an illustration, see Paris and New York 1998, p. 182, fig. 121a.
4. Guffey 2001, p. 209. For the study of the head, see Paris and New York 1998, p. 182, no. 121.

Fig. 33.1
Print after Marie-Françoise Constance Mayer-Lemartinière, *Full-length Portrait of Madame B. Putting on Her Earrings* (also known as *La Toilette*), 1806, oil on canvas, 81.0 x 64.0, Location unknown

Fig. 33.2
Pierre-Paul Prud'hon, *Study of Drapery* (for the painting of Constance Mayer, *La Toilette*), c. 1806, black and white chalk stumped on blue paper, 36.8 x 28.2, Musée du Louvre, Paris, RF 11696

34. Pierre-Paul Prud'hon
Cluny 1758–1823 Paris
Queen Hortense and Her Two Children in a Park, c. 1811
Black chalk, stumped, heightened with white chalk on blue paper, largely faded; black chalk framing lines | Image: 30.3 x 20.5; sheet: 32.7 x 22.8 | Verso, traces of a study of drapery in black chalk | Stamps: bottom left in red ink, monogram of Charles-Boulanger de Boisfremont (L. 353) | Inv. no. 2008-T.16

Provenance: Pierre-Paul Prud'hon (1758–1823), the artist; Charles-Boulanger de Boisfremont (1773–1838), Paris, bequest of the artist in his will (L. 353); Mme Power, née de Boisfremont, his daughter (sale, Paris, Galerie Georges Petit, 15–16 April 1864, no. 8, for 400 francs; Laurent Laperlier (sale, Paris, Drouot, 17–18 February 1879, no. 99, to Mme Lacour, for 1100 francs); Mme Lacour; Léon Ferté (1848–1939), Paris; Private Col-

lection, Paris (sale, Paris, Artcurial, 9 April 2008, no. 138, to de Bayser for the Fondation Custodia); Fondation Custodia, Paris.
Exhibitions: Paris 1874; Paris 1922.
Bibliography: Paris 1874, p. 48, no. 111; Goncourt 1876, p. 68; Burty 1879, p. 150, repr.; Paris 1922, p. 29, no. 149; Guiffrey 1924, p. 172, no. 459; Slayman 1970, p. 126, pl. 106.

Fig. 34.1
Pierre-Paul Prud'hon, *Queen Hortense and Her Children*, c. 1811, black chalk, stumped, heightened with white chalk on blue paper, 31.4 x 21.8, Musée Bonnat, Bayonne, NI 1135

Fig. 34.2
Leonardo da Vinci, *The Virgin and Child with Saint Anne and Saint John the Baptist*, c. 1499–1500, black chalk with touches of white chalk on brownish paper, mounted on canvas on tinted paper, 141.5 x 105.6, Purchased with a special grant and contributions from The Art Fund, the Pilgrim Trust, and through a public appeal organized by The Art Fund, 1962, National Gallery, London, NG 6337

Notes

1. Musée du Louvre, RF 270. A study for the figure of Josephine seated in profile is held by the Fondation Custodia (Inv. no. 2985).
2. Hortense was the daughter of Josephine by General Alexandre de Beauharnais. After de Beauharnais's death, Josephine married Napoleon Bonaparte in 1796. In 1802 the nineteen-year-old Hortense married Napoleon's brother Louis Bonaparte, whom the emperor placed on the throne of Holland in 1806. Louis abdicated four years later, and Queen Hortense, who had spent little time in Holland, remained in France with her sons. Their first son, born in 1802, died at age five. Napoleon-Louis and Charles-Louis-Napoleon were born in 1804 and 1808, respectively.
3. Paris 1979a, p. 85. He used the setting in yet another unrelated work of the same year, a preparatory drawing for *Venus and Adonis* commissioned by Josephine's successor, Marie-Louise of Austria, who married Napoleon in 1810. Musée du Louvre, Paris, RF 29920.

4. Guiffrey 1924, nos. 457–62
5. Cited in Paris and New York 1998, p. 51.
6. "... de la plus large facture et avec les audaces et les brutalités dans le noir que, seuls, ont les grands maîtres"; Goncourt 1876, p. 68.

35. Louis-Jean Desprez
Auxerre 1743–1804 Stockholm
The Slaves of Vedius Pollio Thrown Alive to the Moray Eels, 1777–79
Pen and gray ink, watercolor over traces of black chalk | 22.2 x 15.1 | Inscriptions: verso at center in graphite, "2"; on the mount from the Paignon Dijonval collection, at top, in graphite, "O abla guld" | Watermark: [J.] Honig Zoonen | Inv. no. 1986-T.46

Provenance: M. Paignon Dijonval (1708–1792), Paris; vicomte Charles-Gilbert Morel de Vindé (1759–1842), his grandson, Paris (cf. L. 2520); P. P. Steven, Dover; Gösta Stenman (1888–1947), Stockholm (sale, London, Christie's, 11–13 December 1985, no. 325, repr., as Claude-Louis Châtelet, to Cailleux); Galerie Cailleux, Paris; Fondation Custodia, Paris, acquired 1 July 1986.
Exhibitions: Paris and Geneva 1986; Paris 1994b.
Bibliography: Bénard 1810, p. 170, part of no. 4058; Conisbee 1986, p. 533, fig. 80; Paris and Geneva 1986, no. 18, repr; Roland Michel in Paris 1994b, pp. 100–101, no. 44, repr.; Dupuy-Vachey 2009, pp. 17, 23, 59, 119, 146, repr.

Notes
1. This entry is based on Marie-Anne Dupuy-Vachey's superb scholarship in Dupuy-Vachey 2009.
2. Conisbee 1986, p. 533.
3. Dio/Cary 1914–27, vol. II, book XXIII, p. 341.
4. Roland Michel (in Paris 1994b, p. 100) proposed Piranesi's engraving of the Temple of Clitumnus, Spoleto, in the *Antichità romane*, as a possible source for Desprez's imaginary Villa Pausilypon; see Bettagno 1978, no. 123.
5. See Bruno Chenique's "biochronologie" in Paris 1994b, pp. 212–14.
6. Dupuy-Vachey 2009, pp. 9–14. On the extraordinarily complicated history of this publication, see the summary in Griffiths 2004, pp. 92–97.
7. This sheet was attributed to Châtelet when it appeared at auction at Christie's, London, 11 December 1985, p. 192, no. 325; the attribution to

Fig. 35.1
Louis-Jean Desprez, *Artists Drawing Vedius Pollio's Former Breeding Grounds*, 1777–79, black chalk, pen and brown ink, gray and black wash, and watercolor, 22.4 x 15.0, Allen Memorial Art Museum, Oberlin College, Ohio; Charles F. Olney Fund, 1963.5

Fig. 35.2
Louis-Jean Desprez, *The Victims of Tiberius at Capri*, 1784, pencil, pen and brown ink, brown wash, 34.3 x 23.0, Nationalmuseum, Stockholm, NMH 51/1874:48

Desprez was made by Roland Michel in Paris and Geneva 1986, no. 18.

8. Desprez is first noted among the travelers in Pozzuoli on 26 November 1777; Dupuy-Vachey 2009, p. 27.

9. Ibid., p. 119, note 47; the drawing is now in the Kungliga Akademien för de fria Konsterna, Stockholm (inv. no. P 94:4); see Lamers 1995, pp. 206–7.

10. "Nous avions laissé en passant Després sur un rocher dans la mer . . . Lorsque nous vînmes le prendre, il étoit assailli des vagues qui sembloient lui disputer le portrait des lieux qu'elles chérissent et caressent sans cesse"; Denon, *Voyage d'Italie*, Dupuy-Vachey 2009, p. 58.

11. "L'indigne ami d'Auguste . . . les piscines, ou viviers de Pollion, qui existent encore dans leur entier"; ibid.

12. "Et un troisième de la piscine rétablie comme au tems de Vidius, avec l'odieux et inhumain usage qu'il en faisoit"; ibid., p. 59. Desprez's *Artists Drawing Vedius Pollio's Former Breeding Grounds* in the Allen Memorial Art Museum, Oberlin College, Ohio, formerly catalogued as by Châtelet, has been reattributed to Desprez in Dupuy-Vachey 2009, pp. 119, 145. The author came to a similar assessment on visiting the museum's print room in October 2008, and thanks Andrea Derstine for showing him the drawing and alerting him to Dupuy-Vachey's reattribution.

13. "Cet home . . . les engrassoit du sang et de la chair des Esclaves qu'il faisoit jetter vivants dans les Piscines pour les moindres fautes"; Saint-Non 1781–86, vol. II, p. 163.

14. Roland Michel in Paris 1994b, p. 100, where the sheet was entitled "Scène de Supplice."

15. For Desprez's preparatory pen and wash drawing in the Nationalmuseum, Stockholm (inv. no. 51/1874:48), see the entry by Régis Michel in Paris 1994c, pp. 65–70. Nothing came of the commission, proposed in August 1784, since d'Angiviller found the subject "trop atroce."

16. Dupuy-Vachey 2009, pp. 23, 119.
17. "Le sr. Desprez . . . totalement occupé depuis son retour de Sicile à terminer les desseins des vues qui doivent server à l'ouvrage de M. Laborde, qu'il n'avoit qu'esquissé sur le lieu"; Vien to d'Angiviller, 7 April 1779, in Montaiglon and Guiffrey 1887–1908, vol. XIII, pp. 416–17.

36. Nicolas Lavreince
Stockholm 1737–1807 Stockholm
The Stolen Kiss, c. 1785–90
Pen and black and brown ink, brown and gray wash, heightened with white gouache | 26.1 x 31.5 |
Inv. no. 7492

Provenance: Private Collection (sale, London, Sotheby's, 10 May 1961, no. 57, as *The Amorous Painter*, to Lugt, for £300); Frits Lugt (1884–1970), Paris (L. 1028).
Exhibitions: Amsterdam 1974.
Bibliography: Amsterdam 1974, pp. 58–59, 146, no. 63, repr.; Aaron 1985, p. 28, fig. 11.

Fig. 36.1
Nicolas Lavreince, *The Stolen Kiss*, c. 1780, watercolor and gouache, 6.0 diameter, Nationalmuseum, Stockholm, NMB 724

Fig. 36.2
Jean-Honoré Fragonard, *The Stolen Kiss*, c. 1788, oil on canvas, 45.0 x 55.0, The State Hermitage Museum, Saint Petersburg, GE-1300

Notes
1. For an introduction to the topic, see the excellent article by Smentek 2007; Carlson and Ittmann in Baltimore, Boston, and Minneapolis 1984 remains the standard reference.
2. For examples of their collaboration, see Washington 2003, pp. 116–18, 134.
3. Olausson and Sjöholm 2001, vol. I, p. 379.

4. The alternating sections of the parquet floor in Lavreince's drawing are very close to the example in the great drawing room of the château de Montgeoffroy, Mazé, which follows a design illustrated in André-Jacob Roubo's *L'Art du menuisier*; see Verlet 1967, p. 107. For references to the types of furniture and dress illustrated in Lavreince's *Stolen Kiss*, it is a pleasure to acknowledge Grace Chuang's assistance.

5. For an example of such a worktable, see the *Table de salon ovale en acajou avec tablette d'entrejambe* by Joseph Canabas, in Kjellberg 2002, pp. 158, 164.

6. A similar model is discussed in ibid., pp. 285–86; see, for example, Jean-Baptiste Demay's *Chaise à la Reine*.

7. Ibid., pp. 45–46, for Noel Baudin's *Bergère Louis XVI à dossier médaillon*.

8. Ribeiro 2002, p. 207.

9. Ribeiro 1988, pp. 21, 43. The male and female protagonists of Lavreince's *Gallant Conversation*, c. 1785, in The Wallace Collection, London, wear similar costumes. The women's hairstyles and garments are also comparable to those shown in Adélaide Labille-Guiard's *Self-Portrait with Two Students*, 1785 (The Metropolitan Museum of Art, New York), an authentic portrait of a woman artist in her studio; see Auricchio 2009, pp. 40–42.

10. Rosenberg in Paris and New York 1988, pp. 575–77; Cuzin (1987, p. 224) dates the work to the early 1780s.

37. Joseph Bidauld
Carpentras 1758–1846 Montmorency
View in Rome, c. 1785–90
Watercolor, graphite underdrawing and framing lines | 19.2 x 25.4 | Inv. no. 1983-T.4

Provenance: Stoppenbach & Delestre, London; Fondation Custodia, Paris, acquired 10 March 1983.
Exhibitions: London 1982.
Bibliography: London 1982, no. 2, repr.

Notes

1. He counted among his patrons Joseph Bonaparte; Caroline Murat, queen of Naples; Empress Josephine; and Hortense Bonaparte, queen of Holland. He was also the first landscape painter admitted to the Académie des Beaux-Arts. For a biographical sketch of Bidauld, see Carpentras, Angers, and Arras 1978.

2. This practice would be famously codified by Bidauld's colleague Pierre-Henri de Valenciennes in his treatise of 1800, *Eléments de perspective pratique*. Valenciennes 1800/1973.

3. "avait poussé la passion du paysage jusqu'à ce point d'aller s'établir des mois entiers devant un site . . . de peindre sur place tout le jour . . . en dépit des accidents même de la temperature, et de ne quitter son poste qu'après avoir fini son tableau"; cited in Paris and Mantua 2001, p. 124.
4. "Bidauld! . . . il fut bien un maître et parfois des plus exquis. Telle de ses petites toiles est d'un chef-d'oeuvre . . . Je l'admire, moi, et je le respecte. . . . " Cited in ibid. At the time, Bidauld was considered a conservative academician for his role as a member of the Salon jury in rejecting the work of the young Romantic and naturalist artists Théodore Rousseau and Paul Huet (cats. 48 and 59).

38. Louis-Roland Trinquesse
Bourgogne c. 1746–c. 1800
Portrait of a Man Looking Right, dated 12 October 1797
Red chalk | 23.8 diameter
Inscriptions: at the bottom, signed in red chalk, "desine par Trinquesse. ce 12 .obre 1797."; on the mount, at bottom, in black chalk, "76"; verso, on the mount, in pen and brown ink, "149", and in lead pencil, "95" and "77" (encircled) | Inv. no. 1979-T.14

Provenance: M. X… (sale, Paris, Drouot, 10–11 May 1979, no. 76, to Bruno de Bayser, for the Fondation Custodia); Fondation Custodia, Paris.
Exhibitions: never before exhibited
Bibliography: no known references

Fig. 38.1
Louis-Roland Trinquesse, *Portrait of a Man in a Hat*, 1798, red chalk, Musée du Louvre, Paris, RF 52763

Notes

1. See the articles by Cailleux 1974 and Wilhelm 1974; for his genre painting, Ottawa, Washington, and Berlin 2003, pp. 324–27.
2. For a male académie by him, dated 1770 and inscribed "Figures des Medailles/Quartier de Avril 1770," see Christie's, Paris, 17 March 2005, no. 324.
3. Wilhelm 1974, pp. 55, 58.
4. Duplessis 1857, vol. II, p. 216 (29 August 1789). The engraver Jean-Georges Wille, whom Trinquesse had visited as part of the admission process, noted "qu'il avoit déjà été refusé deux fois."
5. This is the red-chalk *Portrait of a Man in a Hat*, acquired by the Louvre in 2003 and illustrated in fig. 38.1 in this entry, and inscribed "ce 8 fructidor an 6 de la R.," (25 August 1798).
6. The relationship with Bouchardon was suggested by Te Rijdt in Amsterdam and Paris 2003, p. 233. Trinquesse's more formal portrait roundels may also be compared to the cast terracotta medallions of Jean-Baptiste Nini (1717–1786).
7. Paris 1946, p. 48, no. 65; Wilhelm 1974, p. 61, fig. 17.
8. A habit he shared with Gabriel de Saint-Aubin, as noted in Cailleux 1974, p. vi.
9. Wilhelm 1974, pp. 61–64; see the entries on Cochin's portraits of Mariette and Turgot, cats. 15, 16.
10. See, for example, the dashing portrait of the history painter Pierre Guérin (1774–1833), aged twenty-three, in the Musée Carnavalet; see Bottineau 1989, p. 300.
11. As an example, see the portrait of François Reidy de Lagrange, captain of the Gendarmerie, in The Metropolitan Museum of Art, New York; Stein and Holmes in New York 1999a, pp. 220–21.
12. Paris 1946, p. 48, no. 67, *Portrait de l'épouse de Claude-Pierre Clavelin*, "dsiné [sic] par L. R. Trinquesse ce 13 Obre 1797," and no. 68, *Portrait de Claude-Pierre Clavelin*, "desiné par L. R. Trinquesse ce 6 novembre 1797." The *Portrait of Claude-Pierre Clavelin* is also reproduced in Wilhelm 1974, p. 60, fig. 15.
13. Laurent 1907, p. 12, noting that Dom Clavelin was born in 1736, and that he re-entered secular life after the suppression of the monasteries.

39. Jean-Auguste-Dominique Ingres
Montauban 1780–1867 Paris
Medallion Portrait of Julie Forestier, 1806
Graphite pencil, heightened with watercolor and white gouache on transfer paper, mounted on board; oval framing lines in graphite | 9.0 x 7.2 | Inscriptions: at lower right, in graphite pencil: *J.I.* [?] | Inv. no. 2004-T.3

Provenance: Anonymous collection (sale, Senlis, De Muizon-Le Coënt, 9 November 1999, no catalogue); Eric Turquin S.A., Paris; Fondation Custodia, Paris, acquired 18 October 2004.
Exhibitions: Paris, Fondation Custodia, 2005, *Acquisitions 2000–2004* (no catalogue).
Bibliography: Bertin 2001, p. 28 , no. 4a, repr., with image reversed.

Fig. 39.1
Jean-Auguste-Dominique Ingres, *The Forestier Family*, 1806, graphite, 23.5 x 32.2, Musée du Louvre, Paris, RF 1450

Notes

Special thanks are due to Caitlin Henningsen, The Frick Collection, for her substantive contributions to this entry.

1. Anne-Julie Forestier was born in 1782, the daughter of a parliamentary lawyer. She made her debut at the Salon in 1804 as a pupil of a minor master, Jean-Baptiste Debret, and of Jacques-Louis David. For biographical information, see New York 1999b, p. 74.

2. The Louvre drawing is inscribed "Ingres fecit 1806" (Prat 2004, illus. no. 4, p. 77). Two other versions can be found in the Musée de Montaubun (Vigne 1995, illus. no. 2653, p. 474) and the Fogg Art Museum, Cambridge, Mass. (Cohn and Siegfried 1980, illus. no. 33, p. 98). For the relationship between these works and the Louvre prototype, see Naef 1977, pp. 136–43, and Cohn and Siegfried 1980, p. 98.

3. The process is described by Marjorie Shelley in a conservation report for Hubert Duchemein, 24 April 2001, Fondation Custodia files.

4. Stijn Alsteens identified these differences. Following this drawing's acquisition by the Fondation Custodia, he researched its relationship to the Louvre drawing.

5. Lapauze 1910, p. 38. Ingres continues: "J'ai relu cent fois cette charmante écriture au crayon; je vais continuellement de [votre] lettre au portrait. Il me semble vous voir, je vous parle, mais, hélas! Vous ne me répondez pas." He refers to the portrait again on 20 February 1807: "My sweet Julie, I would like to console you the best I can. Separated from you by four hundred leagues and more, dear Julie, you promise me to be a bit more calm, your charming portrait tells me a sweet 'yes', I am crazy about it, it is my most beautiful work." ("ma bonne Julie, je voudrais vous consoler, et le fais du mieux que je peux. Éloigné de vous de quatre cent et plus de lieus [*sic*], vous me promettez d'être un peu plus calme, votre charmant portrait

me dit un joli 'oui' pour vous, j'en suis fou, c'est mon plus bel ouvrage.") Lapauze 1910, p. 112. Before the present drawing was known, scholars considered the Louvre sheet to be the portrait Ingres mentions in these remarks (Cohn and Siegfried 1980, p. 98). It now appears more likely that this individual portrait of Julie is the image to which Ingres refers. This would date the Fondation Custodia drawing to 1806, after the creation of the Louvre work and before October 1806.

6. New York 1999b, p. 74.
7. Ibid., pp. 547–48.
8. Lapauze 1910, p. 197. See also Montauban 1999, pp. 101–2.

40. Théodore Géricault
Rouen 1791–1824 Paris
Forest with Two Figures and a Cow, c. 1813–14
Graphite | 12.7 x 20.4 | Inscriptions: verso, upside down, in graphite, "Bas Breau 10 mai" | Stamps: bottom left in black ink, Coutan-Hauguet-Schubert-L.464); bottom right in blue ink, Nikos Dikeos (mark not catalogued by Lugt) | Inv. no. 2007-T.13

Provenance: Louis-Joseph-Auguste Coutan (1779–1830), Paris; Lucienne Coutan, née Hauguet (1788–1838), his widow; Ferdinand Hauguet (1790–1860), her brother; Maurice-Jacques-Albert Hauguet (1819–1883), his son, Antibes; Marie-Thérèse Hauguet, née Schubert (d. 1883), his widow, Antibes; Henriette Milliet, née Schubert, her sister (L. 464; sale, Paris, Drouot, 16–17 December 1889, no. 210); Nikos Dikeos (1896 or 1899–1987), Lyon (mark not catalogué par Lugt); Edouard Ambroselli, Boulogne-Billancourt; Fondation Custodia, Paris, acquired 16 April 2007.
Exhibitions: never before exhibited
Bibliography: no known references

Fig. 40.1
Théodore Géricualt, *Forest Interior with Thatched Hut*, 1813–14, graphite on cream wove paper, 17.5 x 23.0, The Art Institute of Chicago, Gift of Mr. and Mrs. Tiffany Blake, 1947.35.58v

Notes
1. For a study of this landscape suite, see Tinterow 1990.
2. Letter from Bruno Chenique to Edouard Ambroselli, 27 February 2007, in the files of the Fondation Custodia.
3. For an extensive analysis of the Chicago sketchbooks, see Eitner 1960.

41. Achille-Etna Michallon
Paris 1796–1822 Paris
View from the Vatican, 1818–21
Graphite | 28.3 x 43.6 | Inv. no. 2006-T.32

Provenance: Louis-Joseph-Auguste Coutan (1779–1830), Paris; his widow, Lucienne Coutan, née Hauguet (1788–1838), his widow; Ferdinand Hauguet (1790–1860), her brother; Maurice-Jacques-Albert Hauguet (1819–1883), his son, Antibes; Marie-Thérèse Hauguet, née Schubert (d. 1883), his widow, Antibes; Henriette Milliet, née Schubert, her sister (L. 464; sale, Paris, Drouot, 16–17 December 1889, probably part of no. 289); Private Collection, Egreville; Galerie Artemis, London; Galerie C. G. Boerner, New York; Fondation Custodia, Paris, acquired 29 December 2006.
Exhibitions: Paris 2001.
Bibliography: Paris 2001, p. 10, no. 2a, repr. (as Ingres).

Fig. 41.1
Achille-Etna Michallon, *View of Rome*, 1818–21, lead pencil on tracing paper, 29.6 x 43.6, Musée du Louvre, Paris, RF 14149

Notes
1. Paris 1994a, p. 109
2. Cleaver 1981, p. 360
3. Paris 1994a, p. 109. See also Cleaver 1981, p. 360.
4. Paris 2001, p. 10, no. 2a. On the reattribution, see letter to Mària van Berge-Gerbaud from Tim Bathurst, 6 February 2006 in the files of Fondation Custodia.
5. Cleaver 1981, p. 366, note 9; Artemis Fine Arts.
6. February 2006 in the files of Fondation Custodia.

42. Jean-Baptiste-Camille Corot
Paris 1796–1875 Paris
Landscape with Rocks near Marino, dated 1827
Pencil on paper | 29.2 x 27.3 | Verso, *Sketch with Rocks and Trees* | Inscriptions: lower right of recto in pencil, "Marino Mai 1827" | Inv. no. 2001-T.2

Provenance: Studio of Jean-Baptiste Camille Corot (1796–1875), the artist (L. 461; sale, Paris, Drouot, 31 May–4 June 1875, possibly part of nos. 514, 518, or 519); Thiollier, possibly Félix Thiollier (1842–1914), Saint-Étienne; Mme Bernard Lorenceau; Brame & Lorenceau, Paris; Fondation Custodia, Paris, acquired 12 January 2001.
Exhibitions: Bern 1960; Chicago 1960.
Bibliography: Robaut 1905/1965, vol. IV, p. 24, no. 2570; Bern 1960, no. 102; Chicago 1960, p. 28, no. 149; Jullien and Jullien 1987, pp. 118–19, fig. 9b (recto).

Notes
1. *Bridge at Narni*, National Gallery of Canada, Ottawa, and *La Cervara*, Kunsthaus Zurich.
2. Jullien and Jullien 1987, fig. 9a.
3. Galassi 1991, pp. 179–82.
4. "La fine pointe noir . . . creusait un profond sillon, au risque de traverser la feuille . . . Corot observait: 'J'avais dans ce temps-là de fameux crayons! Ils ne cassaient jamais; ils auraient plutôt emporté un morceau.'" Moreau-Nélaton 1905, pp. 24–25.
5. The Lugt drawing also exhibits the possible influence of the linear style of German fellow artists in Italy who modeled themselves after Albrecht Dürer. Their hatching was wider and less controlled, edging on abstraction (see Galassi 1991, pp. 174–78). This type of vigorous hatching is apparent in the rocks and some of the foliage of the drawing.

43. Louis-Gabriel-Eugène Isabey
Paris 1803–1886 Paris
Boat in a Storm, c. 1828
Pen and brown ink, watercolor heightened with white gouache over black chalk underdrawing on irregularly cut paper | 20.7 x 32.9 | Inscriptions: verso, bottom right, in graphite, "020577" | Inv. no. 2003-T.13

Provenance: Family of the artist; Paul Prouté S.A., Paris; Fondation Custodia, Paris, acquired 28 March 2003.
Exhibitions: Paris 2003a, Paris 2004.
Bibliography: Paris 2003a, p. 52, no. 25, repr.; Paris 2004, pp. 24–25, no. 9, repr.

Fig. 43.1
Etching after Isabey's *The Smugglers*, 1838, etched by J. Rouargue, published by Baillieu, 20.4 x 25.8, *Album Maritime*, National Maritime Museum, London, T.33.P337

Notes

1. The oil was exhibited under the name of *Les Contrebandiers anglais réfugiés dans les rochers*. Location unknown. For the painting, see Miquel 1980, vol. II, p. 137, no. 534.
2. Paris 2004, pp, 24–25, no. 9.
3. London, Minneapolis, and New York 2003, p. 257.
4. The lower right-hand corner of the etching depicts a piece of wreckage, which is perhaps related to the touches of black chalk in that same area of drawing.
5. Baltimore, Birmingham, Ala., and Tacoma 2005, p. 268, no. 72, and London, Minneapolis, and New York 2003, p. 257.

44. Eugène Delacroix
Charenton Saint Maurice 1798–1863 Paris
Near Gibraltar, 1832
Pastel and black chalk | 15.8 x 21.5, with irregular bottom and left edges | Inscriptions: bottom left in graphite, "21 jv / Pres de Gibraltar" | Inv. no. 2005-T.24

Provenance: Paul Meurice (1820–1905), Paris, friend of the artist, by bequest from the artist; Madame Meurice-Clémenceau; Private Collection, Meudon; Eric Turquin S.A.; Fondation Custodia, Paris, acquired 12 December 2005.
Exhibitions: never before exhibited
Bibliography: Arama 2006, p. 23.

Fig. 44.1
Eugène Delacroix, *The Coast of Spain at Salobrena*, 19 January 1832, pastel, 15.8 x 21.2, Musée du Louvre, Paris, RF 9154, f. 4r.

Notes

1. The count's brief was to persuade the sultan of Morocco, Abd-er-Rahman, to cease and desist from aiding the rebel tribesmen under Abd-el-Kader in neighboring Algeria in their ongoing resistance against the French, who had "liberated" the country from the Turks in 1830. The mission was not successful. The ship left from Toulon, France, on 11 January and arrived at Tangier, Morocco, on 24 January.
2. Johnson 1995, pp. 9–19.
3. Although Algeciras was under quarantine at the time owing to an outbreak of cholera, Delacroix and a few of the sailors went ashore. Delacroix recounts how they received their provisions by pitchfork as a cautionary measure against pestilence; Delacroix/Beaumont-Maillet, Jobert, and Join-Lambert 1999, p. 90 (Journal 3-b). This brief glimpse of Spain made a deep impression on him; he wrote in a letter to his friend Pierret, "Tout Goya palpitait autour de moi"; Paris 1963b, p. 109.
4. Ibid., p. 88 (Journal 2-a).

45. Eugène Delacroix
Charenton Saint Maurice 1798–1863 Paris
Study of a Wild Feline Facing Left, c. 1847
Pen and brown ink | 10.2 x 13.0 | Stamp: bottom right corner, cursive initials in red ink, "ED", for artist's estate sale | Inv. no. 2507A

46. Eugène Delacroix
Charenton Saint Maurice 1798–1863 Paris
Study of a Wild Feline Facing Right, c. 1847
Pen and brown ink | 10.1 x 13.0 | Stamp: bottom right corner, cursive initials in red ink, "ED", for artist's estate sale | Inv. no. 2507B

Provenance: Studio of Eugène Delacroix (1798–1863), the artist (L. Suppl. 383a; sale, Paris, Drouot, 17–29 February 1864, no. 496); Gustave Arosa (sale, Paris, Drouot, 27–28 February 1884, part of no. 165 "album"); Emile Wauters (1846–1930), Paris (cf. L. 911 & Suppl.; sale, Amsterdam, Frederik Muller & Cie, 15–16 June 1926, part of no. 54, to Lugt); Frits Lugt (1884–1970), Maartensdijk and Paris (L. 1028).
Exhibitions: never before exhibited
Bibliography: Robaut 1885, p. 445, no. 1771; Lees 1913, p. x, fig. 184, as panthers.

Fig. 45.1
Eugène Delacroix, *Tiger Lying Down*, 1847–49, pen and brown ink, 12.1 x 20.2, Musée du Louvre, Paris, RF 36 803

Notes

1. The drawings were purchased by Frits Lugt from Emile Wauters in 1924 as part of a lot of four animal drawings on three sheets. In one sheet, recto and verso were glued together. The drawings from this sheet were separated after their purchase and sold to Mathey in 1947 and to Neuville in 1948; the other two, which are exhibited here, remain in the collection today (2507 A, B). Archives of the Lugt Foundation, translated from the Dutch by Louisa Wood Ruby.
2. Trapp refers to them as "memory drawings or passages that seem to be doodles"; Amherst 1988, p. 31. For their identification as panthers, see Lees 1913, p. x, fig. 184.
3. The quotation was first cited by George Sand in *Impressions et souvenirs*. Paris, 1873, p. 84. "Quand vous aurez dessiné au trait ma forme sur une ardoise… Pourtant, si vous êtes coloriste, vous viendrez à bout, avec ce simple trait, de faire comprendre que j'ai une épaisseur, un relief, un corps. Comment en viendrez-vous à bout? En n'arrètant pas également partout ce contour, en le faisant très-délié, presque interrompu en certains endroits, en l'accusant en d'autres endroits au moyen d'un second trait et, s'il le faut, d'un troisième, ou encore au moyen d'un trait élargi, engraissé, qui se gardera bien d'être un fil de fer." Translated in Sérullaz 2004, p. 11.
4. "la patte antérieure du lion était le bras monstrueux d'un homme, mais tordu et renversé"; cited in Kliman 1982, p. 447.
5. Ibid., pp. 458–63.
6. On the collaboration of the two artists, see Loffredo 1982.

7. On his return to France, in fact, he traveled with gifts of exotic animals on board from Abd-er-Rahman to King Louis-Philippe, including a lioness and a tiger (Finlay 1964, pp. 66, 247–48, note 88).
8. "Combien il est nécessaire de se secouer de temps en temps, de mettre la tête dehors, de chercher à lire dans la création, qui n'a rien de commun avec nos villes et avec les ouvrages des hommes!"; Delacroix/Pach 1937, p. 130.
9. Paris and Philadelphia 1998, p. 77.

47. Hippolyte-Jean Flandrin or Paul-Jean Flandrin
Lyon 1809–1864 Rome | Lyon 1811–1902 Paris
View from the Summit of Vesuvius, 1838
Watercolor over graphite or black chalk | 13.4 x 18.8 | Inscriptions: verso, top left, in graphite, "du Sommet du Vesuve" | Inv. no. 1989-T.21

Provenance: Mme Hippolyte Flandrin, née Aimée Ancelot (1822–1882), Sèvres, recorded in an album bound in red Morocco leather and bearing the initials "AA"; Paul Flandrin (1902–1936), grandson of the painter Paul-Jean Flandrin; Simone Flandrin-Latron, his widow, Paris; Mme Michel André, her daughter, Reims, 1989; Fondation Custodia, Paris, acquired 9 June 1989.
Exhibitions: Paris 1994b.
Bibliography: Paris 1994b, p. 110, no. 49, repr, as by Hippolyte-Jean or Paul-Jean Flandrin.

Fig. 47.1
Hippolyte Flandrin, *Vesuvius*, 1838, watercolor, Private Collection

Notes
1. There was a third brother, Auguste, who was also an artist.
2. Nantes 2007, pp. 43, 51; Paris and Lyon 1984, p. 11. These two exhibitions helped to restore his reputation.
3. Although he had not won the Rome Prize, Paul-Jean participated in some of the activities of the Academy once Ingres was appointed director in 1835.

4. "Montée au grand cône. Fatigue. Arrivées au sommet . . . Convulsions, chaos horribles . . . Tout le flanc du cône était brûlant. Enfin, nous sommes tous sur le bord regardant au fond une gueule rouge de feu qui aspire et respire des courants d'air avec un bruit horrible!" Flandrin and Froideveaux-Flandrin 1984, p. 125.
5. The lava at Vesuvius contains porphyry, which probably accounts for the deep purple-red color.
6. Flandrin and Froideveaux-Flandrin 1984, p. 124, fig. 51.
7. Paris and Lyon 1984, p. 271, no. 180.
8. Paris 1994b, p. 110.

48. Théodore Rousseau
Paris 1812–1867 Barbizon
Riverbank in the Berri, 1842
Watercolor, brown wash, heightened with oil in brown, blue, and white, over traces of black chalk; pencil framing lines | 28.9 x 43.6 | Stamps: bottom left in black ink, "TH R" for artist's estate sale (L. 2436) | Watermark: [F]ABRIANO
Inv. no. 1990-T.16

Provenance: Théodore Rousseau (1812–1867), the artist (L. 2436 and L. 2437; sale of the artist's estate, Paris, Drouot, 27 April–2 May 1868, no. 195); Galerie de Staël, Paris; Fondation Custodia, Paris, acquired 5 July 1994.
Exhibitions: Paris 1990a; Paris 1994b; Paris 1997b.
Bibliography: Paris 1990a, no. 30, repr.; Paris 1994b, p. 112, no. 50, repr.; Paris 1997b, pp. 18–19, no. 17.

Notes
1. Norwich and London 1982, p. 14–15.
2. Paris 1868, p. 22.

49. François-Marius Granet
Aix-en-Provence 1775–1849 Malvalat (near Aix-en-Provence)
View of Mont Sainte-Victoire from the Terrace of Malvalat, 1844?
Watercolor partially heightened with gum arabic, graphite underdrawing | 10.5 x 16.9 | Inscriptions:

"malavala terrasse" in pencil on the former mount (removed but conserved) | Inv. no. 1995-T.18

Provenance: Pascal Zuber, Paris; Fondation Custodia, Paris, acquired 20 December 1995.
Exhibitions: never before exhibited
Bibliography: Miquel 1975, vol. 1, p. 62, repr.; Fondation Custodia 2000, p. 26.

Fig. 49.1
François-Marius Granet, *View of Mont Sainte-Victoire from the Terrace of Malvallat* (detail).

Notes

1. Granet began painting watercolors steadily after 1830, when he had returned to Paris, and continued when he became the director of the Historic Galleries at Versailles in 1833. When these watercolor views of Paris and Versailles were first exhibited between 1925 and 1936 in France, they sparked a revival of interest in the nearly forgotten artist. Samors 1958, pp. 6–7.
2. For the Provençal school of landscape painting, of which Granet's teacher Jean-Antoine Constantin (1756–1844) was a leading figure, see Montreal 2005, pp. 7–12.
3. New York 1988, pp. ix–x and 69; Samors 1958, p. 147.

50. Johan Barthold Jongkind
Latrop 1819–1891 Grenoble
View of Montmartre, c. 1849
Brush and brown ink, watercolor over black chalk mounted onto Japan paper | 25.7 x 41.5 |
Verso, visible through the mount, a sketch in black chalk of trees, figures, and a house | Inscriptions: signed at lower left, in pen and brown ink, "Jongkind"; center of verso in graphite, "57,55" | Inv. no. 2000-T.1

Provenance: Adolphe Stein (1913–2002), Crans-sur-Sierre and Paris (mark not catalogued by Lugt); Fondation Custodia, Paris, acquired 2 January 2000.
Exhibitions: London 1988; Paris 1996; Paris 2004.
Bibliography: London 1988, no. 90, pl. 55; Paris 1996, p. 65, no. 32, repr.; Blok 2004, pp. 42–43 ; Paris 2004, pp. 33–34, no. 17, repr.; Société Française de Promotion Artistique 2004, p. 25.

Fig. 50.1
Johan Barthold Jongkind, *Self-Portrait under the Sun*, c. 1850, watercolor and brown wash, 20.5 x 16.4, Musée d'Orsay, Paris, RF 11017

Notes
1. Northampton, Mass., and Williamstown, Mass., 1977, p. 25.
2. The Hague, Cologne, and Paris 2004, pp.165–67, 171.
3. My thanks to Camille Mathieu for pointing out the likely feature of this landscape, the gypsum mines, and for suggesting that the tree-covered area may by the Montmartre cemetery.

51. Jean-François Millet
Gruchy 1814–1875 Barbizotn
A Gleaner (study of Ruth for *Harvesters Resting*), 1851–53
Black conté crayon on beige paper | 31.0 x 15.5 | Stamps: bottom right in black ink, "J.F.M" for artist's estate sale (L. 1460) | Inv. no. 3018

Provenance: Jean-François Millet (1814–1875), the artist (L. 1460; sale of the artist's estate, Paris, Drouot, 10–11 May 1875, probably no. 152 or no. 157); Sir William Eden; G. Bellingham-Smith (sale, Amsterdam, Frederik Muller & Cie, 5–6 July 1927, no. 75, to Lugt, for 400 francs); Frits Lugt (1884–1970), Maartensdijk and Paris (L. 1028).
Exhibitions: Paris and Amsterdam 1964; Cherbourg 1975; Williamstown, Mass., Amsterdam, and Pittsburgh 1999 (only exhibited in Williamstown, Mass., and Amsterdam).

Bibliography: Paris and Amsterdam 1964, pp. 141–42, no. 167, pl. 113; Cherbourg 1975, pp. 32–33, no. 17, repr.; Paris 1975, p. 96, under no. 59; Boston 1984, p. 63, under no. 39; Williamstown, Mass., Amsterdam, and Pittsburgh 1999, pp. 58–59, no. 26, repr.

Fig. 51.1
Jean-François Millet, *Harvesters Resting (Ruth and Boaz)*, 1850–53, oil on canvas, 67.3 x 119.7, Museum of Fine Arts, Boston, Bequest of Mrs. Martin Brimmer 06.2421

Notes

1. For the painting, see Boston 1984, pp. 60–63.
2. Ruth, a young Moabite woman who married out of her tribe, remains loyal to her deceased husband's widowed mother, Naomi, rather than returning to her home, supporting them both by gleaning. Ruth was soon recognized for her loyalty and beauty by the landowner, Boaz, who later married her.
3. Herbert has also argued that Millet's depictions of peasant life express a "nostalgia for the pre-industrial past," and his "latent sympathy for the peasant provided a repeated commentary upon the life of the humble and the poor," reminding the bourgeois public of the 1848 uprisings; Herbert 1962, pp. 295–97.
4. Other references cited are Pieter Bruegel the Elder, *The Harvesters* (1565, The Metropolitan Museum of Art, New York) as well as a more contemporary work, Léopold Robert, *Arrivée des Moissonneurs* (1831, Musée du Louvre, Paris). Paris 1975, p. 95.
5. For Millet's working process, see Herbert 1962, p. 302, and Williamstown, Mass., Amsterdam, and Pittsburgh 1999, p. 59.
6. Repro. Sensier and Mantz 1881, p. 143.

52. Jean-François Millet
Gruchy 1814–1875 Barbizon
Landscape near Gruchy, c. 1854?
Pen and brown ink, watercolor | 21.8 x 28.4, irregularly cut | Inscriptions: at lower left, in pen and gray ink, signed "MILLET"; on verso, at lower left, in pencil, "(2)"; at lower right, in blue chalk, "4", crossed out in pencil; below, in pencil, "43 – p9 blanc" (?), partly erased | Inv. no. 2007-T.33

Provenance: Catherine Lemaire (1827–1894), widow of the artist (L. 1815; not in her sale, Paris, Drouot, 24–25 April 1894); Galerie Talabardon & Gautier, Paris; Fondation Custodia, Paris, acquired 21 December 2007.
Exhibitions: Paris 2007b.
Bibliography: Paris 2007b, no. 18, repr.

Notes
1. Sensier and Mantz 1881, p. 154. See also Millet's letter to his friend Campredon, Barbizon, September 1854: "mais j'ai surtout fait une grande quantité de croquis: une centaine environ; et tous, comme je vous le disais, dans le but de me servir"; Lepoittevin 2005, vol. I, p. 83, nos. 147–67.
2. Millet's letter to Sensier, Vichy, 5 July 1866: "quatre-vingt, plus ou moins importants, mais encore a-t-il fallu y toucher"; Lepoittevin 2005, vol. II, p. 133, no. 952-514; and: "J'en ai colorié de petites à l'aquarelle afin de me bien rappeler l'aspect du ton général de ce pays"; ibid., p. 132, no. 948-510. These sheets, with the somewhat angular pen lines and the surprising use of color, are rather reminiscent of the drawing style of Théodore Rousseau, Millet's close friend. In a number of drawings dated between 1860 and 1865 Rousseau also combined pen-and-ink and watercolor; cf. for example Schulman 1997, no. 675-77.
3. Sale, Christie's, New York, 30 October 2002, no. 17, repr. This drawing with the same studio stamp (L. 1815) has the same twentieth-century (?) annotations. However, Sensier's observation (1881, p. 154) that Millet made "des notes sommaires" in the area around Gruchy in 1854 and then recorded them "à la plume et aquarelle" cannot be found in the correspondence.
4. Letter, Vichy, 17 June 1866 (Lepoittevin 2005, vol. II, p. 130, no. 942-505).

53. Charles-François Daubigny
Paris 1817–1878 Paris
View of Paris from the Tour Saint-Jacques, 1852
Graphite with stumping on beige paper | 35.2 x 47.9 | Inscriptions: signed at bottom right in graphite, "C. Daubigny"; verso, traces of charcoal and inscribed in the center in black chalk, "123", possible dealer's mark at bottom right in graphite | Inv. no. 1979-T.7

Provenance: Paul Prouté S.A., Paris; Fondation Custodia, Paris, acquired 2 February 1979.
Exhibitions: Paris 1978
Bibliography: Paris 1978, p. 64, no. 89, repr.; Fidell-Beaufort and Bailly-Herzberg 1975, p. 211, no. 174, repr.; Lasalle 1990, p. 13, repr.

Notes

1. Baron Haussmann served as prefect of the Seine between 1853 and 1870. Already in July 1852, however, Prosper Mérimée observed, "La capitale présente en ce moment un spectacle vraiment curieux; on dirait une ville récemment bombardée. On démolit plus de maisons que l'on bati sous le règne de Louis-Philippe; on accompli les projets les plus grandioses; les rues sont sillonées par des charettes de moellons et de pierre de taille"; cited in Price 1967, p. 11.
2. Although Daubigny is known as a naturalistic landscape painter, he worked as an illustrator to support himself throughout his artistic career (Fidell 1974, p. 7). My thanks to Camille Mathieu for providing additional research on Haussmannization.
3. Moreau-Nélaton 1925, fig. 124.
4. *Mémoires du Baron Haussmann*, vol. III, pp. 535–36, cited and translated in Jordan 1995, p. 200. The Théâtre de la Ville was constructed there on the quai de Gesvres in 1862 as part of the revitalization of the place du Châtelet. On the other side of the Place, west of the rue Saint Denis (located outside the drawing), the Théâtre du Châtelet was built in 1860. The place du Châtelet marked the center of Haussmann's *grande croisée*, the intersection of his two new boulevards, the rue de Rivoli and the boulevard de Sébastopol, which became the main east-west and north-south axes of the new Paris.
5. The gilded statue is the work of Louis-Simon Boizot. The monument is also known as the Fontaine du Palmier for its palm leaf decorations at top. In 1858 the column was moved when the Place du Châtelet was being enlarged (see note 4) and stands today between the two theaters. Daubigny's drawing shows it in its original location. Thanks are due to Cécile Tainturier of the Fondation Custodia for identifying the column.
6. Jones 2004, pp. 308–9.

54. Auguste-Joseph Bracquemond, called Félix Bracquemond
Paris 1833–1914 Sèvres
Portrait of Charles Daubigny (1817–1878), 1853
Lead pencil and graphite | 15.7 x 11.7 | Inscriptions: bottom left in black chalk, "B" | Inv. no. 1994-T.22

Provenance: Patrick de Bayser, Paris; Fondation Custodia, Paris, acquired 4 October 1994.
Exhibitions: Paris, Galerie de Bayser, 1994, *Acquisitions récentes*, no. 43 (no catalogue).
Bibliography: Fondation Custodia 2000, pp. 22, 32, 63, repr.

Fig. 54.1
Auguste-Joseph Bracquemond, called Félix Bracquemond, *Portrait of Daubigny*, 1853, etching, 15.5 x 11.5, Fondation Custodia, Paris, Inv. no. 1996-P.10

Notes

1. Bracquemond was connected to the Impressionist circle through his wife, Marie, and exhibited his work at the Impressionists' exhibitions of 1874, 1879, and 1880. Unlike Marie, Félix did not subscribe to the aesthetic of the movement and remained more closely aligned with the realist tradition. He published his well-known theoretical text, *Du dessin et de la couleur*, in 1885. He was also one of the earliest French appreciators of Japanese prints.
2. He is credited with inventing a type of lift-ground etching called the pen method or pen transfer, and he also revived color etching. See Amsterdam 1993, pp. 9, 11. Furthermore, he probably had an eye to the possible threat of photography to the tradition of reproductive printmaking—a major source of income for him.
3. Félix Bracquemond, "Etude sur la gravure sur bois et la lithographie" (1897) in Bracquemond 2002, p. 208.

55. Horace Vernet
Paris 1789–1863 Paris
Study of Gabions in the Trenches of the Crimean War, 1854–55
Pen and brown ink, brown and gray-brown wash, over traces of graphite on discolored paper | 20.7 x 32.0 | Verso, geometric patterns with notations about color, in graphite | Inscriptions: bottom left, in pen and brown ink, "h Vernet"; on the former mount in pen and brown ink, "H. Vernet étude guerre de Crimée" | Watermark: present but illegible | Inv. no. 1991-T.17

Provenance: Private Collection, Bordeaux; Galerie Fischer-Kiener, Paris; Fondation Custodia, Paris, acquired 3 June 1991.
Exhibitions: never before exhibited
Bibliography: no known references

Notes

1. The term derives from the Italian "gabbione," which translates as "big cage." Although they may be obscure to viewers today, Gabions were undoubtedly familiar to viewers of the time from newspaper articles, photographs, and on-site drawings made during the war.
2. He was the son of the eighteenth-century satirist Carle Vernet and grandson of the landscape artist Joseph Vernet, and, on his mother's side, of the engraver Jean-Michel Moreau (see also cat. 28).
3. Boime 1973, p. 177.
4. "un militaire qui fait de la peinture"; Kelley 1975, p. 161.
5. Rome and Paris 1980, pp. 18–19.
6. For contemporary descriptions of trench conditions and statistics of deaths and hospitalizations, see Keller 2001, pp. 91–93.
7. Rome and Paris 1980, p. 112.
8. *Bataille de l'Alma*, 1857, Musée Fesch, Ajaccio; *L'Assaut du zouave*, 1857, Private Collection, Paris; *Prise du fort de Malakoff*, 1858, Musée Rolin, Autun.

56. Edgar Degas
Paris 1834–1917 Paris
View of the Saône River with the Sérin Bridge near Lyon, 1855
Black chalk on paper | 47.4 x 31.2 | Inscriptions: bottom right in graphite, "du haut du rocher de PierSiz" | Stamps: verso, bottom right in red ink, oval "ATELIER/ ED. DEGAS" (L. 657)
Inv. no. 1997-T.8

Provenance: Studio of Edgar-Hilaire-Germain Degas (1834–1917), the artist (L. 657); Charles E. Slatkin Galleries, New York, sold 1966; Private Collection, Paris, 1967; Fondation Custodia, Paris, acquired 19 March 1997, gift from two anonymous donors on the occasion of the fiftieth anniversary of the Fondation Custodia.
Exhibitions: New York 1966, Paris 1997b.
Bibliography: New York 1966, no. 48, pl. 46, as "Italian Landscape"; Paris 1997b, p. 7, no. 3; Fondation Custodia 2000, p. 25, ill. 27.

Fig. 56.1
Jacob de Heusch, *View of Lyon with Pierre-Scize Fortress*, early 1670s, black chalk, gray wash, brown ink framing lines, 24.6 x 35.3, Fondation Custodia, Paris, Inv. no. 1987-T.47

Notes
1. Pierre-Scize was the residence of the archbishop of Lyon and later served as a prison. It was demolished in 1793. Paris 1994b, p. 72.
2. On the tradition of Lyonnais landscapes, see Stuccilli 2003, pp. 84–94.
3. The Pont Serin was constructed between 1811 and 1815 out of wood. In 1844 five stone arches replaced the wooden construction. (The bridge no longer exists today; the Pont Koenig was built there in 1972.)
4. The Granary was constructed in 1722–28 to hold reserves of wheat for the city of Lyon, but after 1763 it was used by the military. The names of the buildings mentioned here and the quartier are taken from Paris 1997b, p. 8.
5. Dumas 2006, p. 9
6. New York and Houston 1993, pp. 2–3.
7. On the influence of Ingres on Degas, see New York and Houston 1993, pp. 5–6.

57. Edgar Degas
Paris 1834–1917 Paris
Head of a Soldier, c. 1857–59
Watercolor, gouache, and red chalk wash, over graphite | 25.6 x 21.0 | Inscriptions: on the bottom right of the mount, in graphite, "Flor. 1857"; on the verso of the former mat (removed but conserved) in black ink, "Vente Pra/ Paris 1938 / (7 juin)" | Stamp: bottom left in red ink script, "Degas" (L. 658) | Inv. no. 5488

Provenance: Studio of Edgar-Hilaire-Germain Degas (1834–1917), the artist (L. 658; fourth sale of the artist's estate, Paris, Galerie Georges Petit, 4 July 1919, no. 65b, repr.); Albert Pra, Paris (sale, Paris, Galerie Charpentier, 17 June 1938, no. 11, repr.); Knoedler, Paris; Frits Lugt (1884–1970), The Hague and Paris (L. 1028), acquired 5 July 1938.
Exhibitions: never before exhibited
Bibliography: Lemoisne 1946, vol. II, pp. 8–9, no. 25, repr.; Lassaigne and Minervino 1974, pp. 89–90, no. 72, repr.

Cindy Kang, research assistant for the Lugt project, The Frick Collection, discovered the sources for this creative copy and wrote the paragraphs about it.

Notes
1. "Il faut copier et recopier les maîtres, et ce n'est qu'après avoir donné toutes les preuves d'un bon copiste qu'il pourra raisonnablement vous être permis de faire un radis d'après nature"; Ambroise Vollard, *Degas*

(Wildenstein 1924), p. 64; cited in Reff 1963, p. 241.

2. For the classic study on this subject, see Reff 1963.

3. For the creative copy, see Thompson 1992. Degas often copied selected fragments of pictures (Reff 1963, pp. 246–47).

4. Collection of Walter Feilchenfeldt, Zurich, illustrated in Rome 1984, p. 74, no. 18. The secure date of the Zurich drawing suggests a similar date for the Lugt sheet, despite the inscription of 1857 on the mount. Reff has argued that Degas misdated his drawings later in life and that therefore the sheets inscribed 1857 more likely belong to his first documented trip to Florence in 1858–59 (Reff 1963, p. 251).

5. Caneva 2002, p. 255, and Caneva, Cecchi, and Natali 1992, p. 86

6. Degas had copied another portrait by Bronzino at the Uffizi, *Young Girl with a Missal*, in 1858 (Bibliothèque Nationale, Dc 327d réserve, carnet 18, p. 43). This graphite drawing also focuses mainly on the bust and the serious expression of the girl's face, minimizing the details of her dress and accouterments. It is considered a source for his famous *Family Portrait (The Bellelli Family)*, Musée d'Orsay, Paris, RF 2210 (Boggs 1962, p. 12).

7. Degas's appreciation for red chalk drawings is demonstrated by the graphite copy he made of a female portrait in the Uffizi then attributed to Leonardo. He developed this copy into a painting, the *Portrait of a Young Woman* dated 1858–59 and now in the National Gallery of Canada, Ottawa (Paris, Ottawa, and New York 1988, p. 76). Like the Lugt drawing, this work reinvents a Renaissance prototype in a new medium.

Fig. 57.1
Edgar Degas, *Copy after Uccello*, 1859, graphite, 24.0 x 39.0, Private Collection, Zurich

Fig. 57.2
Agnolo Bronzino, *Cosimo I in Armor*, c. 1550s, oil on tin, 15.0 x 12.0, Uffizi, Florence, Inv. no. 855

58. Léon Bonvin
Paris 1834–1866 Meudon
The Plain of Vaugirard, dated 1856
Black chalk with stumping | 17.3 x 26.5 | Verso, traces of black chalk | Inscriptions: bottom right in black chalk, "1856, L. Bonvin" | Inv. no. 2008-T.8

Provenance: Galerie Talabardon & Gautier, Paris; Fondation Custodia, Paris, acquired 29 January 2008.
Exhibitions: Paris 2008.
Bibliography: Paris 2008, no. 18.

Notes
1. Weisberg 1980, pp. 120–24 and Weisberg 1987, pp. 54–58.
2. Bonvin is perhaps better known for his watercolor landscapes, still lifes, and genre scenes executed in a meticulous realist style based on Dutch seventeenth-century masters. William T. Walters collected these works and the Walters Art Museum in Baltimore now holds the most extensive collection of Léon's work in the world.

Fig. 58.1
Léon Bonvin, *Room with Door Open to a Courtyard and Road*, c. 1850s, black chalk, 25.5 x 16.8, Musée du Louvre, Paris, RF 15262

---

59. Paul Huet
Paris 1803–1869 Paris
View near Apt, 1862
Watercolor over black chalk | 22.0 x 35.3 | Inscriptions: bottom right in black ink, "Apt"; on the former mount, in pen and black ink by René Paul Huet, the artist's son, "PAUL HUET / 1803–1869 / 'Apt.1865'" | Stamps: bottom right in red ink, artist's studio (L. 1268) | Inv. no. 1994-T.3

Provenance: studio of Paul Huet (1803–1869), the artist (L. 1268); René Paul Huet (1844–1928), his son; descendants of René Paul Huet; Henrotin

collection; Galerie Antoine Laurentin, Paris; Fondation Custodia, Paris, acquired 1 March 1994.
Exhibitions: Paris 1930; Rouen 1965; College Park, Md., Louisville, Ky., and Ann Arbor, Mich. 1977; New York, Park Avenue Armory, 1994, *Works on Paper* (no catalogue); Paris 1994b.
Bibliography: Paris 1930, no. 73; Rouen 1965, p. 62, no. 186; College Park, Md., Louisville, Ky., and Ann Arbor, Mich. 1977, pp. 148, 150, no. 93, repr.; Paris 1994b, p. 108, no. 48, repr.

Notes
1. College Park, Md., Louisville, Ky., and Ann Arbor, Mich. 1977, p. 144, and New York 1997, p. 7.
2. "J'aspire à causer un peu sérieusement avec cette belle nature de Apt, pour voir si je suis encore bon à quelque chose et un peu autre *qu'une veille ganache*"; Paris 1911a, p. 324.
3. Numerous writers have commented on the proto-Impressionist character of Huet's late work. See, for example, Sheon 1965, p. 442.
4. College Park, Md., Louisville, Ky., and Ann Arbor, Mich. 1977, p. 144.
5. "Le paysagiste est, de tout les artistes, celui qui communique le plus directement avec la nature, avec l'âme même de la nature"; letter to AM.X. 2 September 1868, Paris 1911a, p. 471.

60. Eugène-Emmanuel Viollet-le-Duc
Paris 1814–1879 Lausanne
View of the Alps, dated 1875
Watercolor heightened with yellow gouache over a pencil drawing on blue paper | 14.4 x 23.7
Inscriptions: lower right, in pen and black ink, "au dessus dulac Blanc" and "9 Sept / 75", repeated below in pencil; many inscriptions in pencil above, and in pen and black ink, "Porphire" | Inv. no. 1995-T.12

Provenance: Galerie de Staël, Paris; Fondation Custodia, Paris, acquired 28 April 1995.
Exhibitions: never before exhibited
Bibliography: Fondation Custodia 2000, pp. 29, 31, repr.

Note: Special thanks are due to Joanna Sheers, The Frick Collection, for her substantive contributions to this entry.

Notes

1. The French Ministry of War had published a map of the new French territory in 1865, and Viollet-le-Duc's project was to verify and expand that map. Furthermore, Viollet-le-Duc's publication follows earlier scientific studies of the Alps: Horace-Bénédict de Saussure's *Voyages dans les Alpes* (1779–96), Louis Agassiz's *Études sur les glaciers* (1840), and Alphonse Favre's *Recherches géologiques dans les parties de la Savoie, du Piémont, et de la Suisse, voisines du Mont-Blanc* (1867).

2. Frey interprets his Mont Blanc project as "une vaste allégorie de toutes les restaurations"; Paris 1993, p. 28. See also Middleton in Lausanne 1979, pp. 103, 107–8.

3. Viollet-le-Duc/Bucknall 1877, p. 12.

4. It perhaps represents yellow talcose protogine, a crystalline rock believed at the time to be central to the geological development of the Alps (ibid., p. 115, note 3).

5. On Turner's and Ruskin's watercolors of the Alps, see Hill 1992 and London 1991, respectively. The concept of the Sublime is drawn from Burke 1756.

6. Viollet-le-Duc 1879, p. 302.

7. "Tu en prends à ton aise avec ces roches; cela demande à être dessiné avec précision, et ces formes ne sont pas dues au hazard. Il y a de grandes lignes principales qui'il faut d'abord indiquer; puis, quand elles sont fidèlement tracées, en tenant compte des angles et des inclinaisons, il faut y faire entrer les détails suivant leur importance . . . chaque nature de roche affecte des formes spéciales, et il ne faut pas plus les négliger qu'on ne néglige d'observer les traits d'un visage. . . ." Ibid., p. 256.

8. Viollet-le-Duc/Bucknall 1877, p. 12.

Fig 60.1
Eugène-Emmanuel Viollet-le-Duc, *View of the White Lakes*, 4 September 1875, pencil, watercolor, and gouache, 38.7 x 94.3, Musée d'Orsay, Paris

61. Paul-Gustave Doré
Strasbourg 1832–1883 Paris
View of the Forest at Westbridge, dated 1879
Watercolor and gouache over graphite | 74.3 x 52.7 | Inscriptions: bottom right, in black ink, "G Doré / Wesbridge / 1879" | Inv. no. 1987-T.9

Provenance: Pierre-Yves Gabus, Bevaix (Neuchâtel) (sale, Paris, Drouot, 3 June 1986, no. 93); Paul Prouté S.A., Paris; Fondation Custodia, Paris, acquired 16 February 1987.
Exhibitions: Strasbourg and Paris 1983; Grandson 1985; Paris 1994b.
Bibliography: Strasbourg and Paris 1983, p. 173, no. 177, repr.; Grandson 1985, p. 53, fig. 74, repr.; Paris 1994b, p. 120, no. 54, repr.

Notes

1. Doré exhibited his watercolors for the first time in 1877 at an exhibition at the Cercle de l'Union Artistique de la Place Vendôme. For a thorough discussion of Doré as a watercolorist, see Strasbourg and Paris 1983, pp. 59–67.
2. The catalogue of the exhibition lists three "paysages" but there is not enough information to determine if the Lugt drawing was one of them. Doré did exhibit a large, detailed portrait of his mother in watercolor and gouache in the scale of an oil painting.
3. Repro Strasbourg 1983, p. 173, cat. 176.
4. Fossier identified the trees as beeches. He also relates this work to Doré's illustrations for Shakespeare's *Macbeth*; it recalls the scene in Act V when Birnham Wood "marches" to Dunsinane castle. Paris 1994b, p. 120.
5. Fossier located Westbridge in Sussex county. It should be noted, however, that no such wooded area is known in Sussex. It may refer to a specific footpath in Lavant, though that area is not naturally wooded. I thank Esme Evans, Hon. Librarian of the Sussex Archaeological Society Library, for kindly providing this information.
6. Shoberl 1813, p. 11. My thanks to Emily Kaplan for locating this description.
7. Renonciat 1983, p. 233.

62. Berthe Morisot
Bourges 1841–1895 Paris
Swans on the Lake of the Bois de Boulogne, 1885
Pastel on blue paper (slightly discolored) | 28.5 x 40.0 | Inscriptions: lower right of verso, in lead pencil, "Je certifie que ce pastel / est bien de ma nièce / Berthe Morisot / J. Manet" | Inv. no. 6841

Provenance: Studio of Berthe Morisot (1841–1895), the artist (L. 1826); probably Gabriel Thomas (1854–1932), Paris; Lucien Guiraud; his widow; Institut Pasteur, Paris, bequest of the widow of Lucien Guiraud (sale, Paris, Drouot, 14–15 June 1956, no. 37, to Lugt); Frits Lugt (1884–1970), Paris (L. 1028).
Exhibitions: Paris 1896; Paris 1926.
Bibliography: Paris 1896, p. 34, no. 223; Paris 1926, p. 11, no. 12; Bataille and Wildenstein 1961, p. 55, no. 491, fig. 479.

Notes	
	1. Cited in Washington D.C., Fort Worth, and South Hadley, Mass., 1987, p. 15.
	2. Cited in ibid., p. 57.
	3. The last verse of the poem reads: "Fantôme qu'à ce lieu son pur éclat assigne,/ Il s'immobilise au songe froid de mépris/ Que vêt parmi l'exil inutile le Cygne." Sully Prudhomme's poem "Le Cygne" (1869) is also cited as related to Morisot's works. It describes "L'oiseau, dans le lac sombre où sous lui se reflète/ La splendeur d'une nuit lactée et violette,/ Comme une vase d'argent parmi des diamants,/ Dort, la tête sous l'aile, entre deux firmaments."
	4. For a discussion of the history of the pastel technique, see Monnier 1992, pp. 164–70.

Fig. 62.1
Berthe Morisot, *Swans*, 1885, pastel, 30.0 x 47.0, Musée Marmottan, Paris, Inv. no. 6034

63. Henri-Joseph Harpignies
Valenciennes 1819–1916 Saint-Privé
Studio of the Artist, dated 1909
Watercolor over black chalk | 29.1 x 22.9 | Inscriptions: bottom left in black ink, "Coin de mon Atelier / h¡harpignies"; bottom right in black ink, "Fevrier 1909"; bottom left of verso, in graphite, "Tout blanc"; bottom center in black chalk, an illegible annotation; bottom right, in purple pencil, "Verdun" | Stamps: on verso, HARPIGNIES / VENTE ATELIER R. VERDUN / ORLÉANS – 1978 in an oval, not catalogued by Lugt | Inv. no. 1980-T.31

Provenance: Henri-Joseph Harpignies (1819–1916), the artist; Raymond Verdun (1873–1954), his student, Orléans, by bequest of the artist (mark of Raymond Verdun, not catalogued by Lugt; sale, Orléans, Hôtel des Ventes, 22 October 1978, no. 83, for 6000 francs); Paul Prouté S.A., Paris; Fondation Custodia, Paris, acquired 8 July 1980.
Exhibitions: Paris 1980, Paris 1994b.
Bibliography: Paris 1980, p. 41, no. 98, repr.; Paris 1994b, p. 122, no. 55, repr.

Notes   1. Matisse would play with similar concepts in his famous *Red Studio* of 1911 (The Museum of Modern Art, New York).

Selected Bibliography

AARON 1985
Aaron, Olivier. *Dessins insolites du XVIIIe français*. Paris, 1985.

ADHÉMAR 1950
Adhémar, Helene. *Watteau: Sa vie—son oeuvre*. Paris, 1950.

AMHERST 1988
Delacroix and the Romantic Image: Oriental Themes, Wild Beasts, and the Hunt. Introduction by Frank Anderson Trapp. Exh. cat. Mead Art Museum, Amherst. Amherst, 1988.

AMSTERDAM 1926
Exposition rétrospective d'art français. Edited by Jacqueline Bouchot-Saupique. Exh. cat. Musée de l'État, Amsterdam. Amsterdam, 1926.

AMSTERDAM 1935
Jean Antoine Watteau als tekenaar. Exh. cat. Museum Willet Holthuysen, Amsterdam. Amsterdam, 1935.

AMSTERDAM 1974
Franse tekenkunst van de 18de eeuw uit Nederlandse Verzamelingen. By J. W. Niemeijer, with Peter Schatborn. Exh. cat. Rijksprentenkabinet/Rijksmuseum, Amsterdam. Amsterdam, 1974.

AMSTERDAM 1993
Félix Bracquemond, 1833–1914. Edited by Charlotte van Rappard-Boon. Exh. cat. Van Gogh Museum, Amsterdam. Zwolle, 1993.

AMSTERDAM and PARIS 2003
De Watteau à Ingres: Dessins français du XVIIIe siècle du Rijksmuseum, Amsterdam. By R. J. A. te Rijdt. Exh. cat. Rijksmuseum, Amsterdam; Institut néerlandais, Paris. Paris, 2003.

ANANOFF 1961–70
Ananoff, Alexandre. *L'Oeuvre dessiné de Jean-Honoré Fragonard, 1732–1806*. 4 vols. Paris, 1961–70.

ANANOFF 1964
> Ananoff, Alexandre. "Les Cents Petits Maîtres qu'il faut connaître," *Connaissance des arts*, no. 149 (July 1964): 50–59.

ANANOFF 1965
> Ananoff, Alexandre. "Le Dessin ancien regardé de près," *Connaissance des arts*, no. 161 (July 1965): 84–93.

ANANOFF 1966
> Ananoff, Alexandre. *L'Oeuvre dessiné de François Boucher (1703–1770), catalogue raisonné*. Paris, 1966.

ANANOFF 1980
> Ananoff, Alexandre, with Daniel Wildenstein. *L'opera completa di Boucher*. Milan, 1980.

ANANOFF and WILDENSTEIN 1976
> Ananoff, Alexandre, and Daniel Wildenstein. *François Boucher: Catalogue des peintures*. 2 vols. Paris, 1976.

ARAMA 2006
> Arama, Maurice. *Delacroix. Un Voyage initiatique. Maroc, Andalousie, Algérie*. Paris, 2006.

ATLANTA 2006
> *The King's Drawings from the Musée du Louvre*. By Catherine Loisel and Varena Forcione, with the assistance of George A. Wanklyn. Exh. cat. High Museum of Art, Atlanta. Atlanta, 2006.

AURICCHIO 2009
> Auricchio, Laura. *Adélaïde Labille-Guiard: Artist in the Age of the Revolution*. Los Angeles, 2009.

AVRIL 1980
> Avril, François, ed. *La Donation Suzanne et Henri Baderou au Musée de Rouen: Peintures et dessins de l'École française*. Paris, 1980.

BACOU 1976

Bacou, Roseline. "Bolognese Drawings of the Seventeenth Century [in the Lugt Collection]," *Apollo*, vol. 104, no. 177, new series (November 1976): 382–87.

BACOU 1981

Bacou, Roseline. *The Famous Italian Drawings from the Mariette Collection at the Louvre in Paris.* Translated by Patricia Corbett. Milan, 1981.

BAETJER 1995

Baetjer, Katharine. *European Paintings in The Metropolitan Museum of Art by Artists Born before 1865: A Summary Catalogue.* New York, 1996.

BAILEY 1992

Bailey, Colin B. "'J.-H. Fragonard e H. Robert a Roma' by Jean-Pierre Cuzin; Pierre Rosenberg; Catherine Boulot," in *The Burlington Magazine*, vol. 134, no. 1074 (September 1992): 599–600.

BAILEY 2002

Bailey, Colin B. *Patriotic Taste: Collecting Modern Art in Pre-Revolutionary Paris.* New Haven and London, 2002.

BALTIMORE, BIRMINGHAM, ALA., and TACOMA 2005

The Essence of Line: French Drawings from Ingres to Degas. Edited by Jay McKean Fisher, William R. Johnston, Kimberly Schenck, and Cheryl K. Snay. Exh. cat. Baltimore Museum of Art; The Walters Art Museum, Baltimore; Birmingham Museum of Art, Tacoma Art Museum. Baltimore, 2005.

BALTIMORE, BOSTON, and MINNEAPOLIS 1984

Regency to Empire: French Printmaking, 1715–1814. Edited by Victor I. Carlson, John W. Ittmann. Exh. cat. Baltimore Museum of Art; Museum of Fine Arts, Boston; Minneapolis Institute of Arts. Baltimore and Minneapolis, 1984.

BARCELONA 2006

Jean-Honoré Fragonard (1732–1806): Orígenes e influencias. De Rembrandt al siglo XXI. Catalogue by Jean-Pierre Cuzin, with essays by Jean-Pierre Cuzin, Katharina Schmidt, and Sophie Raux. Exh. cat. CaixaForum, Barcelona. Barcelona, 2006.

BASAN 1775

Basan, Pierre François. *Catalogue raisonné des différens objets de curiosités dans les sciences et arts qui composaient le cabinet de feu M. Mariette.* Paris, 1775.

BATAILLE and WILDENSTEIN 1961

Bataille, Marie Louise, and Georges Wildenstein. *Berthe Morisot. Catalogue des peintures, pastels, et aquarelles.* Paris, 1961.

BAUËR 1959

Bauër, Gérard. *Dessins français du dix-huitième siècle: La Figure humaine.* Paris, 1959.

BEAN 1964

Bean, Jacob. "French Drawings in Dutch Collections," *Master Drawings*, vol. 2, no. 3 (1964): 293–95.

BÉNARD 1810

Bénard. *Cabinet de M. Paignon Dijonval. État détaillé et raisonné des dessins et estampes dont il est composé . . .* Paris, 1810.

BERGE-GERBAUD 1997

Berge-Gerbaud, Mària van. *Rembrandt et son école: Dessins de la collection Frits Lugt.* Paris, 1997.

BERN 1960

Corot. Edited by Hugo Wagner. Exh. cat. Kunstmuseum Bern. Bern, 1960.

BERTIN 2001

Bertin, É. "Premier état du Supplément au Catalogue Naef des portraits dessinés par Ingres," *Bulletin du Musée Ingres*, no. 73 (April 2001): 27–29.

BERTRAND 1991
> Bertrand, Étienne. "Pierre Jean Mariette," *La Revue de l'encadrement et de la dorure*, no. 7 (January/February 1991): 19–25.

BESANÇON 1992
> *La Levrette et le financier: À propos de l'acquisition d'un tableau de François-André Vincent (1746–1816)*. By Matthieu Pinette. Exh. cat. Musée des Beaux-Arts et d'Archéologie de Besançon. Besançon, 1992.

BESANÇON 2006
> *Les Fragonard de Besançon*. By Pierre Rosenberg, with the collaboration of Claudine Lebrun Jouve. Exh. cat. Musée des Beaux-Arts et d'Archéologie de Besançon. Milan, 2006.

BETTAGNO 1978
> Bettagno, Alessandro, ed. *Piranesi: Incisioni, Rami, Legature, Architetture*. 2nd ed. Vicenza, 1978.

BIAIS 1892
> Biais, Émile. *Les Pineau, sculpteurs, dessinateurs des bâtiments du roy, graveurs, architectes (1652–1886)*. Paris, 1892.

BIBLIOTHÈQUE DE L'IMAGE 2002
> Bibliothèque de l'Image. *Le Drapé: Carnet de dessins*. Paris, 2002.

BJURSTRÖM 1982
> Bjurström, Per. *French Drawings: Eighteenth Century*. Drawings in Swedish Public Collections, vol. 4. Stockholm, 1982.

BLOK 1999
> Blok, Rhea. "Tekeningen uit het atelier van Jean Hoüel," *Desipientia*, vol. 6, no. 1 (1999): 42–51.

BLOK 2004
> Blok, Rhea. "Jongkind aquarelliste. Une extraordinaire liberté créatrice," *Dossier de l'Art*, no. 108 (June 2004): 42–53.

BOCHER 1879
> Bocher, Emmanuel. *Augustin de Saint-Aubin*. Gravures françaises du XVIIIe siècle, vol. 5. Paris, 1879.

BOCHER 1882
    Bocher, Emmanuel. *Jean-Michel Moreau le jeune.* Gravures françaises du XVIIIe siècle, vol. 6. Paris, 1882.

BOGGS 1962
    Boggs, Jean Sutherland. *Portraits by Degas.* Berkeley, 1962.

BOIME 1973
    Boime, Albert, "New Light on Manet's *Execution of Maximilian*," *The Art Quarterly*, vol. 36, no. 3 (Autumn 1973): 172–208.

BOORSCH and MARCIARI 2006
    Boorsch, Suzanne, and John Marciari. *Master Drawings from the Yale University Art Gallery.* New Haven, 2006.

BOPPE 1989
    Boppe, Auguste. *Les Peintres du Bosphore au XVIIIe siècle.* Paris, 1989.

BOSTON 1984
    Jean-François Millet. By Alexandra R. Murphy, Susan Fleming, and Chantal Mahy-Park. Exh. cat. Museum of Fine Arts, Boston. Boston, 1984.

BOTTINEAU 1989
    Bottineau, Josette. "La Jeunesse de Pierre Guérin: Étude de quelques dessins," *La Revue du Louvre et des musées de France*, vol. 39, no. 5/6 (1989): 300–309.

BOUCHOT-SAUPIQUE 1953
    Bouchot-Saupique, Jacqueline. *Les Dessins de Watteau.* Paris, 1953.

BOURET 1982
    Bouret, Blandine. "L'Ambassade persane à Paris en 1715 et son image," *Gazette des Beaux-Arts*, ser. 6, vol. 100, no. 1365 (October 1982): 109–30.

BRACQUEMOND 1885
    Bracquemond, Félix. *Du dessin et de la couleur.* Paris, 1885.

BRACQUEMOND 2002
> Bracquemond, Félix. *Écrits sur l'art*. Dijon, 2002.

BRUNEL 1986
> Brunel, Georges. *Boucher*. Paris, 1986.

BRUSSELS and PARIS 1949
> *Le Dessin français de Fouquet à Cézanne*. By Jacqueline Bouchot-Saupique. Exh. cat. Palais des Beaux-Arts, Brussels; Musée de l'Orangerie, Paris. Paris, 1949.

BUFFON 1749–67
> Buffon, Georges Louis Leclerc. *Histoire naturelle, générale et particulière, avec la description du cabinet de roy*. 15 vols. Paris, 1749–67.

BULL 2002
> Bull, Duncan. *Jean-Étienne Liotard (1702–1789)*. Amsterdam, 2002.

BURKE 1756
> Burke, Edmund. *A Philosophical Enquiry into the Origin of Our Ideas of the Sublime and Beautiful*. London, 1756.

BUROLLET 2008
> Burollet, Thérèse. *Pastels et dessins*. Paris, 2008.

BURTY 1879
> Burty, Philippe. "Profils d'amateurs: I. Laurent Laperlier," *L'Art*, vol. 16, no. 1 (1879): 147–51.

BUSIRI VICI 1976
> Busiri Vici, Andrea. "Paesistica Romana di Charles Natoire," in *Antichità viva*, vol. 15, no. 2 (1976): 32–44.

CAILLEUX 1959
> Cailleux, Jean, ed. "Four Studies of Soldiers by Watteau: An Essay on the Chronology of Military Subjects," *The Burlington Magazine*, vol. 101, no. 678/679 (September/October 1959): unnumbered seven-page supplement after p. 366.

CAILLEUX 1960
> Cailleux, Jean. "An Unpublished Painting by Saint-Aubin: 'Le Bal Champêtre,'" *The Burlington Magazine*, vol. 102, no. 686 (May 1960): i–iv.

CAILLEUX 1967A
> Cailleux, Jean. "Apud Mariette et Amicos," *The Burlington Magazine*, vol. 109, no. 773 (August 1967): i–vi.

CAILLEUX 1967B
> Cailleux, Jean. "Newly Identified Drawings by Watteau," *The Burlington Magazine*, vol. 109, no. 767 (February 1967): 56–63.

CAILLEUX 1974
> Cailleux, Jean. "The Drawings of Louis-Roland Trinquesse," *The Burlington Magazine*, vol. 116, no. 851 (February 1974): i–xiv.

CAMBRIDGE, MASS., MALIBU, MONTREAL, and NEW YORK 1980
> *French Drawings from a Private Collection: Louis XIII to Louis XVI*. Edited by Konrad Oberhuber and Beverly Schreiber Jacoby. Exh. cat. Fogg Art Museum, Harvard University, Cambridge, Mass.; The J. Paul Getty Museum, Malibu; Montreal Museum of Fine Arts; National Academy of Design, New York. Cambridge, Mass., 1980.

CAMBRIDGE, MASS., TORONTO, PARIS, EDINBURGH, NEW YORK, and LOS ANGELES 1998
> *Mastery & Elegance: Two Centuries of French Drawings from the Collection of Jeffrey E. Horvitz*. Edited by Alvin L. Clark, Jr., with Margaret Morgan Grasselli, Jean-François Méjanès, and William W. Robinson. Exh. cat. Harvard University Art Museums, Cambridge, Mass.; Art Gallery of Ontario, Toronto; Musée Jacquemart-André, Paris; National Gallery of Scotland, Edinburgh; National Academy Museum and School of Fine Arts, New York; Los Angeles County Museum of Art. Cambridge, Mass., 1998.

CANEVA 2002
> Caneva, Caterina. *Corridoio vasariano agli Uffizi*. Florence, 2002.

CANEVA, CECCHI, and NATALI 1992
> Caneva, Caterina, Alessandro Cecchi, and Antonio Natali. *The Uffizi: Guide to the Collections and Catalogue of All the Paintings*. Boston, 1992.

CARPENTRAS, ANGERS, and ARRAS 1978
> *Jean-Joseph-Xavier Bidauld (1758–1846)*. Edited by Suzanne Gutwirth. Exh. cat. Musées Municipaux, Musée Duplessis, Carpentras; Musée des Beaux-Arts, Angers; Musée des Beaux-Arts d'Arras. Carpentras, 1978.

CASTELOT and DECAUX 1970–75
> Castelot, André, and Alain Decaux. *Histoire de la France et des français*. 13 vols. Paris, 1970–75.

CEDERLÖF 1979
> Cederlöf, Ulf. "On an Unearthed Roman Group Portrait with Sergel, by Esprit Gibelin," *Nationalmuseum Bulletin*, vol. 3, no. 3 (1979): 169–78.

CHAPON 1984
> Chapon, François. *Mystère et splendeurs de Jacques Doucet*. Paris, 1984.

CHAUSSARD 1806
> Chaussard, Pierre Jean Baptiste. *Le Pausanias français ou description du Salon de 1806*. Paris, 1808.

CHENNEVIÈRES 1880
> Chennevières, Philippe de. *Les Dessins de maîtres anciens: Exposés à l'École des Beaux-Arts en 1879*. Paris, 1880.

CHERBOURG 1975
> *Jean-François Millet 1814–1875 et le thème du paysan dans la peinture française du XIXe siècle*. Exh. cat. Musée Thomas Henry, Cherbourg. Cherbourg, 1975.

CHICAGO 1960
Corot 1796–1875. Edited by S. Lane Faison and James Ingram Merrill. Exh. cat. The Art Institute of Chicago. Chicago, 1960.

CHRISTIE'S MONACO 1995
Christie's Monaco. Auction cat. *Dessins de maîtres anciens et du XIXème siècle*. June 30, 1995.

CLEAVER 1981
Cleaver, Dale G. "Michallon et la théorie du paysage," *Revue du Louvre* (May–June 1981): 359–66.

COHN and SIEGFRIED 1980
Cohn, Marjorie B., and Susan L. Siegfried. *Works by J.-A.-D. Ingres in the Collection of the Fogg Art Museum*. Cambridge, Mass., 1980.

COLLEGE PARK, MD., LOUISVILLE, KY., and ANN ARBOR, MICH. 1977
From Delacroix to Cézanne: French Watercolor Landscapes of the Nineteenth Century. By Alain De Leiris. Edited by Carol Hynning Smith. Exh. cat. University of Maryland Art Gallery, College Park, Md.; J. B. Speed Art Museum, Louisville, Ky.; University of Michigan Museum of Art, Ann Arbor, Mich. College Park, 1977.

CONISBEE 1986
Conisbee, Philip. "French Artists at Home and Abroad: London and Paris," *The Burlington Magazine*, vol. 128, no. 1000 (July 1986): 532–35.

COPENHAGEN 1935
L'Art français au XVIIIe siècle. By J. Lejeaux, under the direction of François Boucher. Exh. cat. Palais de Charlottenborg, Copenhagen. Paris, 1935.

COPENHAGEN 1983
Konkylien og Mennesket. By Vibeke Woldbye and Bettina von Meyenburg. Exh. cat. Kunstindustrimuseet, Copenhagen. Copenhagen, 1983.

CORMACK 1970
> Cormack, Malcolm. *The Drawings of Watteau*. London, 1970.

CUZIN 1980
> Cuzin, Jean-Pierre. "Vincent, de l'Académie de France à l'Institut de France," in *La Donation Suzanne et Henri Baderou au musée de Rouen: Peintures et dessins de l'École française*. Edited by François Avril. Paris, 1980, pp. 93–100.

CUZIN 1983
> Cuzin, Jean-Pierre. "De Fragonard à Vincent," *Bulletin de la Société de l'histoire de l'art français*, année 1981 (1983): 103–24.

CUZIN 1987
> Cuzin, Jean-Pierre. *Jean-Honoré Fragonard: Vie et œuvre: Catalogue complet des peintures*. Fribourg, 1987.

CUZIN 1988
> Cuzin, Jean-Pierre. *François-André Vincent, 1746–1816*. Paris, 1988.

DACIER 1929–31
> Dacier, Émile. *Gabriel de Saint-Aubin: Peintre, Dessinateur et Graveur (1724–1780)*. 2 vols. Paris, 1929–31.

DACIER, VUAFLART, and HÉROLD 1921–29
> Dacier, Émile, Albert Vuaflart, and Jacques Hérold. *Jean de Jullienne et les graveurs de Watteau au XVIIIe siècle*. 4 vols. Paris, 1921–29.

DAYOT 1925
> Dayot, Armand. *Carle Vernet: Étude sur l'artiste suivie d'un catalogue de l'oeuvre gravé et lithographié et du catalogue de l'exposition retrospective de 1925*. Paris, 1925.

DE BEAUMONT 1998
> De Beaumont, Kim. "Reconsidering Gabriel de Saint-Aubin (1724–1780): The Background for His Scenes of Paris." Ph.D. diss., Institute of Fine Arts, New York University, 1998.

DE PILES 1708
> De Piles, Roger. *Cours de peinture par principes*. Paris, 1708.

DEHOUSSE, PACCO, and PAUCHEN 1985
> Dehousse, Françoise, Maïté Pacco, and Maurice Pauchen. *Léonard Defrance: L'Oeuvre peint*. Liège, 1985.

DEJEAN 2007
> DeJean, Joan E. "Man of Mode: Watteau and the Gendering of Genre Painting," in *French Genre Painting in the Eighteenth Century*. Edited by Philip Conisbee. Washington, 2007, pp. 39–47.

DELACROIX/PACH 1937
> Delacroix, Eugène. *The Journal of Eugène Delacroix*. Translated by Walter Pach. New York, 1937.

DELACROIX/BEAUMONT-MAILLET, JOBERT, and JOIN-LAMBERT 1999
> Delacroix, Eugène. *Souvenirs d'un voyage dans le Maroc*. Edited by Laure Beaumont-Maillet, Barthélémy Jobert, and Sophie Join-Lambert. Paris, 1999.

DELAROCHE-VERNET 1907
> Delaroche-Vernet, Horace. *Recherches généalogiques sur Horace Vernet, Paul Delaroche et leur famille*. Paris, 1907.

DELIGNIÈRES 1896
> Delignières, Émile. *Catalogue raisonné de l'œuvre gravé de Jacques Aliamet d'Abbeville*. Paris, 1986.

DESCHEEMAEKER 1969
> Jacques Descheemaeker. *La Maison d'Arenberg d'après les archives françaises*. Neuilly, 1969.

DIDEROT 1759, 1761, AND 1763/1984
> Diderot, Denis. *Essais sur la peinture: Salons de 1759, 1761, 1763*. Paris, 1984.

DIDEROT 1767/1995
> Diderot, Denis. *Ruines et Paysages: Salons de 1767*. Paris, 1995.

DIDEROT and D'ALEMBERT 1751–76
> Diderot, Denis, and Jean Le Rond d'Alembert, eds. *Encyclopédie, ou dictionnaire raisonné des sciences, des arts et des métiers*. 28 vols. Paris, 1751–76.

DIDEROT and D'ALEMBERT/GILLISPIE 1751–76/1959
    Gillispie, Charles Coulston, ed. *A Diderot Pictorial Encyclopedia of Trades and Industry: Manufacturing and the Technical Arts in Plates Selected from "L'Encyclopédie, ou Dictionnaire raisonné des sciences, des arts et des métiers" of Denis Diderot*. 2 vols. New York, 1959.

DIJON and LONDON 2004
    Boucher et les peintres du Nord. By Françoise Joulie. Exh. cat. Musée Magnin, Dijon; The Wallace Collection, London. Paris, 2004.

DIMIER 1928
    Dimier, Louis. *Les Peintres français du XVIIIe siècle, histoire des vies et catalogue des œuvres*. Paris, 1928.

DIO/CARY 1914–27
    Cassius Dio. *Dio's Roman History, with an English Translation*. Translated by Earnest Cary, based on the translation of Herbert Baldwin Foster. 9 vols. Cambridge, Mass., 1914–27.

DUCLAUX 1991
    Duclaux, Lise. *Charles Natoire, 1700–1777*. Paris, 1991.

DUMAS 2006
    Dumas, Ann. *Edgar Degas: The Last Landscapes*. London, 2006.

DUNCAN 1973
    Duncan, Carol. "Happy Mothers and Other New Ideas in French Art," *The Art Bulletin*, vol. 55, no. 4 (December 1973): 570–83.

DUPLESSIS 1857
    Duplessis, Georges. *Mémoires et journal de J.-G. Wille, graveur du roi, publiés d'après les manuscrits autographes de la Bibliothèque impériale*. 2 vols. Paris, 1857.

DU PONT DE NEMOURS 1788
    Du Pont de Nemours, Pierre Samuel. *Mémoires sur la vie et les ouvrages de M. Turgot, ministre d'état*. Philadelphia, 1788.

DUPUY, LE MASNE DE CHERMONT, and WILLIAMSON 1999
> Dupuy, Marie-Anne, Isabelle Le Masne de Chermont, and Elaine Williamson. *Vivant Denon, directeur des musées sous le consulat et l'empire: Correspondance, 1802–1815*. 2 vols. Paris, 1999.

DUPUY-VACHEY 2009
> Dupuy-Vachey, Marie-Anne. *Vivant Denon et le voyage pittoresque: Un manuscrit inconnu. Écrits d'artistes de la Collection Frits Lugt*, vol. II. Paris, 2009.

EIDELBERG 1977
> Eidelberg, Martin P. *Watteau's Drawings: Their Use and Significance*." New York, 1977.

EIDELBERG 1995
> Eidelberg, Martin P. "Watteau's Italian Reveries," *Gazette des Beaux-Arts*, ser. 6, vol. 126, no. 1521 (October 1995): 111–38.

EITNER 1960
> Eitner, Lorenz. *Géricault: An Album of Drawings in the Art Institute of Chicago*. Chicago, 1960.

ENGERAND 1896
> Engerand, F. "Modèles et bordures de tapisseries des XVIIe et XVIIIe siecles," *Nouvelles archives de l'art français*, ser. 3, vol. 12 (1896). In *Revue de l'art français ancient et moderne*, no. 4–6, (April–June 1896): 137–48.

FAURE 1961
> Faure, Edgar. *La Disgrâce de Turgot, 12 Mai 1776*. Paris, 1961.

FEUILLET 1926
> Feuillet, Maurice. *Les Dessins d'Honoré Fragonard et de Hubert Robert des Bibliothèque et Musée de Besançon*. Paris, 1926.

FIDELL 1974
> Fidell, Madeleine. "The Graphic Art of Charles-François Daubigny." Ph.D. diss., New York University, 1973.

FIDELL-BEAUFORT and BAILLY-HERZBERG 1975
>   Fidell-Beaufort, Madeleine, and Janine Bailly-Herzberg. *Daubigny*. Paris, 1975.

FINLAY 1964
>   Finlay, Nancy Ann. "Animal Themes in the Painting of Eugene Delacroix." Ph.D. diss., Princeton University, 1964.

FLANDRIN and FROIDEVEAUX-FLANDRIN 1984
>   Flandrin, Marthe, and Madeleine Froideveaux-Flandrin. *Les Frères Flandrin: Trois jeunes peintres au XIXe siècle*. Olonne-sur-Mer, 1984.

FLORENCE and PARIS 1976
>   *Hommage à Titien: Dessins, gravures, lettres autographes de Titien et d'artistes du Nord*. By Bert W. Meijer. Exh. cat. Istituto Universitario Olandese, Florence, Institut Néerlandais, Paris. Paris, 1976.

FOSCA 1928
>   Fosca, François. *Liotard (1702–1789)*. Paris, 1928.

FONDATION CUSTODIA 2000
>   Fondation Custodia. *Acquisitions 1994–99: Collection Frits Lugt*. Paris, 2000.

FONTAINEBLEAU and VERSAILLES 2003
>   *Collections des ducs de Mecklembourg-Schwerin: Animaux d'Oudry*. By Vincent Droguet, Xavier Salmon, and Danièle Véron-Denise. Exh. cat. Musée National de Château de Fontainebleau, Musée National des Châteaux de Versailles et de Trianon. Paris, 2003.

FOUCART-WALTER and ROSENBERG 1987
>   Foucart-Walter, Elisabeth, and Pierre Rosenberg. *Le Chat et la palette: Le Chat dans la peinture occidentale du XVe au XXe siècle*. Paris, 1987.

FRANCIS 1931
>   Francis, Eric C. "Augustin de Saint-Aubin," *The Print Collector's Quarterly*, vol. 18, no. 2 (April 1931): 150–73.

GADY 1994

Gady, Alexandre. "Folie Beaujon et chapelle Saint-Nicolas," in *Rue du Faubourg-Saint-Honoré*. Edited by Béatrice de Andia. Paris, 1994, pp. 354–63.

GALASSI 1991

Galassi, Peter. *Corot in Italy: Open-Air Painting and the Classical-Landscape Tradition*. New Haven, 1991.

GALASSI 1998

Galassi, Peter. "Before Corot," in *Corot, un artiste et son temps: Actes des colloques organisés au Musée du Louvre par le Service culturel les 1er et 2 mars 1996 à Paris et par l'Académie de France à Rome, Villa Médicis, le 9 mars 1996 à Rome*. Edited by Chiara Stefani, Vincent Pomarède, and Gérard de Wallens. Paris, 1998, pp. 397–422.

GELDER 1976

Gelder, J. G. van. "The Animal and His 'Lettres de Noblesse,'" *Apollo*, vol. 104, no. 177, new series (November 1976): 88–95.

GENEVA and DIJON 1984

Dessins genevois de Liotard à Hodler. By Anne de Herdt. Exh. cat. Musée Rath, Geneva; Musée des Beaux-Arts, Dijon. Geneva, 1984.

GENEVA and PARIS 1992

Dessins de Liotard: suivi du catalogue de l'oeuvre dessiné. By Anne de Herdt. Exh. cat. Musée d'Art et d'Histoire, Geneva; Musée du Louvre, Paris. Paris, 1992.

GIBELIN 1807

Gibelin, Esprit-Antoine. *Sur la statue dite le Gladiateur, ou Guerrier Combattant*. Paris, 1807.

GLORIEUX 2002

Glorieux, Guillaume. *À l'enseigne de Gersaint: Edme-François Gersaint, marchand d'art sur le Pont Notre-Dame, 1694–1750*. Seyssel, 2002.

GODFREY 1994
>   Godfrey, Richard T. *Wenceslaus Hollar: A Bohemian Artist in England*. New Haven, 1994.

GONCOURT 1875
>   Goncourt, Edmond de. *Catalogue raisonné de l'œuvre peint, dessiné et gravé d'Antoine Watteau*. Paris, 1875.

GONCOURT 1876
>   Goncourt, Edmond de. *Catalogue raisonné de l'œuvre peint, dessiné, et gravé par Pierre-Paul Prud'hon*. Paris, 1876.

GONCOURT/PETY and GALANTRIS 1881/2003
>   Goncourt, Edmond de. *La Maison d'un artiste*. 2 vols. Paris, 1881. Introductory essays by Dominique Pety and Christian Galantris. Reprint, Dijon, 2003.

GONCOURT and GONCOURT/NEVEUX 1859–75/1927
>   Goncourt, Edmond de, and Jules de Goncourt. *L'Art du dix-huitième siècle*. 3 vols. Postscript by Pol Neveux. Paris, 1927.

GONSE 1889
>   Gonse, Louis. "Honoré Fragonard par M. le baron Roger Portalis," *Gazette des Beaux-Arts*, ser. 3, vol. 1 (January 1889): 74–77.

GORDON 1965
>   Gordon, Douglas. "Recollections of a Collector," *Apollo*, vol. 81, no. 35, new series (January 1965): 36–39.

GRANDSON 1985
>   *Gustave Doré: Réaliste et visionnaire, 1832–1883*. By Philippe Kaenel. Exh. cat. Château de Grandson. Geneva, 1985.

GRAPPE 1929
>   Grappe, Georges Pierre François. *La Vie et l'œuvre de J.-H. Fragonard*. Paris, 1929.

GRASSELLI 1987A
Grasselli, Margaret Morgan. "The Drawings of Antoine Watteau: Stylistic Development and Problems of Chronology." Ph.D. diss, Harvard University, Cambridge, Mass., 1987.

GRASSELLI 1987B
Grasselli, Margaret Morgan. "Watteau's Use of the Trois Crayons Technique," in *Drawings Defined*. Edited by Walter L. Strauss and Tracie Felker. New York, 1987, pp. 181–94.

GRASSELLI 1993
Grasselli, Margaret Morgan. "Eighteen Drawings by Antoine Watteau: A Chronological Study," *Master Drawings*, vol. 31, no. 2 (Summer 1993): 103–27.

GRASSELLI 2000
Grasselli, Margaret Morgan. "Following in Watteau's Line: Some Drawings by Jean-Baptiste Pater," *Master Drawings*, vol. 38, no. 2 (Summer 2000): 159–66.

GRASSELLI 2001
Grasselli, Margaret Morgan. "Pierre Rosenberg and Louis-Antoine Prat: *Antoine Watteau 1684–1721. Catalogue raisonné des dessins*," *Master Drawings*, vol. 39, no. 3 (Fall 2001): 310–34.

GRIFFITHS 2004
Griffiths, Antony. *Prints for Books: Book Illustration in France, 1760–1800*. Panizzi Lectures, 2003. London, 2004.

GROSS 2004
Gross, Hans. *Rome in the Age of the Enlightenment: The Post-Tridentine Syndrome and the Ancien Regime*. Cambridge, 2004.

GRUBER 1994
Gruber, Alain Charles, ed. *L'Art décoratif en Europe, classique et baroque*. Translated by John Goodman. Paris, 1994.

GUFFEY 2001
Guffey, Elizabeth E. *Drawing an Elusive Line: The Art of Pierre-Paul Prud'hon*. Newark, Del., 2001.

GUIFFREY 1924
> Guiffrey, Jean. *L'Oeuvre de P.-P. Prud'hon*. Paris, 1924.

GUIMBAUD 1928
> Guimbaud, Louis. *Saint-Non et Fragonard, d'après des documents inédits*. Paris, 1928.

GUIRAUD 1913
> Guiraud, Lucien. *Dessins de l'école française du dix-huitième siècle provenant de la collection H . . .* Paris, 1913.

HAARLEM 1931
> *Kind en Kunst*. Exh. cat. Frans Halsmuseum, Haarlem. Haarlem, 1931.

THE HAGUE, COLOGNE, and PARIS 2004
> *Jongkind, 1819–1891*. Edited by Sylvie Gache-Patin, John Sillevis, and Götz Czymmek. Exh. cat. Gemeentemuseum, The Hague; Wallraf-Richartz-Museum, Cologne; Musée d'Orsay, Paris. Paris, 2004.

HARTFORD, SAN FRANCISCO, and DIJON 1976
> *Jean-Baptiste Greuze, 1725–1805*. By Edgar Munhall. Exh. cat. Wadsworth Atheneum, Hartford; Legion of Honor, San Francisco; Musée des Beaux-Arts, Dijon. Hartford, 1976.

HASKELL and PENNY 1981
> Haskell, Francis, and Nicholas Penny. *Taste and the Antique: The Lure of Classical Sculpture: 1500–1900*. New Haven and London, 1981.

HASSELT 1964
> Hasselt, Carlos van. "Old Master Drawings in the Lugt Collection," *Apollo*, vol. 80, no. 33, new series (November 1964): 368–78.

HATTIS 1977
> Hattis, Phyllis. *Four Centuries of French Drawings in the Fine Arts Museums of San Francisco*. San Francisco, 1977.

HATTORI 2001
: Hattori, Cordélia. "De Charles de La Fosse à Antoine Watteau: Les Saisons Crozat," *Revue du Louvre et des Musées de France*, vol. 51, no. 2 (2001): 56–65.

HEDLEY 2004
: Hedley, Jo. *François Boucher: Seductive Visions*. Exh. cat. The Wallace Collection, London. London, 2004.

HENNUS 1950
: Hennus, M. F. "Frits Lugt. Kunstvorser—Kunstkeurder—Kunstgaarder." *Maandblad voor beeldende kunsten*, vol. 26 (1950): 75–140.

HENRY 1880
: Henry, Charles, ed. *Mémoires inédits de Charles-Nicolas Cochin sur le comte de Caylus, Bouchardon, les Slodtz*. Paris, 1880.

HERBERT 1962
: Herbert, Robert L. "Millet Revisited—I," *The Burlington Magazine*, vol. 104, no. 712 (July 1962): 294–305.

HESELTINE 1900
: *Drawings by François Boucher, Jean-Honoré Fragonard, and Antoine Watteau in the Collection of J.P.H.* London, 1900.

HILL 1992
: Hill, David. *Turner in the Alps: The Journey through France & Switzerland in 1802*. London, 1992.

HILL 1999
: Hill, Malcolm. *Statesman of the Enlightenment: The Life of Anne-Robert Turgot*. London, 1999.

HONOUR 1972
: Honour, Hugh. "Canova's Studio Practice—I: The Early Years," *The Burlington Magazine*, vol. 114, no. 828 (March 1972): 146–56, 159.

HUMBERT, REVILLIOD, and TILANUS 1897
> Humbert, Édouard, Alphonse Revilliod, and Jan Willem Reinier Tilanus. *La Vie et les oeuvres de Jean Étienne Liotard*. Amsterdam, 1897.

HUYGHE 1971
> Huyghe, René. *Hommage à Frits Lugt*. Paris, 1971.

INGERSOLL-SMOUSE 1928
> Ingersoll-Smouse, Florence. *Pater*. Paris, 1928.

JACCOTTET 1952
> Jaccottet, Philippe. *Le Dessin français au XVIIIe siècle*. Lausanne, 1952.

JACOBY 1979
> Jacoby, Beverly Schreiber. "A Landscape Drawing by François Boucher after Domenico Campagnola," *Master Drawings*, vol. 17, no. 3 (Autumn 1979): 261–322.

JACOBY 1986
> Jacoby, Beverly Schreiber. *François Boucher's Early Development as a Draughtsman, 1720–1734*. New York, 1986.

JEAN-RICHARD 1978
> Jean-Richard, Pierrette. *L'Œuvre gravé de François Boucher dans la collection Edmond de Rothschild*. Paris, 1978.

JOHNSON 1995
> Johnson, Lee. *Delacroix Pastels*. New York, 1995.

JOLY/JOHNSON 1772–89/1988
> Joly, Hugues-Adrien. *Lettres à Karl-Heinrich von Heinecken, 1772–1789*. Edited by W. McAllister Johnson. Paris, 1988.

JONES 2004
> Jones, Colin. *Paris: Biography of a City*. New York, 2004.

JORDAN 1995
Jordan, David P. *Transforming Paris: The Life and Labors of Baron Haussmann*. Chicago, 1995.

JULLIEN and JULLIEN 1987
Jullien, André, and Renée Jullien. "Corot dans les Castelli Romani," *Gazette des Beaux-Arts*, vol. 110, no. 7 (October 1987): 113–19, 127–30.

KARLSRUHE 1999
Jean-Siméon Chardin 1699–1779: Werk, Herkunft, Wirkung. By Dietmar Lüdke. Exh cat. Staatliche Kunsthalle Karlsruhe. Ostfildern-Ruit, 1999.

KELLER 2001
Keller, Ulrich. *The Ultimate Spectacle: A Visual History of the Crimean War*. Amsterdam, 2001.

KELLEY 1975
Kelley, David, *Baudelaire: Salon de 1846*. Oxford, 1975.

KJELLBERG 2002
Kjellberg, Pierre. *Le Mobilier français du XVIIIe siècle: Dictionnaire des ébénistes et des menuisiers*. Paris, 2002.

KLIMAN 1982
Kliman, Eve Twose. "Delacroix's Lions and Tigers: A Link between Man and Nature," *The Art Bulletin*, vol. 64, no. 3 (September 1982): 446–66.

KRAUSE 1996
Krause, Katharina. *Die Maison de Plaisance: Landhäuser in der Île-de-France (1660–1730)*. Munich, 1996.

LA FONTAINE 1664–74/1685
La Fontaine, Jean de. *Contes et nouvelles en vers de Monsieur de La Fontaine*. 1664–74. Amsterdam, 1685.

LA FONTAINE 1664–74/1762
> La Fontaine, Jean de. *Contes et nouvelles en vers*. 1664–74. 2 vols. Amsterdam, 1762.

LA FONTAINE/FERRIER and COLLINET 1664–74/1980
> La Fontaine, Jean de. *Contes et nouvelles en vers*. 1664–74. Edited by Nicole Ferrier and Jean-Pierre Collinet. Paris, 1980.

LA FONTAINE/SELLIERS 1664–74/1994
> La Fontaine, Jean de. *Contes et nouvelles en vers*. 1664–74. Edited by Diane de Selliers. Paris, 1994.

LA FONTAINE/SELLIERS 1668–94/1992
> La Fontaine, Jean de. *Fables*. 1668–94. 2 vols. Edited by Diane de Selliers. Paris, 1992.

LA FONTAINE/SHAPIRO 1664–74/1992
> La Fontaine, Jean de. *La Fontaine's Bawdy: Of Libertines, Louts, and Lechers*. [*Contes et nouvelles en verse*. 1664–74.] Translated by Norman R. Shapiro. Princeton, 1992.

LAMERS 1995
> Lamers, Petra. *Il viaggio nel Sud dell'Abbé de Saint-Non*. Naples, 1995.

LAPAUZE 1910
> Lapauze, Henry. *Le Roman d'amour de M. Ingres*. Paris, 1910.

LASALLE 1990
> Lasalle, Christian. *Charles-François Daubigny*. Paris, 1990.

LASSAIGNE and MINERVINO 1974
> Lassaigne, Jacques, and Fiorella Minervino. *Tout l'œuvre peint de Degas*. Paris, 1974.

LA TRIBUNE DE L'ART 2004
> "Nouvelles brèves: Acquisitions—Paris, Fondation Custodia—Montauban, Musée Ingres," *La Tribune de l'art* (December 12, 2004): <http://www.latribunedelart.com/>.

LAUNAY 1991
> Launay, Élisabeth. *Les Frères Goncourt collectionneurs de dessins.* Paris, 1991.

LAURENT 1907
> Laurent, Jacques. *Cartulaires de l'Abbaye de Molesme, ancien diocèse de Langres 916–1250.* Paris, 1907.

LAUSANNE 1979
> *Viollet-le-Duc: Centenaire de la mort à Lausanne.* Edited by Jacques Gubler. Exh. cat. Musée historique de l'Ancien-Évêché, Lausanne. Lausanne, 1979.

LAVEISSIÈRE 1997
> Laveissière, Sylvain. *Le Cabinet des dessins: Prud'hon.* Paris, 1997.

LAVEISSIÈRE 2005
> Laveissière, Sylvain. "Le Premier Tableau de Prud'hon retrouvé: Allégorie en l'honneur du baron de Joursanvault," *La Revue des Musées de France, Revue du Louvre* (December 2005): 16–18.

LECLAIR 2001
> Leclair, Anne. *Louis-Jacques Durameau, 1733–1796.* Paris, 2001.

LEES 1913
> Lees, Frederic. *The Art of the Great Masters as Exemplified by Drawings in the Collection of Emile Wauters.* London, 1913.

LEGRAND 1997
> Legrand, Catherine. *De Pagnest à Puvis de Chavannes.* Paris, 1997.

LEMOISNE 1946
> Lemoisne, Paul-André. *Degas et son œuvre.* 4 vols. Paris, 1946.

LEPOITTEVIN 2005
> Lepoittevin, Lucien. *Une Chronique de l'amitié. Correspondance intégrale du peintre Jean-François Millet.* Le Vast, 2005.

L'ISLE-ADAM and GRASSE 2001

Fragonard et le voyage en Italie 1773–1774: Les Bergeret, une famille de mécènes. Edited by Frédéric Chappey. Exh. cat. Musée d'Art et d'Histoire Louis-Senlecq, L'Isle-Adam; Musée Jean-Honoré Fragonard, Grasse. Paris, 2001

LOCQUIN 1912

Locquin, Jean. *Catalogue raisonné de l'oeuvre de Jean-Baptiste Oudry: Peintre du Roi (1686–1755).* Paris, 1912.

LOFFREDO 1982

Loffredo, François-Raphaël. "Des recherches communes de Barye et de Delacroix au Laboratoire d'anatomie comparée du Muséum d'Histoire Naturelle," *Bulletin de la Société de l'Histoire de l'Art Français* (December 1982): 147–57.

LONDON 1909A

A Catalogue of the Pictures and Drawings in the National Loan Exhibition in Aid of National Gallery Funds, Held in the Grafton Galleries, London (1909–1910). Exh. cat. Grafton Galleries, London. London, 1909.

LONDON 1909B

A Catalogue of the Pictures and Drawings in the National Loan Exhibition in Aid of National Gallery Funds, Held in the Grafton Galleries, Grafton Street, London, October, November, December, and January 1909–1910. Exh. cat. Grafton Galleries, London. London, 1909.

LONDON 1950

Catalogue of an Exhibition of French Master Drawings of the 18th Century Held for the Benefit of the French Hospital and Dispensary, London. Exh. cat. The Matthiesen Gallery, London. London, 1950.

LONDON 1952

French Drawings from Fouquet to Gauguin. Exh. cat. The Arts Council of Great Britain Gallery, London. London, 1952.

LONDON 1968
: *France in the Eighteenth Century.* By Denys Sutton. Exh. cat. Royal Academy of Arts, London. London, 1968.

LONDON 1977
: *French Landscape Drawings and Sketches of the Eighteenth Century.* Edited by Roseline Bacou, Lise Duclaux, and Jean-François Méjanès. Exh. cat. British Museum, London. London, 1977.

LONDON 1982
: *Nineteenth and Twentieth Century French Drawings and Watercolors.* Exh. cat. Stoppenbach & Delestre, London. London, 1982.

LONDON 1988
: *Master Drawings Presented by Adolphe Stein.* Exh. cat. Douwes Fine Art, London. London, 1988.

LONDON 1990
: *Meisterzeichnungen/Master Drawings 1500–1900.* By Katrin Bellinger, Rhoda Eitel, and Martin Grässle for Katrin Bellinger Kunsthandel, Munich. Exh. cat. Harari & Johns, London. Munich, 1990.

LONDON 1991
: *John Ruskin and the Alps: An Exhibition.* By James S. Dearden. Exh. cat. Fine Art Society, London. London, 1991.

LONDON, MINNEAPOLIS, and NEW YORK 2003
: *Constable to Delacroix: British Art and the French Romantics.* Edited by Patrick Noon. Exh. cat. Tate Britain, London; Minneapolis Institute of Art; The Metropolitan Museum of Art, New York. London, 2003.

LOS ANGELES, HOUSTON, and SCHWERIN 2007
: *Oudry's Painted Menagerie: Portraits of Exotic Animals in Eighteenth-Century Europe.* Edited by Mary Morton, with essays by Colin B. Bailey, Christoph Frank, Marina Belozerskaya, et al. Exh. cat. J. Paul Getty Museum, Los Angeles; Museum of Fine Arts, Houston; Staatliches Museum Schwerin. Los Angeles, 2007.

LOS LLANOS 1995

Los Llanos, José-Luis de. "Les Illustrateurs des contes de La Fontaine au XVIIIe siècle," in *Jean de La Fontaine*. Edited by Claire Lesage. Exh. cat. Bibliothèque nationale de France, Paris. Paris, 1995, pp. 74–95.

LOUKOMSKI and NOLHAC 1930

Loukomski, G. K. and Pierre de Nolhac. *La Rome d'Hubert Robert*. Paris, 1930.

LUGT 1921

Lugt, Frits. *Les Marques de collections de dessins et d'estampes*. Amsterdam, 1921. (Supplement, The Hague, 1956).

LUGT 1950

Lugt, Frits. *Inventaire général des dessins des écoles du Nord: École Nationale Supérieure des Beaux-Arts*. Paris, 1950.

MACDONALD and PINTO 1995

MacDonald, William Lloyd, and John A. Pinto. *Hadrian's Villa and Its Legacy*. New Haven, 1995.

MACGREGOR 2007

MacGregor, Arthur. *Curiosity and Enlightenment: Collectors and Collections from the Sixteenth to the Nineteenth Century*. New Haven, 2007.

MAHÉRAULT 1880

Mahérault, Marie-Joseph-François. *L'Oeuvre de Moreau le jeune: Catalogue raisonné et descriptif avec notes iconographiques et bibliographiques*. Paris, 1880.

MANDROUX-FRANÇA 1983

Mandroux-França, Marie-Thérèse. *Les Mariette et le Portugal*. Paris, 1983.

MARCEL 1914

Marcel, Pierre. *Carnet de croquis par Moreau le jeune: Fac-similé de l'album du Musée du Louvre*. 2 vols. Paris, 1914.

MARIETTE/CHENNEVIÈRES and MONTAIGLON 1851–60
> Mariette, Pierre-Jean. *Abécédario de P.-J. Mariette, et autres notes inédites de cet amateur sur les arts et les artistes.* 6 vols. Annotated by Philippe de Chennevières and Anatole de Montaiglon. Paris, 1851.

MARIETTE/MANDROUX-FRANÇA and PRÉAUD 2003
> Mariette, Pierre-Jean. *Catalogues de la collection d'estampes de Jean V, roi de Portugal.* 3 vols. Edited by Marie-Thérèse Mandroux-França and Maxime Préaud. Paris and Lisbon, 2003.

MARTIGNY 2006
> *The Metropolitan Museum of Art, New York: Chefs-d'œuvre de la peinture européenne.* By Katherine Baetjer. Exh. cat. Fondation Pierre Gianadda, Martigny. Martigny, 2006.

MARTIN 1908
> Martin, Jean. *Catalogue raisonné de l'œuvre peint et dessiné de Jean-Baptiste Greuze: Suivi de la liste des gravures executées d'après ses ouvrages.* Paris, 1908.

MATHEY 1939
> Mathey, Jacques. "Remarques sur la chronologie des peintures et dessins d'Antoine Watteau," *Bulletin de la Société de l'histoire de l'art français* (1939): 150–60.

MATHEY 1959
> Mathey, Jacques. *Antoine Watteau: peintures réapparues, inconnues ou négligées par les historiens, identification par les dessins, chronologie.* Paris, 1959.

MAUCLAIR 1905
> Mauclair, Camille. *Jean-Baptiste Greuze.* Paris, 1905.

MCCULLAGH 1981
> McCullagh, Suzanne Folds. "The Development of Gabriel de Saint-Aubin (1724–1780) as a Draughtsman." Ph.D. diss., Harvard University, Cambridge, Mass., 1981.

MCPHERSON 1990

McPherson, Heather. "Manet: Reclining Women of Virtue and Vice," *Gazette des Beaux-Arts*, ser. 6, vol. 115, no. 1452 (January 1990): 34–44.

MÉJANÈS 1976

Méjanès, Jean-François. "A Spontaneous Feeling for Nature: French Eighteenth-Century Landscape Drawings," *Apollo*, vol. 104, no. 177, new series (November 1976): 396–404.

MELLINI 1999

Mellini, Gian Lorenzo. *Canova: saggi di filologia e di ermeneutica*. Milan, 1999.

MERCIER/DELON and BARUCH 1783–89/1990

Mercier, Louis-Sébastian. "Tableau de Paris," 1783–89, in *Paris le jour, Paris la Nuit*. Edited by Michel Delon and Daniel Baruch. Paris, 1990.

A. MICHEL 1906

Michel, André. *François Boucher*. Paris, 1906.

C. MICHEL 1993

Michel, Christian. *Charles-Nicolas Cochin et l'art des lumières*. Rome, 1993.

MIQUEL 1975

Miquel, Pierre. *Le Paysage français au XIXe siècle 1824–1874: L'École de la Nature*. 3 vols. Maurs-la-Jolie, 1975.

MIQUEL 1980

Miquel, Pierre. *Eugène Isabey 1803–1886: La Marine au XIXe siècle*. Maurs-La-Jolie, 1980.

MIREUR 1911–12

Mireur, Hippolyte. *Dictionnaire des ventes d'art faites en France et à l'étranger pendant les XVIIIe & XIXe siècles*. Paris, 1911–12.

MONGAN 1996
> Mongan, Agnes. *David to Corot: French Drawings in the Fogg Art Museum*. Cambridge, Mass., 1996.

MONNERET 1989
> Monneret, Sophie. *L'Orient des peintres*. Paris, 1989.

MONNIER 1992
> Monnier, Geneviève. "Pastel: Its Genesis and Evolution to the Twentieth Century," in *Drawings: Masters and Methods*, *Raphael to Redon*. Edited by Diana Dethloff. London, 1992, pp. 159–76.

MONTAGU 1837
> Montagu, Mary Wortley. *The Letters and Works of Lady Mary Wortley Montagu*. 2 vols. Edited by James Archibald Stuart-Wortley-Mackenzie Wharncliffe. Paris, 1837.

MONTAIGLON and GUIFFREY 1887–1908
> Montaiglon, Anatole de, and Jules Guiffrey. *Correspondance des directeurs de l'Académie de France à Rome avec les surintendants des bâtiments*. 17 vols. Paris, 1887–1908.

MONTAUBAN 1999
> *Les Élèves d'Ingres*. Exh. cat. Musée Ingres, Montauban. Montauban, 1999.

MONTPELLIER 1996
> *De la nature: Paysages de Poussin à Courbet dans les collections du Musée Fabre*. Exh. cat. Musée Fabre, Montpellier. Paris, 1996.

MONTREAL 2005
> *Right Under the Sun: Landscape in Provence from Classicism to Modernism (1750–1920)*. Edited by Guy Cogeval and Marie-Paul Vial. Exh. cat. The Montreal Museum of Fine Arts. Ghent, 2005.

MOREAU-NÉLATON 1905
> Moreau-Nélaton, Étienne. *Histoire de Corot et de ses œuvres, d'après les documents recueillis par Alfred Robaut*. Paris, 1905.

MOREAU-NÉLATON 1925
> Moreau-Nélaton, Étienne. *Daubigny raconté par lui-même*. Paris, 1925.

MOUREAU 1893
> Moureau, Adrien. *Les Moreau*. Paris, 1893.

MOUREAU and GRASSELLI 1987
> Moureau, François, and Margaret Morgan Grasselli, eds. *Antoine Watteau, 1684–1721: Le Peintre, son temps et sa légende*. Paris, 1987.

MUNGER, ZAFRAN, POULET, et al. 1992
> Munger, Jeffrey H., Eric M. Zafran, Anne L. Poulet, Robert D. Mowry, Ellenor M. Alcorn, Vivian S. Hawes, and Joellen Secondo. *The Forsyth Wickes Collection in the Museum of Fine Arts, Boston*. Boston, 1992.

MUNHALL 1982
> Munhall, Edgar. "Auktion des Jahres: Die Kollektion Mariette," *Du*, vol. 492, no. 2 (1982): 63–65.

MUNHALL 1992
> Munhall, Edgar. *Little Notes Concerning Watteau's* Portal of Valenciennes. New York, 1992.

MYRONE 2005
> Myrone, Martin. *Bodybuilding: Reforming Masculinities in British Art 1750–1810*. New Haven, 2005.

NAEF 1977
> Naef, Hans. *Die Bildniszeichnungen von J.-A.-D. Ingres, I*. Bern, 1977.

NANTES 2007
> *Hippolyte et Paul Flandrin: Paysages et Portraits*. Edited by Cyrille Sciama. Exh. cat. Musée des Beaux-Arts de Nantes. Paris, 2007.

NEW YORK 1966
: *Selected Drawings*. Exh.cat. Charles E. Slatkin Galleries, New York. New York, 1966.

NEW YORK 1988
: *François-Marius Granet: Watercolors from the Musée Granet at Aix-en-Provence*. Edited by Edgar Munhall. Exh. cat. The Frick Collection, New York. New York, 1988.

NEW YORK 1995
: *Fantasy and Reality: Drawings from the Sunny Crawford von Bülow Collection*. By Cara Dufour Denison, with contributions by Stephanie Wiles and Ruth S. Kraemer. Exh. cat. The Pierpont Morgan Library, New York. New York, 1995.

NEW YORK 1997
: *Paul Huet*. Organized by Galerie Antoine Laurentin, Paris. Exh. cat. Bob P. Haboldt & Co., New York. New York, 1997.

NEW YORK 1998
: *Master Drawings, 1500–1900*. Thomas Le Claire, Kunsthandel, XI. Exh. cat. W. M. Brady & Co., New York. New York, 1998.

NEW YORK 1999A
: *Eighteenth-Century French Drawings in New York Collections*. By Perrin Stein and Mary Tavener Holmes. The Metropolitan Museum of Art, New York. New York, 1999.

NEW YORK 1999B
: *Portraits by Ingres: Image of an Epoch*. Edited by Gary Tinterow, Philip Conisbee, and Hans Naef. Exh. cat. The Metropolitan Museum of Art, New York. New York, 1999.

NEW YORK 2007
: *Rococo Exotic: French Mounted Porcelains and the Allure of the East*. By Kristel Smentek. Exh. cat. The Frick Collection, New York. New York, 2007.

NEW YORK 2008
: *Old Master Drawings and Oil Sketches*. Exh. cat. W. M. Brady & Co, New York. New York, 2008.

NEW YORK and EDINBURGH 1987
: *The Art of Drawing in France, 1400–1900: Drawings from the Nationalmuseum, Stockholm*. By Per Bjurström. Exh. cat. The Drawing Center, New York; The National Gallery of Scotland, Edinburgh. London, 1987.

NEW YORK and FORT WORTH 2003
: *The Drawings of François Boucher*. By Alistair Laing. Exh. cat. The Frick Collection, New York; Kimbell Art Museum, Fort Worth. New York, 2003.

NEW YORK, FORT WORTH, and OTTAWA 1990
: *Masterful Studies. Three Centuries of French Drawings from the Prat Collection*. Edited by Pierre Rosenberg. Exh. cat. National Academy of Design, New York; Kimbell Art Museum, Fort Worth; The National Gallery of Canada, Ottawa. New York, 1990.

NEW YORK and HOUSTON 1993
: *Degas Landscapes*. Edited by Richard Kendall. Exh. cat. The Metropolitan Museum of Art, New York; Museum of Fine Arts, Houston. New Haven, 1993.

NEW YORK and LONDON 2005
: *French Drawings from the British Museum: Clouet to Seurat*. By Perrin Stein. Exh. cat. The Metropolitan Museum of Art, New York; British Museum, London. London, 2005.

NEW YORK and LOS ANGELES 2002
: *Greuze the Draftsman*. Edited by Edgar Munhall. Exh. cat. The Frick Collection, New York; The J. Paul Getty Museum, Los Angeles. London, 2002.

NEW YORK and OTTAWA 1999
: *Watteau and His World: French Drawing from 1700 to 1750.* By Alan Wintermute. With essays by Alan Wintermute, Pierre Rosenberg, Margaret Morgan Grasselli, and Colin B. Bailey. Exh. cat. The Frick Collection, New York; The National Gallery of Canada, Ottawa. London, 1999.

NEW YORK and PARIS 2007
: *Gabriel de Saint-Aubin, 1724–1780.* By Colin B. Bailey, Kim de Beaumont, Suzanne Folds McCullagh, Christophe Leribault, Pierre Rosenberg, Marie-Catherine Sahut, and Perrin Stein. Exh. cat. The Frick Collection, New York; Musée du Louvre, Paris. Paris, 2007.

NEW YORK and WASHINGTON 2007
: *Private Treasures: Four Centuries of European Master Drawings.* By Margaret Morgan Grasselli. Exh. cat. National Gallery of Art, Washington; D.C.; The Morgan Library & Museum, New York. New York, 2007.

NEW YORK, DETROIT, and PARIS 1986
: *François Boucher, 1703–1770.* Exh. cat. The Metropolitan Museum of Art, New York; Detroit Institute of Arts; Grand Palais, Paris. New York, 1986.

NORTHALL 1776
: Northall, John. *Travels through Italy.* London, 1776.

NORTHAMPTON, MASS., and WILLIAMSTOWN, MASS. 1977
: *Jongkind and the Pre-Impressionists.* By Charles Crehore Cunningham, Susan D. Peters, and Kathleen Zimmerer. Exh. cat. Smith College Museum of Art, Northampton, Mass.; Sterling and Francine Clark Art Institute, Williamstown, Mass. Williamstown, Mass., 1977.

NORWICH and LONDON 1982
: *Théodore Rousseau 1812–1867.* By Nicholas Green. Exh. cat. Sainsbury Centre for the Visual Arts, Norwich; Hazlitt, Gooden & Fox, London. London, 1982.

OLAUSSON and SJÖHOLM 2001

Magnus Olausson and Jessica Sjöholm. *Nationalmuseum Stockholm : Illustrerad katalog över svenska och övriga nordiska miniatyrer*. 2 vols. Stockholm, 2001.

OPPERMAN 1972

Opperman, Hal N. "Jean-Baptiste Oudry 1686–1755, with a Sketch for a Catalogue Raisonné of his Paintings, Drawings, and Prints." Ph.D. diss., University of Chicago, 1972.

OPPERMAN 1973

Opperman, Hal N. "Oudry aux Gobelins," *Revue de l'Art*, vol. 22 (1973): 57–65.

OPPERMAN 1987

Opperman, Hal N. "The Theme of Peace in Watteau," in *Antoine Watteau (1684-1721), le peintre, son temps et sa legende*. Edited by Francois Moureau and Margaret Morgan Grasselli. Geneva, 1987: pp. 23–28.

ORLÉANS and VEVEY 2006

Entre lumières & romantisme: Dessins du Musée des Beaux-Arts d'Orléans. By Mehdi Korchane. Musée des Beaux-Arts d'Orléans; Musée Jenisch, Vevey. Paris, 2006.

OSBORNE 1985

Osborne, Carol M. *Pierre Didot the Elder and French Book Illustration: 1789-1822*. New York, 1985

OTTAWA, WASHINGTON, and BERLIN 2003

The Age of Watteau, Chardin, and Fragonard: Masterpieces of French Genre Painting. Edited by Colin B. Bailey. Exh. cat. The National Gallery of Canada, Ottawa; National Gallery of Art, Washington, D.C.; Gemäldegalerie, Staatliche Museen zu Berlin. New Haven, 2003.

PALLOT 1993

Pallot, Bill G. B. *Furniture Collections in the Louvre: Chairs and Consoles (Menuiserie), 17th and 18th Centuries*. vol. 2. Dijon, 1993.

PARIS 1771 (LAUTS 1977)
: *Cabinet de Tableaux [the private collection of J-E. Liotard]*. Exh. cat. Paris, 1771. Reproduced on pp. 62–64 in Lauts, Jan. "Jean-Étienne Liotard und seine Schülerin Markgräfin Karoline Luise von Baden," *Jahrbuch der Staatlichen Kunstsammlungen in Baden-Württemberg* (1997): 43–70.

PARIS 1860
: *Catalogue de tableaux et dessins de l'école française, principalement du XVIIIe siècle, tirés de collections d'amateurs et exposés au profit de la caisse de secours des artistes peintres, sculpteurs, architectes et dessinateurs*. By Philippe Burty. Exh. cat. Galerie Martinet, Paris. Paris, 1860.

PARIS 1868
: *Catalogue de la vente qui aura lieu par suite du décès de Théodore Rousseau*. By Théophile Silvestre. Exh. cat. Hôtel Drouot, Paris. Paris, 1868.

PARIS 1874
: *Exposition des œuvres de Prud'hon*. Exh. cat. École des Beaux-Arts, Paris. Paris, 1874.

PARIS 1879
: *Catalogue descriptif des dessins de maîtres anciens exposés à l'École des Beaux-Arts mai–juin 1879*. Exh. cat. École des Beaux-Arts, Paris. Paris, 1879.

PARIS 1896
: *Berthe Morisot*. Exh. cat. Durand-Ruel Galleries, Paris. Paris, 1896.

PARIS 1911A
: *Exposition de l'œuvre de Paul Huet (1803–1869)*. Exh. cat. L'École Nationale des Beaux-Arts, Paris. Paris, 1911.

PARIS 1911B
: *Exposition de la turquerie au XVIIIe siècle*. By Jacques Guérin, Paul Alfassa et André Dubrujeaud. Exh. cat. Musée des Arts Décoratifs. Paris, 1911.

PARIS 1913
: *Catalogue de dessins de l'École française du dix-huitième siècle, Provenant de la collection Heseltine*. By Lucien Guiraud. Exh. cat. Galerie Georges Petit, Salon de M. Stettiner. Paris, 1913.

PARIS 1922
: *Exposition P.-P. Prud'hon*. Exh. cat. École des Beaux-Arts, Paris. Paris, 1922.

PARIS 1926
: *Pastels, aquarelles, dessins, crayons de Berthe Morisot*. Exh. cat. Galerie L. Dru, Paris. Paris, 1926.

PARIS 1930
: *Centenaire du Romantisme: Exposition Paul Huet 1803–1869*. Exh. cat. Musée du Louvre, Paris. Paris, 1930.

PARIS 1935
: *Le dessin français dans les collections du XVIIIe siècle*. Exh. cat. Galerie Beaux-Arts, Paris. Paris, 1935

PARIS 1946
: *Trois siècles de dessin parisien*. Exh. cat. Musée Carnavalet, Paris. Paris, 1946.

PARIS 1951
: *Le Dessin français de Watteau à Prud'hon*. By Gérard Bauër. Exh. cat. Galerie Cailleux, Paris. Paris, 1951.

PARIS 1963A
: *La Peinture française du XVIIIe siècle à la cour de Frédéric II*. By Helmut Börsch-Supan. Exh. cat. Musée du Louvre, Paris. Paris, 1963.

PARIS 1963B
: *Mémorial de l'exposition Eugène Delacroix*. Edited by Maurice Sérullaz. Exh. cat. Musée du Louvre, Paris. Paris, 1963.

PARIS 1967
: *Le Cabinet d'un grand amateur, P.-J. Mariette, 1694–1774: Dessins du XVe siècle au XVIIIe siècle.* Edited by Roseline Bacou. Exh. cat. Musée du Louvre, Paris. Paris, 1967.

PARIS 1968
: *Watteau et sa génération.* By Marianne Roland Michel. Exh. cat. Galerie Cailleux, Paris. Paris, 1968.

PARIS 1974
: *Acquisitions récentes de toutes époques: Fondation Custodia, Collection Frits Lugt.* Exh. cat. Institut Néerlandais, Paris. Paris, 1974.

PARIS 1975
: *Jean-François Millet.* By Robert L. Herbert, Michel Laclotte, and Roseline Bacou. Exh. cat. Grand Palais, Paris. Paris, 1975.

PARIS 1978
: *Catalogue "Centenaire," Dessins originaux anciens et modernes, estampes anciennes du XVe au XVIIIe siècle, estampes originales de maîtres des XIXe et XXe siècles, en vente aux prix marqués chez Paul Prouté S.A.* Exh. cat. Paul Prouté, S.A., Paris. Paris, 1978.

PARIS 1979A
: *Dessins français du XIXe siècle du Musée Bonnat à Bayonne.* Exh. cat. Musée du Louvre, Paris. Paris, 1979.

PARIS 1979B
: *Exposition de dessins et sculptures de maîtres anciens et modernes.* Galerie de Bayser, Paris. Paris, 1979.

PARIS 1980
: *Catalogue "Domenico," Dessins, Estampes Anciennes, Estampes Originales.* Exh. cat. Paul Prouté, S.A., Paris. Paris, 1980.

PARIS 1982A
: *Chaillot, Passy, Auteuil: Promenade historique dans le 16e arrondissement.* Exh. cat. Mairie-annexe du 16e Arrondissement, Paris; Domaine de Bagatelle, Paris; Musée Carnavalet, Paris. Paris, 1982.

PARIS 1982B
> *J.-B. Oudry, 1686–1755.* Exh. cat. Galeries nationales du Grand Palais, Paris. Paris, 1982.

PARIS 1983
> *La Rue de Lille: Hôtel de Salm.* By Claude Ducourtial-Rey and Isabelle du Pasquier. Exh. cat. Institut Néerlandais, Paris; Musée National de la Légion d'Honneur et des Ordres de Chevalerie, Paris. Paris, 1983.

PARIS 1984
> *Acquisitions du Cabinet des dessins: 1973–1983: 81e exposition du Cabinet des dessins.* Musée du Louvre, Paris. Paris, 1984.

PARIS 1986
> *Catalogue "Tintoretto." Dessins originaux anciens et modernes, estampes anciennes du XVe au XVIIIe siècle, estampes originales de maîtres des XIXe et XXe siècles.* Exh. cat. Paul Prouté S.A., Paris. Paris, 1986.

PARIS 1987
> *Dessins français du XVIIIe siècle de Watteau à Lemoyne.* By Roseline Bacou. Exh. cat. Musee du Louvre, Paris. Paris, 1987.

PARIS 1989
> *Maîtres français, 1550–1800: Dessins de la donation Mathias Polakovits à l'École des Beaux-Arts.* Edited by Bruno de Bayser, Marianne Roland Michel, Pierre Rosenberg, et al. Exh. cat. École Nationale Supérieure des Beaux-Arts, Paris. Paris, 1989.

PARIS 1990A
> *Dessins et peintures.* Exh. cat. Galerie de Staël, Paris. Paris, 1990.

PARIS 1990B
> *Hoüel, Voyage en Sicile: 1776–1779.* By Madeleine Pinault. Exh. cat. Musée du Louvre, Paris. Paris, 1990.

PARIS 1992
> *Fragonard et le dessin français au XVIIIe siècle dans les collections de Petit Palais.* By José-Luis de Los Llanos. Exh. cat. Musée du Petit Palais, Paris. Paris, 1992.

PARIS 1993
Viollet-le-Duc et la Montagne. By Pierre A. Frey and Lise Grenier. Exh. cat. Caisse Nationale des Monuments Historiques et des Sites, Paris. Grenoble, 1993.

PARIS 1994A
Achille-Etna Michallon. By Vincent Pomarède, Blandine Lesage, and Chiara Stefani. Exh. cat. Musée du Louvre, Paris. Paris, 1994.

PARIS 1994B
Morceaux choisis: Parmi les acquisitions de la Collection Frits Lugt realisées sous le directorat de Carlos van Hasselt, 1970–94. Edited by Mària van Berge-Gerbaud and Hans Buijs. Exh. cat. Institut Néerlandais, Paris. Paris, 1994.

PARIS 1994C
La Chimère de Monsieur Desprez. Edited by Régis Michel. Exh. cat. Musée du Louvre, Pavillon de Flore, Paris. Paris, 1994.

PARIS 1996
Jongkind 1819–1891. Exh. cat. Galerie Brame et Lorenceau, Paris. Paris, 1996.

PARIS 1997A
Inventaire général des dessins: École française XIII de Pagnest à Puvis de Chavannes. Edited by Catherine Loisel-Legrand et al. Exh. cat. Département des arts graphiques, Musée du Louvre, Paris; Musée d'Orsay, Paris. Paris, 1997.

PARIS 1997B
"La Terre Promise du Beau." Een ode aan de natuur aan de hand van enkele landschapstekeningen uit de Collectie Frits Lugt. By J. de Scheemaker. Exh. cat. Institut Néerlandais, Paris. Paris, 1997.

PARIS 1999
Hadrien, Trésors d'une villa impériale. Edited by Jacques Charles-Gaffiot and Henri Lavagne. Exh. cat. Mairie du 5e arrondissement, Paris. Milan, 1999.

PARIS 2001
> *Ingres & Marcotte: Lettres, documents, dessins, et gravures*. Edited by Maria van Berge-Gerbaud. Exh. cat. Fondation Custodia, Paris. Paris, 2001.

PARIS 2003A
> *Catalogue "Delacroix" Dessins-Estampes*. Exh. cat. Paul Prouté S.A., Paris. Paris, 2003.

PARIS 2003B
> *François Boucher: hier et aujourd'hui*. By Françoise Joulie and Jean-François Méjanès. Exh. cat. Musée du Louvre, Paris. Paris, 2003.

PARIS 2004
> *Jongkind intime. Dessins, estampes et lettres de Jongkind et son entourage dans la Collection Frits Lugt*. By Rhea Blok. Exh. cat. Fondation Custodia, Paris. Paris, 2004.

PARIS 2006
> *Salon du Dessin 2006 Catalogue*. Exh. cat. Palais de la Bourse, Paris. Paris, 2006.

PARIS 2007A
> *Fragonard: Les Plaisirs d'un siecle*. By Marie-Anne Dupuy-Vachey. Exh. cat. Musee Jacquemart-Andre, Paris. Ghent, 2007.

PARIS 2007B
> *Le XIXe siècle*. Exh. cat. Talabardon & Gautier, Paris. Paris, 2007.

PARIS 2008
> *Le XIXe siècle*. Exh. cat. Talabardon & Gautier, Paris. Paris, 2008.

PARIS and AMSTERDAM 1964
> *Le Dessin français de Claude à Cézanne dans les collections hollandaises: Complété d'un choix d'autographes des artistes exposés*. Edited by Carlos van Hasselt. Exh. cat. Institut Néerlandais, Paris; Rijksmuseum, Amsterdam. Paris, 1964.

PARIS and GENEVA 1986
> *Artistes en voyage au XVIIIe siècle.* Galerie Cailleux, Paris; Galerie Cailleux, Geneva. Paris, 1986.

PARIS and GENEVA 2006
> *Suite française, dessins de la collection Jean Bonna.* Edited by Emmanuelle Brugerolles. Exh. cat. École Nationale Supérieure des Beaux-Arts, Paris; Musée d'Art et d'Histoire, Geneva. Paris, 2006.

PARIS and LYON 1984
> *Hippolyte, Auguste et Paul Flandrin: Une Fraternité picturale au XIXe siècle.* Exh. cat. Musée du Luxembourg, Paris; Musée des Beaux-Arts, Lyon. Paris, 1984.

PARIS and MANTUA 2001
> *Paysages d'Italie: Les Peintres du plein air (1780–1830).* Edited by Anna Ottani Cavina. Exh. cat. Galeries Nationales du Grand Palais, Paris; Centro Internazionale d'Arte e di Cultura di Palazzo Te, Mantua. Milan, 2001.

PARIS and NEW YORK 1987/1988
> *Fragonard.* By Pierre Rosenberg. Exh. cat. Galeries Nationales du Grand Palais, Paris; The Metropolitan Museum of Art, New York. Paris, 1987. New York, 1988.

PARIS and NEW YORK 1998
> *Prud'hon, ou, le rêve du bonheur.* By Sylvain Laveissière. Exh. cat. Galeries Nationales du Grand Palais, Paris; The Metropolitan Museum of Art, New York. New York, 1998.

PARIS, OTTAWA, and NEW YORK 1988
> *Degas.* By Jean Sutherland Boggs. Exh. cat. Galeries Nationales du Grand Palais, Paris; The National Gallery of Canada, Ottawa, The Metropolitan Museum of Art, New York. New York and Ottawa, 1988.

PARIS, OTTAWA, and VIENNA 1994
> *Egyptomania: Egypt in Western Art, 1730–1930.* Edited by Jean-Marcel Humbert, Michael Pantazzi, and Christiane Ziegler. Exh. cat. Musée du Louvre, Paris; The National Gallery of Canada, Ottawa; Kunsthistorisches Museum, Vienna. Ottawa, 1994.

PARIS and PHILADELPHIA 1998
: *Delacroix: Les Dernières Années.* By Arlette Sérullaz, Vincent Pomarède, and Joseph J. Rishel. Exh. cat. Galeries Nationals du Grand Palais, Paris; Philadelphia Museum of Art. Paris, 1998.

PARIS, PHILADELPHIA, and FORT WORTH 1992
: *The Loves of the Gods: Mythological Painting from Watteau to David.* By Colin B. Bailey, with the assistance of Carrie A. Hamilton. Exh. cat. Galeries Nationales du Grand Palais, Paris; Philadelphia Museum of Art; Kimbell Art Museum, Fort Worth. New York, 1992.

PARIS, SYDNEY, and OTTAWA 2003
: *François Boucher et l'art rocaille dans les collections de l'École des Beaux-Arts.* By Emmanuelle Brugerolles. Exh. cat. École Nationale Supérieure des Beaux-Arts, Paris; Art Gallery of New South Wales, Sydney; Musée des Beaux-Arts du Canada, Ottawa. Paris, 2003.

PARKER 1931
: Parker, Karl Theodore. *The Drawings of Antoine Watteau.* London, 1931.

PARKER and MATHEY 1957
: Parker, Karl Theodore, and Jacques Mathey. *Antoine Watteau: Catalogue complet de son oeuvre dessiné.* 2 vols. Paris, 1957.

PINAULT SØRENSEN 1996
: Pinault Sørensen, Madeleine. "Le Voyage en Italie de Hoüel (1769–1772)," in *Hommage au dessin: Mélanges offerts à Roseline Bacou.* Edited by Maria Teresa Caracciolo. Rimini, 1996, pp. 501–528.

PLAX 2000
: Plax, Julie-Anne. *Watteau and the Cultural Politics of Eighteenth-Century France.* Cambridge, 2000.

POMIAN 1987
: Pomian, Krzysztof. *Collectionneurs amateurs et curieux: Paris, Venise, XVIe–XVIIIe siècle.* Paris, 1987.

PORTALIS 1889
    Portalis, Roger. *Honoré Fragonard: Sa vie et son œuvre*. Paris, 1889.

POSNER 1973
    Posner, Donald. *Watteau: A Lady at Her Toilet*. New York, 1973.

POSNER 1984
    Posner, Donald. *Antoine Watteau*. New York, 1984.

PRAT 2004
    Prat, Louis-Antoine. *Ingres*. Paris, 2004.

PRICE 1967
    Price, Charles Theodore. "Naturalism and Convention in the Painting of Charles-François Daubigny." Ph.D. diss., Yale University, New Haven, 1967.

RALEIGH and BIRMINGHAM, ALA. 1986
    French Paintings from the Chrysler Museum. Edited by Jefferson C. Harrison. Exh. cat. North Carolina Museum of Art, Raleigh; Birmingham Museum of Art, Alabama. Norfolk, Va., 1986.

REFF 1963
    Reff, Theodore. "Degas's Copies of Older Art," *The Burlington Magazine*, vol. 105, no. 723, (June 1963): 241–38.

RENONCIAT 1983
    Renonciat, Annie. *La Vie et l'oeuvre de Gustave Doré*. Paris, 1983.

RIBEIRO 1988
    Ribeiro, Aileen. *Fashion in the French Revolution*. London, 1988.

RIBEIRO 2002
    Ribeiro, Aileen. *Dress in Eighteenth-Century Europe, 1715–1789*. New Haven, 2002.

ROBAUT 1905/1965
    Robaut, Alfred. *L'Œuvre de Corot: Catalogue raisonné et illustré*. 5 vols. Rev. ed., first published Paris, 1905. Paris, 1965.

ROBAUT 1885
>Robaut, Alfred. *L'Oeuvre Complet d'Eugène Delacroix*. Paris, 1885.

ROETHLISBERGER 2002
>Roethlisberger, Marcel. "Les Collections de Jean-Étienne Liotard," *Zeitschrift für schweizerische Archäologie und Kunstgeschichte*, vol. 59, no. 4 (2002): 385–406.

ROLAND MICHEL 1970
>Roland Michel, Marianne. "Fragonard—Illustrator of the 'Contes' of La Fontaine," *The Burlington Magazine*, vol. 112, no. 811 (October 1970): i–vi.

ROLAND MICHEL 1978
>Roland Michel, Marianne. "De l'illusion à 'l'inquiétante étrangeté': quelques remarques sur l'évolution du sentiment et de la representation de la ruine chez des artistes français à partir de 1730," in *Piranèse et les Français: Colloque tenu à la Villa Médicis, 12–14 mai 1976*. Edited by Georges Brunel. Rome, 1978, pp. 475–98.

ROLAND MICHEL 1984
>Roland Michel, Marianne. *Watteau, An Artist of the Eighteenth Century*. London, 1984.

ROLAND MICHEL 1987
>Roland Michel, Marianne. *Le Dessin français au XVIIIe siècle*. Fribourg, 1987.

ROLAND MICHEL 1996
>Roland Michel, Marianne. "Sur sept médaillons de Fragonard," in *Hommage au dessin: mélanges offerts à Roseline Bacou*. Edited by Maria Teresa Caracciolo. Rimini, 1996.

ROME 1981
>*David e Roma*. Exh. cat. Accademia di Francia a Roma. Rome, 1981.

ROME 1984
>*Degas e l'Italia: Villa Medici*. Edited by Jean Leymarie. Exh. cat. Accademia di Francia a Roma. Rome, 1984.

ROME 1990
: *J. H. Fragonard e H. Robert a Roma*. By Jean-Pierre Cuzin, Pierre Rosenberg, and Catherine Boulot. Exh. cat. Villa Medici, Rome. Rome, 1990.

ROME and MILAN 1960
: *Il Disegno Francese da Fouquet a Toulouse-Lautrec*. Exh. cat. Palazzo Venezia, Rome; Palazzo Reale, Milan. Rome, 1960.

ROME and PARIS 1980
: *Horace Vernet (1789–1863)*. By Yves Taralon and Jean-Marie Pupier. Exh. cat. Académie de France à Rome; École Nationale Supérieure des Beaux-Arts, Paris. Rome, 1980.

ROSENBAND 2000
: Rosenband, Leonard N. *Papermaking in Eighteenth-Century France: Management, Labor, and Revolution at the Montgolfier Mill, 1761–1805*. Baltimore, 2000.

ROSENBERG 1984
: Rosenberg, Pierre. *Vies anciennes de Watteau*. Paris, 1984.

ROSENBERG 2000
: Rosenberg, Pierre. *From Drawing to Painting: Poussin, Watteau, Fragonard, David & Ingres*. Princeton, 2000.

ROSENBERG 2003
: Rosenberg, Pierre. "L'Album Groult, dit aussi album Lepeltier," in *Preussen: Die Kunst und das Individuum*. Berlin, 2003, pp. 29–39.

ROSENBERG and BREJON DE LAVERGNÉE 1986
: Rosenberg, Pierre, with the collaboration of Barbara Brejon de Lavergnée, eds. *Panopticon italiano: un diario di viaggio ritrovato, 1759–1761*. By Jean-Claude Richard de Saint-Non. Rome, 1986.

ROSENBERG and PRAT 1996
: Rosenberg, Pierre, and Louis-Antoine Prat. *Antoine Watteau. 1684–1721: Catalogue raisonné des dessins*. 3 vols. Milan, 1996.

ROSENBERG and PRAT 2002
>   Rosenberg, Pierre, and Louis-Antoine Prat. *Jacques-Louis David (1748–1825): Catalogue raisonné des dessins, Tome I.* Milan, 2002.

ROTTERDAM, PARIS, and NEW YORK 1958A
>   *Van Clouet tot Matisse: Tentoonstelling van franse tekeningen uit amerikaanse collecties van 31 juli tot 28 september in het Museum Boymans te Rotterdam.* By the Committee for the Exhibition of French Drawings from American Collections. Exh. cat. Museum Boymans, Rotterdam; Musée de l'Orangerie, Paris; The Metropolitan Museum of Art, New York. Rotterdam, 1958.

ROTTERDAM, PARIS, and NEW YORK 1958B
>   *De Clouet à Matisse: Dessins français des collections américaines.* By the Committee for the Exhibition of French Drawings from American Collections. Exh. cat. Museum Boymans, Rotterdam; Musée de l'Orangerie, Paris; The Metropolitan Museum of Art, New York. Paris, 1958–59.

ROTTERDAM, PARIS, and NEW YORK 1958C
>   *French Drawings from American Collections: A Special Loan Exhibition, February 3–March 15, 1959.* By the Committee for the Exhibition of French Drawings from American Collections. Exh. cat. Museum Boymans, Rotterdam; Musée de l'Orangerie, Paris; The Metropolitan Museum of Art, New York. Rotterdam, 1959.

ROUEN 1965
>   *Paul Huet (1803–1869).* Exh. cat. Musée des Beaux-Arts, Rouen. Rouen, 1965.

SAINT-NON 1781–86
>   Saint-Non, Jean-Claude Richard de. *Voyage pittoresque, ou, description des royaumes de Naples et de Sicile.* 5 vols. Paris, 1781–86.

SAMORS 1958
>   Samors, Willa Kay. "François-Marius Granet." Ph.D. diss., University of Chicago, 1958.

SANDOZ 1980
>Sandoz, Marc. *Louis-Jacques Durameau, 1733–1796*. Paris, 1980.

SARGENTSON 1996
>Sargentson, Carolyn. *Merchants and Luxury Markets: The Marchands-Merciers of Eighteenth-Century Paris*. London, 1996.

SAUR 1992–2009
>Saur, K.G. *Allgemeines Künstler-Lexicon: Die Bildenden Künstler aller Zeiten und Völker*. 63 vols. Munich and Leipzig, 1992–2009.

SCHAZMANN 1938
>Schazmann, Paul Émile. "Voyage de Constantinople, par le comte de Caylus," *Gazette des Beaux-Arts*, ser. 6, vol. 20, no. 899 (September 1938): 111–26.

SCHERF 2006
>Scherf, Guilhem. *Houdon 1741–1828: Statues, portraits sculptés*. Paris, 2006.

SCHNEIDER/EKKART 1932/1973
>Schneider, Hans, with a supplement by Rudolf E. O. Ekkart. *Jan Lievens: Sein Leben und seine Werke*. Amsterdam, 1973. Reprint of 1932 edition, with supplement.

SCHRODER 1996
>Schroder, Anne L. "Fragonard et le dessin français au XVIIIe siècle dans les collections du Petit Palais," *Master Drawings*, vol. 34, no. 4 (1996): 430–35.

SCHULMAN 1997
>Schulman, Michel. *Theodore Rousseau, 1812–1867. Catalogue raisonné de l'œuvre graphique*. Paris, 1997.

SEIDEL 1890
>Seidel, Paul, "Beiträge zur Lebensgeschichte Jean Baptiste Oudry's," *Repertorium für Kunstwissenschaft*, vol. 13 (1890): 80–110.

SENSIER and MANTZ 1881
> Sensier, Alfred, and Paul Mantz. *La Vie et l'œuvre de J.-F. Millet.* Paris, 1881.

SÉRIEYS 1802
> Sérieys, Antoine, ed. *Lettres de Paciaudi au comte de Caylus.* Paris, 1802.

SÉRULLAZ 1981
> Sérullaz, Maurice. "Musée du Louvre, cabinet des dessins: deux dessins de Watteau," *La Revue du Louvre et des musées de France*, vol. 31, no. 1 (1981): 29–32.

SÉRULLAZ 2004
> Sérullaz, Arlette. *Delacroix.* Milan, 2004.

SHEON 1965
> Sheon, Aaron. "Paul Huet at Rouen," *The Burlington Magazine*, vol. 107, no. 749 (August 1965): 441–42

SHOBERL 1813
> Shoberl, Frederic. *The Beauties of England and Wales: Suffolk; Surrey; Sussex.* Vol. XIV. London, 1813.

SLATKIN 1971
> Slatkin, Regina Shoolman. "Two Early Drawings by François Boucher," *Master Drawings*, vol. 9, no. 4 (1971): 398–403, 447–48.

SLAYMAN 1970
> Slayman, James Hugus. "The Drawings of Pierre-Paul Prud'hon: A Critical Study." Ph.D. diss, University of Wisconsin, Madison, 1970.

SMENTEK 2007
> Smentek, Kristel. "Sex, Sentiment, and Speculation: The Market for Genre Prints on the Eve of the French Revolution," in *French Genre Painting in the Eighteenth Century.* Edited by Philip Conisbee. New Haven and London, 2007, pp. 221–43.

SMENTEK 2008
> Smentek, Kristel. "The Collector's Cut: Why Pierre-Jean Mariette Tore Up His Drawings and Put Them Back Together Again," *Master Drawings*, vol. 46, no. 1 (Spring 2008): 36–60.

SOCIÉTÉ FRANÇAISE DE PROMOTION ARTISTIQUE 2004
> Société Française de Promotion Artistique, ed. *Jongkind*. Special Edition of *Connaissance des arts*. Paris, 2004.

SOLLERS and VIOLETTE 1984
> Sollers, Philippe, and Patrick Violette. *Watteau et les femmes*. Paris, 1984.

SOUTH HADLEY, WASHINGTON, and FORT WORTH 1987
> *Berthe Morisot, Impressionist*. By Charles F. Stuckey, William P. Scott, and Suzanne G. Lindsay. Exh. cat. Mount Holyoke College Art Museum, South Hadley, Mass.; National Gallery of Art, Washington, D.C.; Kimbell Art Museum, Fort Worth. New York, 1987.

STARCKY 1988
> Starcky, Emmanuel. *Inventaire général des dessins des écoles du Nord: Écoles allemande, des anciens pays-bas, flamande, hollandaise et suisse, XVe–XVIIIe siècles: Supplément aux inventaires publiés par Frits Lugt et Louis Demonts*. Paris, 1988.

STEIN 2000
> Stein, Perrin. "Copies and Retouched Drawings by Charles-Joseph Natoire," in *Master Drawings*, vol. 38, no. 2 (Summer 2000): 167–86.

STOCKHOLM 1990
> *Sergel: Nationalmuseum Stockholm*. Edited by Nils-Göran Hökby, Ulf Cederlöf, Magnus Olausson. Exh. cat. Nationalmuseum, Stockholm. Stockholm, 1990.

STRASBOURG and PARIS 1983
> *Gustave Doré, 1832–1883*. Exh. cat. Musée d'Art Moderne, Strasbourg; Musée Carnavalet, Paris. Strasbourg, 1983.

STRASBOURG and TOURS 2003
> *L'Apothéose du geste: L'esquisse peinte au siècle de Boucher et Fragonard*. Edited by Dominique Jacquot, with Florian Siffer and Sophie Join-Lambert. Exh. cat. Musée des beaux-arts de Strasbourg, Palais Rohan, Strasbourg; Musée des Beaux-Arts de Tours. Paris, 2003.

STRAUSS 1978–
> Strauss, Walter L., general ed. *The Illustrated Bartsch*. 96 vols. Norwalk, Conn., 1978–.

STUCCILLI 2003
> Stuccilli, Jean-Christophe. "Paysages urbains à Lyon aux XVIe et XVIIe siècles: L'Europe du nord et son antichambre italienne," *Les Cahiers d'histoire de l'art*, no. 1 (2003): 83–94.

STUFFMANN 1968
> Stuffmann, Margret. "Les Tableaux de la collection de Pierre Crozat: Historique et destinée d'un ensemble célèbre, établis en partant d'un inventaire après décès inédit (1740)." *Gazette des beaux-arts*, ser. 6, vol. 72, nos. 1194–96 (July–September 1968): 11–55.

SUTTON 1976
> Sutton, Denys, ed. "Treasures from the Collection of Frits Lugt at the Institut néerlandais, Paris,"*Apollo*, new series, vol. 104, no. 176 (October 1976): entire issue.

THOMPSON 1992
> Thompson, Richard. "The Creative Copy in Late Nineteenth-Century French Art," in *Drawing: Masters and Methods*, *Raphael to Redon*. Edited by Diana Dethloff. London, 1992.

TINTEROW 1990
> Tinterow, Gary. *Géricault's Heroic Landscapes: The Times of Day*. New York, 1990.

TOKYO and KUMAMOTO 1982
> *François Boucher (1703–1770)*. By Denys Sutton. Exh. cat. Tokyo Metropolitan Art Museum; Kumamoto Prefectural Museum of Art. Tokyo, 1982.

TOKYO and KYOTO 1980
> *Fragonard*. Edited by Denys Sutton. Exh. cat. National Museum of Western Art, Tokyo; Kyoto Municipal Museum. Tokyo, 1980.

TOULOUSE 2001
> *Les Collectionneurs toulousains du XVIIIe siècle: l'Académie Royale de Peinture, Sculpture et Architecture*. By Jean Penent. Exh. cat. Musée Paul-Dupuy, Toulouse. Toulouse, 2001.

TOURNUS 2005
> *Greuze et l'affaire du Septime Sévère*. Essays by Annick Lemoine, Mickaël Szanto, and Udolpho van de Sandt, catalogue entries by Marie-Anne Dupuy-Vachey. Exh. cat. Musée Greuze, Tournus. Paris, 2005.

TRYON 1879–98
> Tryon, George W. *Manual of Conchology: Structural and Systematic, with Illustrations of the Species*. 17 vols. Philadelphia, 1879–98.

TURNER 2001
> Turner, Nicholas. *European Drawings: Catalogue of the Collections* [of The J. Paul Getty Museum.] vol. 4. Los Angeles, 2001.

VALENCIENNES 1800/1973
> Valenciennes, Pierre Henri. *Éléments de perspective pratique*. Paris, 1800. Geneva, 1973.

VALENCIENNES 2004
> *Watteau et la fête galante*. Edited by Martin P. Eidelberg and Patrick Ramade. Exh. cat. Musée des Beaux-Arts de Valenciennes. Paris, 2004.

VASI 1747–61
> Vasi, Giuseppe. *Delle magnificenze di Roma Antica e Moderna*. 10 vols. Rome, 1747–61.

VAUGELADE 2001
> Vaugelade, Daniel. *Le Salon physiocratique des La Rochefoucauld: Animé par Louise Élisabeth de La Rochefoucauld duchesse d'Enville, 1716–1797*. Paris, 2001.

VERLET 1967

Verlet, Pierre. *French Furniture and Interior Decoration of the 18th Century*. London, 1967.

VIENNA 1950

Meisterwerke aus Frankreichs Museen: Zeichnungen französischer Künstler vom Ausgang des Mittelalters bis Cézanne. Exh. cat. Albertina, Vienna. Vienna, 1950.

VIGNE 1995

Vigne, Georges. *Dessins d'Ingres: Catalogue raisonné des dessins du Musée de Montauban*. Paris, 1995.

VIOLLET-LE-DUC 1879

Viollet-le-Duc, Eugène-Emmanuel. *Histoire d'un dessinateur. Comment on apprend à dessiner*. Paris, 1879.

VIOLLET-LE-DUC/BUCKNALL 1877

Viollet-le-Duc, Eugène-Emmanuel. *Mont Blanc: A treatise on its geodisical and geological constitution; its transformations; and the ancient and recent state of its glaciers*. Translated by Benjamin Bucknall. London, 1877.

VOLLARD 1924

Vollard, Ambroise. *Degas*. Paris, 1924.

UTRECHT 1985

Liotard in Nederland. Edited by Frans Grijzenhout. Exh. cat. Centraal Museum, Utrecht. Utrecht, 1985.

WASHINGTON 1978

Hubert Robert: Drawings & Watercolors. By Victor Carlson. Exh. cat. National Gallery of Art, Washington, D.C. Washington, D.C., 1978.

WASHINGTON 1988

Places of Delight: The Pastoral Landscape. By Robert C. Cafritz, Lawrence Gowing, and David Rosand. Exh. cat. National Gallery of Art and The Phillips Collection, Washington, D.C. Washington, D.C., 1988.

WASHINGTON 2003
: *Colorful Impressions: The Printmaking Revolution in Eighteenth-Century France.* By Margaret Morgan Grasselli, with essays by Ivan E. Phillips, Kristel Smentek, and Judith C. Walsh. National Gallery of Art, Washingon, D.C. Washington, D.C., 2003.

WASHINGTON, CAMBRIDGE, MASS., and NEW YORK 1978
: *Drawings by Fragonard in North American Collections.* By Eunice Williams. Exh. cat. National Gallery of Art, Washington, D.C.; Fogg Art Museum, Cambridge, Mass.; The Frick Collection, New York. Washington, 1978.

WASHINGTON, DALLAS, and DETROIT 1976
: *Titian and the Venetian Woodcut.* By David Rosand and Michelangelo Muraro. Exh. cat. National Gallery of Art, Washington, D.C.; Dallas Museum of Fine Arts; Detroit Institute of Arts. Washington, 1976.

WASHINGTON, DETROIT, MINNEAPOLIS, CLEVELAND, LOS ANGELES, DENVER, FORT WORTH, KANSAS CITY, and NEW YORK 1979
: *Old Master Paintings from the Collection of Baron Thyssen-Bornemisza.* By Allen Rosenbaum. Exh. cat. National Gallery of Art, Washington, D.C.; Detroit Institute of Arts; Minneapolis Institute of Arts; The Cleveland Museum of Art; Los Angeles County Museum of Art; Denver Art Museum; Kimbell Art Museum, Fort Worth; William Rockhill Nelson Gallery of Art, Kansas City; The Metropolitan Museum of Art, New York. Washington, D.C., 1979.

WASHINGTON, NEW YORK, MINNEAPOLIS, and MALIBU 1981
: *French Master Drawings from the Rouen Museum: From Caron to Delacroix.* By Pierre Rosenberg and François Bergot. Exh. cat. National Gallery of Art, Washington, D.C.; National Academy of Design, New York; Minneapolis Institute of Arts; J. Paul Getty Museum, Malibu. Washington, D.C., 1981.

WASHINGTON, PARIS, and BERLIN 1984
: *Watteau 1684–1721.* Edited by Margaret Morgan Grasselli and Pierre Rosenberg. Exh. cat. National Gallery of Art, Washington, D.C.; Galeries nationales du Grand Palais, Paris; Schloss Charlottenburg, Berlin. Washington, D.C. 1984.

WEBB 2001
> Webb, Matilda. *The Churches and Catacombs of Early Christian Rome: A Comprehensive Guide*. Portland, Ore., 2001.

WEIMAR, NEW YORK, and PARIS 2005
> *From Callot to Greuze: French Drawings from Weimar*. By David Mandrella, Hermann Mildenberger, Benjamin Peronnet, and Pierre Rosenberg. Exh. cat. Stiftung Weimarer Klassik und Kunstsammlungen, Weimar; The Frick Collection, New York; Musée Jacquemart-André, Paris. Berlin, 2005.

WEISBERG 1980
> Weisberg, Gabriel P. "Léon Bonvin and the Pre-Impressionist Innocent Eye," *Arts Magazine* (June 1980): 120–22, 124.

WEISBERG 1987
> Weisberg, Gabriel P. "Small Works and the Simplified Forms in the Art of Léon Bonvin," *Arts Magazine* (September 1987): 54–58.

WEISBERG-ROBERTS 2005
> Weisberg-Roberts, Alicia Kyana. "Antoine Watteau and the Cultural Value of Drawing in Eighteenth-Century France," 2 vols., Ph.D. thesis, Courtauld Institute of Art, London, 2005.

WESTON 1980
> Weston, Helen. "The Case for Constance Mayer," *Oxford Art Journal*, vol. 3, no. 1 (1980): 14–19.

WHITE 1975
> White, Christopher, "A Rembrandt Copy after a Titian Landscape," *Master Drawings*, vol. 13, no. 4 (Winter 1975): 375–79, 427.

WILDENSTEIN 1960
> Wildenstein, Georges. *The Paintings of Fragonard*. London, 1960.

WILHELM 1974
> Wilhelm, Jacques. "Les Portraits masculins dans l'œuvre de Louis-Roland Trinquesse," *Revue de l'Art*, no. 25 (1974): 55–65.

WILLIAMSTOWN, MASS., AMSTERDAM, and PITTSBURGH 1999
: *Jean-François Millet: Drawn into the Light*. By Alexandra R. Murphy. Exh. cat. Sterling and Francine Clark Art Institute, Williamstown, Mass.; Van Gogh Museum, Amsterdam; Frick Art & Historical Society Center, Pittsburgh. New Haven, 1999.

WILDENSTEIN 1924
: Wildenstein, Georges. *Lancret: Biographie et catalogue critiques*. Paris, 1924.

WILTON-ELY 1994
: Wilton-Ely, John. *Piranesi: The Complete Etchings*. 2 vols. San Francisco, 1994.

WITTKOWER 1977
: Wittkower, Rudolph. *Sculpture: Processes and Principles*. New York, 1977

WYE 1991
: Wye, Kenneth R. *The Encyclopedia of Shells*. New York, 1991.

Index of Artists

Anonymous 7
Joseph Bidauld 37
Léon Bonvin 58
François Boucher 12, 13
Auguste-Joseph Bracquemond,
   called Félix Bracquemond 54
Charles-Nicolas Cochin 15, 16
Jean-Baptiste-Camille Corot 42
Charles-François Daubigny 53
Jacques-Louis David 31
Edgar Degas 56, 57
Eugène Delacroix 44, 45, 46
Louis-Jean Desprez 35
Paul-Gustave Doré 61
Louis-Jacques Durameau 27
Hippolyte-Jean Flandrin or
   Paul-Jean Flandrin 47
Jean-Honoré Fragonard 20, 21,
   22, 23
Théodore Géricault 40
Esprit-Antoine Gibelin 26
François-Marius Granet 49
Jean-Baptiste Greuze 24
Henri-Joseph Harpignies 63
Jean-Pierre-Louis-Laurent Hoüel 25
Paul Huet 59
Jean-Auguste-Dominique Ingres 39
Louis-Gabriel-Eugène Isabey 43

Étienne Jeaurat 9
Johan Barthold Jongkind 50
Nicolas Lavreince 36
Jean-Étienne Liotard 11
Pierre-Jean Mariette 8
Achille-Etna Michallon 41
Jean-François Millet 51, 52
Jean-Michel Moreau le Jeune 28
Berthe Morisot 62
Charles-Joseph Natoire 17
Jean-Baptiste Oudry 14
Jean-Baptiste Pater 10
Pierre-Paul Prud'hon 32, 33, 34
Hubert Robert 19
Théodore Rousseau 48
Gabriel de Saint-Aubin 18
Louis-Roland Trinquesse 38
Horace Vernet 55
François-André Vincent 29
Eugène-Emmanuel Viollet-le-Duc 60
Antoine Watteau 1, 2, 3, 4, 5, 6

Photograph Credits

Fig. 4.1: Réunion des Musées Nationaux / Art Resource, NY
Photograph by D. Arnaudet/Gérard Blot

Figs. 4.2, 16.1, 22.2, 33.2, 44.1: Réunion des Musées Nationaux / Art Resource, NY

Figs. 5.1, 5.2: Stiftung Preussische Schlösser und Gärten Berlin-Brandenburg

Fig. 5.3: © The Trustees of the British Museum

Fig. 6.2
The Morgan Library & Museum, New York

Fig. 7.1:
© Besançon, Musée des Beaux-Arts et d'Archéologie
Photograph by Pierre Guenat

Figs. 8.1, 31.1, 35.2, 36.1: © Nationalmuseum, Stockholm

Fig. 10.1: Image © The Metropolitan Museum of Art, New York

Figs. 11.2, 13.1, 38.1: Réunion des Musées Nationaux / Art Resource, NY
Photograph by Thierry Le Mage

Fig. 12.1: © Museo Thyssen-Bornemisza

Fig. 14.1: Museum Boijmans Van Beuningen, Rotterdam

Fig. 19.1: Collection of The John and Mable Ringling Museum of Art, the State Art Museum of Florida, a Division of Florida State University, Sarasota

20.1: Photograph by Mary Anne Sullivan

20.2: © Bibliothèque Municipale de Besançon

Fig. 21.1: Photograph by Michael Bodycomb

Fig. 22.1: Beinecke Rare Book and Manuscript Library, Yale University, New Haven

Fig. 23.1: Réunion des Musées Nationaux / Art Resource, NY
Photograph by Gérard Blot

Fig. 23.2: © Musée des Beaux-Arts et d'Archéologie, Besançon
Photograph by Pierre Guenat

Figs. 28.1, 28.2, 51.1: Photograph © 2009 Museum of Fine Arts, Boston

Fig. 29.1: © Musée des Beaux-arts et d'Archéologie, Besançon
Photograph by Charles Choffet

Fig. 34.1: © Musée Bonnat, Bayonne- A. Vaquero

Fig. 34.2: © The National Gallery, London

Figs. 39.1, 45.1: Réunion des Musées Nationaux / Art Resource, NY
Photograph by Michèle Bellot

Fig. 40.1: Photography © The Art Institute of Chicago.

Figs. 41.1, 50.1, 58.1: Réunion des Musées Nationaux / Art Resource, NY
Photograph by Madeleine Coursaget

Fig. 43.1: © National Maritime Museum, Greenwich, London

Fig. 57.2: Scala / Art Resource, NY

Fig. 60.1: Réunion des Musées Nationaux / Art Resource, NY
Photograph by Hervé Lewandowski

Fig. 62.1: Giraudon/Bridgeman Art Library

Index

Page numbers in italics refer to illustrations.

Abd-er-Rahman (sultan of Morocco), 248n1, 250n7
Académie de France (Rome). *See* French Academy (Rome)
Académie des Beaux-Arts, 240n1
Académie Royale de Peinture et de Sculpture. *See* Royal Academy
Académie Suisse, 171
Accademia di San Luca (Rome), 200n5
Achenbach Foundation for Graphic Arts (Fine Arts Museums of San Francisco), 228n5
Agassiz, Louis, 263n1
Albani, Francesco
  Diana's Nymphs Disarming Sleeping Cupids, 35
Aliamet, Jacques (after Fragonard)
  À Femme avare, galant escroc (fig. 22.1), 80, *218*
Aligny, Théodore d', 132
Alps (France), 263n4
  See also View of the Alps (Viollet-le-Duc)
Alsteens, Stijn, 131, 243n4
  Altra Veduta di Ripa Grande (1677) (Falda), 199n5
Ambroselli, Edouard (cat. 40), 244
André, Mme Michel (cat. 47), 250
Angiviller, Comte d', 105, 117, 231n11, 231n13, 238n15, 239n17
Anonymous French artist, formerly attributed to Watteau
  Study of a Shell (Murex ramosus Linne) (c. 1720–30) (cat. 7), 42–44, *43*, 195–97
Arenberg, fourth duc d' (Léopold-Philippe-Charles-Joseph), 35
Arosa, Gustave (cat. 45 & 46), 249
Art Institute of Chicago, The, 129
Assejlin, Jan, 206n6
Audran, Claude, III, 27, 53
Aulne, Baron de l'. *See* Cochin, Nicolas, *Portrait of Anne-Robert-Jacques Turgot, Baron de l'Aulne*
Azaincourt, Blondel d', 90

Baderou, Henri, 93, 96, 99, 227n12, 229n1, 229n2
  in cat. 27 provenance, 225
  in cat. 29 provenance, 229
Bale, Charles Sackville (cat. 11), 202
Barbizon school, 22, 129, 145, 179, 182
Barye, Antoine-Louis, 140
Basan, Pierre-François, (cat. 8), 46, 197, 198n6, 198n7
Bassano, Gerolamo
  Deluge, 196n3
Bâtiments (Durameau commission from), 226n3
Baudelaire, Charles, 161
Baudin, Noel
  Bergère Louis XVI à dossier médaillon, 240n7
Bayser, Patrick de (cat. 54), 256
Beauharnais, General Alexandre de, 236n2
Beauharnais, Josephine de, 112, 236n2, 240n1
Beaumont, Kim de, 73
Bellingham-Smith, G. (cat. 51), 253
Berchem, Nicolaes, 206n6
Bergeret de Grancourt, Pierre-Jacques, 83, 84
  in cat. 23 provenance, 220, 221n6
  See also Fragonard, Jean-Honoré, *Portrait of Pierre-Jacques Bergeret* (fig. 23.2)
Bergeret de Grancourt, Pierre-Jacques-Onésyme (father), 83–84, 100, 221n7
Berthélemy, Jean-Simon, 230n2
Bertin, Jean-Victor, 131, 132
Besnard, Albert
  in cat. 24 provenance, 222
  Studies of Bare Feet after Greuze's *La Prière du matin*, 87
Bessborough, Third Earl of (Frederick Ponsonby) (cat. 11), 54, 202
Bessey, M. de, 108, 234n3
Bibliothèque Doucet (cat. 3), 188
Bibliothèque Municipale (Besançon), 73
Bibliothèque Nationale (Paris), 17, 97, 165, 260n6

Bidauld, Joseph
  View in Rome (c. 1785–90) (cat. 37), 22, 119–22, *120*, 240–41
Blanche, Jacques-Émile, 179
Blount, Mme Jos (cat. 16), 210
Boccaccio, Giovanni, 80, 82
Boileau sale (Fragonard art), 218n1
Boisfremont, Charles-Boulanger de
  in cat. 33 provenance, 234
  in cat. 34 provenance, 235
Boisfremont, Émilie de. *See* Power, Mme Émilie (née de Boisfremont) (cat. 33)
Boissieu, Jean-Jacques de, 22
Bonaparte, Charles-Louis-Napoléon (Napoléon III), 112, 155, 236n2
Bonaparte, Joseph, 240n1
Bonaparte, Louis, 236n2
Bonaparte, Napoléon-Louis, 112, 236n2
Bonaparte, Napoléon (Napoléon I), 236nn2–3
Bonington, Richard Parkes, 136
Bonna, Jean, 228n9
Bonna Collection, 59
Bonvin, François, 169
Bonvin, Léon
  Plain of Vaugirard, The, 1856 (cat. 58), 22, *168*, 169, 171, 261
  Room with Door Open to a Courtyard and Road (c. 1850s) (fig. 58.1), 169, 261
Bordeaux-Groult, Pierre (cat. 7), 195
Bouchardon, Edmé, 122, 242n6
Boucher, François, 87, 90, 196n5
  Capriccio View of the Farnese Gardens, 1734, 60
  En camaieu brun (1740), 219n9
  engraving of *Allée Bordered by Trees* (Watteau), 197n2
  and Gobelins tapestries, 207n4
  Head of a Young Woman with Hair Tied Up (1740–41), 59
  Lady Fastening Her Garter ("La Toilette"), A (1742) (fig. 12.1), 56, 59, *204*
  Landscape with Ruins, 60
  Soldier Spreading Alarm in Chilperic's Camp, A, 206n2

[325]

Standing Woman Seen from Behind (c. 1742) (cat. 12), 18, 56, *57*, 59, 203–5
Study of a Cottage (c. 1760) (fig. 13.1), 60, *205*
Study of a Young Woman Tying Her Garter, 56
Venus at Vulcan's Forge (1757), 180
View of a Rustic Habitation (c. 1760) (cat. 13), 22, *58*, 59–61, 205–6
Boulard, Jean-Baptiste, 84, 221n11
Bounieu. *See* Ponce, Nicolas (after Bounieu)
Bourgarel, Georges (cat. 3), 188
Boussac sale (1926), 75
Bracquemond, Joseph, Auguste, *see* Bracquemond, Félix
Braquemond, Felix
Du dessin et de la couleur (1885), 257n1
Portrait of Charles Daubigny (1853) (black chalk and graphite) (cat. 54), 157–58, *159*, 256–57
Portrait of Daubigny (1853) (etching) (fig. 54.1), 158, *257*
Bracquemond, Marie, 257n1
Brame & Lorenceau (Paris) (cat. 42), 246
Bredius, Abraham, 13
British Museum (London), 38, 187n4, 195n10
Bronzino, Agnolo
Cosimo I in Armor, c. 1550s (fig. 57.2), 166, *260*
Young Girl with a Missal, 260n6
Brosses, Charles de, 77, 216n4, 216n8
Bruegel, Pieter, the Elder
Harvesters, The, 254n4
Bryas, marquise de (cat. 1), 185
Buffon, Georges Louis Leclerc, 100, 229nn6–7
Bull, Richard, and daughters (cat. 6), 193

Cabinet d'un grand amateur P.-J. Mariette, Le (1967 exhibition catalogue). *See* Lugt, Frits (Frederik) Johannes
Calmann, Hans Maximilian (cat. 4), 189
Camaratta, Giuseppe (and Jean-Etienne Liotard)
A Frankish Lady from Galata and Her Slave, 1745 (fig. 11.1), 53, 55, *202*
Campagnola, Domenico, 33
Canabas, Joseph
Table de salon ovale en acajou avec tablette d'entrejambe, 240n5
Canova, Antonio, 225n6
Carlson, Victor, 73, 75, 215n4, 8
Caroline Murat, Queen of Naples, 240n1
Carracci, Annibale, 46
Study of a Tree, 198n6
Carracci school, 33
Landscape with Man Seated near a Farm, 189n7
Cartaud, Jean-Sylvain, 45
Caylus, Comte de
and Robert, 215n6
and Watteau, 27, 30, 33, 37, 41, 187n5, 188n4, 190n5, 190n7, 195nn2–3, 197n2
Cercle de l'Union Artistique de la Place Vendôme, 264n1
Chapelle, Madeleine, 127
Charles E. Slatkin Galleries (New York) (cat. 56), 258
Châtelet, Claude-Louis, 116, 237n7, 238n12
Chaufourier, Jean, 46, 198n4
Chaussard, Pierre Jean Baptiste, 229n10
Chaÿs, Louis, 230n2
Chenique, Bruno, 129
Chennevières, Philippe de, 37–38, 192n1
Christian Ludwig II, Duke of Mecklenburg-Schwerin, 63
Christie's (London), 54, 198n6, 237n7
Christie's (New York), 155, 186n3, 211n1, 212n3, 255n3
Christie's (Paris), 213n6
Claude (Le Lorrain), 132
Clavelin, Dom Claude-Pierre, 124, 242nn12–13
Clérisseau, Charles-Louis, 90
Cochin, Charles-Nicolas, 90, 124
Portrait of Anne-Robert-Jacques Turgot, Baron de l'Aulne (1763) (cat. 16), 20, 66, *67*, 69, 210
Portrait of Pierre-Jean Mariette (1756) (cat. 15), 16, 63–64, *65*, 208–9
Colosseum (Rome). *See* Houël, Jean-Pierre Louis Laurent, *View of the Colosseum in Rome*
Conantré, baronne de (cat. 1), 185
Conisbee, Philip, 114

Constable, 171, 172
Constantin, Jean-Antoine, 252n2
Coppenol, Lieven van, 13

Corot, Jean-Baptiste-Camille, 122, 131–32, 158, 179, 182
Bridge at Narni, 246n1
Cervara, La, 246n1
Landscape with Rocks near Marino (1827) (cat. 42), 22, 132, *133*, 135, 246
Sketch with Rocks and Trees, 132
studio of, in cat. 42 provenance, 246
Vallée avec un cavalier et une italienne, 135
Courbet, Gustave, 88, 162, 179
Coutan, Louis-Joseph-Auguste
in cat. 40 provenance, 244
in cat. 41 provenance, 245
Coutan, Lucienne (née Hauguet)
in cat. 40 provenance, 244
in cat. 41 provenance, 245
Coypel, Antoine, 187n9
Crimean War. *See* Vernet, Horace, *Study of Gabions in the Trenches of the Crimean War*
Crozat, Pierre, 33, 37, 45
See also Mariette, Pierre-Jean, *View of Crozat's Gardens at Montmorency*
Cuvier, Georges, 140
Cuzin, Jean-Pierre, 103, 221n1
"Cygne, Le" (Prudhomme), 265n3
Cypierre, M. de (cat. 12), 203

Dambrun, Jean, 80
Le Calendrier des Vieillards (engraving, after Fragonard) (1795) (fig. 21.1), 82, *218*
Daubigny, Charles-François
View of Paris from the Tour Saint-Jacques, 1852 (cat. 53), 22, 155–57, *156*, 255–56
See also Félix Braquemond, *Portrait of Charles Daubigny* (Bracquemond)
Daumier, Honoré, 158
David, Jacques-Louis, 131, 243n1
Sketch of Buildings, 105
studio of, in cat. 31 provenance, 232
View across the Tiber with the Temple of Vesta (1775–1780) (cat. 31), *104*, 105–6, 232–33
View of Rome with the Tower of Milizie and the Church of San Pietro in Vincoli (1775–80) (fig. 31.1.), *106*, 232
David-Weill, D. (cat. 27), 225
Davis, Reginald (cat. 5), 191
Debret, Jean-Baptiste, 243n1
Decameron (Boccaccio), 80, 82

[326]

Decker, Cornelis, 60
Defrance, Léonard, 226n5
Degas, Edgar
 Copy after Uccello, 1859 (fig. 57.1), 166, *260*, 260n4
 Family Portrait (The Bellelli Family), 260n6
 Head of a Soldier (1857–59) (cat. 57), 21, 165–66, *167*, 259–60
 Portrait of a Young Woman (1858–59), 260n7
 studio of, in cat. 56 provenance, 258
 studio of, in cat. 57 provenance, 259
 View of the Saône River with the Sérin Bridge near Lyon (1855) (cat. 56), 22, *163*, 164–65, 258–59
Degas (Vollard), 260n1
Delacroix, Eugène, 100, 171
 Barque of Dante, The, 136
 Coast of Spain at Salobrena, The (1832) (fig. 44.1), *137*, 248
 Near Gibraltar (1832) (cat. 44), 22, 137, *138*, 247–48
 studio of, in cat. 45 & 46 provenance, 249
 Study of a Wild Feline Facing Left (c. 1847) (cat. 45), 21, 139–41, 248–50
 Study of a Wild Feline Facing Right (c. 1847) (cat. 46), 21, 139–41, *140*, 248–50
 Tiger Lying Down (1847–49) (fig. 45.1), *141*, 249
Delafosse, Jean-Baptiste, 99, 228n9
Delaroche, Paul, 153
Demay, Jean-Baptiste
 Chaise à la Reine, 240n6
Denon, Vivant
 Voyage pittoresque ou description des royaumes de Naples et de Sicile, 114, 116, 117, 238nn10–11
Descamps, Jean-Baptiste, 88
Desplaces, Louis, 185n1
Desprez, Louis-Jean
 Artists Drawing Vedius Pollio's Former Breeding Grounds, 1777–79 (fig. 35.1), 116, *238*, 238n12
 Slaves of Vedius Pollio Thrown Alive to the Moray Eels, The, 1777–79 (cat. 35), 114–17, *115*, 237–39
 Victims of Tiberius at Capri, The, 1784 (fig. 35.2), 117, *238*
 Voyage pittoresque ou description des royaumes de Naples et de Sicile, 116, 117

Dessin français (1964 catalogue) (Van Hasselt), 22–23
Dessin français de Claude à Cézanne dans les collections hollandaises, Le (1964 exhibition, Institut Néerlandais, Paris), 14, *14*
Devosges, François, 108, 109
Diderot, Denis, 87, 222n3, 223n5
Didot, Pierre.
 Contes et nouvelles en vers par Jean de la Fontaine, 80, 82, 218n2
Dijonval, M. Paignon (cat. 35), 237
Dikeos, Nikos (cat. 40), 244
Dio, Cassius
 Roman History, 114
Donaldson (cat. 6), 194
Doré, Paul Gustave
 illustrations for *Macbeth* (Shakespeare), 264n4
 Landscape at Westbridge, 176
 London, A Pilgrimage (1872), 176
 View of the Forest at Westbridge (1879) (cat. 61), 22, 176, *177*, 179, 264
Douai album, 201n5
Doucet, Jacques, 39
 in cat. 5 provenance, 191
Doyen, Angélique-Catherine, 46
Duclos, A. J., 71
Dulac, Antoine-Charles, 119
Dumas, Alexander (fils), 109
 in cat. 32 provenance, 233
Du Pont de Nemours, Pierre Samuel, 69, 210n7
Dupuy-Vachey, Marie-Anne, 219n14, 238n12
Durameau, Jacques-Philippe (engraver), 226n4
Durameau, Louis-Jacques
 Continence of Bayard, The, 1776 (fig. 27.1), 94, 226, 226n3
 Interior of a Paper Mill, formerly known as "L'Imprimerie secrète," (c. 1770–80) (cat. 27), 93–96, *95*, 225–27
Dürer, Albrecht, 246n5

École de dessin (Paris), 169, 173
École des Beaux-Arts (Paris), 17, 49, 96, 164, 165, 166
École gratuite de dessin (Dijon), 108
Eden, Sir William (cat. 51), 253
Edgar, Charles-Henri-, comte de Mornay, 137
Emile Wauters, Emile (cat. 45 & 46), 249

En camaieu brun (1740) (Boucher), 219n9
Encyclopédie, 93, 96, 210n3, 227n10
Enville, Duchesse d' (Louise-Elisabeth de la Rochefoucauld), 69, 210
Eric Turquin S.A. (Paris)
 in cat. 39 provenance, 243
 in cat. 44 provenance, 247
Evelyn, John, 33, 189n8
Exposition des dessins des maîtres anciens (1879), 37

Falda, Giovanni Battista
 Altra Veduta di Ripa Grande (1677), 199n5
Farnese Gardens (Rome). See Boucher, François; Vincent, François-André
Favre, Alphonse, 263n1
Feilchenfeldt, Walter, Collection of, 260n4
Féral, Jean (cat. 23), 220
Ferté, Léon (cat. 34), 236
Fine Arts Museums of San Francisco. See Achenbach Foundation for Graphic Arts (Fine Arts Museums of San Francisco)
Fisher, Richard (cat. 2), 186
Flandrin, Auguste, 250n1
Flandrin, Hippolyte-Jean, 164, 165
 Bay of Naples, 145
 Vesuvius, 1838 (fig. 47.1), 145, *250*
Flandrin, Hippolyte-Jean (or Paul-Jean Flandrin)
 View from the Summit of Vesuvius, 1838 (cat. 47), *142*, 143, 145, 250–51
Flandrin, Paul (grandson of Paul-Jean) (cat. 47), 250
Flandrin, Paul-Jean, 143, 145, 250n3
 Environs of Naples, The, 145
Flandrin, Paul-Jean (or Hippolyte-Jean)
 View from the Summit of Vesuvius, 1838 (cat. 47), *142*, 143, 145, 250–51
Fogg Art Museum (Cambridge, Mass.), 88, 243n2
Folie Beaujon (Bergeret's residence, Paris), 84, 221n12
Fondation Custodia (Paris), 15, 20, 22, 50, 67, 114, 236n1
Fondation Custodia (Paris), and artwork provenance
 Bidauld (cat. 37), 240
 Bonvin (cat. 58), 261
 Boucher (cat. 13), 205
 Bracquemond (cat. 54), 256

[327]

Corot (cat. 42), 246
Daubigny (cat. 53), 255
David (cat. 31), 232
Degas (cat. 56), 258
Delacroix (cat. 44), 247
Desprez (cat. 35), 237
Doré (cat. 61), 264
Durameau (cat. 27), 225
Flandrin (cat. 47), 250
Géricault (cat. 40), 244
Gibelin (cat. 26), 224
Granet (cat. 49), 252
Harpignies (cat. 63), 266
Hoüel (cat. 25), 223
Huet (cat. 59), 262
Ingres (cat. 39), 243
Isabey (cat. 43), 247
Jeaurat (cat. 9), 199
Jongkind (cat. 50), 253
Michallon (cat. 41), 245
Millet (cat. 52), 255
Natoire (cat. 17), 211
Oudry (cat. 14), 207
Prud'hon (cat. 32), 233
Prud'hon (cat. 33), 234
Prud'hon (cat. 34), 236
Rousseau (cat. 48), 251
Trinquesse (cat. 38), 241
Vernet (cat. 55), 257
Vincent (cat. 29), 229
Vincent (cat. 30), 230
Viollet-le-Duc (cat. 60), 262
Forestier, Anne-Julie, 125, 243n1, 243n5
See also Ingres, Jean Auguste Dominique, *Medallion Portrait of Julie Forestier*
Forsyth Wickes Collection (Museum of Fine Arts, Boston), 97, 214n2
Fossier, on *View of the Forest at Westbridge* (Doré), 264nn4–5
Foucart, Jacques, 145
Four Seasons (mythological paintings) (Watteau), 37
Fragonard, Jean-Honoré, 70, 75, 93, 94, 100, 103
À Femme avare, galant escroc (c. 1780) (cat. 22), 78, 80–83, *81*, 217–19
À Femme avare, galant escroc (c. 1770) (fig. 22.2), *218*
Ancient Theater at Hadrian's Villa, The, 77
Calendrier des vieillards, Le (c. 1780) (cat. 21), 78–80, *79*, 82–83, 217, 218
Portrait of Fragonard Seated in an Armchair (1789) (cat. 23), 83–84, *85*, 220–21
Portrait of Pierre-Jacques Bergeret (fig. 23.2), 84, 220, 221n9
Self-Portrait, Seen Full Face (late 1780s) (fig. 23.1), 83, 220
Stolen Kiss, The (c. 1788) (fig. 36.2), 119, *239*
View of the Serapeum at Hadrian's Villa (c. 1760) (cat. 20), 76, 77–78, 215–16
France, Anatole, 109
in cat. 32 provenance, 233
Francin, Claude, 131
Frederick the Great, 50
Frederik Muller auction house, 13–14
French Academy (Rome), 103
Bidauld, 121
Coypel, 187n9
David, 106
Desprez, 116
Flandrin, H., 143
Flandrin (P.-J.), 250n3
Hoüel, 90
Ingres, 125, 250n3
Jeaurat, 49
Natoire, 69
Trinquesse, 242n4
Vincent, 100, 103
Watelet, 210n3
Watteau, 38, 187n9
French Revolution, 124
French Royal Collection, 188–189n4
Frits Lugt Collection, 20–22, 223n1, 223n4

Gabus, Pierre-Yves (cat. 61), 264
Gady, Alexandre, 221n12
Gagnaire, Jean-Baptiste-Anne-Geneviève, Baron de Joursanvault (cat. 32), 233
Galassi, Peter, 103, 135
Galata (Turkish colony). *See* Liotard, Jean-Étienne
Galerie Antoine Laurentin (Paris) (cat. 59), 262
Galerie Artemis (London) (cat. 41), 245
Galerie C. G. Boerner (New York) (cat. 41), 245
Galerie Cailleux (Paris)
in cat. 1 provenance, 185
in cat. 10 provenance, 200
in cat. 35 provenance, 237
Galerie de Bayser (cat. 14), 206
Galerie de Staël (Paris)
in cat. 48 provenance, 251
in cat. 60 provenance, 262
Galerie Fischer-Kiener (Paris) (cat. 55), 257
Galerie *Les Autographes* (Paris) (cat. 32), 233
Galerie Talabardon & Gautier (Paris)
in cat. 52 provenance, 255
in cat. 58 provenance, 261
Galerie Terrades (Salon du Dessin, Paris) (cat. 31), 232, 233n4
Gallery Doré (London), 176
Gasc, Charles
in cat. 27 provenance, 225
in cat. 30 provenance, 230
Gavet, Émile, 155
Geoffrin, Madame, 63, 64, 210n3
Geoffrin, Marie-Thérèse. *See* La Ferté-Imbault, marquise de (cat. 15)
Geoffrin, Marie-Thérèse Rodet (cat. 15), 208
Georgian, A (Liotard), 53, 203n3
Géricault, Théodore
Charging Chasseur, The, 127
Forest Interior with Thatched Hut (1813–14) (fig. 40.1), 129, 244
Forest with Two Figures and a Cow (c. 1813–1814) (cat. 40), 127–29, *128*, 244
Raft of the Medusa, The (1819), 127, 136
Times of Day, The (1818), 127
Gersaint, Edme, 44, 56, 197n11, 201n3
Gersaint's Shopsign 1721 (Watteau), 59
Gibelin, Esprit-Antoine
Interior of a Sculptor's Atelier with the Borghese Gladiator (c. 1770) (cat. 26), 90–93, *91*, 224–25
Mémoire sur la statue dite le Gladiateur ou Guerrier combattant (1807), 93
Mythological Scene with Horses (1770) (fig. 26.2), 92, 224
Roman Bacchanalia with Sergel (c. 1770), 224n4
Study for Interior of a Sculptor's Atelier with the Borghese Gladiator (c. 1770) (fig. 26.1), 90, 224
Gibraltar. *See* Delacroix, Eugène, *Near Gibraltar* (Delacroix)
Gillot, Claude, 27
Glomy, Jean-Baptiste, 60
in cat. 12 provenance, 203
in cat. 13 provenance, 205
Gobelins tapestries, 61, 63, 226n3

Goelet, Robert (cat. 19), 214, 214n2
Goncourt, Edmond and Jules de, 15, 35, 39, 71, 93, 94, 158, 227n1
  in cat. 5 provenance, 191, 193n12
  in cat. 27 provenance, 225
Goncourt, Edmond de, 114
  sale of collection (1897), 93
Gougenot, Louis, abbé, 208n9
Goyen, Jan van, 150
Granary of Abundance (Lyon), 165, 259n4
Granet, François-Marius
  View of Mont Sainte-Victoire from the Terrace of Malvalat (1844?) (cat. 49), 146, 147, 149, 251–52
  View of Mont Sainte-Victoire from the Terrace of Malvallat (detail) (fig. 49.1), 252
Graphische Sammlung Albertina (Vienna), 70, 229n3
Grasselli, Margaret, 27, 29, 41, 42, 187n9, 195n8
Greuze, Jean-Baptiste, 99, 109
  Aegina Visited by Jupiter, 87, 88
  Arrest of Sabinus, The, 87
  Danae, 87
  Female Nude with Arms Raised, 88
  Female Nude Kneeling with Outstretched Arms (c. 1765–68) (cat. 24), 18, 86, 87–88, 221–23
  Kneeling Female Nude, Study for "Cimon and Pero: Roman Charity" (c. 1765–68) (fig. 24.1), 88, 222
  Lot and His Daughters, 87
  Prière du matin, La, 87
  Roman Charity (Cimon and Pero), 87, 88
  Seated Female Nude, 88
  Seated Female Nude Leaning Forward, 223n8
Greybeards' Calendar, The. See Fragonard, Jean-Honoré, *Calendrier des vieillards, Le*
Gros, Antoine-Jean, 171
Groult, Camille, 52
  in cat. 7 provenance, 195
  in cat. 10 provenance, 200
  in cat. 23 provenance, 220
Groult, Jean
  in cat. 7 provenance, 195
  in cat. 10 provenance, 200
Groult Album, 52
Gruchy (France). See *Landscape near Gruchy* (Millet)
Guéraud, Pierre (cat. 17), 211

Guercino (Giovanni Francesco Barbieri), 46, 198n6
Guérin, Jacques (cat. 27), 225
Guérin, Pierre, 171, 242n10
Guiffrey, Jean, 234nn3–4
Guiraud, Lucien (cat. 62), 265
Gutekunst & Klipstein (cat. 20), 215

Hadrian's Villa (Tivoli), 216n7, 216n10
  Serapeum, at, 78, 216
  See also Fragonard, Jean-Honoré; Robert, Hubert
Haranger (abbé), 33
Harpignies, Henri-Joseph, 135
  in cat. 63 provenance, 266
  Studio of the Artist (1909) (cat. 63), 180–82, 181, 266
Hasselt, Carlos van, 22, 22
Hattori, Cordelia, 37, 191n8
Hauguet, Ferdinand
  in cat. 40 provenance, 244
  in cat. 41 provenance, 245
Hauguet, Lucienne. See Coutan, Lucienne (née Hauguet) (cat. 40); Coutan, Lucienne (née Hauguet) (cat. 41)
Hauguet, Marie-Thérèse (née Schubert)
  in cat. 40 provenance, 244
  in cat. 41 provenance, 245
Hauguet, Maurice-Jacques-Albert
  in cat. 40 provenance, 244
  in cat. 41 provenance, 245
Haussmann, Baron George-Eugène, 155, 157, 256n4, 256nn1–2
Haussmannization (Paris), 155, 157, 256n2
Hendrick de Keyser art school (Amsterdam), 12
Henrotin collection (cat. 59), 261–62
Herbert, Robert L., 254n3
Heseltine, John Postle
  in cat. 2 provenance, 186
  in cat. 6 provenance, 194
  in cat. 11 provenance, 202
Heusch, Jacob de
  View of Lyon with Pierre-Scize Fortress (early 1670s) (fig. 56.1), 164, 258
Historic Galleries (Versailles), 252n1
Hodgkin, Eliot (cat. 16), 210
Hodgkins, Edwin Marriott (cat. 5), 191
Hooghe, Romeyn de, 219n9, 219n13

Hortense, Queen of Holland, 112, 236n2, 240n1
Hôtel Lévis-Mirepoix (Paris), 20, 20
Hôtel Turgot (Paris), 20, 20, 21
Houdon, 67
Hoüel, Jean-Pierre-Louis-Laurent, 22, 223n1
  View of the Colosseum in Rome (c. 1769) (cat. 25), 88–90, 89, 223
  View of the Gardens of the Villa d'Este, 223n4
  View of the Organ Fountain at the Villa d'Este, 223n4
Houthakker, Bernard (cat. 12), 203
Huet, Paul, 241n4
  studio of, in cat. 59 provenance, 261
  View near Apt, 1862 (cat. 59), 170, 171–72, 261–62
Huet, René Paul (son of Paul), and descendants (cat. 59), 261
Huteau, Lucien (cat. 33), 234

Impressionism, 143, 171, 172, 180, 257n1
Impressions et souvenirs (Sand), 249n3
Imprimerie secrète, L'. See Durameau, Louis-Jacques
Ingres, Jean-Auguste-Dominique, 135
  and Degas, 165
  Delacroix, on, 139
  and Flandrin brothers, 143
  Forestier Family, The, 1806 (fig. 39.1), 125, 243, 243n2, 243n5
  and French Academy, 250n3
  Medallion Portrait of Julie Forestier (1806) (cat. 39), 125–27, 126, 242–44
  and Michallon, 131
Institute for Art History (RKD) (The Hague), 19
Institut Néerlandais (Paris), 12, 14, 14, 15, 20, 20
  official inauguration of, 67
  Paysage évoqué par la plume et le pinceau (1980 exhibition) (See *Paysage évoqué par la plume et le pinceau*.)
Institut Pasteur (Paris) (cat. 62), 265
Isabey, Louis-Gabriel-Eugène, 150
  Boat in a Storm (c. 1828) (cat. 43), 134, 135–36, 246–47
  family of, in cat. 43 provenance, 246
  Les Contrebandiers anglais réfugiés dans les rochers, 247n1
  Smugglers, The, 135, 136, 247n1

[329]

See also Rouargue, J., *Smugglers, The*, engraving after (1838, fig. 43.1)
Italian Renaissance art, 166

J. Paul Getty Museum, The (Los Angeles), 87, 214n2
Jabach collection, 33
Jamonières, M. de
  in cat. 21 provenance, 217
  in cat. 22 provenance, 217
Janinet, Jean-François, 117
Jean-Richard, Pierrette, 23
Jeaurat, Étienne
  Landscape with Two Figures, 199n1
  Prostitutes Being Led off to La Salpetrière (1757), 200n6
  View of the Dogana Vecchia near the Port of Ripa Grande, on the Banks of the Tiber (c. 1724–27) (fig. 9.1), 49, 199
  View of the Tiber, near the Ripa Grande, Rome (c. 1724–27) (cat. 9), 22, 48, 49–50, 198–200
  View of the Tiber at San Bartolomeo, 199n1
Joly, Hugues-Adrien, 63–64
Jongkind, Johan Barthold, 136
  Self-Portrait under the Sun (c. 1850) (fig. 50.1), 150, *253*
  View of Montmartre (c. 1849) (cat. 50), *148*, 149–50, 252–53
Josephine, Empress. *See* Beauharnais, Josephine de
Joursanvault of Beaune, Baron de, 108, 233n1, 234n3
Jullien, André and Renée, 135
Jullienne, Jean de, 38, 59, 185n1, 192n5

Kendall, Richard, 165
Klener, J.
  in cat. 6 provenance, 194
Klever, J.
  in cat. 18 provenance, 212
Klever, Jacoba. *See* Lugt-s Klever, Jacoba (Lugt's wife)
Klever, Josef, 14, 19
Klever-Schmidt, Mme J. (cat. 18), 212
Knoedler (Paris) (cat. 57), 259
Koenigs, Franz, 21
Kunglig Akademien för de fria Konsterna (Stockholm), 238n9
Kunsthaus Zurich, 246n1
Kupferstichkabinett, Berlin. *See* Watteau, Antoine, *Three Soldiers Viewed from Behind* (Kupferstichkabinett, Berlin)

La Bédoyère, Comtesse de, 16
  in cat. 15 provenance, 208
Labille-Guiard, Adélaïde
  Self-Portrait with Two Students (1785), 240n9
Laborde, Jean-Benjamin de, 116, 239n17
  in cat. 21 provenance, 217, 218n1
  in cat. 22 provenance, 217, 218n1
La Caze, Louis, 35
Lacour, Mme (cat. 34), 236
La Ferté-Imbault, Marquise de, 64
  in cat. 15 provenance, 208
La Fontaine, Jean de
  Fables, 207n7
  See also Didot, Pierre, *Contes et nouvelles en vers par Jean de la Fontaine*
La Fosse, Charles de, 37
La Girennerie, Colonel de (cat. 23), 220
La Gourdaine, Martin Norblin de (cat. 1), 185
La Gourdaine Jean-Pierre Norblin de (cat. 1), 185
Lagrange, François Reidy de, 242n11
Lajarriette, M. de (cat. 9), 199
Lajarriette collection (Nantes), 50
Lamothe, Louis, 164, 165
Lancret, Nicolas, 219n13
Lange Vijverberg, Lugt house at (The Hague), *18*, 19
Lapauze, Henry, 127
Laperlier, Laurent (cat. 34), 235
Larmessin, Nicolas de, 219n9
La Rochefoucauld, Louise-Elisabeth de, Duchesse d'Enville, 69
  in cat. 16 provenance, 210
Lasquin, Georges B. (cat. 12), 203
Laveissière, Sylvain, 234n2
Lavreince, Nicolas
  Gallant Conversation, 240n9
  Stolen Kiss, The (c. 1785–90) (cat. 36), 117–19, *118*, 239–40
  Stolen Kiss, The (c. 1780) (fig. 36.1), 119, *239*
"L.B.," Private Collection of (cat. 27), 225
Le Bas, Jacques Philippe, 88
Le Berry (France). *See* Rousseau, Théodore, *Riverbank in Le Berri*
Le Breton, Gaston
  in cat. 21 provenance, 217
  in cat. 22 provenance, 217
Le Brun, Charles, 45
Lebrun, Jean Baptiste Pierre (cat. 5), 191
Leclair, Anne, 93–94, 226n7
Le Claire, Thomas (cat. 25), 223
Légion d'honneur, 182
Legros, Alphonse, 158
Lemaire, Catherine (cat. 52), 255
Le Nôtre, André, 45
Leonardo da Vinci, 260n7
  Virgin and Child with Saint Anne and Saint John the Baptist, The (c. 1499–1500) (fig. 34.2), 112, *236*
Léopold-Philippe-Charles-Joseph, fourth duc d'Arenberg, 35
Lépicié, Nicolas-Bernard, 93
Lille, rue de (Paris), 67
Lindon, M. (cat. 4), 189
Liotard, Jean-Étienne
  in cat. 11 provenance, 201
  Frankish Woman from Galata and Her Servant (c. 1740–42) (cat. 11), 53–55, *54*, 201–3
  Frankish Woman from Galata (c. 1740–42) (fig. 11.2), 55, *202*
  Georgian, A, 203n3
  Servant Presenting Tea to Her Seated Levantine Mistress, 55, 203n6
  Veiled Turkish Woman (1738), 203n9
Liotard, Jean-Étienne (and Giuseppe Camaratta)
  A Frankish Lady from Galata and Her Slave (1745) (fig. 11.1), 54–55, *202*
Locatelli, Andrea, 90
Loo, Carle van, 94
Lorenceau, Mme Bernard (cat. 42), 246
Lorrain, Claude, 121
  Evening Landscape (c. 1640–55), 19, *19*
  Sunrise (c. 1640–55), *18*, 19
Louis-Philippe, King of France, 137, 161, 250n7, 256n1
Louis XIV, 33
Louis XV, 50, 63
Louis XVI, 20, 67, 119
Ludwig II, Christian, Duke of Mecklenbourg-Schwerin (cat. 14), 207
Lugt, Frits (Frederik) Johannes
  and art collecting, 13, 14–17, 18–19, 20–22

Cabinet d'un grand amateur
  P.-J.Mariette, Le (1967 exhibition
  catalogue), 16
children, 19
death of, 22
Dessin français de Claude à Cézanne
  dans les collections hollandaises, Le
  (1964 exhibition, Institut Néerlandais, Paris), 14, *14*
first art purchase, 13
Marques de collections de dessins & d'e-
  stampes, Les (1921 book), 12, 16, 17
marriage of, 13
at Oberlin College (Ohio), 19
photograph of (1967), *17*
photograph of, with wife (1910), *13*
photograph of, with wife (1967), *22*
photograph of (age 10), *12*
Rembrandt biography, 13, *12*
Répertoire des catalogues de ventes
  publiques (1927–68), 12, 17
Répertoire (Supplément), 19
residences, *18, 19, 20*
self-portrait (1901), *13*
Wandelingen met Rembrandt in en om
  Amsterdam (book), 14
Lugt, Frits (Frederik) Johannes, and
  artwork provenance
Anonymous (formerly attributed to
  Watteau) (cat. 7), 195
Boucher (cat. 12), 204
Cochin (cat. 15, 16), 208, 210
Degas (cat. 57), 259
Delacroix (cat. 45, 46), 249
Fragonard (cat. 20, 21, 22, 23), 215,
  217, 220
Greuze (cat. 24), 222
Lavreince (cat. 36), 239
Liotard (cat. 11), 202
Mariette (cat. 8), 197
Millet (cat. 51), 253
Moreau (cat. 28), 227
Morisot (cat. 62), 265
Pater (cat. 10), 200
Robert (cat. 19), 214
Saint-Aubin (cat. 18), 212
Watteau (cat. 1, 2, 3, 4, 5, 6), 185,
  186, 188, 189, 191, 194
Lugt-Klever, Jacoba (To) (Lugt's wife),
  13, 19
photographs of, *13, 21, 22*

"M. X." (cat. 38), 241
Maartensdijk estate (Utrecht), *18, 19*
Mallarmé, Stephane

"Le Vierge, le vivace . . . ", 180, 265n3
Malvalat, Le Petit (Granet's country
  house), 149
  See also Granet, François-Marius,
  View of Mont Sainte-Victoire from the
  Terrace of Malvalat
Manet, Édouard, 158, 162
Mannerist art, 166
Marie-Louise of Austria (wife of
  Napoleon I), 236n3
Mariette, Pierre-Jean, 16–17
autographed letter, by, 20, *21*
Cabinet d'un grand amateur
  P.-J.Mariette, Le (Lugt, 1967
  exhibition catalogue), 16
Landscapes with Rocks and Trees,
  198n6
Lugt's study, on, 64
on Oudry, 63, 208n10
Portrait of P.-J. .Mariette (after
  Cochin) (1765) (A. de Saint-Aubin),
  16, *16*
Portrait of Pierre-Jean Mariette (after
  Cochin) (fig. 15.1) (A. de Saint-
  Aubin), 64, *208*, 209n7
Portrait of Pierre-Jean Mariette
  (1756) (cat. 15) (Cochin), 63–64, *65*,
  208–9
View of a Park, c. 1724 (fig. 8.1), 46,
  198, 198n8
View of Crozat's Gardens at
  Montmorency (1724) (cat. 8), 18,
  45–46, *47*, 197–98
on Watteau, 33, 188n2
Mariette, Pierre-Jean II (cat. 8), 197
Marigny, Marquis de, 212n2, 212n4,
  214n1
Marino (Rome). See Corot, Jean-
  Baptiste-Camille, Landscape with
  Rocks near Marino (Corot)
Marius Paulme collection, 18
Marville, Charles, 155
Mathey, Jacques, 42, 44, 189n10
Mathey, purchase of Delacroix draw-
  ing, by, 249n1
Matisse, Henri
  Red Studio (1911), 266n1
Maurice Feuillet, Maurice, 193n13
Mauritshuis (The Hague), 13, 19
Mavrocordato (Prince of Moldavia), 53
Mayer-Lemartinière, Marie Françoise
  Constance, 109–10, 234n1
Mayer-Lemartinière, Marie Françoise
  Constance, print after
  Full-length Portrait of Madame B.

Putting on Her Earrings (also known
  as La Toilette), 1806 (fig. 33.1), 110,
  235, 235n3
Mecklenbourg-Schwerin, Duke of, 63
Méjanès, Jean-François, 230n2, 231n9
Mellan, Claude, 18
Meller, S. (cat. 18), 212
Mensing, Anton, 13
Mercier, Sebastian, 73, 213n9
Mercure de France (pub.), 44, 196n11,
  206n2
Merimée, Prosper, 256n1
Meryon, Charles, 158
Metropolitan Museum of Art, The
  (New York), 50, 60, 87, 201n1,
  240n9, 242n11, 254n4
"Metsu manner" (painting style), 122
Meulemeester, Jean-Paul de (cat. 13),
  205
Meurice, Paul (cat. 44), 247
Meurice-Clémenceau, Madame
  (cat. 44), 247
Michallon, Achille-Etna, 132
  View from the Vatican (1818–21) (cat.
    41), *130*, 131–32, 245
  View of Rome (1818–21) (fig. 41.1),
    131, *245*
Michallon, Claude (father), 131
Michel, Christian, 209n7
Michel, Roland, 237n4, 238n7
Millet, Jean-François, 135
  in cat. 51 provenance, 253
  Gleaner, A (Study of Ruth for
    Harvesters Resting) (1851–53)
    (cat. 51), 151–53, *152*, 253–54
  Harvesters Resting (Ruth and Boaz)
    (fig. 51.1), 151, *254*
  Landscape near Gruchy (c. 1854 (?))
    (cat. 52), 153–55, *154*, 254–55
  Sower, The, 153
Milliet, Henriette (née Schubert)
  in cat. 40 provenance, 244
  in cat. 41 provenance, 245
Monet, Claude, 150
Montagu, Lady Mary Wortley, 55,
  203n10
Montgeoffroy (Mazé), château de,
  240n4
Montigny, Comte de, 203n3
Montmartre (Paris). See Jongkind,
  Johan Barthold, View of Montmartre
Montmorency (France). See Mariette,
  Pierre-Jean; Watteau, Antoine
Moreau, Catherine-Françoise, 97, 99,
  227n3, 228n5

[331]

portraits of (*see* Moreau, Jean-Michel)
Moreau, Gabriel-François (bishop of Mâcon), 108
Moreau, Jean-Michel (known as Moreau le Jeune), 258n2
  Artist's Daughter Asleep (facing left, The), (c. 1772) (fig. 28.2), 97, *228*
  Artist's Daughter Asleep (facing right), The (c. 1772) (fig. 28.1), 97, *228*
  Portrait of the Artist's Daughter (British Museum), 228n5
  Portrait of the Artist's Daughter (San Francisco), 228n5
  Portraits of the Artist's Daughter Asleep (c. 1772) (cat. 28), 97–99, *98*, 227–28
Moreau-Nélaton, Étienne, 135, 246n4
Morel de Vindé, Vicomte Charles-Gilbert (cat. 35), 237

Morgan Library & Museum, The (New York), 42, 44, 203n9
Morisot, Berthe
  studio of, in cat. 62 provenance, 265
  Swans, 1885 (fig. 62.1), 179, *265*
  Swans on the Lake of the Bois de Boulogne (1885) (cat. 62), 21–22, *178*, 179–80, 265
Muller, Frederik, 13–14
Munhall, Edgar, 87, 88
Musée Atger (Montpellier), 212n6
Musée Bonnat (Bayonne), 88
Musée Carnavalet (Paris), 124, 200n6, 242n10
Musée Cognacq-Jay (Paris), 37
Musée de Montauban, 243n2
Musée des Beaux-Arts (Besançon), 77, 216n3
Musée des Beaux-Arts (Grenoble), 94
Musée des Beaux-Arts (Orléans), 56
Musée des Beaux-Arts (Rouen), 99, 229n2, 231n10
Musée des Beaux-Arts (Tours), 200n5
Musée des Beaux-Arts (Valence), 225n7
Musée d'histoire naturelle (Paris), 140
Musée d'Orsay (Paris), 260n6
Musée du Louvre (Paris)
  and Albani, 35
  and Boucher, 180
  Cabinet des Dessins, 23
  and Carracci, 198n6
  and Degas, 165

and Delacroix, 140, *249*
and Fragonard, 221n2
and Greuze, 87, 223n8
and Hoüel, 223n3
and Ingres, 125
and Isabey, 135
Lugt's commission from, 17
and Mariette, 64
and Michallon, 131
and Pater, 201n4, 5
and Poussin, 151
and Prud'hon, 110, 236n1, 236n3
and Robert, Léopold, 254n4
and Trinquesse, 242n5
and Vernet, 97
and Watteau, 59, 193n11
and Zoubaloff album, 129
Musée Fabre (Montpellier), 87
Musée Fesch (Ajaccio), 258n8
Musée Hyacinthe-Rigaud (Perpignan), 71
Musée Magnin (Dijon), 195n7
Musée Municipal (Chaumont), 87
Musée Rolin (Autun), 258n8
Museum Boijmans Van Beuningen (Rotterdam), 21
Museum of Fine Arts (Boston), 45, 73, 97, 151, 209n10, 227n1
Museum of Modern Art, The (New York), 266n1
Museum voor Schone Kunsten (Ghent), 35

Napoleon I. *See* Bonaparte, Napoleon (Napoleon I)
Napoleon III. *See* Bonaparte, Charles-Louis-Napoleon (Napoleon III)
National Gallery of Art (Washington, D.C.), 231n10
National Gallery of Canada, The (Ottawa), 199n1, 246n1, 260n7
Nationalmuseum (Stockholm), 46, 195n7, 198n8, 224n4, 238n15
Natoire, Charles-Joseph, 103, 105
  Farmhouse at Frascati, A (1757), 211n1
  View of San Giovanni e Paolo and San Gregorio, 69
  View of San Giovanni e Paolo in Rome (1757) (cat. 17), *68*, 69–70, 211–12
  and Vincent, 231n11, 231n13
Neoclassicism, 171
Neuville (purchase of Delacroix drawing, by), 249n1
Nini, Jean-Baptiste, 242n6

Oberlin College (Ohio), 19
Oger, Jean-Joseph, 226n4
Old Master paintings, 100, 106, 151, 165, 166, 180, 218n3
Oppenort, Gilles-Marie, 52
Opperman, Hal, 61
Orford, Earl of. *See* Walpole, Horace (Fourth Earl of Orford)
Orleans, duc d'. *See* Louis-Philippe, King of France
Orléans, Hôtel des Ventes (cat. 63), 266
Oskar Reinhart Foundation Museum (Winterthur, Switzerland), 55
Oudry, Jean-Baptiste
  in cat. 14 provenance, 206
  Chasses royales de Louis xv, 61
  "Deux Taureaux et une grenouille, Les," 207n6
  Landscape with Bulls Fighting (1751) (cat. 14), 61–63, *62*, 206–8
  Lions and Bears Fighting (1745) (fig. 14.1), 61, *207*
Ovid. *See Metamorphoses* (Ovid)

Paillet, Eugène (cat. 23), 220
Palazzo Giustiniani (Rome), 75
Paris, Haussmannization of. *See* Haussmannization (Paris)
Pâris, Pierre-Adrian, 75
Parker, Karl Theodore, 42, 44, 189n10
Pater, Jean-Baptiste
  Soldiers before an Inn, 50
  Soldier Walking to the Right, 201n5
  Standing Man, 201n5
  Standing Soldier with a Pipe (c. 1725–30) (cat. 10), 50–52, *51*, 200–201
  Studies of a Soldier with a Rifle, 201n5
  Troops at Rest (c. 1725–30) (fig. 10.1), 50, *200*
Paulme, Marius
  in cat. 21 provenance, 217
  in cat. 22 provenance, 217
  in cat. 28 provenance, 227
Paul Prouté S.A. (Paris)
  in cat. 43 provenance, 247
  in cat. 53 provenance, 255
  in cat. 61 provenance, 264
  in cat. 63 provenance, 266
Petithory, Jacques
  in cat. 17 provenance, 211
  in cat. 30 provenance, 230
Petit Palais, 17, 80, 219n4

Petit Salon (Goncourts), 39
Petit Salon (Jacques Doucet), 39
Philips Family collection, The, 215n4
Piat, A.
　in cat. 21 provenance, 217
　in cat. 22 provenance, 217
Pierre, Jean-Baptiste-Marie, 94, 105, 231n12
Pierre-Scize fortress (Lyon), 164, 259n1
Piles, Roger de, 33, 60–61, 206n7
Pinault, Madeleine, 90
Pineau Sørenson, Dominique, 99
Piranesi, Giovanni Battista, 60, 78, 237n4
Place du Palais Bourbon (Paris), 20
Poisson, Philippe, 29, 187n4
Polakovits collection (École des Beaux-Arts), 49
Ponce, Nicolas (after Bouniou)
　Innocence Watched over by Fidelity (fig. 28.3), 99, *228*, 228n10
Ponsonby, Frederick. *See* Bessborough, Third Earl of (Frederick Ponsonby)
Ponsonby, William, 53
Portail, (Jacques) André, 18
Portalis, Baron Roger, 93
Posner, Donald, 41
Poussin, Nicolas, 121, 132
　Summer: Ruth and Boaz, 151
Power, Mme Émilie
　(née de Boisfremont)
　in cat. 33 provenance, 234
　in cat. 34 provenance, 235
Pra, Albert (cat. 57), 259
Prat, Louis-Antoine, 38, 39, 41, 42, 186n4, 187n2, 188n1, 188n3, 192n3, 193nn9–11, 195n10, 196n4
Prat collection (Paris), 223n4
pre-Impressionism, 150
Prix de Rome. *See* Rome Prize
Prouté, Paul (cat. 9), 199
Provençal school of landscape painting, 147, 252n2
Prudhomme, Sully
　"Cygne, Le," 265n3
Prud'hon, Pierre-Paul, 18
　in cat. 33 provenance, 234
　in cat. 34 provenance, 235
　The Cellist, half-length, three-quarter back view, turned toward the left (1777–78) (cat. 32), 107–9, *107*, 233–34
　Empress Josephine at Malmaison, 112, 236n1
　Queen Hortense and Her Children (c. 1811) (fig. 34.1), 112, *236*
　Queen Hortense and Her Two Children in a Park (c. 1811) (cat. 34), 112–14, *113*, 235–37
　Seated cellist, front view (curate of Baron de Joursanvault) (1777–78) (fig. 32.1), 108, *233*
　Study for a Curtain (c. 1806) (cat. 33), 109–10, *111*, 234–35
　Study of Drapery (for the painting of Constance Mayer, *La Toilette*) (c. 1806) (fig. 33.2), 110, *235*
　Venus and Adonis (c. 1811), 236n3

Reff, Theodore, 260n4
Regnault, Nicolas-François, 119
Rembrandt Harmenszoon van Rijn
　artistic influence on Rousseau, 147
　Landscape with Bear Devouring a Goat (fig. 3.1), 33, *189*
　Lugt's biography, on, *12*, 13
　portrait of Lieven van Coppenol, 13
Renaissance tradition (art), 158, 164, 166, 260n7
Renard, Jean-Augustin, 116
Répertoire des catalogues de ventes publiques (1927–68) (Lugt). *See* Lugt, Frits (Frederik) Johannes
Reza Beg, Mehemet (Persian ambassador), 29, 30
Ribeiro, Aileen, 56, 204n1
Ricci, Seymour de (cat. 5), 191
Rijksmuseum (Amsterdam), 12–13, 193n9
　Dessin français de Claude à Cézanne dans les collections hollandaises, Le (1964 exhibition), 14
Rijksprentenkabinet (Amsterdam), 23
Ringling Museum (Sarasota), 75
Ripa Grande (Rome). *See* Falda, Giovanni Battista; Jeaurat, Étienne
"R.M," Private Collection of (cat. 12), 203
Robert, Hubert, 70, 100
　Antiquities of the Capitoline Museum, 225n7
　artistic influence on Vincent, 103, 105
　Farmyard with Two Figures by a Well, 214n2
　Fountain in the Garden of the Villa d'Este (1760), 215n4
　Fragonard's work acquired by Lugt as this name, 77
　Landscape with Stairs, 73
　Vaulted Garden, The, c. 1760 (fig. 19.1), *75*, 214
　View of an Italian Garden, c. 1760 (cat. 19), 73–75, *74*, 214–15
　View of The Serapeum at Hadrian's Villa, 1765 (fig. 20.2), 78, *216*
Robert, Léopold
　Arrivée des Moissonneurs (1831), 254n4
Rodrigues, Eugène, 197, 211
　in cat. 3 provenance, 188
　in cat. 8 provenance, 197
　in cat. 17 provenance, 211
Romanticism, 127, 136, 166, 171, 175
Rome Prize, 116, 122, 125, 131, 143, 250n3
Rosenband, Leonard N., 226n8
Rosenberg, Pierre
　on David, 232n2
　on Fragonard, 78, 216n2, 221n5
　and Mariette catalogue, 209n10
　on Oudry, 61, 207n1
　on *Study of a Shell* (Anonymous), 42, 196n4
　on Watteau, 38, 39, 41, 186n2, 186n4, 187n2, 188n1, 188n3–4, 192n3, 193nn9–11, 195n10
Rothschild, Edmond de, collection, 59
Rouargue, J.
　Engraving after Isabey's *The Smugglers*, 1838 (fig. 43.1), 136, *247*
Roubo, André-Jacob
　Art du menuisier, L', 240n4
Rousseau, Jean-Jacques
　Émile ou de l'éducation, 99, 228n12
Rousseau, Théodore, 135, 150, 241n4, 255n2
　in cat. 48 provenance, 251
　Riverbank in Le Berri (cat. 48), 22, *144*, 145, 147, 251
Roux, Dr. (cat. 32), 233
Royal Academy
　and Boucher, 60
　and Chaufourier, 46
　and Cochin, 64
　and Greuze, 87
　and Trinquesse, 122
Rubens, Peter Paul, 108
Rublé, baronne de (cat. 1), 185
Ruisdael, Jacob van, 147, 150
Ruskin, John, 175
Rustenhoven (country estate near Utrecht), *18*, 19

[333]

Ruth and Naomi (biblical figures), 151, 254n2
See also Millet, Jean-François

Sablet, F. *See* Jeaurat, Étienne
Sablet, Jean-François
Fisherman in an Italian Landscape during a Storm (c. 1793) (fig. 9.2), 50, 199
Saftleven, Cornelis, 206n6
Saint, Daniel (cat. 5), 191
Saint-Aubin, Augustin de, 64, 99, 124
Portrait of Pierre-Jean Mariette (after Cochin), 16, *16*, (fig. 15.1), 64, *208*, 209n7
Saint-Aubin, Gabriel de, 209n10, 242n8
Boulevard, Le (c. 1760) (cat. 18), *18*, 71–73, *72*, 212–13
Boulevard, Le (c. 1760) (fig. 18.1), 71, *213*, 213n7
Meeting on the Boulevard, The, 71
Society Promenade, 71
Spinning Factory (1776–77), 96
Street Scene, 71, 213n6
Sainte-Victoire, Mont. *See* Granet, François-Marius, *View of Mont Sainte-Victoire from the Terrace of Malvalat*
Saint-Hilaire, Étienne Geoffroy de, 140
Saint-Martin (art dealer), 193n12
Saint-Morys collection, 201n5
Saint-Non, Abbé de, 73, 77, 116, 117, 214n1, 216n5, 219n3
on Vedius Pollio, 238n13
Salles, Pierre, 67
Salon de la Correspondance, 122
Salon (Paris), 110, 122, 145, 147, 182, 241n4
of 1738, 219n13
of 1748, 60
of 1765, 77
of 1777, 66
of 1804, 243n1
of 1806, 110
of 1812, 127, 131
of 1819, 136
of 1822, 136
of 1824, 171
of 1827, 132
of 1850, 153
of 1853, 151
Sand, George, 249n3
Sandwich, Earl of, 53
San Giovanni e Paolo, church of. *See* Natoire, Charles-Joseph, *View of San Giovanni e Paolo in Rome; see also* Vasi, Giuseppe

Sanssouci Palace (Potsdam), 50
Saussure, Horace-Bénédict de, 263n1
Schelfhout, Andreas, 150
Schloss Charlottenburg, Staatliche Schlösser und Gärten (Berlin), 38, 39, 59
Schlossmuseum (Weimar), 212n6
Schubert, Henriette. *See* Milliet, Henriette (née Schubert)
Schubert, Marie-Thérèse. *See* Hauguet, Marie-Thérèse (née Schubert)
Schwerin, gallery at, 208n12
Schwerin archives, 63
Schwiter, Baron Louis Auguste de (cat. 24), 222
Séné, Jean-Baptiste-Claude, 84, 221n11
Sensier, Alfred, 153, 255n2
Serapeum, at Hadrian's Villa (fig. 20.1), 78, *216*
See also Fragonard
Sergel, Johann Tobias, 92, 93, 225n11
Sérin, Pont (Lyon), 163, 259n3
Seurat, Georges, 171
Shelley, Marjorie, 243n3
Siege of Sebastopol. *See* Vernet, Horace, *Study of Gabions in the Trenches of the Crimean War*
Société des Amis des Arts (Paris), 135
Société des Aquafortistes Français, 158
Société des Aquarellistes Français, 176, 182, 264n2
Société des Peintre-Graveurs Français, 158
Sotheby's (New York), 201n1, 201n5, 231n10
Städelsches Kunstinstitut Frankfurt, 212n6
State Hermitage Museum (Saint Petersburg), 71, 197n2, 223n3
Stefani (on Michallon), 131
Stefano da Verona, 15, *15*
Stein, Adolphe (cat. 50), 253
Stenman, Gösta (cat. 35), 237
Stettiner & Co. (Paris)
in cat. 2 provenance, 186
in cat. 6 provenance, 194
in cat. 11 provenance, 202
Steven, P. P. (cat. 35), 237
Stoppenbach & Delestre (London) (cat. 37), 240

Sublime, 175
Suvée, Jean-Benoit, 230n2, 234n1
Symbolism, 179

Taine, Hippolyte, 140
Tainturier, Claire, Mme (cat. 32), 233
Temple of Vesta (Rome). *See* David, Jacques-Louis, *View across the Tiber with the Temple of Vesta*
Tessin, Carl Gustav Tessin, 42, 56
Teylers Museum (Haarlem), 193n9
Thaw Collection, The (The Morgan Library & Museum, New York). *See* Morgan Library & Museum, The, (New York)
The Hague (The Netherlands), 19
Lugt's home, in, *18*, 19
Mauritshuis (*See* Mauritshuis (The Hague)
Rembrandt exhibition, in (1898), 13
Thibault, Anatole-François. *See* France, Anatole
Thiollier, possibly Félix Thiollier (cat. 42), 246
Thomas, Gabriel (cat. 62), 265
Thomassin, Henri-Simon, 185n1
Titian, 33, 35
Tour Saint-Jacques (Paris). *See* Daubigny, Charles-François, *View of Paris from the Tour Saint-Jacques*
Trinquesse, Louis Roland, 196n5
Guérin, Pierre, portrait of, 242n10
Lagrange, François Reidy de, portrait of, 242n11
Portrait de Claude-Pierre Clavelin (1797), 242n12
Portrait de l'épouse de Claude-Pierre Clavelin (1797), 242n12
Portrait of a Man in a Hat, 1798 (fig. 38.1), 124, *241*, 242n5
Portrait of a Man Looking Right (1797) (cat. 38), 122–24, *123*, 241–42
Troy, Jean-François de, 56
Turgot, Anne-Robert-Jacques
See also Cochin, Charles-Nicolas; Watelet, Claude-Henri
Turner, J. M. W., 175

Uffizi Galleries (Florence), 166, 260nn6–7

Valenciennes, Pierre-Henri de, 131
Eléments de perspective pratique, 131, 240n2

[334]

Michallon and Bertin were students of his, 132
Valenciennes (France), 27
Van Dyck, Sir Anthony
   Jupiter and Antiope, 35
Vasi, Giuseppe
   Chiesa dei SS Giovanni e Paolo, from *Delle magnificenze di Roma Antica e Moderna* (1753) (fig. 17.1), 70, *211*
Vatican. See *View from the Vatican* (1818–21) (Michallon) (cat. 41)
Vaugirard (Paris). See *Plain of Vaugirard, The* (Bonvin)
Vedius Pollio, 114
   See also Desprez, Louis-Jean, *Slaves of Vedius Pollio Thrown Alive to the Moray Eels, The* (1777–79) (Desprez)
Verdun, Raymond (cat. 63), 266
Vernet, Carle, 97, 99, 258n2
Vernet, Horace
   Assaut du zouave, L' (1857), 258n8
   Bataille de l'Alma (1857), 258n8
   Prise du fort de Malakoff (1858), 258n8
   Study of Gabions in the Trenches of the Crimean War (1854–55) (cat. 55), 97, *160*, 161–62, 257–58
Vernet, Joseph, 90, 97, 124, 258n2
Veronese, Paolo, 196n3
Verschuur, Wouterus, 12
Vesuvius, Mount, 251nn4–5
   See also Flandrin, Paul-Jean, *View from the Summit of Vesuvius*
Vien, Joseph-Marie, 117
Villot, Frédéric (cat. 12), 203
Vincent, François-André
   Artists in a Landscape, near Tivoli (1773) (cat. 30), 22, *102*, 103, *105*, 230–31
   Artist Sketching in the Farnese Gardens (1773) (fig. 30.1), 103, *231*
   Classical Statue in a Niche (1774), 231n10
   Head of a Young Woman (1782), 229n3
   Portrait of Diane, Greyhound of Bergeret de Grancourt (1774) (fig. 29.1), 100, *230*
   Sheet of Studies for Aria and Poetus (1784), 229n3
   Studies of Cats and a Donkey (1772) (cat. 29), 22, 99–100, *101*, 229–30
   View of an Italian Park (c. 1774), 231n10
   View of Steps Leading to the Villa Doria Pamphili, 231n10
   View of the Gardens of the Villa Negroni (1773) (fig. 30.2), 103, *231*
   The Young Man at the Villa Doria (1774), 231n10
Viollet-le-Duc, Eugène-Emmanuel
   Histoire d'un dessinateur: comment on apprend à dessiner, 175, 263n7
   Massif du Mont Blanc, Le, 173, 262n1
   View of the Alps, 1875 (cat. 60), 173–75, *174*, 262–63
   View of White Lakes, 4 September 1875 (fig. 60.1), 175, *263*
Visconti, Ennio Quirino, 93
Vivant, Dominique, 97
Vleughels, Nicolas, 49, 103
Vogtherr, Christoph, 50
Vollard, Ambroise
   Degas, 260n1

Walferdin, Hippolyte
   in cat. 23 provenance, 220, 221n12
   in cat. 24 provenance, 222
Wallace Collection (London), 240n9
Walpole, Horace (Fourth Earl of Orford) (cat. 11), 201
Walters, William T., 261n2
Walters Art Museum (Baltimore), 261n2
War of the Spanish Succession, 27, 50
Watelet, Claude-Henri
   Art de peindre, L' (1760), 210n3
Watelet, Claude-Henri (after Cochin)
   Portrait of Anne-Robert-Jacques Turgot, Baron de L'Aulne (1763) (fig. 16.1), 66, *210*
Watteau, Antoine
   Actor Philippe Poisson, The (1715), 187n4
   Allée Bordered by Trees, 197n2
   À Montmorency, 197n2
   as artistic influence, 50, 52, 59, 100
   Autumn, 37
   Bacchante Lying on the Ground, 37
   Embarkation to Cythera (detail) (1718, Berlin) (figs. 5.1 and 5.2), 38–39, *192*, 192n5
   Embarkation to Cythera (Louvre), 38
   Entretiens badins, 38
   Escorte d'équipages, 186n3
   Figures françoises et comiques (1715), 29
   Four Seasons (mythological paintings), 37
   Gersaint's Shopsign 1721, 59
   in Groult Album, 52
   Jupiter and Antiope (c. 1717) (fig. 4.1), 35, 37, *190*, 190n1
   Landscape with Bear Devouring a Goat (c. 1715–16) (cat. 3), 18, *32*, 33, 188–89
   Lugt's collecting, of, 15–16
   Perspective, La (c. 1717), 45
   Recruits Going to Join the Regiment (fig. 1.1), 27, 29, *185*, 186n7
   Seated Young Woman (c. 1718) (fig. 6.2), 42, *194*
   Sheet of Eight Heads, with a Right Hand Holding a Mask, 193n10
   Shepherds, The, 38
   Standing Man (Persian) (1715) (cat. 2), 15, 29–30, *31*, 186–87
   Study for a Satyr about to Attack (c. 1717) (cat. 4), *34*, 35, 189–91
   Studies of a Woman and a Woman Holding Her Apron (c. 1717–18) (fig. 5.3), 39, *192*, 192n9
   Studies of Seven Heads (c. 1717–18) (cat. 5), 15, *36*, 37–39, 191–93
   Study of a Nude Man Kneeling and Holding Drapery (c. 1717) (fig. 4.2), 35, *190*
   Study of a Semi-Nude Woman Seated on a Chaise Longue, 195n10
   Study of Two Persian Diplomats (1715) (fig. 2.1), 29, 30, *187*
   Three Soldiers Advancing (fig. 1.2), 29, *185*
   Three Soldiers Carrying Muskets, 29
   Three Soldiers Viewed from Behind, 29, 186n7
   Three Standing Soldiers (c. 1715) (cat. 1), 27–29, *28*, 52, 185–86
   Three Studies of Soldiers, 29, 186n7
   Two Cousins (c. 1716), 59
   Two Studies of Women (c. 1716–17), 195n7
   Woman Reclining on a Chaise Longue (c. 1718) (cat. 6), 15, 20, 39–42, *40*, 193–95
   Woman Reclining on a Chaise Longue (c. 1718) (fig. 6.1), 41, 42, *194*
   Young Woman in a Bonnet on a Chaise Longue (c. 1714–15), 195n7
Wauters, Émile, 249n1
Westbridge (Wales). See Doré, Paul Gustave, *View of the Forest at Westbridge*
Wille, Jean-George, 242n4
Williams, Eunice, 75, 215n8

[335]

Wintermute, Alan, 42
Witte, Mme de (cat. 1), 185
Wittel, Gaspar Van
  Vedute, 200n5
World War I, 14
World War II, 19

Yale Center for British Art (New Haven), 189n8

Zanetti, Antonio, 198n6
Zoubaloff album (Louvre), 129
Zuber, Pascal (cat. 49), 25